A Year in Colossians

A 365-Day Devotional Commentary

DAVID J. LANDEGENT

DEDICATION

This book is dedicated to my parents, John and Audrey Landegent,
who taught me a love for God and God's Word.

Introduction

ON READING DEVOTIONALS

My faith has not only been strengthened by the Bible, but also by devotional books designed to help me understand and apply what I was reading in the Bible.

Devotional books come in a wide variety of styles, all of which deal with Scripture differently.

- *Thematic devotionals* trace a certain subject matter or topic, such as spiritual gifts or financial stewardship. Not surprisingly, the topic sets the agenda, with the biblical text serving in a supporting role—which sometimes means the context is neglected.
- *Life situation devotionals* are designed for a target audience and its needs, such as teenagers, single moms, or those dealing with cancer. The biblical texts are viewed from that certain perspective.
- *Illustration devotionals* cater to the many readers who are looking for a memorable little story or metaphor that will illuminate one aspect of a Bible text. Unfortunately, people often remember the illustration more than the biblical text.
- *Scattershot devotionals* jump all over the Bible from day to day. Because each day's reading is totally unrelated to the next, there is no continuity. Readers pick up snippets of biblical truth, but often miss the big picture.

All these devotional books have fed God's people, myself included. They do the best they can within the constraints of a short reading. But I was always hoping for more, and I'm guessing that others have had the same desire.

I wanted a devotional that stayed with a given book of the Bible for an extended period of time so that I could catch the flow of its truth. I also wanted a devotional that focused on what the biblical text meant to its original readers before jumping to what it might mean for me. So I decided to write the kind of devotional that I would like to use myself, which resulted in the book you're now reading.

This is actually my second book on Colossians. Not long ago I published a very large book called *Colossians: A Commentary*. It was so large—about 1000 pages—that it only made sense to publish it as an ebook instead of in a printed format. I wrote it so that anyone could understand the details of Colossians, even those who did not know Greek or have a seminary training in theology. But I also was aware that many would find a 1000-page commentary intimidating. So I decided to turn that book into a daily devotional that would take the reader through Colossians phrase-by-phrase. That meant reducing 1000 pages to 365 pages, which I was able to accomplish by keeping the meat of that book intact, but trimming away much of the background research.

By the way, in providing background information I will sometimes refer to the Greek OT, which is known as the Septuagint. Without this resource it would be difficult to compare the usage of OT *Hebrew* words with NT *Greek* words. But with the Septuagint, which we know was available to Paul, comparisons are easier to make. I will also refer to the Apocrypha and other ancient Jewish books, not because I regard them as inspired, but because the ideas in these books were part of the thinking in Paul's day.

If, after using this devotional book, you would like to know even more about Colossians, you are welcome to purchase my commentary inexpensively at many online stores that sell e-books. It's called *Colossians: A Commentary* and is published through WestBow Press. If you've already purchased the commentary, there is not much new here, but it is presented in a "bite-sized" format.

FORMAT OF THIS DEVOTIONAL

Following this introduction, you will find a new translation of Colossians, which I will use throughout the commentary. The whole letter is printed in its entirety at the beginning so that you can read it straight through. I also provide some footnotes with that translation to briefly explain some of the translation decisions that differ markedly from the NIV, ESV, or NRSV.

Readers will quickly notice that I did not render my translation with smooth English phrases. Instead, the translation is a bit stiff. That's by design. I tried as much as possible to make the sentences as long as Paul made them (notice that Col 1:3-8, for example, is all one sentence), to put the words in the same order as in the Greek, and not add too many words that were not there. My goal was also to keep grammatical elements the same from Greek to English—so nouns were translated as nouns, adjectives as adjectives, verbs as verbs, etc. In addition, I attempted to be consistent in translating commands as commands, infinitives as infinitives (verbs with "to" in front of them) and participles as participles (verbs that often end with "ing"). And when the same word was used more than once in the letter, I tried to translate it the same way in most cases. When I felt it necessary to add clarifying words that were not in the text, I placed those words in brackets. Sometimes a single Greek word could only be translated accurately with a phrase, so I would sometimes hyphenate the phrase so that the reader would know this was originally one Greek word.

The translation and the devotional proper is divided into fifteen sections that trace the flow of Colossians.

Within each section, the first day or so will provide an overview of that section as a whole. The rest of the daily readings in that section follow the verses phrase by phrase—and sometimes the devotional will spend more than one day on the same phrase.

At the conclusion of each section, a day will be devoted to singing the truths learned in that section by means of new lyrics set to a familiar hymn or praise song. I did this to remind myself (and maybe you) that God's truth is not just for entering our heads, but also our hearts. Music has a way of doing just that. It's my conviction that if you can't sing your beliefs to God or about God, then it's questionable how true or important they really are.

Other than the days which feature a song, all the daily readings include a short portion of the Colossian verses near the top of the page, with that day's key phrase in bold print. At the bottom of the page, you will also be invited to offer a short prayer of response to God's Word.

At the very end, a bibliography and footnotes are provided to give credit to those who are quoted, and also to point readers toward further study.

THE BOOK OF COLOSSIANS

The apostle Paul was called by God to lead the way in bringing the good news of Jesus to those who were not Jews. He was an unlikely candidate for this position, because at one time he had been so zealous for traditional Jewish ways that he actively persecuted the followers of Jesus. But that

3

completely changed when the Risen Lord confronted him on the Damascus Road and gave him his new calling.

Paul was faithful to that calling and worked diligently in preaching the gospel—to the Jews first, and then to the non-Jews—especially in various cities of Asia Minor, Macedonia and Greece. Nearly everywhere he went, a church was formed from those who came to believe in Jesus. Although Paul did not often remain long in one place—mostly because of persecution, but also because of the Spirit's leading—he did not want to leave these new believers to fend for themselves. In order to continue nurturing them in the faith, Paul: (1) prayed for them; (2) made return visits when he was able; (3) appointed leaders from within the congregation; (4) sent his own ministry team members to give guidance; and (5) wrote letters to further encourage them in following Jesus.

Often Paul sent letters to the churches that he himself had founded (as is true of 1-2 Corinthians, Galatians, Ephesians, Philippians and 1-2 Thessalonians), but in the cases of Romans and Colossians, he wrote to churches he had never visited before.

Even though some scholars doubt it, Paul (along with Timothy in some way) is the author of this letter (consult my companion book, *Colossians: A Commentary* if you are interested in knowing more about this). The most likely scenario is that Paul had been released from the confinement written about at the end of Acts, was later re-arrested, and then he wrote this letter.

While some might think Colossians should read like a book meant to satisfy the needs of the scholarly world for new ideas clothed in academic rigor, it's often forgotten that Colossians is a letter written to ordinary (often uneducated) believers in the first century. As Tidball said, "This letter was written to farmers and traders in wool who would have had no formal education and many of whom would have been illiterate. The readers were ordinary people—not post-Enlightenment theological graduates—eking out an existence in a precarious world."[1] It's also telling that Paul wrote a letter, not an essay. Letters, unlike essays, were not sent to engage in academic arguments. Rather, letters served many different purposes, and in the case of Colossians some of those purposes included unifying relationships, conveying information, celebrating and defending truth, giving advice and warnings, making corrections, sharing love, and strengthening faith.

Many scholars assume the letter was mostly written to warn the Colossians of a dangerous set of ideas and practices circulating in their church. Various names for this teaching have been used. Some of the names are too strong (heresy), while others are too weak (error). It's common to call it a false teaching, but this might imply that it was (1) a systematic set of ideas taught by (2) official teachers who (3) didn't really believe it themselves, but were only deceiving others for some kind of selfish gain. It's also common to think that (4) these false teachers (like the ones spoken of in Galatians or 2 Corinthians) came in from the outside.

But all of these impressions are wrong. First, it's not clear that the false teaching in Colossae is systematic, nor that it consists mostly of ideas. It rather seems to be a smorgasbord of both ideas and practices drawn from Jewish and pagan sources. Whatever seemed to be "working" spiritually was added to the mix. Second, there is no indication that official teachers or leaders were promoting this false teaching. It's more likely that individual Christians simply began sharing and promoting their spiritual experiences and ideas in a way that was not helpful to the church. Third, while it's common for NT writers (and other writers of that era) to attribute bad motives to false teachers, we do not find much of that talk in Colossians. Paul seems to recognize that, while these people may be wrong in what they say and do, most of them are *sincerely* wrong and have no consciously underhanded purposes in mind. Finally, there is no indication in Colossians that the people who are promoting wrong ideas and practices had come from the outside. It appears to be a homegrown distortion of the faith. So I will mostly be referring to these wrong beliefs and practices as a distortion, and those who follow it I will be calling distortionists.

Paul deals with this distortion most explicitly in Col 2:6-23, making the following points: it's an empty and deceptive philosophy dependent on human tradition and the elemental orders of the world, rather than on Christ (Col 2:8). It focused on special days and diets (Col 2:16), angels (and perhaps other spiritual powers), visions (Col 2:18) and rules that required harsh treatment of the body in order to bring some kind of "fullness" to one's faith (Col 2:20-23). And all this was presented in a way that made the other members of the Colossian church feel like they did not measure up by comparison (Col 2:16, 18).

How did this distortion arise? The scenario that seems most likely to me is that some Colossian believers had initially found great satisfaction in their newfound faith, but they quickly became aware that they still had problems and sins which they had hoped to have put behind them. Something seemed to be missing, and so they sought something more, something higher or deeper than what they had so far found in Christ. When some of them experienced new supernatural phenomena (such as visions of heavenly worship and encounters with angels), they were so delighted that they sought spiritual techniques to help them experience this again. Thus, they tried observing special days, fasting, and other forms of humbling oneself (taken from Jewish and pagan practices) in an attempt to subdue the body and experience the spiritual world. Whatever appeared to be effective in helping them to experience "more" in their faith, they would then share with others, urging them to adopt the same practices and experience the same supernatural visions—and also giving the impression that if others did not follow their advice, then maybe their faith was deficient. Unfortunately, in their efforts to experience more of the supernatural, these people quickly lost sight of Christ and all the fullness he brings. Whether intentionally or not, they ended up looking beyond Christ to other sources of spiritual power—which probably explains why Paul talks about supernatural powers more in this letter than any other. Thus, Paul had to combat this tendency by emphasizing strongly that the Colossian believers already had in Christ alone everything they needed to experience God's fullness.

While it's true that this distortion dominates chapter two, it's not so clear that the whole letter is written against the distortionists. Perhaps these wrong-headed ideas and practices created the need and urgency for Paul to write to the Colossians in the first place, but he had so much more to say to them than what *not* to believe.

If any general purpose can be discerned in Colossians, it is that of encouraging these new believers. Paul has not met them, but he knows they—like all believers living as a religious minority in a suspicious or hostile society—need encouragement. He mentions this purpose in Col 2:1-2 ("For I want you to know how great a struggle I have over you and those in Laodicea...in order that their hearts might be encouraged") and also in Col 4:8 (in that Tychicus was sent "in order that you may know the things concerning us and that he may encourage your hearts").

THE AUTHOR OF THIS DEVOTIONAL

In case you're wondering who wrote this devotional, I am an evangelical Christian (who also happens to be a pastor in the Reformed Church in America). I believe Colossians is part of God's Word revealed by the Lord for the sake of individual Christians as well as the church. Although Paul was not conscious of it at the time, I believe that the process described in 2 Pet 1:21 (concerning the OT prophets) also applies to Paul's letters: he was moved by the Holy Spirit to express the Word of God. These words to the Colossians were not only spoken by Paul and written by his secretary, but they were also breathed-out by God and thus are profitable for teaching, reproving, correcting, training and equipping God's people (2 Tim 3:16-17). I do not regard the book of Colossians, therefore, as a dead document from the past, a literary corpse that needs to be dissected so that we can write an autopsy concerning what was healthy or diseased about it. Rather, I am convinced that the book of Colossians is the Word of God, alive and active, sharper than any two-edged sword (Heb 4:12). We may be the ones reading and interpreting this book, but in a more profound sense it is reading and interpreting us.

So for all those readers who seek to hear, understand and obey the Word of God, the book of Colossians comes as a divine gift, written by Paul, inspired by the Spirit and presently moving into our open hearts. I trust that those who use this devotional will be delighted, convicted and encouraged by all they discover in this letter, so that their faith in Jesus will grow and their love for him will abound.

—

I want to thank all those who have encouraged me in my writing, especially my parents to whom this book is dedicated, and also my wife, Ruth Ann, to whom my Colossians commentary was dedicated.

I also want to thank Rev. Miguel Cruz who helped me in the editing of this devotional.

A translation
Colossians

Words placed inside [brackets] are not in the Greek text, but are implied by the grammatical indicators of the Greek language. Some words are hyphenated to indicate that they are one word in Greek.

GRACE TO YOU (1:1-2)

[1] *Paul (an apostle of Christ Jesus through the will of God) and Timothy (a brother);* [2] *to those in Colossae, the holy-ones[1] and faithful brothers [and sisters] in Christ; grace to you and peace from God our Father.*

PRAYERS OF THANKS (1:3-8)

[3] *We give-thanks to God, the Father of our Lord Jesus Christ, at all times when praying for you,* [4] *having heard of your faith in Christ Jesus and the love which you have for all the holy-ones* [5] *due to the hope being kept for you in the heavens, which you previously heard about in the word of truth, the good-message[2]* [6] *which is making itself present to you—even as in all the world it is fruit-bearing and growing, so also among you, since the day you heard and knew the grace of God in truth,* [7] *just as you learned from Epaphras, our beloved fellow-slave, who is a faithful servant of Christ for us,* [8] *the one who informed us of your love in the Spirit.*

PRAYERS OF ASKING (1:9-14)

[9] *Because of this, we also, from the day we heard, have not stopped praying for you and asking in order that you may be filled with the knowledge of his will in all wisdom and Spirit-oriented[3] understanding,* [10] *to walk worthily of the Lord in every form of pleasing, in every good work fruit-bearing and growing in the knowledge of God,* [11] *being empowered with all power in accordance with the might of his glory in all endurance and patience with joy,[4]* [12] *giving-thanks to the Father for qualifying you for a share of the inheritance of the holy-ones in the light,* [13] *[the Father] who delivered us from the authority of darkness and relocated [us] to the*

---

[1] Both the traditional translation "saints" and my translation "holy-ones" could be misleading to modern readers, but the latter is closer to the mark of what Paul is getting at. I follow this same translation also in Col 1:4, 12, 26. See the devotions for January 8 and 9.
[2] Most translations use "gospel" here, but that seemed like too church-y of a word. It is a compound noun that means good-news or good-message. This word is also used in Col 1:23.
[3] Most translations use the term "spiritual," but Paul is not talking about something that comes from the human spirit, but God's Spirit, thus the adjective "Spirit-oriented." I follow this same translation in Col 3:16.
[4] Translations differ on whether the phrase "with joy" belongs with endurance and patience (ESV, NRSV) or with the next verse's reference to thanking (NIV). I have chosen the former. See the February 11 devotional.

kingdom of the Son of his love— [14] *in whom we have redemption, the forgiveness of our sins—*

JESUS' MINISTRY: THE LAUDATION (1:15-20)
[15] *[the loved Son], who is the image of the unseen God, the firstborn of all creation,* [16] *for in him were created all things in the heavens and on the earth, the seen things and the unseen things, whether thrones or lordships or primal-powers,*[5] *or authorities; all things through him and toward him have been created;* [17] *and he is before all things, and all things in him stand together.*[6] [18] *And he is the head of the body (the church), the Primal-Power,*[7] *the firstborn from out of the dead ones, in order that in all things he [himself] would be firsting,*[8] [19] *for in him all the fullness was pleased to dwell* [20] *and through him to reconcile all things toward him— having-made-peace through the blood of his cross—whether things on the earth or things in the heavens.*

JESUS' MINISTRY TO THE COLOSSIANS (1:21-23)
[21] *And you, once being alienated and enemy-minded in evil works,* [22] *he now reconciled in his body of flesh through death, to present you as holy and unblemished and blameless before him,* [23] *if indeed you remain in the faith, being foundationed and settled, and not moving from the hope of the good-message which you heard, which has been proclaimed to every created-being under heaven, of which I, Paul, have become a servant.*

PAUL'S MINISTRY (1:24-29)
[24] *Now I rejoice in sufferings for you, and I fill up that which remains to be completed*[9] *of the afflictions of Christ in my flesh, for [the sake of] his body, which is the church,* [25] *of which I have become a servant according to the*

---

[5] Most translations go with "rulers" here, but the fact that this word can be translated as either "ruler" or "beginning" implies that it refers here to supernatural powers that came into being early in creation. I tried to convey both ideas with the term "primal-power." I followed this same translation in Col 2:10 and 15.

[6] Most translation say that all things "hold together" in Christ, but the root meaning of the word here is about standing. See March 14 devotional.

[7] Most translations use "beginning" here, and that is one of its two primary meanings. Jesus is indeed the Beginning, and that would fit the context of creation. But the fact that Paul just used this same word to refer to other spiritual powers in verse 16 implies that Jesus is *the* Primal-Power above them all. See March 18 devotional.

[8] The word here is a verb, but the English language does not have an equivalent verb. We often end up using a verb with an adjective to say something like being first or being supreme. I was looking instead for a more active way to say that and so I coined a new verb, "firsting." See March 21 devotional.

[9] Most commentaries translate this phrase "that which remains to be completed" as "what is lacking," but this translation implies some kind of deficiency in what Christ has done. See April 20 and 21 devotionals.

household-management-plan[10] *God has given to me—for you—to fill-out the word of God,* [26] *the mystery which was being concealed from ages and from generations, but now is revealed to his holy-ones,* [27] *to whom God willed to make known what are the riches of the glory of this mystery among the nations,*[11] *which is, Christ in you, the hope of glory;* [28] *whom we declare, warning every person and teaching every person in all wisdom, so that we may present every person complete*[12] *in Christ;* [29] *[a goal] for which I toil, striving by means of his energy, which is energizing me with power.*

PAUL'S MINISTRY TO THE COLOSSIANS (2:1-5)

[1] *For I want you to know how great a struggle I have over you and those in Laodicea and as many as have not seen my face in the flesh,* [2] *in order that their hearts would be encouraged, having been drawn together in love and toward all the riches of the full assurance of understanding, toward the knowledge of the mystery of God, [which is] Christ,* [3] *in whom all the treasures of wisdom and knowledge are concealed.* [4] *This I say so that no one may con you with a convincing*[13] *word.* [5] *For even if I am absent in the flesh, yet in spirit I am with you, rejoicing and seeing your orderly-formation and the solidarity of your faith in Christ.*

A COMMAND AND A WARNING (2:6-8)

[6] *As you therefore have received the Christ—Jesus the Lord—walk in him,* [7] *having been rooted and being built up in him, and being established in the faith just as you were taught, overflowing in thanksgiving.* [8] *Watch out that no one will be captivating you through philosophy and empty deceit which are according to human tradition, according to the elemental-orders*[14] *of the world, and not according to Christ;*

ATTACHED TO CHRIST (2:9-15)

[9] *for in him [that is, in Christ] dwells bodily all the fullness of the deity,* [10] *and you have been filled in him, who is the head of all primal-powers and authorities,* [11] *in whom also you were circumcised with a circumcision made-without-hands, by the stripping of the body of flesh in the*

---

[10] The word used here is translated in many different ways. It comes from putting the word for "house" together with the word for "law." To preserve those concepts, I went with "household-management plan" instead of the more typical translations like stewardship (ESV) or commission (NIV, NRSV). See April 24 devotional.

[11] Most translations use the term "Gentiles" here, but this is not a term used outside of Christian circles. The actual word Paul used here is the usual word for nations.

[12] Most translations use the word "mature" here, but this misses the connection of the Greek word to ideas about reaching a goal.

[13] The ESV and NRSV render this as "plausible," which is a good translation, but I was trying to preserve a word-play in the Greek between the words for conning and convincing.

[14] There is a disagreement among translations and commentaries about whether this word is about spirits (NRSV, ESV, 2011 NIV) or principles (original NIV). I have attempted a translation that encompasses both ideas. See devotions for June 3-5.

circumcision of Christ, [12] having been jointly-buried with him in baptism, in whom also you were jointly-raised through faith in the energizing-work of God who raised him from the dead ones. [13] And you, being dead in the transgressions and the uncircumcision of your flesh, he [God] made you jointly-alive with him [Christ], having granted-grace[15] to us for all transgressions. [14] Wiping-away the handwritten debt-note against us, which opposed us with its decrees, he [God] has taken it from center-stage,[16] having nailed it to the cross. [15] Having stripped the primal-powers and the authorities, he [God] exposed them openly, triumphantly-parading them in him [Christ].

DETACHED FROM CHRIST (2:16-23)

[16] Therefore, let no one judge you in eating and drinking or in respect to a festival or a new-moon or sabbaths, [17] which are a shadow of coming things, but the body[17] [that cast the shadow is] of Christ. [18] Let nobody disqualify you, insisting on humbling-practices[18] and worship of angels, claiming-access to the things which he has seen, vainly being puffed up by his mind of flesh, [19] and not gripping the head, from whom all the body, being supplied and drawn together through its joints and connecting-tissues, grows with growth from God.

[20] If you died with Christ to the elemental-orders of the world, why, as though living in [that] world, would you come under its decrees, [21] "Do not touch; do not taste; do not contact!" [22] all of which goes to decay with use? [Such decrees are] according to the commandments and teachings of men, [23] which indeed are a word having wisdom in self-willed-worship and humbling-practices, the unsparing-treatment of the body, but they are without honor[19] [in going] against the filling-full of the flesh.

SEEK THE THINGS ABOVE (3:1-4)

---

[15] Most translations speak of forgiveness in this verse, but Paul does not use the normal word for forgiveness here. Instead he uses a word that is related to grace. He does the same in Col 3:13. See June 29 devotions.

[16] Literally, this says "taken it from the middle," and most translations render it as "set aside" (ESV and NRSV) or taken it away (NIV). I wanted to preserve the literal idea of the middle. See July 3 devotions.

[17] The word here is the one used for "body" throughout Colossians, but many translations opt for a different contrast with shadow by speaking of reality (NIV) or substance (ESV, NRSV).

[18] Paul uses the normal word for "humility" here, which he usually uses in a positive sense (as he does in Col 3:12). But here (and Col 2:23), he means it in a negative sense. Translators struggle with how to render this: asceticism (ESV), false humility (NIV), self-abasement (NRSV). Since it's referring to practices that are designed to humble oneself, such as fasting, I have opted for "humbling practices."

[19] Most translations refer to value here, which is another meaning of the word, but its more common meaning is honor. The connection is that we honor that which we value.

[1] *If therefore you were jointly-raised with Christ, seek the things above, where Christ is, sitting at the right-hand of God. [2] Think the things above, not the things on the earth. [3] For you died and your life is hidden with Christ in God; [4] when Christ (your life) is revealed, then also you—with him—will be revealed in glory.*

COMMANDS FOR LIFE IN THE CHURCH (3:5-17)

[5] Necrotize[20], therefore, the parts [of you which are] of the earth: sexual-sin, impurity, passion, bad desire, and greed (which is idolatry)— [6] because of these the wrath of God comes. [7] In these you also once walked when you were living in them; [8] but now, you, throw-off all these: wrath, anger, bad things, slander, filthy-talk from your mouth. [9] Lie not to each other, having stripped off the old man with his practices, [10] and having clothed [yourself] with the new [man], which is being renewed in knowledge according to the image of the one who created him. [11] Here there is not Greek and Jew, circumcision and uncircumcision, barbarian, Scythian, slave, free, but all and in all is Christ.

[12] Clothe [yourselves], therefore—as God's chosen-ones, holy and being loved—with the heart of compassion, kindness, humility, gentleness, patience, [13] bearing with one another and granting-grace to each other if ever anyone has a grievance. Just as the Lord has granted-grace to you, so should you [grant-grace to others]. [14] Over all these things, [put on] love, which is the connecting-tissue of completeness.

[15] And let the peace of Christ, to which you were called in one body, arbitrate in your hearts; and be thankful. [16] Let the word of Christ dwell in you richly, teaching and warning each other in all wisdom with psalms, hymns and Spirit-oriented songs, singing by grace[21] in your hearts to God. [17] And in all of whatever you do—in word or in work—[do] all things in the name of the Lord Jesus, giving-thanks to God the Father through him.

COMMANDS FOR LIFE IN THE HOME (3:18-4:1)

[18] Women,[22] submit to [your] men as fitting in the Lord. [19] Men, love [your] women, and do not be embittered against them.

[20] Children, obey [your] parents in all things, for this is well-pleasing in the Lord. [21] Fathers, do not provoke your children, lest they become dispirited.

---

[20] Most translations render this as "put to death," but I thought it better to coin a word that's based on the Greek word. See devotions on September 6-8.

[21] Most translations render this as singing "with gratitude," but the word used here mostly commonly means "grace." See October 23 devotions.

[22] There is no separate Greek word for wife or husband. I followed the more literal meaning here of women and men, with the context revealing their marital status.

^{22} *Slaves, obey in all things [your] lords*^{23} *according to the flesh, not by way of "only-when-watched service," as people-pleasers, but in sincerity of heart, fearing the Lord.* ^{23} *In whatever you do, work from the soul, as for the Lord and not for men,* ^{24} *knowing that from the Lord you will receive the reward of the inheritance. Slave for the Lord Christ,* ^{25} *for the one doing wrong will receive-back what he did wrong—and there is no partiality.* $^{4:1}$ *Lords, give justice and equal-treatment to [your] slaves, knowing that you also have a Lord in heaven.*

COMMANDS FOR LIFE IN THE WORLD (4:2-6)
^{2} *As for prayer—attend to it, being-watchful in it with thanksgiving,* ^{3} *praying at the same time even for us in order that God would open for us a door for the word, to speak the mystery of Christ for which I have been bound,* ^{4} *in order that I may reveal it as is necessary*^{24} *for me to speak.* ^{5} *Walk in wisdom before those "outside," snapping up the time.*^{25} ^{6} *Let your word always [be spoken] in grace, being seasoned with salt, [so as] to know how it is necessary for you to respond to each one.*

GRACE BE WITH YOU (4:7-18)
^{7} *Tychicus, the beloved brother and faithful servant and fellow-slave in the Lord, will make known to you all the things about me.* ^{8} *Him I sent to you for this [reason]: in order that you may know the things concerning us and that he may encourage your hearts.* ^{9} *[I sent him] along with Onesimus, the faithful and beloved brother, who is one of you; they will make known to you all the things here.*

^{10} *Aristarchus my fellow-prisoner-of-war greets you, [as does] Mark, the cousin of Barnabas (about whom you have received commands; if he comes to you, welcome him),* ^{11} *and Jesus called Justus—these alone being from the circumcision who are [my] fellow-workers in the kingdom of God, [and] who have been a comfort to me.* ^{12} *Epaphras, who is one of you, a slave of Christ Jesus, greets you, always striving for you in his prayers in order that you may stand, complete and being fully-assured in all the will of God.* ^{13} *For I testify for him that he experiences much hardship for you and those in*

---

[23] The Greek word often translated as "master" is the same word used to describe Jesus as Lord. I preferred to keep the wording consistent in order to contrast the Lord with the lords. I made this same translation decision in Col 4:1. See devotions for November 14 and 22.
[24] Most translations of this word here (and in Col 4:6) go with words like "ought" or "should," but I think that is a weak translation, for Paul is talking about divine necessity. See December 5 devotions.
[25] The King James Version rendered this as "redeem the time," and modern translations speak of making the best use of time (ESV) or making the most of every opportunity (NIV). It's not a time-management word, however, but a market-place word associated with snatching up a bargain. See December 9 devotions.

Laodicea and those in Hierapolis. [14] Luke the beloved physician greets you, and [so does] Demas.

[15] Greet the brothers [and sisters] in Laodicea and Nympha and the church in her house. [16] And when this letter is read to you, make [arrangements] in order that it be read in the church of the Laodiceans, and that you read the one [forwarded] from Laodicea. [17] And say to Archippus, "See to the service which you received in the Lord in order that you may fulfill it." [18] The greeting is [written] in my—Paul's—hand. Remember my chains. Grace be with you.

ABBREVIATIONS

OT BOOKS

Gen	Genesis
Ex	Exodus
Lev	Leviticus
Num	Numbers
Dt	Deuteronomy
Josh	Joshua
Judg	Judges
Ruth	Ruth
1 Sam	1 Samuel
2 Sam	2 Samuel
1 Kgs	1 Kings
2 Kgs	2 Kings
1 Chron	1 Chronicles
2 Chron	2 Chronicles
Ezra	Ezra
Neh	Nehemiah
Est	Esther
Job	Job
Ps	Psalms
Prov	Proverbs
Eccles	Ecclesiastes
Song	Song of Songs
Isa	Isaiah
Jer	Jeremiah
Lam	Lamentations
Ezek	Ezekiel
Dan	Daniel
Hos	Hosea
Joel	Joel
Amos	Amos
Obad	Obadiah
Jonah	Jonah
Mic	Micah
Nah	Nahum
Hab	Habakkuk
Zeph	Zephaniah
Hag	Haggai
Zech	Zechariah
Mal	Malachi

APOCRYPHA

1 Mac	1 Maccabees
2 Mac	2 Maccabees
4 Mac	4 Maccabees
Sol	Psalms of Solomon
Wisdom	Wisdom of Solomon

NT BOOKS

Mt	Matthew
Mk	Mark
Lk	Luke
Jn	John
Acts	Acts
Rom	Romans
1 Cor	1 Corinthians
2 Cor	2 Corinthians
Gal	Galatians
Eph	Ephesians
Phil	Philippians
Col	Colossians
1 Thess	1 Thessalonians
2 Thess	2 Thessalonians
1 Tim	1 Timothy
2 Tim	2 Timothy
Titus	Titus
Philemon	Philemon
Heb	Hebrews
Jms	James
1 Pet	1 Peter
2 Pet	2 Peter
1 Jn	1 John
2 Jn	2 John
3 Jn	3 John
Jude	Jude
Rev	Revelation

OTHER

ESV	English Standard Version
KJV	King James Version
LXX	Septuagint (Greek OT with Apocrypha)
NETS	New English Translation of the Septuagint
NIV	New International Version
NRSV	New Revised Standard Version
NT	New Testament
OT	Old Testament

Opening greetings: grace to you

Colossians 1:1-2

January 1-14

¹ Paul (an apostle of Christ Jesus through the will of God) and Timothy (a brother); ² to those in Colossae, the holy-ones and faithful brothers [and sisters] in Christ; grace to you and peace from God our Father.

Letters are about forming and strengthening personal relationships. Colossians is no different. The main figures in the network of relationships discussed in this letter are God the Father, Jesus, Paul and his co-workers, and the Colossian believers. We also hear of how these parties are impacted by relationships with those who distort the truth, various spiritual powers, and unbelievers.[2]

First, this letter reveals *God's* relationships. There is the relationship between the Father and the Son as they work together in creating the world and bringing salvation and reconciliation. But God is also in relationship with: Paul whom he called to be an apostle; the Colossian believers for whom God has worked salvation and who continues to work for them and in them; the powers who were created and subdued by Christ; the distortionists who have cut off their relationship with Christ; and the unbelievers sought out by the Lord through the preaching of the gospel.

In addition to God's relationships, we also read about *Paul's* relationship with the Colossian believers (he prays for them, works to present them complete in Christ, and asks them to pray for him) and with unbelievers for whose sake he preaches the gospel. We hear nothing about Paul's relationship with the distortionists, other than his rejection of their teachings.

Besides their relationship with God and Paul, the *Colossians* themselves are also in relationship with one another (and Paul will emphasize what it also means for them to be in Christ in their homes). They have no need to be in relationship with the powers, nor do they need to heed the judgments of the distortionists. They are called, however, to support Paul's gospel ministry to a lost world, as well as reach out to that lost world themselves.

One might get the impression in looking at these relationships that they are all equally important, but the Christ-centered approach of Colossians means that Jesus is the one who ties all these relationships together (for "all things in him stand together," Col 1:17). Colossians is not just about Jesus; it is about Jesus in relationship to all others.[3]

Lord Jesus, I'm thankful for my own network of relationships, and I pray that you would be the tie that binds them all together.

> [1] *Paul (an apostle of Christ Jesus through the will of God) and Timothy (a brother);* [2] *to those in Colossae, the holy-ones and faithful brothers [and sisters] in Christ; grace to you and peace from God our Father.*

Most cultures have standard ways of greeting one another when writing. Until the rise of email and text-messages, Americans often began letters with "Dear *x*," or "To whom it may concern." Compared to that standard, letters in Paul's day began more abruptly. They would simply state the name of the writer, the name of the recipient, followed by a brief word of greeting: "*x* to *y*, greetings." The two main exceptions to this would be official letters in which formal titles would be included, and letters written to dear friends in which terms of endearment would be used.[4] Paul manages to follow both exceptions here, for he includes an official title (apostle) *and* terms of endearment (holy-ones and faithful brothers in Christ).

Paul also finds other ways to tweak standard letter-writing forms in order to express important truths. Garland observes from the opening of Colossians that "The author is no ordinary person but one who writes with apostolic authority from God . . . The recipients are not ordinary people but a consecrated society established by God . . . The greetings are not ordinary good wishes but blessings that have become a spiritual reality through the death and resurrection of Jesus."[5]

Although Paul addresses his letter to some new believers who lived long ago and far away, there is a very real sense in which he is addressing us today. This letter is part of God's inspired and written Word, meaning that it was and is God-breathed (2 Tim 3:16-17). It not only spoke, but it still speaks as the living and active voice of God.

Jesus once compared God's Word to a seed that falls on hard soil, shallow soil, weedy soil, and good soil (Mt 13:3-9, 18-23). He summons us to listen with good, fertile ears. If we would update this parable to contemporary emailing practices, we would say: "If you get an email from God, don't treat it like spam and toss it in the trash unread. Don't let it get lost in a gigantic backlog of old emails. Don't read it and file it away for a future response that you never make. Instead, read it now and respond to it now. The Lord is writing to you."

Lord, speak to me each day by means of your Word. Give me ears to hear it and a heart to do it.

[1] **Paul** *(an apostle of Christ Jesus through the will of God) and Timothy (a brother)*

In all of his letters, the apostle begins with his Roman name (Paul) instead of his Jewish name (Saul). There is no evidence for the widely-held belief that God changed Paul's name when he became a Christian. More likely, Paul always had both names. Among Jews, the apostle likely called himself Saul, especially since both the apostle and the Israelite king of that name were from the tribe of Benjamin. But when among non-Jews, the apostle probably went by his Roman name of Paul. It's also possible Paul did not use his Jewish name when traveling throughout the Roman empire because the Greek word *saulos* was a term for walking in a provocatively sexual way, similar to our English word "strut."[6]

There are a number of "famous" people in the New Testament, like Peter, James, John, John the Baptist, Mary, Priscilla and Aquila. There are also a few infamous people, like Judas, Herod, and Pilate. But besides Jesus, the most well-known figure of all was Paul. His story is given a prominent place in the book of Acts, and the bulk of the NT letters come from his hand.

If Paul lived in our day, we would likely attempt to treat him like a Christian celebrity. His books would be best-sellers. His video series would be used in adult Sunday School classes. He would be a headline speaker at Christian conferences held in luxury hotels. Or at least that's the mold we'd try to squeeze him into. But if we treat Paul like a superstar, we will neglect our own responsibility to shine like stars in the universe (Phil 2:15). If we treat Paul like an idol, we will become idle ourselves, just sitting around admiring his work and avoiding our own calling.

Paul was not interested in celebrity status. He wanted the gospel to prosper, but not himself. Celebrities want to be known, to be powerful, and to hobnob with other famous people. Paul had other goals: to know Christ, and the power of his resurrection and the fellowship of his sufferings (Phil 3:10). And for the sake of reaching that goal, Paul was willing to suffer poverty, hardship, persecution, and dishonor. He would rather be a fool than a celebrity in the eyes of the world (1 Cor 4:10).

Paul's letter, then, does not contain juicy celebrity gossip from the first century. Instead he is challenging each of us to know Jesus and live in him.

Lord Jesus, use Paul's letter to challenge me to know you, to live by your power, and to suffer for your kingdom.

*¹ Paul **(an apostle of Christ Jesus** through the will of God) and Timothy (a brother)*

In the opening line in nine of his thirteen letters, Paul describes himself as an apostle. The term "apostle" (*apostolos*) was used in secular and religious contexts to refer to people who had been sent, usually with authority, to accomplish some mission. In much of the NT, the term was reserved for the original Twelve disciples chosen and sent by Jesus. According to Mk 3:14-15, for instance, Jesus named the Twelve the "apostles" because they would be "sent out" (using the corresponding verb *apostellō*) with authority to preach and cast out demons.

Gradually, however, the meaning of "apostle" shifted from the Twelve *who were sent* by Jesus to the Twelve *who provided a foundational message* for the church. So it's fitting that the names of the apostles appear on the foundation stones of the New Jerusalem in Rev 21:14.

Paul thought of himself as an apostle in both senses of the word. He was *sent* by the Lord to preach to the nations and he *provided a gospel foundation* for those who accepted his message. Oddly enough, even when Paul was in prison, unable to be sent anywhere, his apostolic work actually affected even more people through his letters, which still speak to us today.

Today's church must also be apostolic in the same two senses: founded upon the witness of the apostles and sent to a needy world with that message. We do not want to be a missional church that is so intent on successfully reaching the lost that we wrongly bend the truth handed down from the apostles. Nor do we want to become so entrenched in preserving the apostolic foundation that we neglect the church's mission. Rather, we want to be apostolic in the same way Paul was: to press on in the Lord's mission to a lost world with a message that aligns with the foundational truth of Jesus.

The foundation has already been laid by the apostles, with Jesus as its cornerstone (Eph 2:20). There is no need, then, for us to keep laying a new foundation. But there is a need for the church and all the followers of Christ to go wherever the Lord sends us with that foundational truth. You may not be one of the Twelve apostles, but you are one of millions who make up the apostolic church. You are sent today into a lost world, desperately in need of the gospel. Will you go on the Lord's mission, or will you only pursue your own agenda? Where will you go today for the Lord?

Here am I, Lord, send me.

[1] *Paul (an apostle of Christ Jesus **through the will of God**) and Timothy (a brother)*

Not everyone thought Paul was an apostle. He had to defend his apostleship against itinerant preachers who questioned his credentials, especially in his letters to the Corinthians. According to Paul, he was an apostle because, like the Twelve, he had seen the risen Jesus (1 Cor 9:1), performed signs and wonders (2 Cor 12:12), suffered for the sake of the gospel (1 Cor 4:9), and most importantly, he was appointed by Jesus himself to that responsibility. A self-appointed apostle is a contradiction in terms; true apostles can only be sent by the Lord.

Thus, Paul knew himself to be an apostle "through the will of God" (Col 1:1; see also 1 Cor 1:1, 2 Cor 1:1, Eph 1:1, 2 Tim 1:1), who called (Rom 1:1) and commanded him (1 Tim 1:1, Titus 1:1-3) to assume this role. His appointment was "not from men nor through men, but through Jesus Christ" (Gal 1:1). It was the will of God.

The will of God, of course, covers morality. But here, Paul is thinking more of God's missional will for accomplishing his purposes for the world. God is not merely calling Paul to keep the Ten Commandments, but to accomplish a mission for him.

Some might wonder if Paul liked to call himself an apostle for the prestige of it. But the only other words Paul uses to describe himself in the opening lines of his letters are slave (Rom 1:1; Phil 1:1; Titus 1:1) and prisoner of Christ (Philemon 1). For Paul, then, an apostle is not a dominating force or a self-appointed leader exerting his will on others, but a servant who follows the will of God. While we might regard "apostle" as a title of authority, Paul likely interpreted the term as a reminder that he was under authority—under the authority of the Lord who had sent him out.

This is true for each of us. Whether we have a title or not, whether we are a leader or not, as Christians we live under the authority of Jesus. We are called to do the will of God—not only the moral will of God by reflecting his character in our thoughts, words and actions, but also the missional will of God for our life.

God's will for Paul was for him to be an apostle. God also has a will for you. What has God appointed you to do and be in this season of your life? Whatever God's moral or missional will might be for you, the main thing is that you obey that will.

Show me your ways, O Lord, teach me your paths, lead me in your truth.

¹ Paul (an apostle of Christ Jesus through the will of God) **and Timothy (a brother)**

This letter not only comes from Paul, but also from his co-worker Timothy, whom Paul met on his second missionary journey (see Acts 16:1-3). Timothy, his Jewish mother Lois, and grandmother Eunice (but not Timothy's Greek father) likely had become Christians in Lystra, and the members of that church had commended Timothy to Paul. After having Timothy circumcised to avoid offending the Jews, Paul took him along as a traveling companion. Whenever Timothy is mentioned in his letters, Paul speaks highly of him and mentions him more frequently than any other co-worker (see 1 Cor 4:17; 16:10; Phil 2:22; 1 Thess 3:2; 1 Tim 1:2).

Paul was not a "Lone Ranger" apostle. He almost always worked—and wrote—in tandem with others. The only letters in which Paul's name alone appears in the opening line are Romans, Ephesians, and his personal letters to Timothy and Titus. Those who are included as co-writers in the other letters are Sosthenes (1 Corinthians), Timothy (2 Corinthians, Philippians, 1 and 2 Thessalonians and Philemon), Silas (1 and 2 Thessalonians) and some co-workers (Galatians).

Paul, of course, is the chief author. While he begins and ends his letters with plural pronouns (like we, us and our), Paul mostly refers to himself with singular pronouns (like I, me and my). Yet we should not imagine that Paul wrote like many do today—in a quiet place, by himself, in one sitting. His co-workers likely had more input in a process that may have involved multiple drafts.[7] Timothy may have even been involved in the actual putting of ink to parchment, since Paul's hands were in chains (see Col 4:18).

Because of his co-workers, Paul was able to resist the very common temptation to go it alone in the life of faith. Sometimes we go it alone because other people are such a bother, or it seems easier to do it ourselves, or we want to avoid accountability, or we want to receive all the glory if our endeavor succeeds. Resist that urge. To fully do the will of God, do not rely solely on your own understanding, energy or skills. Instead rely on the Lord and on the Christian sisters and brothers the Lord has placed in your life. They can help you accomplish God's will for your life, and you can help them accomplish God's will for theirs.

Savior, your yoke is easy and your burden is light, and it's all because you and the people you send into my life are helping carry the load. Thank you.

*[1] Paul (an apostle of Christ Jesus through the will of God) and Timothy (a brother); [2] **to those in Colossae,** the holy-ones and faithful brothers [and sisters] in Christ; grace to you and peace from God our Father.*

This letter was written to the Christians in Colossae, an ancient town in the mountainous valley of the Lycus River, about 120 miles east of Ephesus, the capital of the province. Immediately to the south of Colossae was a high ridge of difficult-to-cross mountains, but the Lycus valley provided the easiest route through them to connect eastern and western Asia Minor.

About 400 AD, the Greek historian Xenophen called Colossae "an inhabited city, prosperous and large," with a thriving textile industry that produced dark reddish wool. By Paul's day, however, Colossae's importance appears to have diminished.

The religious environment of Colossae was shaped by a strong paganism. Coins minted in Colossae at this time testify to the worship of deities like Isis, Serapis, Helios (a sun god), Demeter, Artemis and Men (a moon god), to name a few. The area was a center of magic and superstition. But there were also many Jews there. In 213 BC, a Greek ruler transported 2000 Jewish families to the Lycus Valley to bring some political stability. By 62 BC at least 11,000 free Jewish males were living in the same district as Colossae. These Jews not only influenced the pagans around them, but the Jews were also strongly influenced by the magical practices of the pagans.

In spite of the many Jews in this region, the Colossian church was most likely composed of former pagans. I say that because Paul will later state that they had lived in the uncircumcision of the flesh (Col 2:13) and formerly worshiped idols (Col 3:5-7), which would not be a fitting description of Jews. In addition, Paul never once quotes the OT or refers to the OT Law in this letter, which he would be more likely to do if he were addressing Jews.

In our day, some might mourn the fact that our nation and our neighborhoods are much more religiously mixed than in the past. But our situation is not nearly as pluralistic as what Paul faced in Colossae and other communities in the Roman empire. And yet, in spite of the religious plurality, the gospel of Christ was able to make headway and transform the world. The gospel can do the same today. In fact, we should view today's pluralism as a blessing in that the Lord is sending the nations to our doorsteps for us to bear witness to the light of Christ.

Creator of all,, you have sent us into the world with your good news. Thank you also for sending the world to us that we might be your witnesses.

> [1] *Paul (an apostle of Christ Jesus through the will of God) and Timothy (a brother);* [2] *to those in Colossae,* **the holy-ones** *and faithful brothers [and sisters] in Christ; grace to you and peace from God our Father.*

Paul not only describes himself as an apostle in the opening of this letter; he also describes the letter's recipients as "holy-ones" (*hagios*). This is often translated as "saints," but that term is tainted by the widespread notion that saints are a small subset of believers who have an above-average dedication to the Lord. Paul, however, regards *all* believers as *hagios.* Unfortunately, the term "holy-ones" also can be misleading because many can hardly hear the word "holy" without thinking "holier than thou," the kind of people who use their self-righteousness to condemn others.

Many people have such negative opinions of "holy" because they view holiness as a human endeavor instead of a divine gift. They believe holiness is a human accomplishment: a righteousness achieved by mustering the spiritual energy to pray more frequently, obey God more readily, love others more deeply, and forgive more quickly than the average person. If they appear to be sincere and successful in all this, we praise them as saints. If they seem to be insincere or unsuccessful in this, then we criticize them as "holier than thou" hypocrites. For Paul, however, being holy is a gift bestowed by God and it is often mentioned in this letter (see Col 1:4, 12, 22, 26; 3:12).

Set-apartness was the original idea behind holiness. Primarily it is God who is set apart; God is the Holy One, beside whom there is no other comparable god or creature (Isa 43:10-15). God is uniquely eternal, powerful, wise, righteous and good. But even though God is set apart from all others, God longs to share his holiness, to draw all humanity (even sinful humanity) into the circle of his holy love. So through the actions of God in establishing and maintaining a relationship with humanity through Christ, people can also be holy. We could think of it as relational holiness, for it only takes on reality in relationship with the holy God. Apart from this relationship, we are unholy; but in relationship with God through Christ, we too are set apart as holy.

Perhaps you do not regard yourself as holy and do not even *want* to be thought of as holy. But if you are in Christ, God thinks of you that way. Even though the word often gets misused today, do not reject this gift from the Lord. In Christ, you are holy, which we will explore even further tomorrow.

Holy Lord, I deserve many labels — sinner, hypocrite, liar, egotist, coveter — but I thank you for calling me holy and placing me among your holy people.

¹ Paul (an apostle of Christ Jesus through the will of God) and Timothy (a brother); ² to those in Colossae, the holy-ones and faithful brothers [and sisters] in Christ; grace to you and peace from God our Father.

There are three facets to holiness.

(1) Possessional holiness. God "sets us apart" as holy by choosing us "to be his people, his treasured possession" (Dt 7:6, NIV). That verse goes on to say that God's people are special to the Lord not because we deserve it, but simply because the Lord loves us. Israel, Jesus, the church—we are holy to the Lord, set apart as his special treasure (see also Col 3:12).

(2) Moral holiness. God also "sets us apart" as holy by transforming us to reflect his own character. As the Lord said to Israel, "if you will indeed obey my voice and keep my covenant...you shall be to me a kingdom of priests and a holy nation" (Ex 19:5-6, ESV). Although the law alone cannot make God's people morally holy, the work of Jesus can. Through the sacrifice of Christ, God *reckons* us as morally holy (it's called justification), and through Jesus' gift of the Holy Spirit, God actually *grows* moral holiness within us (in a process called sanctification). Due to the goodness of Jesus flowing into our lives like life-giving sap flowing from the vine to the branches (Jn 15:1-17), we are able to move toward obedience. People are not holy because they behave themselves, but only because they are in Christ, and Christ is at work in them.

(3) Missional holiness. In addition, God "sets us apart" to join him in his mission. Israel was holy, set apart to be a blessing to the nations (Gen 22:18). Jesus was holy, set apart to seek and save the lost. And the church is holy, set apart to proclaim and live out the gospel (1 Pet 2:9). When the church is set apart for God's mission, it does not mean that we are better than the lost world, but that we are called to love that lost world.

These are three facets of holiness, and only when all three are in play can holiness be whole. It just won't do, for instance, if we aim to be morally holy without sensing our value to God. Or if we go on a mission for God, but neglect moral holiness.

And remember, all three facets only take on reality in relationship to God. We are not holy-ones because we belong to the church, live morally, and are active in good causes. We are only holy when we belong to *God*, reflect *God's* moral character, and join *God* in his mission.

Lord, I don't want to merely "take time to be holy," as if it were a part-time endeavor. I want to be holy, treasured by you, transformed by you and active with you.

*¹ Paul (an apostle of Christ Jesus through the will of God) and Timothy (a brother); ² to those in Colossae, the holy-ones **and faithful brothers [and sisters]** in Christ; grace to you and peace from God our Father.*

Paul commends his readers as faithful brothers and sisters (the plural word for brothers in Greek can also include women). Of the 127 times Paul mentions brothers, he is almost always referring to brothers and sisters in the faith, not biological kindred. Such talk is not found in the OT because prior to the coming of Jesus, the biological connection was the primary criterion for determining who could be counted as a brother.

But one of the astonishing things Jesus did was to set aside the importance of a biological connection in the family of God. In Christ, Jews and non-Jews could be brothers and sisters together. Outside of Christ, they would only be a conglomerate of humanity, members of competing ethnic and economic groups. But in Christ, Jews and non-Jews are all adopted into God's family of faith.

It's likely that the family-feel of the church was a contributing factor to its early rapid growth. Those who felt socially isolated would have been especially attracted to the love and concern of the followers of Jesus. By functioning as a family, the church became the primary source of a believer's identity, relationships, behavior patterns, values, and loyalty. In a cruel, competitive world, it gave people a place to belong.

While it's true that some trade guilds in the eastern Roman Empire also called each other brothers, most of their members came from the same social class and gender. In the church, however, people from many different classes and ethnic groups became brothers and sisters in Christ. This closeness among those who would not normally associate together was so striking that some opponents of the church thought all this family talk was evidence that Christians practiced incest.

In spite of his frequent references to brothers in his letters, Col 1:2 is the only time Paul addresses recipients of a letter in this way. Perhaps he wanted to assure the Colossians that even though they had never met, he did not regard them as his fan club, his servants, or his underlings. They were his family.

Maybe you do not call each other "brother" or "sister" in your own local church. But whether you state it overtly or not, the important thing is that you treat one another as family—with loyalty, love and faithfulness.

I praise you, Heavenly Father, that you have provided me with a spiritual home and a family of faith.

*¹ Paul (an apostle of Christ Jesus through the will of God) and Timothy (a brother); ² to those in Colossae, the holy-ones and faithful brothers [and sisters] **in Christ;** grace to you and peace from God our Father.*

Paul describes his readers as being in two locations: they are *in Colossae* and they are *in Christ* (a parallel hidden by some translations). Their cultural location in Colossae certainly shapes the believers who live there, but what determines their identity even more is their spiritual location in Christ. For Christians, no matter where they live, they are in Christ.

Paul refers to believers being "in Christ" over 80 times in his letters. For him, Jesus is more than someone to trust and obey, for those terms imply a measure of distance between the believer and Christ. Rather, Paul believes we participate in Christ, living within him, moving so much in union with him that what happens to him in some sense happens to us as well.

Paul points out what this means in other letters. "In Christ" we are alive to God (Rom 6:11), beyond condemnation (Rom 8:1), enriched (1 Cor 1:4), a new creation (2 Cor 5:17), set free (Gal 2:4), God's children (Gal 3:26), chosen before time began (Eph 1:4), redeemed and forgiven (Eph 1:7), brought near to God (Eph 2:13), at peace (Phil 4:7), assured of faith (1 Tim 3:13), recipients of grace (2 Tim 1:9), saved (2 Tim 3:15), and much more.

Colossians reaffirms these same truths. In this letter Paul focuses on being "in Christ" (1:2, 28), "in the Lord" (3:18, 20; 4:7, 17), "in whom" (1:14; 2:3, 11-12), "in him" (1:16-17, 19; 2:6-7, 9-10) and "with Christ" (2:12-13, 20; 3:1, 3-4)—English translations may vary slightly from this list. Colossians especially shows that in Christ we also experience his death, burial, and resurrection (Col 2:11-13, 20; 3:1-4).

Christians often talk about the importance of inviting Jesus into your heart and life. He stands at the door and knocks, calling us to let him in (see Rev 3:20). This important verse was critical in my own coming to faith. But sometimes we take this great truth of Christ living in our hearts and twist it. We end up thinking of Jesus as nothing but our own little household god confined to the small world that orbits inside our skulls. But Jesus doesn't just want to be in *your* life (a truth declared in Col 1:27); he also calls you to come into *his* life. He calls you move out beyond yourself and experience the wide, open spaces of who he is and what he is doing. Some of us have been playing inside our own hearts for too long. It's time to enter a new place by living in the Lord.

"Out of my bondage, sorrow and night, Jesus, I come; Jesus, I come. Into Thy freedom, gladness and light, Jesus, I come to Thee."

> *[1] Paul (an apostle of Christ Jesus through the will of God) and Timothy (a brother); [2] to those in Colossae, the holy-ones and faithful brothers [and sisters] in Christ;* **grace to you** *and peace from God our Father.*

As he does in most of his letters, Paul gives an opening blessing to the recipients. By definition, a blessing conveys what it expresses. Just as the Word of God is alive and active (Heb 4:12), able to accomplish that for which it is sent (Isa 55:10-11), so a word of blessing accomplishes what it says; God blesses us through it. Paul is not praying, promising or wishing for something to be true for them. He simply declares what is the case—as the blessing is heard or read, God's people are receiving good things.

Paul's blessing is based upon a creative word-play. Instead of using the common verb for greeting (*chairō*), Paul replaced that verb with a similar-sounding noun, *charis*, which means "grace." Word-play is an important part of proclaiming the gospel, a way to "take captive every thought to make it obedient to Christ" (2 Cor 10:5, NIV). Words which had been neutral or even hostile to the gospel message can be shifted in meaning or replaced in order to declare the gospel. Some believers might wince when they see commercialized versions of this spiritual wordplay (as can be seen in thousands of gospel-toting tee-shirts in America), but even these represent attempts to turn language back to its original purpose of glorifying God. So with the exchange of a few letters, Paul transforms greeting into grace, *chairō* into *charis*. It's the power of language put into service for Jesus, the Word of God.

Paul mentions grace in every single one of his letters. Its most basic meaning includes the granting of love, kindness and good-will. Paul uses it to refer to God's love as a gift, not something that one earns or deserves. While it includes the idea of forgiveness, grace also points to overflowing generosity on all fronts.[8] Without the undeserved gift of God's grace, we would only be unholy and faithless enemies of the gospel.

Although the explicit references to grace are few in Colossians (only four total), it is nonetheless grace which lies behind Paul's discussions of the person and work of Christ, as well as the false and true means of living in a holy way. The book as a whole originates in grace, reveals grace, and conveys grace. May the Lord bless you today with his grace.

Gracious Savior, I have no right to your grace, but you have blessed me with it anyway. Thank you for empowering me to live by your grace each day.

*¹ Paul (an apostle of Christ Jesus through the will of God) and Timothy (a brother); ² to those in Colossae, the holy-ones and faithful brothers [and sisters] in Christ; grace to you **and peace from God our Father.***

Paul not only gives his readers a word of grace, but following Jewish custom, he also imparts a word of peace, which appears in the opening address of every one of his letters.

Paul's letters often associate peace with reconciliation with God ("Therefore, since we have been justified by faith, we have peace with God through our Lord Jesus Christ," Rom 5:1, ESV) and reconciliation with others ("If possible, as far as it depends on you, live peaceably with all," Rom 12:18, ESV). This peace comes as a gift from God (Rom 15:13), through the work of Jesus on the cross, who not only preached peace (Eph 2:17), but is peace embodied ("For he himself is our peace," Eph 2:14, NIV).

We will encounter the term "peace" twice more in Colossians: when Paul speaks of Jesus reconciling all things through his blood on the cross (1:20), and when Paul calls on the believers to let Christ's peace rule in their hearts so they can live in peace as one body in Christ (3:15). So when Paul blesses his readers with peace, he is not merely thinking of us individually experiencing an inner calmness, but instead he is wanting us to live together in reconciliation with God and others, to experience even now the final wholeness God intends for creation.

The source of this peace (and grace) is God the Father. This name for God was widely used by Christians because of Jesus' own practice. As the Son of God, he called God his Father, and now all those who have been adopted into God's family can also speak to God in the same way (see Jn 1:12-13). As our Father, God has the power needed and the compassion required to grant peace to his children.

Since so many of the phrases and terms in Paul's opening address can also be found in his other letters, we might wonder if they had just become clichés. But that doesn't appear to be the case for Paul. Rather, he is so enlivened by the new reality brought by Jesus that he cannot introduce himself without mentioning his apostleship. He cannot write to other believers without rejoicing in their new status. He cannot greet them without bestowing the grace and peace of God. May we never succumb to a spiritual boredom over these divine miracles.

Take from me, Lord Jesus, the lifelessness of lethargy and boredom, and in its place grant me your energizing peace.

We Are Holy in the Lord

to the tune of Easter Hymn: *Christ the Lord is Ris'n Today*
© 2010 David J. Landegent

We are holy in the Lord—alleluia
Here with God, we are restored—alleluia
Grace and peace to us belong—alleluia
Through these gifts God makes us strong—alleluia

We're a fam'ly formed in Christ—alleluia
Faithful to His sacrifice—alleluia
Grace and peace to us belong—alleluia
Through these gifts God makes us strong—alleluia

Prayers of thanks

Colossians 1:3-8

January 15-28

[3] We give-thanks to God, the Father of our Lord Jesus Christ, at all times when praying for you, [4] having heard of your faith in Christ Jesus and the love which you have for all the holy-ones [5] due to the hope being kept for you in the heavens, which you previously heard about in the word of truth, the good-message [6] which is making itself present to you—even as in all the world it is fruit-bearing and growing, so also among you, since the day you heard and knew the grace of God in truth, [7] just as you learned from Epaphras, our beloved fellow-slave, who is a faithful servant of Christ for us, [8] the one who informed us of your love in the Spirit.

Paul had a thriving life of prayer, especially on behalf of the churches. He, of course, prayed about their problems, asking God to intervene. But even more importantly he prayed with gratitude for how God was already operating in their lives. And Paul let them know of his gratitude. He begins with expressions of gratitude in all of his letters except three (Galatians, 1 Timothy and Titus). In Colossians, Paul's report of thankfulness consists of one long sentence running from verses 3-7. (By the way, long flowery sentences were characteristic of Asiatic rhetoric, which would be fitting when writing to a church in Asia Minor.)[9]

Here and elsewhere Paul never thanks his readers directly, but instead reports that he gives thanks to God for what God is doing in their lives. This is in keeping with Paul's general approach of seeing God involved in everything. It's not merely the case that the Colossians are doing good things and Paul thanks *them* for it. Rather, it is God who is working good things in the Colossians, and Paul gratefully calls attention to it. And by doing so, he brings encouragement to the Colossians. When someone says, "thank you for helping out," we feel appreciated, but when they say, "I thank God for you," we feel even more appreciated and are delighted to know God is using us in his work.

Prayers of thanks were not nearly as common among the pagans as among the Jews. The pagans preferred instead to express gratitude through votive offerings.[10] In those times in which they did say thanks, it was usually for some physical benefit like rain or health. Paul, however, focuses on spiritual benefits, such as how a church's faith is flourishing and making an impact on the world. The next time you're tempted to complain, you might want to instead thank the Lord for what he's doing in your midst.

Open our eyes, Lord, so we can see your hand at work in the people around us and thank you for it.

³ **We give-thanks to God**, *the Father of our Lord Jesus Christ, at all times when praying for you*

Giving thanks is a prominent theme in Colossians. It appears six times in this letter—in the form of a verb (1:3, 12; 3:17), a noun (2:7; 4:2), and an adjective (3:15). Although Paul might use these same words slightly more often in his longer letters, on a per word basis Colossians refers to thanksgiving twice as often as those longer letters.

It was tempting to translate "We give-thanks to God" as "We say *gracias* to God" because that Spanish word does a better job than the English word in preserving the important connection between the Greek words for grace and thanks. In Greek, grace is *charis* and is found within the word for giving thanks, *eucharisteō*. It's unfortunate that this linguistic connection between grace and thanks is not strong in the English language. The connection still shows itself, but barely, in words like gratitude, grateful, and gratis, and in the phrase "saying grace" to describe a thankful prayer given before a meal. The Spanish word for "thank you," *gracias*, more readily reminds us of grace. *Gracias* is the fitting response to grace.

Paul sees God's grace at work in the Colossian believers and so he says *gracias* to God. The Colossians did not come to faith in Christ because they were spiritually astute. Nor did they trust in Jesus because Paul himself was so persuasive. They only came to the Lord because of God's grace, and so Paul can only respond with *gracias*.

In his other letters, Paul was also thankful for deliverance from sin (Rom 6:17; 7:25); victory over death (1 Cor 15:57); the spread of the gospel (2 Cor 2:14-15); co-workers (2 Cor 8:16); spiritual gifts (1 Cor 14:18); and his own appointment and empowerment for ministry (1 Tim 1:12).

Today people often think of thankfulness as an internal attitude. But Paul grew up in a Jewish atmosphere in which thanksgiving was an act of public praise for the purpose of inviting others to join in.[11] The same psalmist who says: "I will bless the Lord at all times; his praise shall continually be in my mouth," then adds, "Oh, magnify the Lord with me, and let us exalt his name together" (Ps 34:1, 3, ESV). In the same spirit, Paul reports his gratitude as an encouragement for the Colossians to also be thankful to the Lord. He encourages us to join in this as well.

I am glad, O God, to join with the millions of others who even now are offering their prayers of thanks to you.

*³ We give-thanks to God, **the Father of our Lord Jesus Christ,** at all times when praying for you*

In Colossians, thanking God means thanking the Father: 1:3 (God, the Father of our Lord Jesus Christ); 1:12 (the Father); and 3:17 (God the Father). This is actually different from Paul's other letters. When Paul specifies who is to be thanked in his other letters, it's nearly always just "God." The only exceptions to this are: Eph 5:20, which expresses thanks to God the Father; 1 Tim 1:12, where Christ Jesus our Lord is thanked; and Rom 1:8 and 7:25 where Paul thanks God through Jesus Christ.

It's unclear why Paul makes this change in Colossians, but it's a helpful variation. Today many people in public settings express thanks to a generic god. For example, an athlete might credit "the Lord" for her success on the soccer field. A musician might thank "God" for his musical achievements at an awards ceremony. When hearing such words, we can't help but wonder, which lord is she talking about, which god is being given the glory. Paul leaves us in no doubt here. He's thankful to the God who is the Father of our Lord Jesus Christ. There's nothing generic about this God.

This is important for Paul to state because he will soon deal with the issue of other gods, lords, powers, and authorities—an issue that appears more frequently in this letter than in any other. In an environment full of other rivals to the throne, then, it is necessary to "take a swim in the Specific Ocean," as we say at our house. Paul was not just thankful to any god, deity, or supernatural power, nor are we. We give thanks only to God the Father of our Lord Jesus Christ.

In fact, it's only because Jesus is the Son of the Father that we can be sons and daughters of the Father at all. There may be a sense in which God is our Father simply because he made us (see Mal 2:10). But because of sin, we actually had no standing in God's family. Nevertheless, the Father desired to draw us to himself, and he made that possible by sending his Son. So now all who believe in Jesus are given "the right to become the children of God" (Jn 1:12, NIV) and are adopted into God's family (Eph 1:5; Rom 8:12-17). In Christ, the Father of Jesus is now our Father too. Thanks be to God; thanks be to God the Father of our Lord Jesus Christ!

Bless you, Heavenly Father, for adopting us into your forever family through Jesus your eternal Son.

³ *We give-thanks to God, the Father of our Lord Jesus Christ, **at all times when praying for you***

Paul often uses all-encompassing words like "all" and "always" in reference to prayers and thankfulness. Paul is "always" thankful (1 Cor 1:4; Phil 1:3; Col 1:3; 1 Thess 1:2; 2 Thess 1:3; 2:13; Philemon 4) and "always" prays (Rom 1:10; Phil 1:4; 2 Thess 1:11; 2 Tim 1:3) for "all" of them (Rom 1:8; Phil 1:4; 1 Thess 1:2) for "all" the ways God has blessed them (1 Cor 1:5; Philemon 6), because their lives have impacted "all" God's people (Eph 1:15; Col 1:4; 1 Thess 1:7; 2 Thess 1:3; Philemon 5); and "all" the world (Rom 1:8; Col 1:6; 1 Thess 1:8). One might dismiss Paul as a chronic exaggerator in this, but more charitably we might think of Paul as praising a God whose work knows no bounds.

Some translations give the impression that Paul always prays or gives thanks without stopping to eat or sleep. This cannot be what Paul means. His life of prayer is not formed through an endlessly repeated check-list of praises and concerns that he works through. This would be trading the legalism of the Pharisees for a legalism in Christ. There would be no good news in that.

Paul did not write these words to the Colossians to say, "I have successfully checked off your name on my prayer list every day" or even every hour. He is simply saying that the abounding grace of God has flowed from God through the Colossians to Paul, and he continues to live in that mighty river of grace by responding in prayer. His prayer arises not from guilt or worry, but from the experience of God's grace. Even in the action of prayer, he experiences the grace of being welcomed, loved, and heard by God. Thus, thankfulness is not a place Paul visits on occasion; it is the environment in which he lives. His waking moments are filled with gratitude for what God is doing in the Colossian believers and others like them.

And the good news is that whether we pray at all times or not, God listens at all times, for as Jesus said to the Father, "I knew that you *always* hear me" (Jn 11:42, ESV, italics mine). And further, Jesus himself "*always* lives to intercede" for us (Heb 7:25, NIV, italics mine).

So when you read about Paul's continual prayer, don't look on it as one more standard that you'll fail to live up to. Instead, rejoice that you can speak with the Father at any time and he will listen.

I thank you, Father, that you always hear me.

> *3 We give-thanks to God . . . 4 having heard of your **faith** in Christ Jesus and the **love** which you have for all the holy-ones 5 due to the **hope** being kept for you in the heavens, which you previously heard about in the word of truth, the good-message*

Paul gets more specific concerning what it is about the Colossians that makes him grateful to God, and it can be summarized by the trio of faith, love and hope. Some refer to the members of this trio as virtues, but I would rather avoid that term, for it carries the connotation of moral perfections that arise through human effort. After all, "virtue" stems from *vir*, the Latin word for "man." But faith, hope and love are to be characterized by their object and their source (which is God), not by the human accomplishments of believing, loving and hoping.[12]

Paul also places this trio together (in varying order) in Rom 5:1-5, 1 Cor 13:13, Gal 5:5-6, Eph 1:15-18, 1 Thess 1:3 and 5:8. In the three instances of the trio appearing in the opening section of thanks (Ephesians, Colossians and 1 Thessalonians) all follow the order of faith, love and hope. When the object of faith, love, and hope is specified (which is not often), then faith is in the Lord, love is for God's people, and hope is also in the Lord.

Some writers interpret the elements of this trio in terms of time. Emil Brunner once said, "We live in the past by faith; we live in the future by hope; we live in the present by love."[13] There is a measure of truth in his words, yet each member of the trio stands in relationship to all aspects of time. *Faith* continues in the present as an ongoing relationship of trust in the Lord, even as it counts on the past acts and promises of the Lord to face the future. And even though *hope* is based on what God has done in the past and keeps us going in the present, yet it definitely focuses on the future when all the "not yet" truths of the kingdom will become "now" truths. Likewise with *love*—it may build on the memories of the past and endure into eternity (1 Cor 13:8), but its reality is best seen in daily living with God's people and others.

Lord Jesus, thank you for granting to me the gift of faith, the assurance of hope, and the power of love.

> *³ We give-thanks to God . . . ⁴ **having heard of your faith in Christ Jesus** and the love which you have for all the holy-ones ⁵ due to the hope being kept for you in the heavens, which you previously heard about in the word of truth, the good-message*

Paul is grateful to God because even though he has never met the Colossian believers, he has heard of their faith. He has heard of their conversion to this new faith, as well as their continued growth in it (see Col 1:5-6). Theirs was not the kind of faith that sprouted quickly and then shriveled, like a seed planted on shallow soil (see Mt 13:20-21). Rather, it took root and grew (Col 2:7).

Here Paul emphasizes that we do not put our faith in a spiritual slogan, a teaching, a Christian idea, or even in faith itself. Rather, our faith is in a person, a person named Jesus (see also Col 2:5, 12). At its core, the Christian faith is a relational matter. Even when we speak of having faith in a "thing" (like the Bible), it's still a relational matter because that Bible comes from God. Our trust in the Bible is based on our trust in the God who spoke it and who still speaks it today. So who is this Jesus in whom the Colossians have faith? Very shortly, Paul will spell this out (Col 1:15-20).

While Paul might be thankful that each individual Christian in Colossae has his or her own faith in Jesus, here he observes how they trust in Jesus *together*. He has heard how they, as a church, have expressed that trust. Their faith was not merely an internal thing, hidden in the hearts of isolated believers. Rather, they placed their trust in someone outside of themselves (Jesus) and did this in conjunction with others. They knew that an isolated faith cannot thrive in the same way that the faith of a community of believers can. Together the Colossians lived out a life of faith, and somebody noticed it enough to let Paul know.

If someone were watching you, would they be able to tell that you trusted in Jesus, so much so that they'd remark to others about it? Or even more in keeping with the words of Paul, if someone were observing your *church*, would they be able to tell that you trust in Jesus together? Would it be so stirring to them that they'd let others know of your church's faith? Today I'm afraid that often the only two signs of a church stepping out in faith are (1) they walk out of their homes to go to a weekly service, and (2) they vote to take out a loan on a building project. There must be other ways to tell that a church is placing its trust in Jesus Christ.

Lord Jesus, I trust you. We trust you. Cause our trust to grow even more.

*³ We give-thanks to God . . . ⁴ having heard of your faith in Christ Jesus **and
the love which you have for all the holy-ones** ⁵ due to the hope being kept
for you in the heavens, which you previously heard about in the word of
truth, the good-message*

Another reason for Paul's gratitude to God is that the Colossian Christians
excel in love (*agape* in Greek). Paul credits this love, not to the naturally
affectionate personalities of the believers there, but to the work of God in
their lives. Later, in verse 8, Paul will point out that their love happens "in
the Spirit," for love is a fruit of the Holy Spirit (Gal 5:22-23).

Although the word *agapē* existed before Paul's time, it was not used
much until he and other Christians latched onto it. Perhaps Paul used this
term, rather than other Greek words for love, in order to avoid confusing
the unique qualities of Christian love with other varieties of love prevalent
in his culture—and ours.[14]

Paul especially rejoiced to see how the Colossians showed love to one
another. This would not have come naturally, because they were not flaw-
less, easy-to-love saints, but ordinary flawed believers just like you...and
just like all the people in your church. Yes, all God's people are called to
moral holiness, but even if we are not far along in that calling, we are still
his holy-ones, set apart and treasured by God. And if we're treasured by
God, it's only fitting that we treasure one another as well.

Modern readers might be taken aback by the fact that Paul and other
NT writers do not speak much of loving those who are not Christians. There
are, of course, general calls to love others, and Jesus did command us to love
our enemies, and our neighbors. Yet most NT references about love focus
on loving fellow Christians (such as Jn 15:12; Rom 12:10; Eph 4:2; 1 Thess
4:9; Philemon 5; Heb 13:1; 1 Pet 4:8; 1 Jn 4:7). This does not mean that the
church should become inwardly focused, loving each other to the exclusion
of others. Rather, the love shared among the believers is to be so intense
and so unusual in an indifferent or hostile culture that it cannot help but
draw others to Christ. Love flowed so freely in the church that it overflowed
to the world. As Paul said in 1 Thess 3:12, "May the Lord make you increase
and abound in love for one another *and for all*" (ESV, emphasis mine).

*We call on you, Savior of the world, to pour out your love into our hearts so
that it flows to all your people and to all your world.*

*³ We give-thanks to God . . . ⁴ having heard of your faith in Christ Jesus and the love which you have for all the holy-ones ⁵ **due to the hope being kept for you in the heavens,** which you previously heard about in the word of truth, the good-message*

Although we might think that faith and love would cause the Colossians to have hope, Paul actually says the opposite here. Their hope is what causes them to have faith and love. Hope is what helps them press on when hardships make it difficult to trust Jesus or love others. If there is no hope of eternal life with God, there is less motivation to devote oneself to relationships that will end. But when hope is present, then people not only find the strength to get up in the morning, but also the strength to pour themselves into their relationships—both divine and human.

Many people regard hope as roughly equivalent to a wish. For them to say, "I wish it would rain" or "I hope it will rain," is to say the same thing. This wishful kind of hoping, however, is only a subjective thing, something we'd like to see happen even though we have no reason to believe it will. Biblical hope, however, is different. It's an *internal* confidence in an *external* being named God that something will take place. Psalm 71 reveals both sides of this coin. The psalmist has an *internal* hope ("But I will hope continually," verse 14, ESV) because the Lord is his *external* hope ("For you, O Lord, are my hope," verse 5, ESV). Subjective feelings of hope are wonderful, but they mean nothing if our hope is placed in the wrong object or person. What validates hope is not the intensity of our internal optimism about the future, but the reliability of the One in whom we have placed our hope.

Our *internal* hope may be kept in our hearts, but our *external* hope is far more secure because it is kept in heaven. Our feelings of hopefulness will come and go, but our actual hope remains constant because it's in heaven, where it cannot perish, spoil or fade (see 1 Pet 1:4). And it's kept in heaven because that's where Jesus is (Col 3:1); our real hope is always connected to him. Hopes that have nothing to do with Jesus will soon wither like a branch cut off from a vine. Only in Christ do our hopes live.

My hope is in you, Lord—not in my own optimism or self-generated confidence. You are my hope and my strength.

[3] We give-thanks to God . . . [4] having heard of your faith in Christ Jesus and the love which you have for all the holy-ones [5] due to the hope being kept for you in the heavens, **which you previously heard about in the word of truth,** *the good-message*

The Colossians have hope because they had heard and believed the "word of truth" about Jesus. Unfortunately, many have struggled with the whole notion of truth. They echo the question of Pilate, "What is truth?" (Jn 18:38).

According to the Bible, truth is a relational word intended to convey the reliability and faithfulness of those who speak it. The same Hebrew word often translated as truth (*emeth*) is even more often translated as faithful and trustworthy, words which describe a relationship. Even the English language still conveys this relational aspect of truth. When someone is described as a *true* friend, it does not mean that they report accurate information, but that you can rely on them to stand by your side. Likewise, Jesus Christ is the true God, not only in distinction from false gods, but also in that he can be relied upon to be true to us. Similarly, the gospel is true not only because it conveys accurate data, but even more because it introduces us to the Lord who is trustworthy. The relational aspect of truth is especially prominent when Jesus claims in Jn 14:6 that he not only speaks the truth; he *is* the truth. Therefore, the gospel is a message of truth because it puts us into relationship with the One who is the Truth.

Modern ideas fail to recognize the relational importance of truth. The modernists who think truth is about quantifiable facts and figures have forgotten about people. The relativists who think everyone's truth is true quickly reach the relationship-killing conclusion of "you go your way and I'll go mine." The skeptics who think nobody's truth is true only see others as arrogant people who need to be knocked down a peg or two. And the postmodernists who insist, "my truth is true" or "our truth is true," only see others as truth-competitors who must be defeated. All these concepts of truth are relationally-challenged.

Because this relational element is often missing from contemporary ideas about truth, many are afraid that truth is nothing but an oppressive set of data cobbled together so that one party can gain control over others. To them, this oppressive truth is nothing but advertising slogans and political propaganda. But Paul instead sees the truth as a relational word from the Lord, an invitation to experience the reality of his grace. The Colossians have found delight in this truth, and so do we.

Send out your light and truth, and let them lead me, Lord—to you.

*³ We give-thanks to God . . . ⁴ having heard of your faith in Christ Jesus and the love which you have for all the holy-ones ⁵ due to the hope being kept for you in the heavens, which you previously heard about in the word of truth, **the good-message***

The message of Jesus is not only a *true* word; it's also a *good* word. Here Paul uses the term *euaggelion* (a Greek compound noun formed from the stem *eu-* meaning "good" and *aggelia*, meaning "message"), which is often translated as "gospel."

Paul liked this term *euaggelion*: nearly 80% of the 76 times it is used in the NT are in his writings. He preached it (Rom 1:15), declared it (1 Thess 2:2), shared it (1 Thess 2:8), proclaimed it (Gal 2:2; Col 1:23; 1 Thess 2:9), and defended it before the nations (Phil 1:7, 16). It was good because the proclamation of Jesus' life, death and resurrection brought peace, salvation and eternal life to all who heard it.

Unfortunately, some Christians only proclaim a *stern* message of morality instead of the *good* message of Christ. In recent years, these Christians have become so intent on speaking against various societal sins, that they have twisted the gospel into a joyless and heavy-handed attempt to impose this morality on others. The world is not hearing the goodness of the good news from these misguided believers.

But we must also acknowledge that even when Christians do succeed in proclaiming the goodness of the good news, many sinful hearts will still reject it. Those who love the darkness rather than the light (see Jn 3:19-20) only hear the good news as an attack on their favorite idols—whether those idols be a beloved nation, material prosperity, favorite superstition, popular celebrity, or cherished addiction.

Thanks be to God, however, that this is not true of everyone. Some (like the Colossians) believe the good news, find freedom from sin and can thus live in the faith, love, and hope found in Christ. For them, the good news never becomes tiresome old news. Unlike those who quickly get bored with the latest ideas and move on to other novelties, the Christian simply bores deeper into the same deep well of the gospel. And if we persevere in drilling into the same gospel message, we will find inexhaustible aquifers of living water. Don't get bored with the good news—just bore a little deeper.

Lord, you're so good. Your message is good, your grace is good, your purposes are good. You're so good to me.

*[3] We give-thanks to God . . . [4] having heard of your faith in Christ Jesus and the love which you have for all the holy-ones [5] due to the hope being kept for you in the heavens, which you previously heard about in the word of truth, the good-message [6] **which is making itself present to you—even as in all the world** it is fruit-bearing and growing, so also among you, since the day you heard and knew the grace of God in truth,*

The word of truth—the good message about Jesus—is not some far-off thing spoken from distant lands or ages past. Rather, "the word is near you, in your mouth and in your heart" (Rom 10:8, quoting Dt 30:14, ESV). It has made itself present to the Colossians and us. The Greek verb here conveys both movement (the gospel is coming to you) and staying power (the gospel is remaining among you). It's not a "come-and-go" message.

Paul points out that this coming and staying power of the gospel did not just happen among the Colossians, but is happening all over the world. Paul will soon state this even more boldly when he says that the gospel has been "proclaimed to every created being under heaven" (Col 1:23).

Given that the Christian population at this point in history was small, we might be tempted to dismiss Paul's words about the gospel's worldwide growth as an exaggeration. Historians of that era, like Josephus and Tacitus, barely mention the Christians at all. Yet exaggeration, if we call it that, has an important role in the Scriptures. There are many places in which Scripture asserts that which seems to be way out of proportion to reality.

For instance, the claims of the psalmists—that the throne of the kings of Judah will last forever (Ps 89:4) or that Jerusalem was established as the joy of the whole earth (Ps 48:1-2)—would have seemed laughable to the surrounding empires. Likewise, when Jesus claims that those who trust in him will never thirst again (Jn 4:14) and won't even die (Jn 11:26), he seems to be claiming too much.

Yet what we might call exaggerations are actually current truths moving toward full reality in the future. When Paul says that we believers are holy (see Col 1:2), it may seem like an exaggeration to those familiar with our unholy ways, but it's a truth that will become even more fully true in the future. Likewise, here in verse 6, Paul sees that the gospel is already impacting the whole world, even though that will become more true when God's kingdom comes in its fullness. Like yeast, the gospel is working its way discreetly throughout the whole loaf of the world (see Mt 13:33).

Infiltrate my mind, O Lord, and our world, with your words of sweetness and light.

*³ We give-thanks to God . . . ⁵ due to the hope being kept for you in the heavens, which you previously heard about in the word of truth, the good-message ⁶ which is making itself present to you—even as in all the world **it is fruit-bearing and growing, so also among you, since the day you heard and knew the grace of God in truth,***

The good news of Jesus is not only present all around the world, but it is present in a "fruit-bearing and growing" way. Paul is not talking about institutional growth, resulting in new structures and regulations. He is not talking about economic growth with an increase in revenue or market-share. Nor is he talking about territorial growth, which often involves the use of force. Instead Paul's metaphor has agricultural roots, thus conveying the kind of growth that is alive and organic. When the gospel grows organically, faith, love, and hope spring to life in individuals, churches and communities.

Notice that Paul does not say that *believers* are bearing the fruit (although he will say that in Col 1:10). Nor are *he and his co-workers* bearing the fruit. Instead, it is the *gospel* itself which is bearing the fruit. Although we might say things like, "The farmer grows the fruit," in actuality the farmer only tends to the fruit. God alone can make fruit grow.

Without the fruit-bearing power of God's Word, believers can try all kinds of techniques to make their faith or their churches grow, but they will fail. "As the branch cannot bear fruit by itself, unless it abides in the vine, neither can you, unless you abide in me...apart from me you can do nothing" (Jn 15:4, 5b, ESV). As Paul noted in 1 Cor 3:5-10, he may plant and Apollos may water, but it is God who gives the growth.

Paul may be echoing themes from Genesis 1. Just as God's word bestowed fruitfulness on humanity in the first creation ("be fruitful and multiply," Gen 1:28), so now through Christ he bestows fruitfulness on his new creation—us. We ourselves are the first fruits brought forth by the Word of truth (see Jms 1:18).

The propaganda of the Roman Empire often claimed to bring fruitfulness to the world—seen especially in the vine themes carved into much of their official architecture. Yet Paul felt no need to refute their puny claims. Instead, he rejoices in the much more astounding fruitfulness of God's Word. That's where the real action is.

Grow the fruit of the Spirit, Lord Jesus, in my life and in my church, so there will be an abundant harvest of love, joy, peace, and patience.

[6] *. . . it is fruit-bearing and growing, so also among you, since the day you heard and knew the grace of God in truth,* [7] **just as you learned from Epaphras, our beloved fellow-slave, who is a faithful servant of Christ for us,** [8] **the one who informed us of your love in the Spirit.**

Although the gospel moves on its own power, it nearly always does so through human representatives. For the Colossians, this happened through a man named Epaphras.

Obviously, Paul did not think of himself or the Twelve apostles as the only ones who could proclaim the gospel. In fact, he rejoices that others can proclaim the gospel because it means that God's message still goes forth even as Paul and the other apostles face imprisonment and death.

Scholars conjecture that Epaphras first became a believer after hearing Paul preach during his long stay in Ephesus, the largest city in the province of Asia (see Acts 19). Epaphras then returned to his hometown of Colossae (see Col 4:12) to share this good news. Whatever Epaphras' story may have been, Paul clearly regards him as a valued worker, calling him a "beloved fellow-slave" and "faithful servant of Christ."

The implication of the term "fellow-slave" is that Paul also regards himself as a slave, a slave of Jesus (Rom 1:1; Gal 1:10; Phil 1:1; Titus 1:1). In spite of widespread cultural aversion to slavery, the frequency and ease with which Christians regarded themselves as slaves and servants of Christ is due to the fact that Jesus had turned the values of the world upside down. He's the one who said in Mk 10:43-44 that those who would be great in God's kingdom would function as servants and slaves.

Much as we rightly object to the whole idea of slavery, then, there is a real sense in which we are the Lord's slaves. We were bought with a price (1 Cor 6:20); we are called to obey; we are not free to do whatever we feel like doing. Yet, as the Lord's slaves, we are free, we are loved, we are blessed. To paraphrase the paradoxes of 1 Cor 1:25—slavery to God is more liberating than the freedom of men.

In looking back, then, on Paul's words of thanksgiving, we learn this about the gospel, as summarized by William Barclay: it is good news from God, true, universal, productive, full of grace and humanly-transmitted.[15]

Thank you, Lord and Redeemer, for freeing us to serve you. We gladly obey your call to join all the others who share your message with a world in bondage.

For the Gift of Faith in Christ
to the tune of Dix: *For the Beauty of the Earth*
© 2010 David J. Landegent

For the gift of faith in Christ, thank You, Father, bless-ed Lord.
For His gracious sacrifice, may You always be adored.
We have heard Your word of truth;
It is growing, bearing fruit.

For the gift of caring love, thank You, Father, from the heart
When it's love that's from above, walls of hatred fall apart
We have heard Your word of truth;
It is growing, bearing fruit.

For the gift of steadfast hope, thank You, Father; we're secure
Through all trials, we can cope, since Your promises are sure
We have heard Your word of truth;
It is growing, bearing fruit.

Prayers of asking

Colossians 1:9-14

January 29-February 25

> [9] *Because of this, we also, from the day we heard, have not stopped praying for you and asking in order that you may be filled with the knowledge of his will in all wisdom and Spirit-oriented understanding, [10] to walk worthily of the Lord in every form of pleasing, in every good work fruit-bearing and growing in the knowledge of God, [11] being empowered with all power in accordance with the might of his glory in all endurance and patience with joy, [12] giving-thanks to the Father for qualifying you for a share of the inheritance of the holy-ones in the light, [13] [the Father] who delivered us from the authority of darkness and relocated [us] to the kingdom of the Son of his love— [14] in whom we have redemption, the forgiveness of our sins—*

In eight of his nine letters to churches, Paul reported that he was thankful to God for them. In five of those letters, including this section of Colossians, he also told them that he was praying to God for them.

In contemporary usage, the words "prayer" and "pray" refer to any words of communication with God (including praise, thanks, confessions of sin, promises made, expressions of sorrow and anger, and asking for God to act). The primary meaning of the term "prayer," however, is about asking. In fact, the English words "prayer" and "pray" at one time referred not only to asking God for things, but to any kind of asking. For example, an Englishman in an earlier time might say to another, "What time is it, I pray thee?"

Paul led an active prayer life, especially praying for the churches, and he called for those churches to be faithful in prayer too. In fact, when they were separated by distance, prayer functioned as the main link between Paul and these believers. This understanding fits with Dietrich Bonhoeffer's thought that we relate to others through Christ, for he is the mediator not only between us and God, but also between ourselves and others.[16] When we cannot communicate directly with other believers, we can still relate to them through prayer, with Jesus serving as the mediating link.

Paul never discusses prayer techniques. He does not talk about when to pray, how long to pray, what words to use to increase the effectiveness of prayer or the importance of praying "in the name of Jesus." Paul doesn't want to spend much time talking about prayer. He just wants to do it and he asks the churches to do the same.

Heavenly Father, today I offer no excuses for my prayer life. I only want to pray, asking you to empower your people and your church with your grace.

[9] ***Because of this***, *we also, from the day we heard, have not stopped praying for you and asking in order that you may be filled with the knowledge of his will in all wisdom and Spirit-oriented understanding*

Paul switches from the *thankful*-prayers of verses 3-8 to the *asking*-prayers of verses 9-14. The two paragraphs are connected by the words "because of this." Because of his thankful prayers, Paul is now prompted to offer up asking-prayers. It's as if the requests were an echo of his gratitude. And you can see that echo when comparing verses 3-8 with 9-14:

- *Since the day they believed.* When Paul heard of their faith, he began to thank God for them (verses 3-4) and to pray for them (verse 9).
- *At all times.* Paul thanks God for the Colossians "at all times" (verse 3) and he has "not stopped praying" for them either (verse 9).
- *Knowledge.* Paul is thankful for their knowledge of God's will (verse 6) and prays for them to have that knowledge even more (verse 9).
- *Fruit-bearing.* Paul is grateful that God's word was fruitful among them (verse 6), and he prays that they, too, would bear fruit (verse 10).
- *Thankfulness.* Paul was thankful for the Colossians (verse 3), and he prays that they would be thankful as well (verse 12).

This order is counterintuitive. Many people think the process goes like this: we ask, God responds, and then we give thanks. But that scenario presupposes that it is our prayers which start the process. Some even think God is dependent upon our prayers to act, as if his hands were tied until we fold our hands in prayer. But Paul's order is this: God gives, we thank, and then we ask for more. It all starts with God.

Sometimes it may seem as if God is doing nothing until we boldly claim a promise or cry out for his attention, but God has always been at work long before we ever thought about prayer. His action always precedes our prayer.

And this truth affects the anxiety level of our asking-prayers. It's a heavy burden to bear if we think God won't do anything until we get the process rolling and pray in the right way. But asking-prayers lose their anxious character when they flow from a thankfulness for what God has already been doing for us.

What a joy it is, Lord, to know that you have been abundantly pouring out your grace long before I offered any prayers.

> [9] *Because of this,* **we also, from the day we heard, have not stopped praying for you and asking** *in order that you may be filled with the knowledge of his will in all wisdom and Spirit-oriented understanding*

Paul lets the Colossians know that his prayers for them are not sporadic, but continual. He does not stop praying for them, nor for other churches and believers (see similar words in Rom 1:9; Eph 1:16; 1 Thess 1:2; 3:10; 2 Thess 1:11; and 2 Tim 1:3). He will not allow anything to block his prayers, such as "busyness, other priorities, a fatalistic approach to life, a low view of God's ability to transform a situation, and a lack of compassion."[17]

Paul's continual prayer conforms to what Jesus commanded in Lk 18:1—that his followers "should always pray and not give up" (NIV). Jesus urged continual prayer so that in spite of persecution, the Son of Man will find faith on the earth (Lk 18:8b). This same concern for strengthening faith shapes Paul's prayers. In his letters, we read little about health and nothing about the issues that often occupy our prayer meetings and prayer chains, like finding jobs, safety in travels, good weather, comfort for the grieving, or good participation at church events. Instead Paul's prayers focus on faith—that the Colossians would understand God's will, walk worthily of the Lord, bear good fruit, be empowered to endure and be full of gratitude.

Why are our prayer concerns so different from Paul's? Maybe it's self-centeredness. Eugene Peterson once wrote, "Left to ourselves, we are never more selfish than when we pray. With God as the Great Sympathizer, the Great Giver, the Great Promiser, we go to our knees and indulge every impulse for gratification."[18]

Or maybe it's because we tend to confine our prayers to those matters over which we feel powerless. We pray about jobs, travels, weather and health because we know we have little control over those matters. But we (falsely) think we do have control over the strength of our faith. With a little optimism and determination, we can be spiritually healthy...or so we tell ourselves.

But Jesus and Paul knew better. Our faith is weak. It can only survive through God's strength, not our own. Paul goes to God in prayer concerning the faith of the Colossians because a living, growing faith is not a human accomplishment, but an amazing work of God. Pray now for your faith and for the faith of others.

Lord, I believe; help my unbelief. Lord, we believe; help our unbelief.
Send your Spirit to strengthen our faith.

*⁹ Because of this, we also, from the day we heard, have not stopped praying for you and asking **in order that you may be filled** with the knowledge of his will in all wisdom and Spirit-oriented understanding*

Paul next strings together a series of clauses to specify what it is that he is asking God to provide for the Colossians, things which neither he nor the Colossians can provide for themselves. The main thing he asks is that the Colossians would be filled.

This is the first of many times Paul will mention fullness and filling in this letter. He will talk about being filled with knowledge (1:9); the fullness of God in Christ (1:19; 2:9); fullness of suffering (1:24); God's word being filled-out (1:25); full assurance (2:2; 4:12); believers being filled (2:10); the fullness of the flesh (2:23); and the fulfillment of ministry (4:17). Paul will also describe some distorted teachings in Colossae as being empty (2:8). We will later see that this distortion presented itself as a deeper and fuller version of the gospel, but Paul demonstrates that in Christ believers already have all the fullness they will ever need.

Sometimes people are filled with evil (Rom 1:29) and hypocrisy (Mt 23:28), but the Bible also notes how God's people can be filled with good things from God: grace (Jn 1:16), the Holy Spirit (Eph 5:18), goodness and knowledge (Rom 15:14), the fruit of righteousness (Phil 1:11), and the knowledge of God's will (Col 1:9).

Paul's thoughts about filling and fullness are reinforced in verses 9-11 through his fivefold use of the word "all" and "every" (both English terms translate the Greek word *pas*). In order to be truly filled, we believers need to be filled not just with *partial* wisdom and understanding, but "with the knowledge of his will in *all* wisdom and Spirit-oriented understanding" (verse 9). We must not only walk worthily in *some* forms of pleasing, but "in *every* form of pleasing" (verse 10). We not only walk by faith in a *few* good works, but "in *every* good work" (verse 10). We are not just equipped with *some* power, but "with *all* power" (verse 11). We not only press on with *a bit of* endurance and patience, but "in *all* endurance and patience" (verse 11). Believers need all the fullness the Lord can provide, and God is eager to do so (see Jms 1:5).

Fill me now, fill me now; Jesus, come and fill me now.

*⁹ Because of this, we also, from the day we heard, have not stopped praying for you and asking in order that you may be filled **with the knowledge of his will in all wisdom and Spirit-oriented understanding***

Those who have heard and believed the "word of truth" about God (Col 1:5) need to know more. Those who have been reborn need to be retrained.[19] They may come to know the Lord in the instant of conversion, but growing in that knowledge is a lifelong journey. That's why Paul prays for the Colossians to grow in knowledge, wisdom and understanding. The life of the mind is important for Christian living.

Knowledge, wisdom and understanding can cut in two directions, either reinforcing or undermining our relationship with God. As finite human beings, we have limited knowledge. As sinners, we repress the true knowledge of God and construct a self-serving set of "alternative facts." And religious people are not immune to the mind-distorting effects of sin. Even as Christians we can get off track by using our knowledge in loveless and arrogant ways. Or we might gather more data about God and yet never put it into practice or grow in our relationship with the Lord.

But the problem of distorted knowledge is not resolved by an escape to the world of feelings. Instead, distorted knowledge is overcome by the true knowledge. And this true knowledge comes from God (Rom 11:33), characterizes the Son (Isa 11:2; Jn 14:6) and is revealed to us by the Spirit (1 Cor 2:9-10). The phrase "Spirit-oriented understanding" in today's verse means that true knowledge comes from God's Spirit, not the human spirit (as the common translation "spiritual wisdom" might wrongly suggest).[20]

People are often attracted to forms of religious knowledge that do not demand a change of lifestyle, but Paul does not want this for us. He is not asking that we would gain a theoretical or mystical knowledge of God which has little impact on the way we live. Instead, Paul prays for us to have the kind of relational knowledge of God that leads us to both know and do God's will. And this kind of knowing happens through prayer.

At times Paul will *command* his readers to know God's will (see Eph 5:17), but even more effective is *praying* that they would grow in that knowledge. By getting to know the mind of God in prayer, God's own character and purposes "rub off" on us. In prayer, we are not only asking God to listen to us, but we are also learning to listen to God.

Lord Jesus, I'm laying down my own self-serving knowledge
to know and serve you instead.

> [9] *...asking in order that you may be filled with the knowledge of his will in all wisdom and Spirit-oriented understanding,* [10] ***to walk*** *worthily of the Lord in every form of pleasing, in every good work fruit-bearing and growing in the knowledge of God*

What is the purpose of being filled with the knowledge of God's will? So that we might walk worthily of the Lord. To refer to the way one lives as "walking" is a very Hebrew way of looking at life. To live is to walk.

Some versions choose to translate walking as "living," but it's best to keep the walking imagery for at least four reasons: (1) The image of walking helps us see life as a journey instead of a stationary existence. Karl Barth said the Holy Spirit "does not put the Christian at a point or in a position. He sets him on the way, on the march."[21] (2) Walking conveys that obedience is an ongoing activity. (3) The OT reminds us that we never walk alone: God walks ahead of us and beside us as he accompanies us on the way (see Lev 26:12). (4) "Walking," says Gorman, "implies involvement in the world—mission—not existence in an isolated holy huddle."[22]

Many OT verses speak of either walking in the way of the Lord or walking after other gods. Of special interest is how the Israelite kings were judged by how they walked. David, Jehoshaphat and Josiah were said to walk in the way of the Lord, but most of the kings did not. That's because they did not have the Spirit of God working within them. So God prophesies of a future day when "I will put my Spirit within you and cause you to walk in my statutes and be careful to obey my rules" (Ezek 36:27, ESV).

That day of Spirit-empowered walking arrived with the coming of Jesus. Paul uses the verb for walking thirty-two times and never once refers to literal walking. Instead, he speaks of walking in newness of life, walking according to the Spirit, walking in the light, walking in love, walking by faith, and more. He also warns against walking in sinful, deceptive ways as enemies of the cross. In Colossians, he will use the word four times to speak of walking worthily of the Lord (1:10), walking in Christ (2:6), not walking in evil ways (3:7), and walking wisely in evangelism (4:5).

It should not surprise us that Paul talks about walking so much. After all, Paul met the Lord on the road to Damascus and spent many years of his life walking throughout the Roman Empire to bring the gospel. Life was a journey of faith for Paul. Even when he was stuck in some prison, he thought of himself as walking in a way that would draw others to Christ.

Lord Jesus, we are not your fans, sitting in easy chairs, rooting for your cause. We are your followers. Call us to rise up and walk with you.

> [9] *...asking in order that you may be filled with the knowledge of his will in all wisdom and Spirit-oriented understanding,* [10] *to walk **worthily of the Lord** in every form of pleasing, in every good work fruit-bearing and growing in the knowledge of God*

Paul prays for his readers to walk worthily of the Lord (an idea he repeats in Eph 4:1 and 1 Thess 2:12; see also Phil 1:27). While the Greek adjective for "worthy" could mean something is either "deserving" or "fitting," the adverb used here ("worthily") only refers to fittingness in the NT. It is fitting for people who are walking with the Lord to have their conduct match their faith.

In our consumerist culture the whole concept of worth is very tied in our minds to commercial transactions. We shop around in an attempt to discover what is most worthy of a purchase. If it's a good deal, we say, "it's worth it," but if the price is too high, we observe that "it wasn't worth it." We, the consumers, become the assessors of what is worthy and what is not. Unfortunately, if we carry that consumerist attitude into the realm of faith, then we make ourselves the final arbiters of good and evil, with God reduced to a deity trying to persuade us to buy his goods. "Worthy is the Lamb that was slain" would mean nothing more than "I, as a consumer, have decided that I'll continue in my brand-loyalty to Jesus because he offers me a good deal."

But Paul is not drawing on the world of commerce when talking about worth, for God is worthy of praise and obedience whether we recognize it or not. Our assessment of God is not what makes God worthy. Instead, God's own character and actions are what make God worthy of our praise and obedience. Worth is not to be determined by the world of commerce, but the world of worship. Whether God's salvation package feels like a "good deal" or not, it's always fitting for us to walk in a way that glorifies him.

It's also notable that the Bible's frequent references to "worthy" and "worthily" are found in contexts of hospitality (see Rom 16:2 and 3 Jn 6). It is important for hosts and guests to treat each other in a fitting manner. Therefore, since we are "in Christ," we are his guests and must conduct ourselves accordingly. Or we might think of ourselves as the hosts, with Christ in us, in which case, we must act in fitting ways. Whenever you walk in the company of Jesus, some forms of conduct are more fitting than others. Paul's prayer is for us to figure out what that is and follow through.

Lord, it is completely unfitting for me walk with you and yet insist that you follow my lead. You are worthy of my praise and obedience.

*[9] ... asking in order that you may be filled with the knowledge of his will in all wisdom and Spirit-oriented understanding, [10] to walk worthily of the Lord **in every form of pleasing**, in every good work fruit-bearing and growing in the knowledge of God*

Walking worthily of the Lord might sound like having to live up to the demands of a stern God. But this next phrase reveals God's heart. Walking worthily of the Lord is all about giving God pleasure. Just as hosts and guests don't merely go through the motions of hospitality, but genuinely want to please one another, so we do the same in our walk with God. We want to be good traveling companions with the Lord and enjoy each other's company.

The idea of bringing God pleasure is surprisingly common in the Bible, often in the context of sacrifices, prayers and worship. In the OT, the Lord is pleased with the aroma of sacrifices, but in the NT God is pleased when we offer ourselves as living sacrifices (Rom 12:1). Sometimes God seems to do whatever he pleases and the rationale is not obvious to us, but more often God takes pleasure in our obedience and righteous behavior. Best of all, the Lord not only takes pleasure in righteous actions, but he also takes pleasure in the people doing the actions—people like Enoch, David and Hezekiah. The Heavenly Father especially takes pleasure in Jesus his Son (as he said at Jesus' baptism and transfiguration). And by extension, the Father is also pleased to save those who are in Christ and give them the kingdom (Lk 12:32).

Fittingly enough, if God takes pleasure in us, then we want to do the things that give him pleasure in return. Just as Jesus did not come to please himself (Rom 15:3), but the One who sent him (Jn 8:29), "so we make it our goal to please him" as well (2 Cor 5:9, NIV). But pleasing God does not involve some great human effort on our part, for "it is God who works in you both to will and to work for his good pleasure" (Phil 2:13, ESV). Paul would not have to pray about learning to please God if we could do it on our own. But through prayer we not only come to know what is pleasing to God, but also are given the power and the desire to do it. Then we can pray in the words of Christian singer Terry Talbot, "pleasing You pleases me."

Thank you, Father, for delighting in me as your child. May my words and actions this day bring pleasure to your heart.

> [9] *...asking in order that you may be filled with the knowledge of his will in all wisdom and Spirit-oriented understanding,* [10] *to walk worthily of the Lord in every form of pleasing,* **in every good work** *fruit-bearing and growing in the knowledge of God*

Paul often spoke forcefully against those who think salvation can be achieved through the works of the law: "By works of the law, no human being will be justified in [God's] sight" (Rom 3:20, ESV), for God "saved us, not because of works done by us in righteousness" (Titus 3:5, ESV).

But even though works cannot save, Paul still calls us to do them. In the very context of saying that we are not saved by any works we have done, he will also say that we are called to a holy life: God "saved us and called us to a holy life, not because of our works but because of his own purpose and grace" (2 Tim 1:9, ESV). And in the very context of declaring that we are saved by grace through faith and not by works, Paul quickly adds that "we are God's handiwork, created in Christ Jesus to do good works" (Eph 2:8-10, NIV).

Although God takes no pleasure in someone trying to save themselves through their works, he is pleased when those who are already saved by his grace do good works. Jesus begins a good work in us, so we also can do good works (Phil 1:6). That's why Paul prays for the Colossians to walk worthily of the Lord in every good work. Elsewhere, Paul encourages good works by saying that God is able to make all grace abound so that we will abound in every good work (2 Cor 9:8), and God will strengthen us in every good work (2 Thess 2:16-17). Paul also approved works of service (Eph 4:12), fruitful works (Phil 1:22), and works produced by faith (1 Thess 1:3; 2 Thess 1:11).

These good works would include acts of helping others, giving to the poor, visiting the sick, etc. But we should not think of our good works as one of many components in our compartmentalized lives. Since all of life is to be lived "in the name of the Lord Jesus" (Col 3:17), then all of life should be a good work filled with good works.[23]

Again, the reason Paul is *praying* about this is that good works are not self-generated. They are God's work in us, which is why it's important for us to follow Paul in praying for the Lord to produce such works.

Lord, you began a good work in me. Please continue that work so that I may participate in all the good things you are doing in this world.

> [9] *...asking in order that you may be filled with the knowledge of his will in all wisdom and Spirit-oriented understanding,* [10] *to walk worthily of the Lord in every form of pleasing, in every good work **fruit-bearing and growing in the knowledge of God***

In verse 6 Paul stated that the *gospel* was fruit-bearing and growing. Here Paul prays that the *Colossians themselves* would be fruit-bearing and growing. It's a case of fruit producing fruit. Apple trees produce apples, which have seeds, which grow into more trees and more apples. The fruit of the gospel produces new believers, who also grow more fruit.

The Colossians can take no credit for bearing fruit. Apart from Christ, they were only able to bear the fruit of death (Rom 7:5). But once a person is united with Christ, then the living fruit of the Spirit can grow—like love, joy, and peace (see Gal 5:22-23). These fruits, of course, are not merely internal qualities alone, but are internal qualities that show up in visible forms. Just as there are no invisible fruits on a tree or bush, "there are no invisible fruits" in the life of a Christian.[24]

Fruit-bearing is such a helpful way of conceptualizing righteous living. When we realize what Jesus has done for us, it's tempting to think that we are independent beings who can formulate and carry out how best to respond to his love—congratulating ourselves when we do well and kicking ourselves when we fail. But that's the wrong approach, for in the Christian life, we are not independent beings who merely respond to Jesus. Through the work of the Spirit, we are connected to Jesus like a branch is connected to a vine or tree. We draw our very life and productivity from this deep relational connectedness to him. As Jesus said in Jn 15:4-5, "No branch can bear fruit by itself...I am the vine; you are the branches. If you remain in me and I in you, you will bear much fruit" (NIV).

Our fruitfulness demonstrates that God is indeed ruling over his kingdom. When ancient kings conquered new territories, they would take fruit trees back home and plant them in their royal orchards in order to display their power and wisdom. The Assyrian king Tiglath-pilesar I, for instance, boasted, "I took rare orchard fruit which is not found in my land (and therewith) filled the orchards of Assyria."[25] Similarly, God takes delight in displaying his power and wisdom through the fruitfulness of people newly won to his kingdom.

I am thankful, Lord Jesus, that I am not apart from you, and nothing can separate me from you. Grow your fruit in my life, I pray.

> [9] *...asking in order that you may be filled with the knowledge of his will in all wisdom and Spirit-oriented understanding, [10] to walk worthily of the Lord in every form of pleasing, in every good work fruit-bearing and growing in the knowledge of God, [11]* **being empowered with all power in accordance with the might of his glory** *in all endurance and patience with joy, [12] giving-thanks to the Father for qualifying you for a share of the inheritance of the holy-ones in the light*

Paul knew that in his own ministry, "the surpassing power belongs to God and not to us" (2 Cor 4:7, ESV). That's why he prays for God's empowerment for all believers. Here Paul pulls together three "power words" (empowered, power and might) to make his point. He does a similar thing in Eph 6:10 (ESV)—"Finally, be strong in the Lord and in the strength of his might".

It's not just any power that we need. Paul is not talking about legal authority, psychological fortitude, or social power. Rather, it's a power that moves in accordance with the might of God's glory. The reference to glory indicates that it is not just the *quantity* of power that is important, but the *quality* and source of that power; it comes from God and operates in the way God operates.[26] By putting power and glory together (as often happens in the Bible), we know that all the power and glory of the coming kingdom is already available to the followers of Jesus through prayer. We are already living in the atmosphere of that powerful and glorious future.

God's power is seen in the work of the Holy Spirit (Eph 3:16), the gospel (Rom 1:16), the resurrection of Jesus—and our resurrection with him (1 Cor 6:14). This does not mean, however, that Spirit-empowered Christians now move from one mighty success to another. In some strange but wondrous way, God's power is especially seen in the weakness of Jesus on the cross (1 Cor 1:23-24) and in our being weak with him (2 Cor 12:9). Jesus "was crucified in weakness, yet he lives by God's power. Likewise, we are weak in him, yet by God's power we will live with him" (2 Cor 13:4, NIV).

Paul's main concern in Col 1:11, then, is that God would grant his power to the Colossians so that the other good things he prayed for them would happen. Without God's power, sinful humans are unable to walk worthily of Lord, or to please God, or to bear fruit in every good work. But with God's power, abundant fruit can grow.

> *Lord, I am full of weakness, but that has never stopped you from accomplishing mighty things. Send your Spirit's power today.*

*⁹ ...asking in order that you may be filled... ¹¹ being empowered with all power in accordance with the might of his glory **in all endurance** and patience with joy, ¹² giving-thanks to the Father for qualifying you for a share of the inheritance of the holy-ones in the light*

If a genie appeared to grant you the power to do anything, you would likely choose the power to eliminate suffering from your life or from the lives of others. You would think, then, that when God makes his power available to believers, we would use it to overpower and vanquish any troubles that might rob us of heavenly bliss. But the elimination of suffering is not why God grants us power. Instead, all the resources of divine power are brought together to help us *endure* suffering, not *eliminate* it.

This is surprising because we usually think that it's only powerless people who have to put up with suffering. But instead, it's the powerful followers of Christ who are called to endure.

The word for "endurance" (*hupomonē*) is about enduring and persisting in faith through a bad experience and not giving up when the going gets tough. Sometimes it is translated as persistence or perseverance. Endurance leads us to hope. According to Rom 5:3, endurance produces character, which in turn produces hope. But the opposite can also be true: hope leads us to endurance (1 Thess 1:3). Just as the sight of the finish line can cause a hurting athlete to press on anyway, so the future hope we have in Christ causes believers to press on through pain.

But endurance is not only needed for getting through suffering. It's also for pressing on in doing good when we're tempted to grow weary in it (Gal 6:9). Without endurance, righteousness would become a part-time activity, an occasional and unreliable—and ultimately hypocritical—display of godliness. In order for righteousness to reflect God's character, it must endure. That's why 1 Cor 13:7 does not say, "love has the capacity to occasionally put up with a few things." Rather, "love endures all things." Fortunately, to endure in righteousness is not an impossible task, for the Lord not only *calls* us to endure, but he also *empowers* us to do so.

Lord Jesus, there are times I want to give up because of pain or weariness.
Give me instead a steadfast spirit to press on.

61

> ^{9} ...*asking in order that you may be filled...* ^{11} *being empowered with all power in accordance with the might of his glory in all endurance* **and patience** *with joy,* ^{12} *giving-thanks to the Father for qualifying you for a share of the inheritance of the holy-ones in the light*

While endurance (*hupomonē*) is generally about persisting through bad circumstances, patience (*makrothumia*) is more about being patient with annoying people. *Makrothumia* is formed from two other Greek words put together: *makros* (meaning long or far) and *thumos* (meaning breath, temper or anger). As opposed to being short-tempered, a patient person is long-tempered and slow to anger.

The King James Version translated it as "long-suffering." According to Lewis Smedes, this is not a call to be a perpetual victim. "Suffering long is not the same as suffering endlessly...Love suffers long so that time can be created for redemptive powers to do their work."[27]

First and foremost, God is the one who is patient and slow to anger. In Ex 34:6 (NETS) the Lord describes himself as "compassionate and merciful, patient [*makrothumos*] and very merciful and truthful" (a description repeated at least eight more times in the OT). The patience of the Lord hit home for Paul when God showed him mercy on the Damascus Road. It was through that incident that "Christ Jesus might display his immense patience as an example for those who would believe in him" (1 Tim 1:16, NIV).

But it's not just the Lord who is patient. God's people are also called to show patience toward others: "whoever is patient has great understanding, but one who is quick-tempered displays folly" (Prov 14:29, NIV). Some verses about patience could be interpreted to mean that it is nothing more than a prudent, humanly-achievable practice. But the NT emphasizes that because God is patient with us, then God's Spirit can grow patience within us as well (Gal 5:22).

According to Col 1:11, we need divine power to journey with God in a patient manner. Patience is necessary in our relationships with God and others. We must even show patience toward ourselves. The knowledge of God we seek may come to us slower than we expect. The reward of doing good work may be delayed. The fruit we expect to see growing in our lives may take a while to appear. Yet we press on with patience because God empowers us to do so.

Gracious God, I love it when you and others are patient with me. Empower me to return the favor by giving me a long temper.

*[9] ... asking in order that you may be filled... [11] being empowered with all power in accordance with the might of his glory in all endurance and patience **with joy,** [12] giving-thanks to the Father for qualifying you for a share of the inheritance of the holy-ones in the light*

The last phrase of this verse, "with joy," is also an important qualifier for Paul. It would not do for the followers of Jesus to endure in a grim manner, setting their jaws to press on with a miserable task. It would not be fitting if the followers of Jesus were patient in a despondent way, as if to sigh, "I guess we'll just have to put up with this, too." Although endurance and patience are necessary for coping with the trials that accompany our walk with God, Paul prays that our coping would be filled with joy.

In their paraphrase of this verse, Walsh and Keesmaat not only link joy with endurance and patience, but also with this verse's earlier prayer for power: "Joyful thanksgiving is deeply empowering."[28] Without joy, a suffering person can easily slide into an attitude of perpetual victimhood. Without joy we no longer live life; it only happens to us. We no longer seize the day; we are seized by the day. We no longer grab the bull by the horns, but are gored by the bull. But divine joy has the capacity to liberate and empower us to live as God called us to live.

Paul himself lived out this joy. When he and Silas were unjustly beaten and thrown into prison, they did not grumble and groan as most people would do. They did not respond with only calmness (as would their contemporaries, the Stoics, who regarded endurance as a virtue).[29] Rather, they went beyond endurance by bursting into joyful song. Paul rejoiced in his sufferings (Rom 5:3; 2 Cor 6:10; Phil 2:17; Col 1:24), called on churches to rejoice no matter what the circumstance (Phil 4:4; 1 Thess 5:16), and celebrated whenever he saw believers doing just that (1 Thess 1:6, 2 Cor 8:2).

In distinction from a *natural* happiness that only occurs whenever good things happen, and an *unnatural* euphoria that avoids reality, Paul prayed for—and lived out—a *super-natural* joy that was a fruit of the Spirit (Gal 5:22).

Lord Jesus, happiness is nice. Euphoria can be pleasurable. But what I really need from you is joy, the kind of joy that paints even my suffering with the colors of your kingdom.

> [9] *...asking in order that you may be filled...* [11] *being empowered with all power in accordance with the might of his glory in all endurance and patience with joy,* [12] ***giving-thanks to the Father*** *for qualifying you for a share of the inheritance of the holy-ones in the light* [13] *[the Father] who delivered us from the authority of darkness and relocated [us] to the kingdom of the Son of his love—* [14] *in whom we have redemption, the forgiveness of our sins*

With verse 12, Paul is coming full circle in the opening part of his letter. He began by reporting his own thankful prayer (verse 3), and now he ends with a prayer for the Colossians to join him in thankfulness. We might as well practice a life of gratitude, because the day is coming when there will be no more need to ask God for anything in prayer; all our needs will be met in the eternal presence of God. In eternity, all prayer will consist only of praise and thanksgiving.

By ending his string of requests for his readers with a call to be thankful, Paul is reminding us that the Christian life is not about producing something *for* God. Rather, it's about gratefully receiving *from* God. We can only bear the fruit we have *received* from the Spirit. We can only grow in the knowledge we have *received* from God's revelation. We can only be empowered to endure with the power we have *received* from the Lord. Thus, we live in thankfulness for all we have *received* from the Father.

Thankfulness also implies that there are some things (listed in verses 12-14) that we do *not* have to ask for. And that's because we have already received them, and their reality in our lives is fully established.[30] For instance, Paul is *not* praying for the Colossians to qualify for their share of God's inheritance—God has already qualified them for it through Christ (verse 12). Likewise, Paul is *not* praying for the Colossians to be delivered from the authority of darkness and relocated into the Son's kingdom—God has already relocated them (verse 13). Nor is Paul praying for the Colossians to be redeemed and forgiven—they are already redeemed and forgiven in Christ (verse 14). There are some things the Colossians do not yet fully possess, such as knowledge and power, but there are other things they already do possess in Christ, namely, the spiritual blessings described in verses 12-14. Thanks be to God, there is no need to ask for what you already have in Christ.

Thank you, heavenly Father, that my walk with you is not measured by how much I've produced for you, but how much I've received from you.

> [9] *...asking in order that you may be filled...* [11] *being empowered with all power in accordance with the might of his glory in all endurance and patience with joy,* [12] *giving-thanks to the Father **for qualifying you** for a share of the inheritance of the holy-ones in the light*

The implication of the word "qualifying" is that apart from the work of God, we are not qualified for God's kingdom. We do not have the credentials needed to do a certain task or the qualifications needed to receive a gift or reward. But God has graciously qualified us, which is why it is appropriate for Christians to be thankful to the Father. Instead of being anxious about whether we qualify, we are to be grateful that we are already qualified.

This is also the thought behind Jesus' words in Lk 12:32 (NIV), "Do not be afraid, little flock, for your Father has been pleased to give you the kingdom." Because God has given us the kingdom (or, as Paul says here, qualified us for the kingdom), we do not have to be anxious about life's provisions—which was Jesus' main point—but neither do we have to be anxious about eternity. Such a gift transforms anxiety into gratitude.

With these words Paul may be counteracting the distorted teaching that he criticizes in chapter 2. These distortionists had been creating anxiety among the Colossian believers, telling them they were not qualified for the kingdom unless they followed some new practices (Col 2:18).[31] Paul thoroughly disagrees, for he knows that no human actions or set of doctrines qualifies us for God's inheritance. That's God's work.

The verb for "qualifying" was used only one other time by Paul, when he was defending his apostolic qualifications in 2 Cor 3:5-6. His message there could easily fit here as well. If we were to paraphrase that text and apply it to the Colossians, it might read this way: "Not that you are qualified in yourselves to receive the inheritance of the kingdom, but your qualification comes from God. He has qualified you for a share of that inheritance."

In the next verses (13-14) Paul will spell out further what God did to make us eligible for this inheritance. When living under the authority of darkness, we were not qualified, but by delivering us from darkness and moving us to the kingdom of the Son, we became qualified. This qualifying act of God is not something any of us can demand as our right. It's God's gift to us.

Father, by myself I am unqualified to serve you, to represent you, or to live with you forever. I'm thankful that I'm not by myself, but I'm in Christ.

> [9] *...asking in order that you may be filled...* [11] *being empowered with all power in accordance with the might of his glory in all endurance and patience with joy,* [12] *giving-thanks to the Father for qualifying you **for a share of the inheritance** of the holy-ones in the light*

An heir is usually a family member. So, in order for us to be qualified for a share in the Lord's inheritance, we must somehow be adopted into God's family. Even though we have not yet received our full inheritance from God, we can be grateful that we have already been fully qualified to do so.

Receiving an inheritance is not something we deserve or earn. While many children may think it's their right to receive an inheritance from their parents, the parents are under no obligation to give them one. An inheritance—whether from one's biological parents, another human being, or from God—is always a gift. For this reason, Paul calls us to be amazed and thankful that God has qualified us for an inheritance.

The Colossian Christians, most of whom were not Jews, would be especially amazed by this gift. The Jews had been in God's family for so many centuries that it would be easy for them to assume they were heirs. But for non-Jewish Christians, their experience was like being invited to a neighbor's family reunion, and then discovering that there will be a reading of a will at this reunion, and they're in the will! What?! An amazing gift![32]

Paul does not specify here what the inheritance is. In the OT, God gave an inheritance of land to the Israelites (a very common theme). But in the NT, we do not inherit land, but a kingdom—a glorious and unending life with our God and King. We already have a taste of this inheritance through the Holy Spirit who serves as a guarantee of what is to come (Eph 1:13-14). But the fullness of our inheritance awaits us in in the future.

Lest anyone think of this inheritance, however, as some purely spiritual, ethereal reality, disconnected from our life on earth, we do well to listen to Russell Moore: "If the kingdom is what Jesus says it is, then what matters isn't just what we neatly classify as 'spiritual' things. The natural world around us isn't just a temporary 'environment,' but part of our future inheritance in Christ."[33] The next major section of Colossians (1:15-20), which speaks of Jesus as Creator and Lord of all things, will reinforce this truth.

Thank you, Jesus, for welcoming me into your forever family. You died so I could inherit eternal life, and you rose from the dead so that I could inherit that eternal life with you.

*⁹ ...asking in order that you may be filled... ¹¹ being empowered with all power in accordance with the might of his glory in all endurance and patience with joy, ¹² giving-thanks to the Father for qualifying you for a share of the inheritance **of the holy-ones in the light**, ¹³ [the Father] who delivered us from the authority of darkness and relocated [us] to the kingdom of the Son of his love*

The inheritance belongs to the holy-ones who dwell in the light. A few scholars interpret this to be a reference to angels around God's throne, but this is unlikely because in the other 40+ times that Paul refers to the holy-ones (like in Col 1:2), he always means the human followers of Jesus.

This reference to the holy-ones being "in the light" may be a reference to a heavenly reward of "great light in that world which has no end" (as the apocryphal *2 Baruch* 48:50 puts it). But Paul's description of the "holy-ones in the light" is not just about believers who have died and now dwell in heaven (or will do so in the future). It's also about the present state of believers, who have already been transferred from darkness to light (see Col 1:14). Living in the light is our current situation, and letting that light shine is our present mission. As 1 Pet 2:9 puts it, we are "a holy nation...that you may declare the praises of him who called you out of darkness into his wonderful light" (NIV).

When the NT refers either to *being* the light or being *in* the light, there is often a missional thrust to it. This is true for both Jesus and his followers. When Jesus is born, Zechariah prophesies that he will be a light for revelation to the nations (Lk 2:32); and when he begins to minister in Galilee, those living in darkness see a great light (Mt 4:16). Jesus is the light shining in the darkness, giving light to all—even to those who resist it (Jn 1:4, 9; 3:19-21; 8:12; 9:5; 12:46).

This is why he called his followers to put their trust in his light and thus become sons of light (Jn 12:36). Then they too would be the light of the world, letting their light shine so others may see (Mt 5:14-16). Even if we once were in darkness, says Paul in Eph 5:8-9 (ESV), "now you are light in the Lord. Walk as children of light, (for the fruit of light is found in all that is good and right and true)." We may be waiting for the day of the Lord's return, but the light of that day is already shining on us, and we can reflect it to others today. Brighten the corner where you are.

Shine, Jesus, shine. Let the light of your face shine in our hearts to give the light of the knowledge of the glory of God.

> [12] *giving-thanks to the Father for qualifying you for a share of the inheritance of the holy-ones in the light,* [13] ***[the Father] who delivered us*** *from the authority of darkness and relocated [us] to the kingdom of the Son of his love—* [14] *in whom we have redemption, the forgiveness of our sins—*

One of the striking aspects of verses 13-14 is the way they echo the language of the Exodus. The verb here for being delivered (*rhuomai*) is the same one used in the Greek translation of Exodus, which states that the Israelites were delivered from slavery (Ex 6:6), from the death of the firstborn (Ex 12:27) and from Pharaoh's pursuing army (Ex 14:30).

When the Israelites were later exiled from the Promised Land, many OT prophets also prophesied of a *second* exodus. According to Jer 16:14-15, people will one day associate God more with how he brought Israel out of exile than how he brought them out of Egypt. Isa 11:1-11 even implies that the coming Messiah will make this new exodus happen.

Now that Jesus the Messiah has come, Paul is telling us that this second exodus is actually our story. Just as God had *delivered* Israel from the *darkness* of Egypt by *moving* them to their *inheritance* of a new *kingdom* (the Promised Land), so now the Father has *delivered* us from the *darkness* of evil by *moving* us to our *inheritance* in the *kingdom* of his Son.

"Deliver" is a good translation of *rhuomai*, especially since even its English connotations fit the context well. For one thing, "deliverance ministries" in contemporary Christian language are ministries that focus on helping people overcome their bondage to evil spirits. Paul is discussing similar realities when speaking of our deliverance from the authority of darkness.

Secondly, the English word "delivery" includes the notion of moving something from one place to another, as in delivering a package. Again, Paul is emphasizing here how God has moved us from an evil dominion to a righteous kingdom. There's an evacuation from darkness to light.

Finally, the root meaning of the English word—but admittedly not the Greek word—is connected to the idea of liberation ("deliver" is related to the Latin for setting free, *liberare*), which is also fitting. If our walk with God lacks this atmosphere of freedom, then all we're doing is pacing the floor of a religious jail cell. It's for freedom Christ has set us free (Gal 5:1).

Deliver me, Lord, from all the trappings of religion that only ensnare me in addictive, compulsive darkness. Set me free that I might follow you.

¹² *giving-thanks to the Father for qualifying you for a share of the inheritance of the holy-ones in the light,* ¹³ *[the Father] who delivered us* **from the authority of darkness** *and relocated [us] to the kingdom of the Son of his love*

The Father has delivered us—not just from sin and death, but also from "the authority [*exousia*] of darkness [*skotos*]." Paul is referring to demonic powers, like "the prince of the power [*exousia*] of the air, the spirit that is now at work in the sons of disobedience" (Eph 2:2, ESV).

In God's marvelous plan, the only way for people to be rescued from this death-dealing authority of darkness was for his Son to submit to the darkness and die our death on the cross. In this way Jesus stripped the powers of their dominion (see Col 2:15), and someday he will destroy them completely (1 Cor 15:24).

This deliverance from darkness to light was especially meaningful to Paul, because he literally experienced this on the Damascus Road. Christ had blinded him to reveal the darkness in his soul, and then restored his sight through the laying on of hands (Acts 9:1-18). So it's no surprise that the wording in Col 1:13 reflects Jesus' assignment given to Paul on the Damascus Road: he was sent to the nations "to open their eyes and turn them from darkness [*skotos*] to light and from the power [*exousia*] of Satan to God" (Acts 26:18, NIV).

In Colossians this deliverance from dark powers is a cause for thanksgiving and celebration. In Eph 6:12-18, however, this deliverance is a call to arms. Deliverance does not mean we are disengaged from the battle against the Evil One. Rather, God delivers us in order to enlist us in his cause. We may have been relocated from darkness to the kingdom of light, but not so we can live as far from the border skirmishes as possible. Rather, we remain at the frontlines to rescue others under Satan's dominion, "for we do not wrestle against flesh and blood, but against...the authorities [*exousia*], against the cosmic powers over this present darkness [*skotos*]."

But a call to arms and a call to thankfulness are not unrelated. Spiritual battles are not won through cries of anger, shouts of vengeance, or outbursts of intimidation. They are won through songs of thanksgiving. Just ask Jehoshaphat who won a great battle by means of a squadron of musicians singing, "Give thanks to the Lord, for his love endures forever" (2 Chron 20:21, ESV).

Your light shines into the darkness, O Lord, and we are so thankful that the darkness cannot overcome it.

*[12] giving-thanks to the Father for qualifying you for a share of the inheritance of the holy-ones in the light, [13] [the Father] who delivered us from the authority of darkness **and relocated [us]** to the kingdom of the Son of his love*

The Father did not simply remove believers from the dominion of darkness, only to leave them in the "no man's land" of exile. Rather, God brought them out in order to bring them in.[34] He relocated us to his heavenly kingdom.

This is not the first time God has moved his people. God moved Abraham to Palestine. God moved Jacob's family to Egypt and then later back to Palestine under the leadership of Moses. Centuries later God moved Israel to Assyria and Babylon, only to return some of them to their home-land decades later. And just as God had moved Israel out from under the darkness of Egypt and into the kingdom of David, so now God has moved us from the authority of darkness to the kingdom of Jesus, the Son of David. No longer are we abused subjects of a dark empire; now we are well-loved citizens of a new kingdom.[35] The Colossians needed to hear this, because their confidence had been shaken by those who questioned their qualifications (see Col 2:16, 18). Paul reassured them (and us) by declaring we have already been moved to God's kingdom.

By using geographic terms here, Paul highlights the drama of salvation. It's not merely agreeing to proper doctrines about God. It's more than being reconciled to God. Rather, salvation also means being evacuated from dangerous territory and brought to a new homeland. It's a move from darkness to God's light, a move from bondage to God's freedom, a move from a vulnerable dependency on evil to a new allegiance to God's kingdom, from condemnation to forgiveness. It's high drama.

How conscious we are of this drama, however, varies much from one believer to the next. Some (like Paul and the Colossians) experience a vivid transition from darkness to light, as tangible as moving from Babylon to Palestine. Others, however, have no consciousness of dramatic movement at all, which is often the case for those raised in the faith from infancy. Their situation is like that of the children of immigrants. The very young have no remembrance of moving, but even without the memory of it, the life-changing fact remains that they are in a new location. The main thing to celebrate, then, is not how conscious we are of being relocated from darkness to light, but the fact that we have indeed been relocated.

I praise you, Sovereign Lord, for moving me into your kingdom. Whether I remember the event or not, what matters is that I'm in a new place with you.

*[12] giving-thanks to the Father for qualifying you for a share of the inheritance of the holy-ones in the light, [13] [the Father] who delivered us from the authority of darkness and relocated [us] **to the kingdom** of the Son of his love*

Compared to Jesus, who spoke of the kingdom at least 126 times, Paul only mentions it 14 times—usually to talk about who will or will not inherit it (as in 1 Cor 6:9). For Paul, the kingdom represents the future reality of God's complete rule, with believers already walking in that reality and motivated by its future completion to press on in their mission.

There may be a couple reasons Paul doesn't emphasize kingdom talk. For one, Jesus spoke mainly to Jews who longed for the coming King and kingdom. But Paul focused on non-Jews in the Roman Empire, and from their perspective, kings (like Herod) were a step down from the emperor, and kingdoms were smaller in scope than the empire. So Paul would rather talk about Jesus as Lord (a term that the emperors liked to use for themselves). Secondly, for Paul, Jesus himself now functions as the kingdom. As the church father Tertullian stated, "In the gospel Christ Himself is the kingdom of God" (*Against Marcion* 4.33.8). In Jesus, the King and the kingdom merge together.

In contemporary Christianity, many are calling for Christians to re-emphasize kingdom-talk because it provides a larger frame of reference for understanding what it means to follow Jesus. Kingdom-talk opens our minds to seeing Jesus as Lord over all things—not just over our souls or the church. Instead the kingdom of God means that Jesus is also Lord over politics, economics, the arts, the environment, justice concerns, science, technology and more. In the famous words of Abraham Kuyper, "There is not a square inch in the whole domain of our human existence over which Christ, who is Sovereign over all, does not cry, 'Mine!'"[36]

While these ideas are wonderful and true, most of the kingdom language in the NT does not provide explicit support for such a position. Instead the focus of the kingdom is on repentance, healings and exorcisms, obedience and righteousness, the gospel message, judgment, sacrifices, children, rebirth and even its non-worldly status (Jn 18:36). To be sure, God's kingdom does encompass *all* things (as Col 1:15-20 affirms), but in our eagerness to declare the all-encompassing kingdom of God, we dare not neglect the King of the kingdom.

Great Lord and King, all things belong to you, and even though I have been resistant, I acknowledge that all of me belongs to you as well.

> ^{12} *giving-thanks to the Father for qualifying you for a share of the inheritance of the holy-ones in the light,* ^{13} *[the Father] who delivered us from the authority of darkness and relocated [us] to the kingdom **of the Son of his love***

Because Paul focuses on the King more than the kingdom, he is quick to describe the kingdom as belonging to the Father's well-loved Son.

This connection between being a king and being a divine son was common in the ancient world. Kings were regarded as gods in human form, or at least as sons of the gods. So when God reluctantly allowed Israel to adopt the kingship model as their system of government, the language of divine sonship was also adopted, although in a limited way intended to preserve the oneness of God. For instance, the Lord says to the Anointed One, a king descended from David, "You are my Son; today I have begotten you" (Ps 2:7, ESV). The psalm goes on to command the rulers of the earth to kiss the Son who will rule over all (Ps 2:12).

In the NT such language now applies to Jesus, on an even more literal level. For example, an angel announces the divine sonship of Jesus to Mary (Lk 1:31-35). The Father confirmed the divine sonship of Jesus at his baptism (Mt 3:17) and at his transfiguration (Mt 17:5). Peter formally confessed Jesus to be the Son of the Living God in Mt 16:16. Jesus himself made the same claim, especially in the gospel of John (see a cluster of sayings in Jn 5:19-27 for just one set of examples).

Paul's calling was particularly focused on the sonship of Jesus. After he was converted, "at once he began to preach in the synagogues, that Jesus is the Son of God'" (Acts 9:20, NIV). Paul himself confirmed this in Gal 1:16— God "was pleased to reveal his Son to me that I might preach him among the Gentiles" (ESV). He tells the Romans that God commissioned him to preach "the gospel of his Son" (Rom 1:9, NIV). In 2 Cor 1:19, Paul refers to "the Son of God, Jesus Christ, who was preached among you by us" (NIV).

To say that Jesus is the Son who rules over the kingdom is not just a term of endearment or political hype. Jesus is in essence the Son of God and thus the King of all creation, as will be even more evident in Col 1:15-20.

We worship You, Jesus, as the Son of God, and we pledge allegiance to you as our King.

*[12] giving-thanks to the Father for qualifying you for a share of the inheritance of the holy-ones in the light, [13] [the Father] who delivered us from the authority of darkness and relocated [us] to the kingdom **of the Son of his love***

Look up all the verses that refer to Jesus as the Son and you will discover a number of recurring themes besides the Son-kingdom connection.

The Son-love connection. We expect sons to be loved by their fathers, and the same is true with Jesus. In the Greek translation of the OT, the same words for "son" and "love" are found together twenty-nine times—the most significant of which would be Isaac being loved by Abraham (Gen 22:2), and Solomon being loved by the Lord (2 Sam 12:24-25). Jesus is also loved by his Father, as was declared at Christ's baptism and transfiguration. "The Father loves the Son and has placed everything in his hands" (Jn 3:35, NIV).

The Son-inheritance connection. Ordinarily, sons and daughters are regarded as heirs of their parents; this is also true of Jesus the Son. Right after God called the king his Anointed Son, he promised him the nations as his inheritance (Ps 2:7-8). In the Parable of the Tenants, Jesus is the Son who is killed by the rebellious tenants in the vain hope that they would then seize his inheritance (see Mt 21:33-45). In Christ the Son, we also become God's children and heirs (see Gal 4:6, Rom 8:17, and Col 1:12).

The Son-atonement connection. It's surprising how often the NT refers to the death of the Son (such as Rom 8:32 about God not sparing his Son but giving him up for us all) and that the Son's death brought forgiveness (for God "sent his Son as an atoning sacrifice for our sins," 1 Jn 4:10, NIV). The next verses in Colossians will make this same connection. It's unclear why the death of the Son is needed. The most likely link is to the near-sacrifice of Isaac by his father Abraham. Some rabbis regarded this as an atoning sacrifice, but the NT never makes this explicit.

The NT also connects the Son to: the giving of life ("God sent his one and only Son into the world, so that we might live through him," 1 Jn 4:9, ESV); spiritual warfare ("The reason the Son of God appeared was to destroy the devil's work," 1 Jn 3:8, NIV); and knowledge ("the Son of God has come and has given us understanding, so that we may know him who is true," 1 Jn 5:20, ESV). These themes are also found in the immediate context of Col 1:13. To call Jesus the Son, then, is no idle cliché, but a powerful expression of who Jesus is and what he came to do.

Lord Jesus, you truly are the Christ, the Son of the Living God, and we are so grateful that in you we also may be sons and daughters of the Father.

> ^{13} *[the Father] who delivered us from the authority of darkness and relocated [us] to the kingdom of the Son of his love—* ^{14} ***in whom we have redemption,*** *the forgiveness of our sins—*

By being relocated to the kingdom of the Son, we now live in Christ. And when we are in Christ, we are in the sphere of redemption.

Redemption is a word associated with the process of setting a slave or captive free. If we look back to verse 13, the identity of the enslaving power would be the demonic darkness, but if we look ahead to the next phrase, the enslaving power could also be thought of as sin. The two go together: the powers of darkness enslave people to sin.

Redemption is described as an "already and not yet" reality, a present and future reality. In the present, those who had at one time been in the stranglehold of sin have already been loosened by Jesus. Although all have sinned, believers "are justified freely by his grace as a gift, through the *redemption* that is in Christ Jesus" (Rom 3:23-24, NIV, italics mine). The present reality of redemption is why Paul uses the present tense in Col 1:14 to state that believers "have" redemption. It's not only something they will have in the future, but they have it right now. Since Jesus is our redemption (1 Cor 1:30), then when we are in Christ, we have redemption.

But the redemption of believers also has a "not yet" quality. Jesus told his disciples that in the Last Days they should look up "because your redemption is drawing near" (Lk 21:28, NIV); it's still coming. Even those who are redeemed still "groan inwardly as we wait eagerly for...the redemption of our bodies" (Rom 8:23, NIV).

What holds the present and future reality of redemption together is the Holy Spirit. The Spirit is a deposit, a down-payment of our future inheritance of the fullness of redemption. According to Eph 1:14, the promised Holy Spirit "is a deposit guaranteeing our inheritance until the redemption of those who are God's possession" (NIV). Later, in Eph 4:30, Paul warns us, "do not grieve the Holy Spirit of God, by whom you were sealed for the day of redemption" (ESV).

So are we redeemed already, or are we looking forward to being redeemed in the future? Yes. We are both. The doors of our prison are open, but we keep drifting back for a peek at where we used to live. Someday the whole prison will be blown to pieces.

For freedom, Christ Jesus, you have set us free. Give me the determination to stand firmly in that liberty.

^{13} *[the Father] who delivered us from the authority of darkness and relocated [us] to the kingdom of the Son of his love—* ^{14} *in whom we have redemption, **the forgiveness** of our sins—*

In Christ we also live in a kingdom marked by forgiveness. The word used here (*aphesis*) refers to some kind of release. In the Greek translation of the OT, it's often about a release from oppression and economic debt. The Year of Jubilee, when all debts were cancelled, was called the Year of *Aphesis* in the Greek OT (see Lev 25:13; Isa 61:1-2).

Although being released from sin is not the focus of the OT, it's completely the reverse in the NT. Nearly every one of the 17 NT references to *aphesis* is about the release, or forgiveness, of sins. Surprisingly, however, the idea of forgiveness is not prominent in Paul's letters (nor do Peter and John use this word). Paul only uses this noun here and Eph 1:7, and he only uses the corresponding verb for forgiving in Rom 4:7 when quoting Ps 32:1.

Why does Paul pay so little attention to this word for the forgiveness of sins? Possibly it's because *aphesis* is so associated with debt cancellation that it could give the wrong impression that forgiveness does nothing but erase a bad mark from your record, without bringing an inner change. It's a word that quickly pulls us in the direction of commerce and financial transaction, and even toward the idea that we might be able to do something to pay off our debt. The fact that *aphesis* could be taken in the wrong way may explain why Paul usually prefers a different word for forgiving, *charizomai*, which is related to *charis*, the word for grace. It's a word Paul will use later in Col 2:13 and 3:13. When it comes to forgiveness, Paul would rather emphasize gift-giving over debt-cancelling. It's more than a transaction, but an overflowing of love.

But even though Paul does not emphasize *aphesis*, his use of it here shows that it's still a great word for describing God's grace. *Aphesis* means that we have been released from the burden of spiritual debt and been given an inheritance instead (verse 12). *Aphesis* also means that instead of being captured by demonic powers, we have been released from their hold on our lives (verse 13)—for as Jesus said in Lk 4:18, he was anointed to proclaim release (*aphesis*) for the captives. And instead of living in bondage to sin, *aphesis* means that we have been set free from them as well.

There may be times, Lord, that I misuse your wonderful gift of forgiveness. Whenever I receive that wonderful gift, set my heart in the right direction.

> [13] *[the Father] who delivered us from the authority of darkness and relocated [us] to the kingdom of the Son of his love—* [14] *in whom we have redemption, the forgiveness **of our sins**—*

When Paul speaks of sin, he usually talks about singular "sin," not plural "sins." Of the 64 times Paul uses the word sin, it's only in the plural 12 times. That's because for him, SIN in the singular (I'll put it in uppercase in today's devotion to help clarify this) is like an evil power within us that is greater than the sum of its parts. SIN entered the world through one man (Rom 5:12), and outside of Christ all are now in its power (Rom 3:9).

So what can conquer this juggernaut called SIN? While forgiveness is an appropriate term for how God deals with particular sins (plural)—forgiving lies, greed, lust, etc.—something stronger is needed to overcome the massive power of SIN. And that something stronger is the death of Jesus (Rom 8:2-3) and our death with him (see Col 2:11-12).

Here in Col 1:14, however, Paul *does* refer to sins in the plural, and for good reason. Paul usually shows us the big picture—the drama of salvation played out between the power of SIN and Christ. But Paul knows it's also good for us to look at the little picture of how Jesus deals with us and the particular sins we have committed.

Not that we want to take the path of the Pharisees, cataloging, ranking, and nit-picking over all the little actions that could possibly be wrong. Still, we are living in a dream world if we only talk about SIN in general without ever examining the specific sins in our own hearts that need forgiveness. Paul usually calls attention to the forest that's on fire with SIN, but we must also pay attention to each tree that's aflame as well, the particular sins of our daily lives.

The prostitute who anointed Jesus' feet, for example, did not love Jesus because she had received an abstract forgiveness for generalized SIN in her life. Instead she loved much, because "her sins, which are many [!] are forgiven" (Lk 7:47, ESV).

So we rejoice that the Lord not only conquers SIN in general, but also forgives us for a multitude of sins in particular. Although we were dead in our sins (Eph 2:1), "Christ died for our sins" (1 Cor 15:3, NIV) and "gave himself for our sins" (Gal 1:4, NIV). In Christ, the big war is won and SIN is defeated. But also through Christ, all the smaller battles and skirmishes against specific sins are being won as well.

My Lord and Savior, I thank you for defeating sin on my behalf. Please forgive and overcome the sins that remain in me.

This is My Heart's Prayer
to the tune of *For You I Am Praying*
© 2010 David J. Landegent

This is my heart's prayer that you'd be filled with knowledge
With wisdom and insight into the Father's will,
And in each day's journey you'd bring the Lord great pleasure,
So fruitful in good works—God's purposes fulfilled.
For you I am praying, for you I am praying,
For you I am praying—I'm praying for you.

I pray that you'd be empowered for endurance,
Withstanding each hardship with joyful gratitude.
For God qualified you, with all the saints in glory
To be heirs of blessings—eternal, bright and good.
For you I am praying, for you I am praying,
For you I am praying—I'm praying for you.

I am not anxious, but confident when praying,
For we have been rescued from realms so dark and grim.
And now we've been transferred to Jesus' holy kingdom,
In him, there's redemption—forgiveness of our sins.
For you I am praying, for you I am praying,
For you I am praying—I'm praying for you.

Jesus' ministry: the laudation

Colossians 1:15-20

February 26-April 1

> [15] *[the loved Son], who is the image of the unseen God, the firstborn of all creation,* [16] *for in him were created all things in the heavens and on the earth, the seen things and the unseen things, whether thrones or lordships or primal-powers, or authorities; all things through him and toward him have been created;* [17] *and he is before all things, and all things in him stand together.* [18] *And he is the head of the body (the church), the Primal-Power, the firstborn from out of the dead ones, in order that in all things he [himself] would be firsting,* [19] *for in him all the fullness was pleased to dwell* [20] *and through him to reconcile all things toward him—having-made-peace through the blood of his cross—whether things on the earth or things in the heavens.*

This section proclaims the centrality of Jesus for the Christian faith. We are not simply God-ians, but Christ-ians. If Jesus had only been a good moral teacher, we could dismiss Paul's words as an inappropriate, over-the-top expression of praise. But because Jesus is the Son of God, these words demonstrate that he is at the core of what God is doing in our world.

Although some call this section a poem or hymn, it really does not seem to fit those labels, so I will be calling it a laudation, words that give glory, laud and honor to the King of kings and Lord of lords.

Even though this laudation exalts Jesus, it does not consist of a set of abstract ideas about his divine qualities, such as "Jesus is all-knowing, all-powerful, gracious, etc." Instead we find a storyline here that praises Jesus by declaring who he is through what he has done. Although some elements are missing from the plot, yet the main story tells us that in the distant past, Jesus created all things (verse 15-16). However—in some way not spelled out here—creation fell away and needed Christ to bring reconciliation and make peace. This he accomplished by coming to earth to die on the cross (verses 19-20). Shortly after that he rose from the dead and formed an assembly of followers as his body to carry on this work of reconciliation (verse 18). Currently, Jesus is holding all things together (verse 17), "heading" up the church, ruling over all things (verse 18), and continuing the work of reconciliation begun at the cross (verse 20). As for the future, Jesus' title of firstborn from the dead (verse 18) signals the future restoration of all creation.

Thus, Paul provides a sweeping view of Jesus' relationship with all things, from the dawn of creation to the new creation at the end of time.

Lord Jesus, it's so easy for me to focus on myself and my circle of loved ones. Awaken me to the magnitude of all you are doing in your world.

Read the laudation again — Colossians 1:15-20

Paul is writing to a church that lived in a culture whose religious ideas ranged from superstition to high-minded philosophy. Parts of his laudation would speak to both ends of that spectrum.

On the superstitious end, various inscriptions, amulets, and documents show that the pagans of that region went to great lengths to placate evil supernatural powers and to call on good powers to rescue them.[37] The Colossian believers, leaving this fear-based religion behind, would learn much from the laudation about Jesus being the Lord of all these powers.

The laudation also speaks to more philosophical pagans, especially those from the adherents of Stoicism. First, Paul said that all things were created "in him [Christ]...through him...and for him" (Col 1:16). The Stoics used similar phrases to describe Nature. The second century Stoic and emperor Marcus Aurelius said to Nature, "from you are all things, in you are all things, and toward you are all things" (*Meditations* 4.23). Yet, a similar grammatical form does not make for a similar thought. Aurelius is not celebrating the power, glory, and orderliness of Nature, but is only resigning himself to the fact that we appear (all things come from Nature); we're here (all things exist in Nature); and we disappear (all things return to Nature). Aurelius' words of resignation to an impersonal force, then, have nothing in common with Paul's good news of the glory and triumph of Jesus over all things.

Second, Paul declares here that all things are held together in Christ (Col 1:17). Similarly, the Greek philosophers also spoke of what holds all things together. But again, using the same phrases does not necessarily mean Paul and the philosophers had the same understanding. For Paul, the universe is held together by a person named Jesus. For the Stoics, it was a more impersonal force that held all things together. So when the Stoics said their generic god held all things together, it was only a statement meant to encourage resignation to the way things are. But when Paul declared that Jesus holds all things together, it's the good news that the universe is in the care of a Savior who loves it deeply.

Paul and the Greek philosophers do share a common cultural language, and Paul adapted it as part of his evangelistic strategy of becoming all things to all people that he might win some (1 Cor 9:22). But his meaning is very different from what the philosophers were saying.

I am so thankful, Sovereign Lord, that as I make my way through life, I am not simply adjusting to cosmic forces; I am living in your hands.

Read the laudation again — Colossians 1:15-20

The Jews believed that talking about God having a Son would jeopardize their foundational belief in the oneness of God. But the oneness of God in Jewish writings is richer than simple math would suggest. When Paul assigned some divine actions to Jesus, he was making a move very similar to what is found in Proverbs 8-9, the apocryphal books of the Wisdom of Solomon and Sirach, and the extensive writings of a first century Jewish philosopher named Philo. These writings assigned divine actions to personifications of the Word or Wisdom (usually portrayed as a woman). Here are some of the many obvious comparisons:

Jesus in Col 1:15-20	Other Jewish writings
the image of God	"Wisdom is the image of his [God's] goodness" (Wisdom) • "the image of God is the Word" (Philo)
the firstborn of creation	"The Lord created me as the beginning of his ways" (Prov 8:22, NETS) • "the divine word, [is God's] own firstborn son" (Philo)
all was created in him	"I was beside him like a master workman" (Prov 8:30, ESV) • Lady Wisdom is "the fashioner of all things" (Wisdom)
he is before all things	"Ages ago I was set up, at the first, before the beginning of the earth" (Prov 8:23, ESV) • "From eternity, in the beginning, he created me, and for eternity I shall not cease to exist" (Sirach)
all things hold together in him	"By his [God's] word all things hold together" (Sirach) • "The word of the living God...holds all things together, and binds all the parts" (Philo)

Why did Paul closely echo these writings? Well, just as these Jewish writers could speak of the Word and Wisdom as a person without casting doubts on the oneness of God, so Paul was doing the same in talking about Jesus. Jesus was everything that the Jewish writings said of Wisdom and Word...and more.[38] But here are two crucial differences: (1) The Jewish writers speak of wisdom and word *as if* they were persons; Jesus is a person, not a personification. (2) The Jewish writings had nothing to match the second half of the laudation; they don't associate Wisdom or Word with resurrection, reconciliation, a cross, or a church. Word and Wisdom were involved in creation (as was Jesus), but only Jesus brings the new creation.

Thank you, Father for sending more than a personification of wisdom and truth. Even better, you sent your only begotten Son.

Read the laudation again — Colossians 1:15-20

The first followers of Jesus sought the right words to describe who Jesus was. He was obviously human, with a body that could be seen, heard, and touched (1 Jn 1:1-3). He grew up in a town they could visit and had a family they had met. And yet they knew something was different about him. Although some people thought of him as evil because of what he claimed about himself, the sinful people he associated with, and some of the unusual ways he interpreted the OT, yet the disciples never saw any immorality or unrighteousness in him. Even more amazing to them was Jesus' authority over the created world and the demonic world. And then there were Jesus' own divine claims about himself, claims so outrageous that he was either crazy, evil or telling the truth (lunatic, liar or Lord, as C. S. Lewis put it).[39]

But the teaching of the OT made Jesus' claims a difficult pill to swallow. There were no obvious verses in the OT suggesting that God had an eternal son or that this son would come as a human being and die for sinners. It's not surprising that Jesus' claim to be the Son of God earned him the charge of blasphemy by the Jewish authorities. What really convinced Jesus' followers of his divine sonship, however, was his resurrection. When that happened, they fell to their knees and worshiped him as Lord.

Paul's laudation fits well with the words and deeds of Jesus found in the rest of the NT. Here and everywhere in the NT, Jesus is the one who reveals the Father, who has power over creation and the powers-that-be, who calls and leads his people, who works to bring reconciliation, who died on the cross to make peace, and who rose from the dead to open the door for the new creation. According to Paul's laudation, Jesus is not a charismatic wonder-worker, interesting sage, or Jewish revolutionary, but the eternal Son of God.

Paul was not the only early disciple to reach such lofty conclusions about Jesus' identity. John 1:1-14 dares to describe Jesus as the Word of God who was with God and is God from the very beginning, creating all things, and coming from the Father's side into our world in human flesh, full of God's grace and truth. Similarly, Heb 1:1-4 calls Jesus the Son who reveals the Father in the last days, is heir of all things, made the universe, radiates God's glory, represents God's being, sustains all things, has provided purification for sin, and rules over all things at God's right hand. We follow a mighty Lord.

The world may not understand you, Jesus, but we rejoice in what you've revealed of yourself to us, and are eager to share it with others.

Read the laudation again — Colossians 1:15-20

Some people might be surprised by the sudden appearance of this stirring laudation in the book of Colossians. But Paul commonly inserted words of exalted praise for Jesus into all kinds of discussions. For example, when talking about the advisability of eating meat, he proclaims the larger truth of belonging to Jesus in life and in death (Rom 14:7-12). When discussing his travel plans, he announced that all God's promises are "yes" and "Amen" in Christ (2 Cor 1:18-22). In the middle of talking about eating food offered to idols (1 Cor 8:6), the integrity of his ministry (2 Cor 5:11-21), marital roles (Eph 5:21-33), or making a financial appeal (2 Cor 8:8-9), Paul easily launched into words of praise for Jesus. And he does the same here.

One unique element here is that Paul's words for exalting Jesus are more extensive than in his other letters. Usually the words of praise for Jesus are brief, and then Paul returns to the matter at hand. The six verses of Col 1:15-20, however, are packed with important descriptions of Jesus and his work.

But in spite of the unusual length, nearly everything in the laudation is paralleled in Paul's other letters. Paul elsewhere refers to Jesus as the image of God (2 Cor 4:4); the firstborn (Rom 8:29); the Creator (2 Cor 5:17); the Lord over all other powers (Rom 8:38; 1 Cor 8:5-6); the one through whom we live (1 Cor 8:6); the head of the church (Eph 4:15); the first one risen from the dead to lead the way for others (1 Cor 15:20, 23; 1 Thess 4:16); the one having fullness (Eph 4:12-13); the reconciler (Rom 5:10; 2 Cor 5:18-20); and the one who brought forgiveness by his blood (Rom 3:25; 5:9; Eph 1:7). By concentrating these phrases together, Paul has produced a powerful paragraph of praise for Jesus.

Paul's habit of suddenly bursting into words of praise, even in the most ordinary moments of life, is a call for us to be ready to do the same. Since Jesus stands at the center of all creation, then anything and everything can remind us of something about which we can rejoice in the Lord.

Lord Jesus, it often takes special moments and times of worship for me to lift my heart to you in praise. Open my eyes to see your glory even in the ordinary as well.

Read the laudation again — Colossians 1:15-20

Later in Colossians we'll learn that some of the believers were anxious about the quality of their faith. False teachers were suggesting that Christ was only a partial savior. If they wanted to experience the fullness of salvation, they needed to contact other supernatural powers and observe rules about holy days and diets (see Col 2:16-23).

To counteract this threat and bolster the confidence of the believers, Paul declares here the supremacy of Jesus. How do we know we have been transferred from the domain of darkness to the kingdom of the Son (Col 1:13)? Because the Son created and rules over all other powers (Col 1:16). How do we know that the things of creation (like food) are not undermining our faith? Because Jesus has made all things (Col 1:16). How do we know we have redemption and forgiveness of sins (Col 1:14)? Because the Son is reconciling all things through the blood of his cross (Col 1:20).

Anxious Christians, like the Colossians, commonly focus on themselves and their own concerns. But the laudation awakens us to the reality that we are not the center of the universe; Jesus is. We cannot confine the scope of Jesus' work to our own heart or our own church. Rather, this laudation shows us a Jesus who is in relationship to "all" things. In fact, the Greek for "all" is used eight times in these six verses. Count them. Once the laudation is concluded, Paul will refer to his readers once again (Col 1:21-23), but for now he wants us to look up and see Jesus as Lord of all things.

Up until the laudation, the emphasis of Colossians has been on God the Father. Jesus has been mentioned often, but most of the action has been either done by the Father or directed toward the Father. The Father gives grace and peace (verses 2 and 6), fills us with the knowledge (verses 9-10), strengthens us with power to endure (verse 11), qualifies us to share in an eternal inheritance (verse 12), rescues us from darkness and brings us into the kingdom of the Son (verse 13). And for our part, we thank the Father (verses 3, 12) and pray to the Father (verses 9-12). But from here on out the letter portrays Jesus as the focal point of God's redemptive plan.

Self-centeredness has no place in the Christian life. Rather, we are called to be Jesus-centered. In him, through him, for him—that's how we live.

Everlasting Lord, pull me out of my own self-constructed universe with all its worries and fears by lifting my eyes to see you in all your glory.

Read the laudation again — Colossians 1:15-20

Paul's laudation has a definite poetic style, even if the Greek words don't rhyme or have a rhythmic beat.

For one thing, there is a definite grammatical pattern here indicated by the repetition of small phrases. Verses 15-16 start with the phrase "who is," followed by the lines "for in him," and then "through him" and "toward him." This exact same pattern is seen in verses 18b-20 (but not always reflected in translations, including mine): "who is...for in him...through him...toward him." In between these two "stanzas" are verses 17-18a, both of which start with the phrase "and he is." But in spite of these patterns, it's not a tightly-organized poem, for the stanzas vary significantly in length.

Another indication of the laudation's poetic quality is the existence of parallel meanings that echo one another. This was a common feature of Jewish poetry (see Ps 24:1 for an example of this). Paul does something like this in his laudation with the first part dealing with creation (verses 15-17), echoed by the second half highlighting the new creation (verses 18-20):

A. **Jesus' divinity**: Jesus is the image of God (15a) — all the fullness of God dwells in Jesus (19).
B. **Jesus as the firstborn**: Jesus is the firstborn of all creation (15b) — Jesus is the firstborn from the dead (18c).
C. **Jesus and all things**: all things in heaven and earth created in Christ (16a) — all things in earth and heaven reconciled in Christ (20).
D. **Jesus and the powers**: Jesus created all the primal-powers (16b) — Jesus himself is *the* Primal-Power (18b).
E. **Jesus holding things together**: Jesus holds all creation together (verse 17) — Jesus as the head holds the church together (verse 18a; 2:19).

But even here the parallels are not perfect. The parallels in the two "halves" occur in reverse order—almost. Instead of following the order of ABCDE–EDCBA, Paul writes ABCDE-EDBAC (with C moved to the end). It seems Paul was not that interested in impressing us with a perfectly symmetrical poem. What he wanted to impress upon us was the majesty and glory of Jesus.

Even if the laudation's structure is difficult to figure out, Paul clearly wants us to see that for both creation and the new creation, Jesus is the center point of it all.

Lord Jesus, all of creation revolves around you and your purposes of grace. I want to be a willing part of that revolution.

*¹⁵ [the loved Son], **who is the image of the unseen God,** the firstborn of all creation*

Jesus is exalted, not only because of what he has done, but especially for who he is: he is the image (*eikōn*) of God. As children resemble their parents because of shared genes and shared life together, so Jesus shares the same Trinitarian DNA, so to speak, of his heavenly Father.

But we must be clear about what this means. Jesus is not a *commercial* image or logo, a false façade designed to sell something.⁴⁰ Rather, he wants to give us something, and it's something genuine and true—a visible revelation of the heavenly Father. Jesus provides open and visible access to his unseen Father.

Neither is Jesus a mere *symbolic* image or an inferior copy of God. Heb 10:1 describes an *eikōn* as real and substantive, just the opposite of a shadow. So as the *eikōn* of God, Jesus does not merely symbolize God, but expresses and lives out the reality of God in our midst.

In addition, Jesus is not an *idolatrous* image, for he is the Creator and not the creature. If Jesus had been a created being, it would be wrong to worship him. But as the Creator, he is the image of God worthy of all praise.

Jesus is not merely made *in* the image of God; he *is* the image of God (see also 2 Cor 4:4, 6). Adam and Eve and all humanity with them were made *in* God's image (Gen 1:26-27). And in a certain sense, Jesus is what humanity was created to be. But in another sense, Jesus is greater than humanity, not just *bearing* the image of God, but *being* the image of God.

But whether we're talking about humanity or Christ, the main focus of the image of God is that of having dominion. Right after God said, "Let us make man in our image," he charged them to have dominion (Gen 1:26). Just as ancient kings set up images of themselves to establish their claim over territories, so God created people in his image to establish his rule over earth. Likewise, Jesus bears God's image in all its fullness by having dominion over creation. That's why, after describing Jesus as the image of God, Paul immediately turns to speak of Jesus' power over all creation in verses 15b-17.

So when Isaiah 40:18 asks, "What image will you compare God to?" Paul gives the answer—Jesus, the Son of God.

Lord Jesus, I have no need for you to show me the Father. When I see you, I see the Father, his power, and his grace.

¹⁵ *[the loved Son], who is the image of the unseen God,* **the firstborn of all creation**

The sonship of Jesus not only means he is God's image, but also God's firstborn (see Rom 8:29 and Heb 1:1-6 for other examples of how sonship, image, and firstborn go together in describing Jesus).

In most OT references to the firstborn, the time element is obvious: the firstborn is the first male offspring born to a human family or to livestock. But if we were to focus on the time element in Col 1:15, we might fall into the error of thinking that Jesus was created first and then everything else. But if Jesus was the same as Lady Wisdom, who claimed, "The Lord brought me forth as the first of his works" (Prov 8:22, NIV), then worshiping Jesus would mean we were worshiping a created being, which is idolatry.

In wrestling with this, the early church found help in the term "begotten"—Jesus was begotten not made. When you beget something, said C. S. Lewis, you beget something that's the same kind as yourself. Humans beget humans, beavers beget beavers, birds beget birds. But when you make something, you make something *unlike* yourself. Humans make radios, beavers make dams, birds make nests. So when the Father has a "firstborn" only-begotten Son, he is begetting someone like himself. Jesus, then, is not the first created being, but the eternal Son of God.⁴¹

Paul, then, is not focusing on the time element when he calls Jesus the firstborn. Instead he's emphasizing the power and authority of the firstborn. According to ancient custom, the firstborn was honored with a double portion of the inheritance, and the firstborn prince was the heir to the throne (2 Chron 21:3). Firstborn honors, however, did not always go to the son who was born first. For instance, the fourth-born Judah was considered the leader of Israel, a firstborn bull (Dt. 33:16-17). Likewise, God said of the last-born King David, "I will also appoint him my firstborn, the most exalted of the kings of the earth" (Ps 89:27). In this respect, "firstborn" is similar to the American title, "First Lady." The First Lady is not Eve, but the wife of the current (male) president.

So even though the title contains the word "first," it's not a reference to time, but a reference to honor. Likewise, the firstborn of all creation is not about Jesus being created first, but to his being the number one ruler of creation.

Lord Jesus, you are the first-born, and we are glad to be your brothers and sisters in your forever family.

> [15] *[the loved Son], who is the image of the unseen God, the firstborn of all creation,* [16] **for in him were created all things** *in the heavens and on the earth, the seen things and the unseen things*

The laws of physics, said C. S. Lewis, can explain what will happen when one billiard ball hits another ball, but they cannot explain who hit the ball or why. Likewise, science can explain many things, but it cannot explain the who and why of creation.[42] For those answers we must turn to Jesus. All things were created in him, a truth echoed by Jn 1:3 and Heb 1:2.

Skeptics think that Paul, John, and the writer of Hebrews are getting carried away in their estimation of Jesus, transforming the simple prophet from Nazareth into a cosmic Christ that goes beyond what's in the Gospels. But the miracles recorded in the Gospels—multiplying food, commanding storms, restoring sight to the blind, healing diseases, and raising the dead—clearly demonstrate Jesus' power over creation. And he has this power because he is its Creator.

The words of Col 1:13 about God delivering us from darkness and moving us to the kingdom of the Son might give the impression that Jesus' kingdom has its limits, that there is another kingdom making its own claims. But the dominion of darkness has no true claim on anything or anyone. Jesus made all things and thus has a claim over every single thing, large and small, from galaxies to atomic particles. It all belongs to him. At the Stake known as the cross, Jesus especially staked his claim to take back the world he had made. He exercises authority over all things, and in turn, all things are answerable to him. His is a kingdom without boundaries, for there is nothing outside of his realm.

The last part of this verse declares that all things were created *through* and *toward* Jesus, but here Paul observes that everything has also been created *in* him. Nothing has an independent existence; everything lives and moves and has its being within God's ultimate purposes for the Son.

To say all things were created in Christ also suggests that creation is an act of gracious, undeserved love. While we might think grace is all about salvation and forgiveness, it's more extensive than that. Everything Christ does is an act of grace, whether that act be healing a lame man, dying on the cross for sinners, or creating the world. Grace is Christ's free favor bestowed on his creation. Said Adrio König, "In making us, he bestows an incomparable favor on us: the opportunity to be his creatures."[43]

I thank you, Lord, that I am fearfully and wonderfully made by you. I experience your grace today simply because I exist.

[15] *[the loved Son], who is the image of the unseen God, the firstborn of all creation,* [16] *for in him were created all things* **in the heavens and on the earth, the seen things and the unseen things**

It's important to Paul that Jesus is Creator of both heaven and earth. It's a truth that supports him in his opposition to the Colossian distortion.

First, consider the importance of Jesus creating the *earth*. The religious impulse of many people, ancient and modern, assumes that God is only interested in the spiritual, not the physical. They like God creating the heavens, but they're not so sure about the earth with all its weak, finite, and gross things. The Colossian distortion leaned in this direction.

Paul, however, will not allow anyone to spiritualize the work of Jesus, as if he were only responsible for creating the good spiritual realities of heaven, and not the grossly material things of earth. The material world and the physical body are not enemies of God, nor are they obstacles to faith. The distortionists may have believed that a "harsh treatment of the body" would be spiritually beneficial (see Col 2:20-23), but Paul knows better: Jesus made the world and took on human flesh himself (see Col 2:9).

But it's also important to say Jesus created the *heavens*. Some people think of Jesus as only one of many supernatural beings. When the distortionists, for instance, boasted of their heavenly visions and angel worship (Col 2:18), they thought they were entering into a realm larger than Christ, a supermall of salvation with Christ manning only one little kiosk. But Jesus is not to be confined to a small corner of a larger reality. He *is* the larger reality. As the Creator, he not only has the whole world in his hands, but also the entirety of the heavens and all the powers within it.

That God made heaven and earth is a key weapon in opposing idolatry. Jer 10:11-12 says, "The gods who did not make the heavens and the earth, will perish from the earth and from under the heavens. But God made the earth by his power...and stretched out the heavens by his understanding" (NIV). Col 1:16 would agree. For Jesus to make the heavens and the earth means that he rules over all other pretenders to the throne—as the rest of this verse will attest.

Prov 30:4 asked, "Who has gone up to heaven and come down?...Who has established all the ends of the earth? What is his name, and what is the name of his son? Surely you know!" (NIV). We now know the name of the Creator's son—Jesus.

The heavens and the earth testify to your glory, Lord Jesus. I pray for eyes and ears to hear their testimony.

*¹⁶ for in him were created all things in the heavens and on the earth, the seen things and the unseen things, **whether thrones or lordships or primal-powers, or authorities***

Some people approach the all-encompassing creative work of Jesus from a sentimental perspective. They find it heart-warming to think of Jesus creating their favorite things, like ocean waves and pepperoni pizza. Indeed, Jesus did make everything, but in spite of the prominence of the word "all," Paul is especially thinking of Jesus creating the things that are large and in charge, the powers-that-be listed in this part of verse 16.

This does not mean that the news media are right, that only the movers and shakers matter, and the rest of creation is comparatively insignificant. But it does acknowledge that the powers-that-be have a profound effect on the rest of creation, often in a negative way. So it's important to see that Jesus made these powers; they must answer to him; and they are not to be worshiped.

It's significant that all four terms used here for the powers can also be used more accurately to describe God—and God's Son.[44] There may be thrones, lordships, primal-powers, and authorities, but more importantly God is on the *throne* as *Lord*; God is the *Primal-Power* with *authority* over them all. Whenever the powers forget this (whether they be demonic or political), they become nothing. If rulers try to raise their thrones to the level of God's throne (like the king of Babylon in Isa 14:13-19), they become nothing but empty chairs. If the lordships stage a coup against the Lord, they become slaves. If primal-powers try to oust the Primal-Power, they lose all their might. If authorities attempt a revolt against God, they are quickly deauthorized. They have no independent authority to rule.

Many heresies in the second century embellished Paul's list of powers, attempting to map out how they were structured, assigning them names, rankings, job descriptions, and territories. They believed that with such knowledge they could harness these powers for their own advantage. That's a misuse of Paul's list. He was only trying to say that no matter what terms or titles you give them, every power in the universe—without exception—was created by Jesus and answerable to him.[45] As Walsh and Keesmaat say, Jesus is "their source, their purpose, their goal, even in their rebellion."[46] So there is no reason to call on a variety of good powers to fight off evil powers. All power is in the hands of Jesus, and we are to seek his help only.

Jesus, in spite of what the media reports about so-called 'movers' and 'shakers,' we gladly praise you as the sovereign Lord over all things.

^{16} *for in him were created all things in the heavens and on the earth, the seen things and the unseen things, **whether thrones or lordships or primal-powers, or authorities***

The question arises: are the powers-that-be supernatural or political in nature? Yes. They're both. The visible governing powers on earth; the structural realities that shape economies, traditions, and institutions; the invisible angelic powers in the heavens; the unseen demonic powers from the abyss—Jesus created them all. He also rules over them (Col 2:10, Eph 1:21), does not allow any of them to separate us from God's love (Rom 8:38-39), will judge them for oppressing people (Ps 82), and will eventually remove them from power (1 Cor 15:24). *Good* powers cannot add to what we have in Christ, nor can *evil* powers undo what we have in Christ.[47]

Most likely Paul is especially thinking of supernatural powers, because according to archaeological findings, the people in the region of Colossae were far more anxious about the harm that could be caused by them than by the political authorities. Thus, in Eph 6:12, Paul says, "For we do not wrestle against flesh and blood, but against the rulers, against the authorities, against the cosmic powers over this present darkness, against the spiritual forces of evil in the heavenly places" (ESV).

But even if Paul was thinking mostly of *supernatural* powers, it would be unwise to say the laudation has nothing to do with *political* powers. The supernatural powers and earthly powers often interact and feed off of each other, as can be seen in the mixture of demons and kings in the book of Revelation. Yet Christians should be very cautious in labeling any particular political group they don't like as a tool of satanic powers.[48] We must remember Paul's words in Rom 13:1 that human governments are established by God and ruled by Christ.

This does not mean Jesus approves the current arrangements of power in the world and provides legitimacy for every corrupt kingdom or empire. Not at all. Instead, as Walter Wink said, "at one and the same time [Jesus] *upholds* a given political or economic system," "*condemns* that system" when it goes in the wrong direction, and "*presses for its transformation.*"[49] Because he created them, Jesus holds the powers responsible for failing in their duties, and he has and will triumph over them (see Col 2:15 for the surprising way he wins the victory).

Lord, this day I pray for my nation. Uphold it by your providence, judge it for its injustices, and transform it by your Spirit.

> [16] *for in him were created all things in the heavens and on the earth, the seen things and the unseen things, whether thrones or lordships or primal-powers, or authorities; **all things through him** and toward him have been created.*

English teachers will tell us that it's usually best to use active verbs instead of passive verbs. Rather than saying, "the ball was thrown by the boy," we should say, "the boy threw the ball." This rule may be grammatically helpful, but it overlooks the fact that sometimes a passive verb more precisely expresses the truth. I mention this because of how Paul expresses Jesus' role in creation. Although I would like to use an active verb here to say, "Jesus created all things," Paul—intentionally or not—describes creation with a passive verb—"all things through him and toward him have been created." Perhaps Paul thought an active verb would sound as if Jesus were creating on his own, apart from God the Father. By using a passive verb and the prepositions in, through, and toward, Paul and the other writers want us to know that Jesus was a co-worker with the Father in creating all things, very similar to the role of Lady Wisdom in Proverbs 8.

But what does it mean for creation to happen *through* the Son? Paul frequently said that various actions were done to believers "through" Christ. "Through" Jesus, believers receive grace and eternal life, are justified freely, have peace with God, are saved from God's wrath, are reconciled to God, are more than conquerors, are adopted as God's children, are filled with the fruit of righteousness, and much more. And not only that, but the whole universe was also created through Christ.

This thought is not unique to Colossians. As Paul stated in 1 Cor 8:6, "Yet for us there is one God, the Father, from whom are all things came and for whom we exist, and one Lord, Jesus Christ, *through* whom are all things and *through* whom we exist" (ESV, italics mine). See also John 1:3, 10 and Hebrews 1:2.

Jesus is the conduit through whom the Father's creative power flows in making all things. Jesus is the instrument or agent by which the Father does his creative work. Jesus is the crown prince through whom the Father's authority moves for creating a kingdom which is as large as all the universe. Nothing came into existence independently, but only through the power of Jesus the Son.

Through you, Lord Jesus, I live and move and have my being—and so does everything else. Thank you for your generosity to us all.

> [16] *for in him were created all things in the heavens and on the earth, the seen things and the unseen things, whether thrones or lordships or primal-powers, or authorities; all things through him **and toward him have been created.***

Not only were all things created *in* Christ and *through* Christ, but they were also made *for* (*eis*) him, as many translations put it. The Lord doesn't make the world simply so it's there, but so that it's there for a purpose.

To say all things were made "for" Jesus does not, however, mean that he is a pampered prince or dictator, sitting back while everyone falls all over themselves trying to please him. Then we would only have a divine version of "it's all about me." But self-centeredness is not the Lord's way: he richly provides *for* our enjoyment (1 Tim 6:17).

We'd be closer to the mark if we think of *eis* as indicating a purpose. Jesus said to Pilate, "for [*eis*] this purpose I was born and for [*eis*] this purpose I have come into [*eis*] the world—to bear witness to the truth" (Jn 18:37, ESV). Similarly, we were created for Jesus and his purposes.

Another possible translation of *eis* is "toward." Toward" indicates a movement in a certain direction, and if it's toward a *person* that we move, we are moving in a relational direction. This is why the NT often uses the word *eis* to talk about having love *for* or *toward* others

So to say that all things are created *toward* Jesus (as we find in Col 1:16) means that all things are oriented toward Jesus the Son, moving toward him and his kingdom purposes. The universe does not operate by chance; instead, it operates with the purpose of moving toward Christ. Nothing exists for its own sake, but for the sake of Jesus.

Given the relational aspect of this preposition, it's no surprise to read that God calls us toward (*eis*) the fellowship of his Son (1 Cor 1:9) that we have set our hope toward (*eis*) Christ (2 Cor 1:10), that the church is to grow toward (*eis*) Christ the head (Eph 4:15), and that Christ is working to reconcile all things toward (*eis*) himself (Col 1:20).

Jesus, then, not only stands as the *first cause* of the creation (all things were made *through* him), but also as the *final goal* of creation (all things were made *toward* him, moving in his direction). Jesus came first and now leads the way into the future with all things moving toward him in the parade (see 2 Cor 2:14). Jesus is truly the beginning and the end, the Alpha and the Omega (Rev 22:13), the first cause and final goal of all creation.

Lord Jesus, I live for you and I live toward you. Help me to keep my bearings and orient my daily life in your direction.

¹⁷ **and he is before all things,** *and all things in him stand together.*

The other key word in this phrase is "before," which translates the Greek preposition *pro*. In both Greek and English "before" can refer to time ("this event happened prior to—or before—that one"), space ("this object was placed in front of—or before—that one"), and even priority ("before you pay attention to anything else, note this"). *Pro* is most often used in the NT in reference to time, as is the case in this verse.

Paul's conception of Jesus existing *before* creation was possibly modeled after Lady Wisdom's claim to have been appointed for creative work "before the beginning of the earth...before the mountains had been shaped...before he [God] made the earth" (Prov 8:23-27, ESV). The Greek translation of the OT uses the word *pro* six times in those verses.

When the NT uses *pro* in terms of time, sometimes it simply refers to one ordinary action happening before another action, but often it's about the order of *significant* events. Most relevant to Col 1:17 are those NT verses about things that existed or happened before the creation of the world. For example, before creation was formed: Jesus lived in glory with the Father (Jn 17:5); Jesus was loved by the Father (Jn 17:24); there existed a secret wisdom destined for the glory of believers (1 Cor 2:7); believers were chosen in Christ (Eph 1:4); believers were given grace in Christ (2 Tim 1:9); eternal life was promised (Titus 1:2); and glory and majesty belonged to God through Jesus (Jude 25). But these things could only happen because Christ was also in this "before" time. Without Christ's prior existence there is no prior chosenness or grace for the people of God. Paul is celebrating in verse 17, then, that before anything else came into existence, Jesus lived.

This truth is known as the pre-existence of Jesus. It means that Jesus is not a mere human being who only came into existence at birth, nor is he a created being who existed before he was born. Instead, Jesus existed with the Father from all eternity, participating in the creation of the world, and also being a willing participant in the Father's plan of salvation. As Paul said in Phil 2:5-11, Jesus was equal with the Father before the world was made, but he did not cling to the divine privileges he had from the beginning, but emptied himself of them in order to become a human being, a willing servant, and a sacrifice for sin.

I thank you, Father, that Jesus was not an after-thought, a later addition to your plans, but that he has lived and reigned with you from all eternity. I live in that assurance.

¹⁷ *and he is before all things, **and all things in him stand together.***

Because they lived in an earthquake zone in a superstitious part of the world, ordinary pagans in Paul's day regarded the universe as an unstable place. At any moment, creation could be turned into catastrophe by various powers-that-be.[50] But Paul assures them there's no need to fear—Jesus is holding it together, or more literally, causing it to stand together.

Translations vary. Some opt for "hold together," an attractive option because it conveys an image of an ongoing relationship in which "he's got the whole world in his hands." Other translations go with "establish," but that conveys a sense of an action that is now completed, as if Jesus had established all things from the start, and then left them to their own devices. That's why I prefer the Greek root of this term which speaks of standing together instead of falling apart. But standing together is not like maintaining a status quo. As F. F. Bruce said, Christ "upholds the universe not like Atlas supporting a dead weight on his shoulders, but as One who carries all things forward to their appointed course."[51]

Jesus is on the perimeter, binding all things together like sheaves for the harvest, so that nothing falls down flat and useless. Jesus is in the center, providing a point of gravity so that all things are able to stand as they are directed toward him. In an internet-oriented world that deeply longs to connect to others, Jesus is the wireless connection.[52] Jesus provides the life-giving energy that sustains all things. There are no rogue elements in creation which have escaped his influence, direction, power, or grace.

Ultimately, however, these word pictures of a binding cord, the force of gravity, or a wireless connection are not enough. What causes the universe to stand together is not some principle or physical law (as the Stoics in Paul's day thought, or some scientists in our day), but a man who had been crucified and raised from the dead. As Garland says, the principle uniting the universe has a heart, a purpose, and a face.[53] If what held the universe together were a principle or physical law, then ultimately everything would be impersonal. But since Jesus is the unifier, then all reality takes on a personal character marked by the love of God.[54]

Jesus did not create the world and let it go. Nor did Jesus create all things and then give them over to the authority of other supernatural powers. Rather, Jesus continues to sustain all things. As H. C. G. Moule said, he is the bond that makes the universe "a cosmos, not a chaos."[55]

Lord Jesus, may all my thoughts, words and actions orbit around you and your grace.

¹⁸ And he is the head of the body (the church)

With this verse, we come to the second half of the laudation. The first half focused on the *beginning* when God created all things through Christ. Here in the second half, Paul focuses on the *end*, when all things will be reconciled through Christ in the new creation. Paul is not saying, however, that creation merely provides the platform-stage for the drama of salvation. Creation has value in itself. Nor is Paul leaving creation behind in the second half of the laudation. Rather, he is indicating that the fallen creation will return to all it was meant to be—and it will happen through God's Son.

The two halves of the laudation, then, do not mean we should split creation from new creation, the physical from the spiritual, or the secular from the sacred. Rather, they belong together in Christ, and so they also belong together in the lives of those who are in Christ.

Paul has just said that all things stand together in Christ (Col 1:17), but he recognizes that creation is no longer standing as it once did, nor as it someday will. He knows that a better day will come for creation, and his hope is based on the fact that some elements of creation are already up on their feet, standing together as the new creation in Christ. It's the church.

And Jesus is the head of this body called the church. Later in this letter Paul will tell us that one of the main functions of Jesus as head of the body is to support and hold it together by ligaments and sinews (Col 2:19). So Jesus not only holds all *creation* together, but he also holds together the *new creation* as embodied in the church.

The scope of Jesus' reign has not suddenly become smaller, as if he had created all things (the first stanza of this laudation), but now has settled for only operating within the church (the second stanza). His lordship over the church and all creation go together. Through the church God's purposes for a new creation are gaining a foothold in the universe. The church is a mustard seed that will grow into a tree of universal dimensions (see Mt 13:31-32; Mk 4:30-31; Lk 13:18-19), bearing fruit all over the world (see Col 1:6). Dunn calls the church a small version of the new creation; it's a greenhouse for growing the shoots that will be planted throughout creation.

Grow your kingdom, Lord, within your church, even the local church that I belong to, so that all the world may come to know your gracious rule.

97

¹⁸ And he is the head of the body (the church)

Some philosophers in Paul's day thought of the universe as the body of God. Zeus was the head and the universe was his body. Similarly, the Jewish philosopher Philo said that the body of the universe needed the eternal divine Word to be its guiding head.

Because of this, some people wonder if Paul originally meant that Jesus was the head of the body of the universe, but someone else later added the words "the church." There's no evidence of this at all, but it appeals to some people because of their general dislike of the institutional church. Compared to the lovely thought of Jesus as the head of the universe, it might seem distasteful to attach him to this pitiful group known as the institutional church.

But this is Paul's point exactly, for the NT presented Jesus as the Son of God who draws near to the lowly and despised (see Mt 11:25; 12:20; Mk 2:15-17), with the church especially regarded as a prime example of this. The church was not filled with wise, powerful, noble somebodies, but with foolish, weak, and lowly nobodies. (1 Cor 1:26-28).

Paul is the only NT writer to use the word picture of the "body" to describe the church (see also Rom 12:4-5; 1 Cor 12; Eph 1:22-23; 4:16; 5:23-27; Col 3:15). The idea behind this image may have come to him after meditating on Jesus' words to him on the Damascus Road. When Jesus asked why Paul was persecuting *him* (Acts 9:4-5), Paul became profoundly aware of how much Jesus identifies himself with his people; their hurts are his hurts. What happens to Christ's embodied people, then, also happens to Christ (such as persecution). And the reverse also holds true—what happened to the embodied Christ happens to his people (such as being crucified and raised with him).

Since the bodily experiences of Christ and the church are so closely connected, it's not a far step to think of the believers as being the body of Christ. Jesus himself hinted at this when he said, "Anyone who welcomes you welcomes me" (Mt 10:40, NIV), and "Whoever listens to you listens to me" (Lk 10:16, NIV). Add to this Jesus' words about how we are to abide in him and he in us (Jn 15:4; 17:21), and you can see how Paul could think of the church as the body of Christ.

Jesus, show me today how I—along with your church—can serve as your hands and feet, ears and mouth, muscles and shoulders in this needy world.

¹⁸ And he is the head of the body (the church)

In 1 Corinthians 12, Paul was thinking the whole body was Christ and not just the head. The head was just one of the body's many interrelated parts (1 Cor 12:21). But in Colossians (and Ephesians) Paul also finds it helpful to think of Jesus as the head of the body.

Interpreters commonly regard the head as the control center of the rest of the body. In the OT, "head" often serves as another word for leader (see Judg 10:18 for just one example). In the NT book of Revelation, a head is mostly regarded as the location of a crown, implying that the head is the location of authority. Submission to the head is also part of the discussion of the roles of men and women (1 Cor 11:3-10 and Eph 5:21-33).

Yet there is no call for heads to dominate or force submission on others. In fact, Christ shows himself to be the kind of head that loves, cares, and sacrifices for the body. Too often, people react against the idea of someone being the head because it sounds so authoritarian. But they forget that the head is attached to the body. Head and body are so intimately connected, that both of them affect each other continually. The head is not located in a separate palace issuing edicts for the body to obey. The head and body are alive and thrive together.

Although Jesus does issue commands as the head of the church, and he calls for us to submit to those commands, he is not a boss who stands far off issuing orders. He is not the head of the church like an aloof CEO maximizing his portfolio, or a dictator amassing power. He is the head of the church like the head of a body, organically connected to us to bring life.

It should come as no surprise, then, that many of the incidental references to the head in the NT are found in the context of suffering. John the Baptist lost his head. Jesus had nowhere to lay his head (Mt 8:20). Disciples can face persecution without fear because God knows the number of hairs on their head. Jesus' own head was crowned with thorns and beaten. Jesus is the Head who suffers for the sake of his body.

The church, then, exists only in its relationship to Christ. Without Christ as the Living Head, the church is only a corpse, a headless cadaver, a decapitated carcass—not a living body. But when the body *is* connected in a vital way to its Head, then the power of life flows from Jesus to the church, so that it is an embodiment of God's justice, holiness and grace.

We are your church, O Lord. Lead us and love us, guide us and provide us with all we need to live in you.

[18] And he is the head of the body (the church), the Primal-Power, the firstborn from out of the dead ones, in order that in all things he [himself] would be firsting,

Paul continues to describe the power and glory of Jesus by calling him the *archē*. Most frequently this word is translated as "the beginning." Such a translation would fit well in this context, for verse 17 had just said that Jesus existed before anything else, and soon verse 18 will declare that Jesus is first. If this is what Paul meant, he would be in the same company as Rev 21:6, where Jesus claimed to be "the Alpha and the Omega, the Beginning [*archē*] and the End" (NIV). Using the opening words of Genesis, we could reach the stunning conclusion that in the beginning, that is, in Christ the Beginning, God created the heavens and the earth.

But there is another meaning for *archē* in the Bible that fits this context, for it can also be translated as a title for rulers and supernatural powers. The Greek translation of 1 Chron 29:12, for instance, used this word twice to say that the Lord was the ruler of all rulers. This meaning for *archē* can still be found in the English language in words like "arch-angel." In nine of the other ten times Paul uses *archē*, he's talking about these primal-powers (Rom 8:38; 1 Cor 15:24; Eph 1:21; 3:10; 6:12; Col 1:16; 2:10, 15; Titus 3:1). In fact, Paul has just used this term in verse 16 as a reference to the primal-powers when he listed the powers created by Jesus.

It seems reasonable, then, for Paul to use *archē* here to paint a contrast between Christ and these other primal-powers. Unlike the other primal-powers, Paul praises Jesus as the ultimate Primal-Power. While many of the other powers had failed in their mission to maintain justice and order in God's creation (see Ps 82:1-6), Jesus has succeeded. He is not merely one primal-power among many others, but *the* Primal-Power ruling over all the others.

This would have been especially important for Paul to say if the Colossian distortion regarded Jesus as only one of many primal-powers and angelic beings who were necessary to experience the fullness of salvation. Even today many people act as if the powers-that-be have more effect on politics, the economy, the mood of the times, and even their own personal situation, than Jesus does. But to all those who either fear, admire, or trust the powers-that-be, then and now, Paul extols Jesus as the Primal-Power over all others (which we will see further in Col 2:10 and 15).

Lord, sometimes I'm afraid of all the powers-that-be in this world. Grant to me an increasing vision of how you rule over them all.

*[18] And he is the head of the body (the church), the Primal-Power, **the firstborn from out of the dead ones,** in order that in all things he [himself] would be firsting,*

Jesus is the firstborn of creation (verse 15). However, because of human sin, creation was on a fast track toward death. So what did Jesus do about this? Well, instead of pulling creation from the brink of death, Jesus charged right off the cliff, leading the way to certain death for himself and dragging the world with him. Jesus, however, did not remain dead, but by his resurrection, he became the firstborn from the dead.

Although firstborn sons were given extra privileges in Israel, the biblical track record of firstborns is not enviable. Almost to a man, the named firstborn sons in OT history are a troubled lot. Esau lost his blessing; Jacob's oldest son Reuben was cursed by his father; Joseph's firstborn Manasseh was passed by for a blessing; Aaron's eldest son Nadab died while offering a sacrifice wrongly, Jesse's oldest son Eliab was not anointed as king, David's firstborn Amnon was killed by his step-brother. In the story of the Exodus, it is the firstborn who lose their lives if they are not protected by lamb's blood. So while ancient society regarded the firstborn as the chosen ones born for privilege, the biblical stories often treat the firstborn as if they were chosen for rejection, cursing, and death.

This was also Jesus' fate. As a firstborn, Jesus was chosen to be loved by his Father, but also chosen to be forsaken by God on the cross (Mk 15:34). He was chosen to be blessed, but also chosen to become a curse for us (Gal 3:13). Jesus was chosen to rule the world, but also chosen to be the servant of all (Mt 20:28). Jesus was chosen to be the high priest, but also to be the sacrificial offering of atonement (Heb 9:11-12). Jesus was chosen to live in righteous union with his Father, but he also took on the likeness of sinful flesh (Rom 8:3). Jesus was chosen to live, but he was also chosen to die for the sins of the world (Jn 10:10-11).

So even though the prophet Micah said it would do no good to offer his firstborn for his transgression (Mic 6:7), in the NT that's exactly what God did for us, offering his firstborn for our transgressions. Thus, when Jesus was crucified, John saw it as a fulfillment of Zech 12:10 (NIV): "They will look on me, the one they have pierced...and grieve bitterly for him, as one grieves for a firstborn son."

Thank you, Jesus, for all that you endured for the sake of sinners like me, willing to come under a curse so that we could be blessed.

¹⁸ And he is the head of the body (the church), the Primal-Power, **the firstborn from out of the dead ones,** *in order that in all things he [himself] would be firsting,*

Jesus was not only God's firstborn who died, but even more importantly he was resurrected as the firstborn from the dead. In a pagan society that regarded the body as a prison house of the soul, the message of Jesus' resurrection did not sound like good news (see Acts 17:32). The majority of Jews, however, regarded the resurrection of the dead as a primary sign of God's end-times purposes being fulfilled (see Dan 12:2).

So when Jesus rose from the dead, his disciples knew the last days had arrived. The future had broken into the present. Jesus is not only the *Primal*-Power who created the world in the beginning, but also the *Final*-Power, leading God's people into the future. It's a strange part of our language that we say of those who have already died that they have gone *before* us. They are not behind us, stuck in the past. They are before us, ahead of us. That's even more true of the resurrected Jesus; he has gone before us, the firstborn from the dead, signifying that others will be raised later. As Walsh and Keesmaat put it, Jesus is "the head of the resurrection parade."[56]

Paul often maintains that what happens to Jesus happens to us too, including resurrection. Irenaeus, a theologian from the second century, said that when a child is born, usually the head emerges first, and then the rest of the body follows. Since the Head of the body is already resurrected as the firstborn of the new creation, the rest of the body will follow.[57] Likewise, if the firstborn son is raised to life, the rest of the family will be raised as well. Jesus put it very simply in Jn 14:19, "Because I live, you also will live" (NIV). While many had been assuming the end-times resurrections would happen all at once, there is actually a lapse between Jesus' own end-time resurrection and the end-times resurrection of all others, thus giving time for people to come to faith.[58]

It is Jesus' resurrection which distinguishes him from all other powers-that-be. No other power can reverse the old creation's death spiral. They may be able to give the illusion of holding that spiral in check, but they cannot stop or reverse the gravity of death, and, in fact, these powers often contribute to the deathliness around us. Jesus, by contrast, is re-creating this world through his own resurrection power.

Living Lord, I am filled with hope knowing that your resurrection signifies the resurrection of all your people.

> [18] *And he is the head of the body (the church), the Primal-Power, the firstborn from out of the dead ones, **in order that in all things he [himself] would be firsting***

The most common translations of the key verb here are that Jesus would "be first" or "have the supremacy." But these phrases are too passive, as if the action is over and now Jesus merely exists in the state of having won first place—like a has-been athlete known only for his victories in days gone by. To me the best option is to follow the Greek and translate "first" as a verb instead of an adjective. In this way Jesus is firsting forth.

We see Jesus' firsting activity throughout Paul's laudation. Jesus goes first by creating all things, leading the way in forming life and establishing its grace-full and playful orderliness (Col 1:15-17). Jesus goes first by being the head of the body, leading the way in how that body (his church) serves in the world. Jesus goes first by ruling and overruling as the Primal-Power over all other powers-that-be. And of course, Jesus goes first by rising from the dead—blazing the trail up the mountain of God's kingdom, with his footsteps causing a landslide of grace to rumble in our direction and change the landscape of our world. Jesus is firsting forth, and he is still firsting forth (as the present tense of this verb suggests).

As Jesus "firsts" forth, he does so in an unexpected way. He did not want to be first so he could be "king of the mountain," looking down on everyone else. Jesus does not lord it over others or "have the supremacy" (as the NIV puts it) in the way that a white supremacist group wants to be supreme. Instead Jesus follows his own teaching: if anyone would be first, that person must become last, the servant of all (as noted in Mt 20:16).

And we see Jesus' servant heart throughout the laudation. He is first over creation by serving and providing for it. He is head over the church by giving his life for it. He rules as the Primal-Power by surrendering himself to crucifixion at the hands of the powers-that-be. Even in the resurrection, Jesus continues as a servant, for he is the Master who will serve his servants (Lk 12:37). Jesus is firsting, but he is firsting on our behalf.

Sometimes believers talk about making Jesus first in our lives (as a variant of seeking first the kingdom of God). But this sounds as if were up to us make Jesus number one. But we don't have to make Christ number one; he already is number one. When Jesus is first in our lives, we are only lining up with the reality God has already provided: Jesus is first.

Lord Jesus, I acknowledge you as first over all things. Please line up my life with that reality.

[18] *And he is the head of the body (the church), the Primal-Power, the firstborn from out of the dead ones, in order that in all things he [himself] would be firsting,* [19] **for in him all the fullness was pleased to dwell**

Paul returns to the theme of Jesus' divinity here, but he uses the concept of fullness to describe it. Although the verse does not specify that Paul is talking about the fullness of God, he will clarify this with similar words in Col 2:9. Jesus is not a mere sketch, summary, or lifeless portrait of God.[59] Rather, the very God who said, "Do I not fill heaven and earth?" (Jer 23:24, NIV) was pleased to dwell in Jesus, a man who lived, died and rose again only a few years before Paul wrote this letter.[60]

A comparison of this verse with Phil 2:5-11 reveals an interesting dynamic of being empty and full. Phil 2:6-7 praises Jesus because, even though he was in the form of God, he was willing to empty himself in order to take on human likeness and die on the cross. Col 1:19, however, approaches this from the other end—the one who was willing to empty himself was nonetheless filled with the fullness of God. It's the willingness to empty himself that best reveals the fullness of God.

Because fullness and filling are common ideas in Colossians, Paul may be directing his comments against the distortionists. They may have taught that God's fullness could only be experienced through a multitude of spiritual powers. Nonsense, says Paul. All the fullness of God dwells in Christ, so there is none left to be portioned out to other spiritual powers.

It is significant that the fullness of God was *pleased* to dwell in the Son. More than a third of the NT uses of pleasing are about how the Father is pleased with the Son, as he says at Jesus' baptism and transfiguration (Mt 3:17; 17:5). Since God is pleased with his Son, then the best way for us to live in a God-pleasing way is to be "in Christ" the Son ourselves.

Also notable is that God was pleased to *dwell* in the Son, not as a passing guest, but a permanent resident. Jesus is no flash-in-the-pan Savior, who makes his mark and then disappears from the scene. Rather, he continues to be the center of God's purposes for the world. Just as God was pleased to dwell on Mt. Zion (Ps 68:16, which uses nearly identical words), so God is pleased to dwell in his Son, filling him with a glory that even surpasses that of the Temple (see 1 Kgs 8:10-11).

I seek to be filled, Jesus, with the same fullness of the Spirit that caused you to empty yourself for others.

*[19] for in him all the fullness was pleased to dwell [20] **and through him to reconcile** all things toward him—having-made-peace through the blood of his cross—whether things on the earth or things in the heavens.*

Although nothing had been said earlier in this laudation about a rupture in the relationship between God and creation, it is through Jesus that this rupture can be healed and reconciliation take place.

If you were to look up the 16 NT references to reconciliation, you would discover two things: 13 of them came from Paul's writings, and all but one of his references are about reconciling with God. Reconciliation with God was not often found in Jewish writings and almost never in Greek and Latin writings. That's because, says Cranfield, "The relation between deity and man was not conceived of in ancient paganism as the deeply personal thing it is in the Bible."[61]

Paul's understanding of this reconciliation was very different from what the rest of the culture meant by the term. According to Pao, "Instead of the guilty party initiating the process of reconciliation, Paul emphasizes that it is God, the offended party, who took the initiative while humans were still sinners (Rom 5:8, 10). Equally striking is Paul's emphasis on the death of Christ, which accomplished this act of reconciliation, rather than on reparations made by the offending humanity."[62]

In contemporary usage, reconciliation happens in two main ways. In *direct* reconciliation, one or both parties take steps to restore the relationship. In *third-party* reconciliation, another party steps in to restore a relationship. Some assume the gospel is about a third-party reconciliation. God and sinful humanity are the parties in conflict, and then Jesus comes along as a third-party negotiator. Jesus' role is to persuade a reluctant God to show some mercy and to convince a reluctant humanity to have a little faith. But this is a flawed picture of reconciliation.

First, even though Jesus is called a mediator, he is not a third-party mediator. Jesus the Son does not approach a resistant Father, trying to bring him to the negotiating table. Instead, it's the Father who wants to restore his relationship with humanity. It's the Father who moved directly toward reconciliation by sending Jesus as his representative to a resistant humanity. To use the preposition of verse 20, God worked "through" Jesus to bring reconciliation.

Thank you, Father, for caring enough about us to seek reconciliation with us. Draw us nearer to you.

[19] *for in him all the fullness was pleased to dwell* [20] *and through him to* *reconcile **all things toward him***

Col 1:16 proclaimed that all things were made *in, through,* and *toward* Christ. Now these same three prepositions are used in verses 19-20 to say that all the fullness of God was *in* Christ and was working *through* Christ to reconcile all things *toward* Christ.

Paul is not using the term "all things" to mean only "all people" or "all different kinds of people." All things refers to all the things created by Jesus in verse 16, including the non-human part of creation. This inclusion of all creation means that reconciliation is not an escape from the physical world, but a movement towards God's reclamation and renewal of creation. Crea- tion "is not merely a stage on which the drama of human redemption takes place but is itself fully bound up in the story of redemption and libera- tion."[63] Someday the reconciled creation will no longer be the arena of death and decay, but of abundant life and vibrant growth.

Because Paul speaks of Jesus' relationship to "all things" and not just humanity, it's easy to see why some hear in these words a call for Jesus' followers to care for creation and resist those who deface it. As much as that is a good message, we cannot forget that Paul's own focus is not on environmental pollution, but on how faith can be polluted by worshiping various cosmic powers. Our passion for Jesus' world should not outweigh our passion for Jesus himself. We worship the Creator, not the creation (Rom 1:25).

Also, this extension of reconciliation to the whole creation does not undercut God's special concern for humanity. Immediately after this lauda- tion, Paul narrows his focus to God's reconciliation of humanity—and the Colossians in particular (Col 1:21-22). Jesus did not do his reconciling work in the flesh of a bird or beast, but in human flesh. That's because the resto- ration of humanity is the central concern of the story of Jesus, and the rest of creation gladly gets included in that story.

Even though it is a good and necessary thing for people to be good stewards of creation, the emphasis of the laudation is not on what *we* need to do, but on what *God* is doing through Christ. Human actions to protect and clean up the environment—as wonderful as those actions are—will not bring about the reconciliation of "all things."

Thank you, Lord, for this homeland called creation. In whatever way I can *participate in your work in this world, show me the way.*

*[19] for in him all the fullness was pleased to dwell [20] and through him to reconcile **all things toward him***

Astonishingly, reconciliation in verse 20 is far broader than what we find elsewhere in the NT. The spectrum of reconciliation can be illustrated thus:

Col 1:20	2 Cor 5:19	Rom 11:15	Eph 2:16	2 Cor 5:18	Rom 5:9-11	Col 1:22
all things	the world	non-Jewish world	Jews & non-Jews	us (believers)	those justified	believers in Christ

These verses have figured prominently in discussions about whether few or many will be saved. But rather than emphasizing one end of the spectrum over the other, we need to incorporate the entire spectrum (just as Colossians does on both extremes). There are two dangers here.

On the one hand, if we camp on the right end of the spectrum and ignore the left end, then we'll be tempted to confine the work of Jesus to saving a few souls (like ourselves) from a fallen world, instead of seeing the magnitude of what Jesus has done. Then we'll see our mission more in terms of keeping unqualified people out of the kingdom than announcing the good news that they can be reconciled with God.

Paul doesn't want to fall into that trap. He doesn't directly address the issue of whether few or many will be saved. He offers no census profile of Judgment Day. He knows, as G. C. Berkouwer said, that "every 'ascertainment' of who is outside becomes boundless self-exaltation."[64]

Rather, Paul's eyes are focused on Jesus, exalting him in the highest possible terms. He does not want to portray Jesus as only partially effective in his saving work. He does not want to give the impression that Adam had a greater impact than Jesus on the history of the world—as if Adam affected everyone, while Jesus only affected some. No, what Jesus has done on the cross is not just a heart-changer, but a world-changer, even though some will foolishly refuse the very reconciliation God has achieved for them.

Even if we should be wary of the danger of universalism (which we'll consider tomorrow), we should not lose sight of the grand truth that filled Paul with praise. He is amazed that God is not at war with sinful humanity, nor is he alienated from the very creation that he placed under a curse because of sinful humanity. Instead, God has, through his Son, turned toward the whole world with grace, mercy, and peace.

There's a wideness in your mercy, O God. I want to praise you for it instead of being afraid of it.

*[19] for in him all the fullness was pleased to dwell [20] and through him to reconcile **all things toward him***

While some set up camp on the right end of yesterday's spectrum, others camp on the left end and conclude that everyone will be saved (an idea known as universalism). When this happens, we start to ignore important biblical truths about faith, sin, God's wrath, hell, the need for evangelism, and Jesus being the only Savior. But how can we believe verse 20 without resorting to universalism? Whole books have been written on the subject, so we can only offer some initial thoughts.

(1) The two ends of the spectrum appear contradictory, but Paul believes they belong together. Here Paul declares the reconciliation of *all things* to Christ in Col 1:20, but in verses 21-23 he states that this reconciliation is for *those who continue in their faith*, implying that those who have no faith or break from it will not experience this reconciliation.

(2) The same Paul who made these "all things reconciled" statements could also speak of God's wrath which will fall upon "all" sinners who do not trust in Jesus (see Rom 1:18; 2:12; 1 Thess 4:6). Nothing in Paul's broad conception of reconciliation suggests that Christ has canceled Judgment Day or will transform it into a surprise Reconciliation Day.

(3) Here Paul coined a new word for reconciliation (*apokatallassō*), perhaps because other words for reconciliation didn't quite fit what Jesus had done. In English, reconciliation normally means that a relationship has moved from hostility to love. This may be true of those who trust Jesus, but it doesn't seem to be the right word for what happens to creation (which was not hostile toward God in the first place) or what happens to those people or powers who refuse to trust in Jesus. Paul needed a word that said God accomplished a positive thing with respect to the entire universe without saying that everything and everyone is now saved and forgiven.

(4) 1 Tim 4:10 (NIV) may provide us with a model for what Paul means when he speaks of "all" being reconciled: "we have put our hope in the living God, who is the Savior of all people, and *especially of those who believe*" (emphasis mine). We could perhaps say a similar thing here: God is pleased through Christ to reconcile all things, *especially those who believe*. Some may think this spin on Paul's "all" statements wrongly undercuts the largeness of Paul's gospel. Possibly. But it might also help us understand the reconciliation of all things better.

Protect us, Lord, from the laziness of universalism that tempts us to forget our mission in this world and just let it go its own way.

*¹⁹ for in him all the fullness was pleased to dwell ²⁰ and through him to reconcile all things toward him—**having-made-peace** through the blood of his cross—whether things on the earth or things in the heavens.*

The verb for "having-made-peace" implies that peace does not merely exist, but it must be made and done, formed and performed, created and carried out. Jesus is the one sent by the Father to make this peace. Without the action of Jesus, the alienation between God and humanity (as well as between Jews and the nations) would continue to fester, but the action of Jesus creates a peace where there had been no peace. Thus, echoing his own Beatitude (Mt 5:9), Jesus shows himself to be the Son of God because he is a peace-maker.

The Greek word for peace (*eirēnē*) is viewed from many different angles in Paul's letters: peace in general as a gift from God (especially in his greetings and closing benedictions), peace of mind (Rom 8:6), peace with others (Rom 14:19), and peace with God (Rom 5:1). Today's verse focuses on being at peace with God. Any anger God may have had toward us as sinners is gone and in Christ our relationship with God is restored.

Jesus is not the only one who claimed to make peace. Julius Caesar was called the peace-maker, and later this became an official title for Roman emperors.⁶⁵ But what a difference between Christ and the Caesars! The emperors imposed their peace through military action and killing rebels by means of crucifixion. Jesus, however, brought peace, not by crucifying anyone, but by being crucified himself.

In military terms, "pacification" is about making peace through the use or the threatened use of force. This was a specialty of the Roman empire. A barbarian once said of the Romans, "To plunder, butcher, steal, these things they misname empire: they make a desolation and they call it peace." Similarly, Caesar Augustus once said, "The provinces of the Gauls, the Spains and Germans...I reduced to a state of peace." *Reduced* to a state of peace—this seems a far cry from Paul's words about reconciliation. Such pacification sounds more like the famous line from the Vietnam war, "It was necessary to destroy the village in order to save it."

But Jesus did not come to steal, kill, and destroy. He came to bring life and peace (see Jn 10:10). His goal in making peace is not that we grudgingly submit to God's superior force. Rather, he wants to welcome us into the family of the Father, where we will experience fullness of love and joy.

Lord, you have made peace where there once was chaos and turmoil, hatred and anxiety. Thank you for making peace with me and in me.

*[19] for in him all the fullness was pleased to dwell [20] and through him to reconcile all things toward him—having-made-peace **through the blood** of his cross—whether things on the earth or things in the heavens.*

Peace did not happen because God began to think differently about us. God has always yearned for fallen humanity with love and compassion, mixed with sorrow and anger. What brought peace was not new thoughts on God's part, but the new action of the bloody sacrifice of God's Son.

Blood was instrumental in initiating the old covenant made with Israel. To avoid the consequences of the tenth plague (the death of firstborn sons), the Israelites brushed lamb's blood on the doorframes of their homes (Ex 12:13). Later, when God formalized the covenant at Sinai, Moses took sacrificial "blood, threw it on the people and said, 'This is the blood of the covenant that the Lord has made with you in accordance with all these words'" (Ex 24:8, NIV).

Blood also initiated a new and better covenant through Christ. At his last Passover, Jesus took a cup and said, "This is my blood of the covenant, which is poured out for many" (Mk 14:23-24), as happened the next day on the cross. Thus, Jesus mediated a new covenant with "sprinkled blood that speaks a better word than the blood of Abel" (Heb 12:24, NIV).

A well-known hymn declares, "There is Power in the Blood." NT writers agreed. Some focused on the power of Jesus' blood *to cleanse us*. Everything must be cleansed by blood (Heb 9:22), including our conscience (Heb 9:14), so that we are purified from all sin (1 Jn 1:7).

Others emphasized the power of Jesus' blood *to set us free*. Just as the Israelites were freed from slavery through the blood of the Passover lamb, so Jesus "has freed us from our sins by his blood" (Rev 1:5, NIV) and from our lifelong slavery to the fear of death (Heb 2:14-15). By the blood of the Lamb we were ransomed from futile ways (1 Pet 1:18) and from the devil who had enslaved us (Rev 12:11).

Still others emphasize the power of Jesus' blood *to restore relationships,* replacing hostility with reconciliation and peace. We are justified by the blood of Jesus (Rom 5:9), so that "you who once were far off have been brought near by the blood of Christ. For he himself is our peace" (Eph 5:9).

All three images of salvation can be found in Colossians 1: Jesus' blood brings *cleansing forgiveness* (Col 1:14), *liberating redemption* from the authority of darkness (Col 1:13-14), and reconciling atonement (Col 1:20).

We may not understand how it "works," Jesus, but we rejoice in the power of your blood to cleanse us, free us, and draw us to you.

*¹⁹ for in him all the fullness was pleased to dwell ²⁰ and through him to reconcile all things toward him—having-made-peace **through the blood** of his cross—whether things on the earth or things in the heavens.*

Although both Old and New Testaments testify that blood is necessary for forgiveness, redemption, and reconciliation, many still wonder if the Scriptures are correct. To them, a blood sacrifice seems to be unnecessarily cruel and violent.

But the role of blood in salvation will always be puzzling until we really believe the truth of Rom 6:23, "the wages of sin is death" (NIV). As long as we think sin only deserves a time-out, a stern reprimand, or a short-term negative consequence, we will be baffled by the necessary role of death in God's plan for salvation. But when we realize that sinning causes a person to forfeit his or her life, then and only then will we recognize that sin can only be dealt with through death. Either the sinner must die, or God will send someone to die in the sinner's place. To speak of the blood of Jesus is to speak of his death in our place, so that sin could be vanquished. Without the shedding of blood, those who sin remain unclean, in slavery, and disconnected from God. But with the shedding of blood, there is forgiveness, redemption, and reconciliation.

Some have wondered if the sending of God's Son to die is divine child abuse. But this would only be so if they were not working together for our salvation. Both Father and Son suffered, admittedly in different ways, but they both experienced separation from one another. And they both had the same purpose in taking this road of suffering, namely, to reconcile all things to the triune God. Jesus did not die as an unwilling victim of his Father's abusive behavior. No, Jesus came to die.

Another objection to Paul's gospel comes from those who prefer a more ethereal kind of salvation in which cosmic harmony happens by serenely meditating on spiritual realities instead of through a violent and bloody death. Perhaps the Colossian distortionists would fit into that camp. (Notice their discomfort with the body in Col 2:20-23.) But Paul would object strenuously. As the laudation has been telling us, Jesus did not just create spiritual realities and beings. He created all things, even the gross world of body fluids, like blood, sweat, tears, semen, and urine. Body fluids like blood are an important part of God's created reality, and here we see blood function in a redemptive way.

Lord Jesus, even if the sight of blood makes me feel squeamish, I thank you for your willingness to offer your blood on my behalf.

[19] *for in him all the fullness was pleased to dwell* [20] *and through him to reconcile all things toward him—having-made-peace through the blood **of his cross**—whether things on the earth or things in the heavens.*

If we wonder where the blood of Jesus was offered as a sacrifice, we need not look for some sacred altar in a temple. Rather, Jesus' blood was offered on a cross. While we are accustomed to beautiful crosses of gold hanging from necklaces and on the walls of lovely church buildings, for the people of Paul's day the cross was a horrendous form of capital punishment, best described as barbaric, cruel, and obscene.[66] The only contemporary form of death that conveys this same sense of dread would be a beheading.

It is an amazing thing to find the cross in this laudation. So many of the phrases have been about the power and glory of Jesus, but here we see that the true source of Jesus' power and glory was his lowly and shameful death. It is in his willingness to be brought low that Jesus most fully reveals that he is God Most High and worthy of praise (see Isa 53:7-12 and Phil 2:5-11).

Even though Paul says the cross was a critical component of the gospel (1 Cor 2:2; Gal 6:14), he only refers to it by name twenty times. Maybe he didn't want to go overboard in using such a scandalous word. And when Paul does speak of the cross, it's often about us being crucified with Christ. Salvation does not come by *trying,* but by *dying*—dying with Jesus.

It is the book of Colossians, however, that is most responsible for spelling out Paul's belief in the saving impact of the cross. Just as we saw with the word "blood," the cross also brings: (1) forgiveness (the debt-note against us was wiped away at the cross in Col 2:13-14), (2) redemption from slavery (the primal-powers were overcome at the cross in Col 2:14-15), and (3) reconciliation (as in our current verse).

Although the violent and shameful death of God's Son on the cross could have prompted God to seek vengeance, instead it was God's way to bring reconciliation. In English, crosses get associated with "crossroads," the intersection of lines at right angles. Perhaps we could think of Jesus' cross as a crossroad where all things come together to meet with God. As Jesus said in Jn 12:32, "And I, when I am lifted up from the earth, will draw all people to myself" (NIV).

Savior, I dare not come to the cross and then leave it behind. Rather, I hold your cross always before me, for what you did there shapes my life.

*[19] for in him all the fullness was pleased to dwell [20] and through him to reconcile all things toward him—having-made-peace through the blood of his cross—**whether things on the earth or things in the heavens.***

With this final phrase, Paul is balancing out the two stanzas of his laudation. The first stanza spoke of Jesus as the Creator of all things in heaven and on earth (Col 1:16). The second stanza highlights the new creation in which Jesus will reconcile all things on earth and in heaven.

This is important because Paul wants us to understand that the new creation is not a smaller version of the first creation, as if God were only partly successful in his mission of reclaiming the whole world. The new creation is just as all-encompassing as the first creation. In fact, the new creation is larger than the first one, for it includes a much larger population and a fuller, richer world than was the case in Eden. According to Rev 21:26, the New Jerusalem will also include redeemed versions of the creative work of humanity, for the kings will bring into it the glory and the honor of the nations. The work of Jesus on the cross did not affect only a remnant of creation, but the entire creation.

Again, Paul's language here could be twisted by some in the direction of universalism, but that is not what he's teaching. Instead of addressing who will be saved in the end, Paul is emphasizing who saves in the end. It is Jesus who saves, reconciles, redeems, and forgives, and we dare not minimize his work by putting limits upon it. We leave it in God's hands what it means for Jesus to reconcile all things to God, and for our part we testify to what Christ has done and is doing on behalf of fallen humanity and all creation.

As we conclude our examination of the laudation, the old warning about missing the forest for the trees may apply. We have looked with so much detail at each phrase that we may be in danger of missing the overall point. Paul did not write these words in order to satisfy our curiosity about divine things. Rather, each phrase is written to point us toward Jesus. What we need is not a better idea of Jesus; we need Jesus. Because the Colossian distortion was encouraging the Colossian believers (and all of us) to look elsewhere for the fullness of salvation, Paul shows us again that all we need is found in the Son of God.

Our most appropriate response to the laudation, then, is to join in its words of praise.

May all the glory be yours, O Lord. May heaven and earth be filled with the knowledge of you to the same extent as the waters cover the sea.

Christis the Image of our God

to the tune of Ellacombe: *I Sing the Mighty Power of God*
© 2008 David J. Landegent

Christ is the image of our God, the Firstborn of His works.
For by Him all these things were made, both things in heav'n and earth
Both seen and unseen, thrones and pow'rs, all things for Him were made
He is before all of these things, in Him they stand and stay

Christ is the Head of His own church; the Alpha One is He.
He lives, the Firstborn from the dead, so He might reign supreme.
For God was pleased to dwell in Him, and through His saving work
To reconcile all to Himself, in heaven and on earth.

Jesus' ministry to the Colossians

Colossians 1:21-23

April 2-17

[21] And you, once being alienated and enemy-minded in evil works, [22] he now reconciled in the body of his flesh through death, to present you as holy and unblemished and blameless before him, [23] if indeed you remain in the faith, being foundationed and settled, and not moving from the hope of the good-message which you heard, which has been proclaimed to every created-being under heaven, of which I, Paul, have become a servant.

In verses 15-20, Paul did not speak directly to the Colossians, but instead focused on exalting Jesus. In this section, Paul returns to addressing the Colossians. Paul is also returning to themes he was writing about before the laudation, as can be seen in the following chart:

1-2   Paul is an apostle of Jesus
3-8   Thanks for faith, hope, and the gospel proclaimed to the world
9-14   The Colossians were lost, but are now redeemed by the Son
15-17   The Son is the firstborn over all creation
18-20   The Son is the firstborn over the new creation
21-22   The Colossians were lost, but are now reconciled by the Son
23a   Remain in faith and hope in the gospel proclaimed everywhere
23b   Paul is a servant of the gospel

This chart shows Paul writing as if he's stepping in a certain direction and then backing out in the reverse order of the way he stepped in, which was a common writing technique in his day.

With the laudation, Paul wanted his readers to move beyond their own salvation experience in order to see the bigger picture. We need to see that the gospel was not just about us, but about Jesus and what he is doing in relation to the whole creation.

But as important as the big picture is, Paul does not want us to think we are little nobodies in the grand scheme of God's kingdom. Therefore, in verses 21-23, he returns to where he had left off in verses 13-14. While there is always a danger in proclaiming a gospel that is too small (from which the laudation protects us), there is also a danger in proclaiming a gospel so large that people cannot see its relevance for their own lives. According to Fitch, effective evangelism "demands a continual traveling back and forth from the grand scope of all that God is doing in Christ to the simple offer of salvation to the stranger and back again."[67]

I am filled with wonder, Lord, that even though the entire universe is in your hand, you know my name and include me in your family.

> *²¹ And you, once being alienated and enemy-minded in evil works, ²² he now reconciled in the body of his flesh through death, to present you as holy and unblemished and blameless before him...*

Paul begins by describing what the Colossians had been prior to coming to faith in Christ. When he had earlier described their former state, it was a mixture of being both *victims* (who needed deliverance from their bondage to the authority of darkness, Col 1:13) and *victimizers* (who needed to be forgiven of sins, Col 1:14), with the emphasis falling on the former. Here, however, Paul emphasizes how the Colossians had brought this sorry state upon themselves...and we do too.

First, Paul describes us as being alienated, separated from God by our sinful desires and hardness of heart. It was not God who had moved away from us. Rather, through Adam's sin and our own, we had put ourselves outside God's family and kingdom. But there is still hope, for as Paul says in Rom 5:8, "but God demonstrates his love for us in this: While we were still sinners, Christ died for us" (NIV).

Paul further describes us as being "enemy-minded"—not having the mind of Christ, but a depraved mind hostile toward God. Many of those who are God's enemies, however, might not think of themselves this way. The Jews who rejected Jesus thought they were doing God's will. Some false teachers thought the same. But whether one is purposely opposing God or not, the fact remains that those who resist Jesus are enemies of God. But again, there is hope. Just as Jesus called us to love our enemies, so he came to love his enemies as well; and that was us.

Our hostility however, is not just in our minds, but also shows up in "evil works." In a reverse version of Phil 4:8, the fallen human mind will think on whatever is false, ignoble, wrong, impure, unlovely, notorious, sinful and shameful—and these thoughts will give birth to evil actions (see Jms 1:13-15)..

Paul's description of life without Christ applies even to so-called "nice" sinners.[68] Some sinners live with their minds in the gutter, acting in utterly depraved, vicious and perverted ways. But many sinners are high-minded, respected citizens who do good deeds in their communities. Yet both are enemies of God. Overcoming this hostility to God does not lie in cleaning up our minds or correcting our behavior. Instead, our only hope is in Christ.

Thank you, Lord, for being gracious to me even when I acted like your enemy.

*²¹ And you, once being alienated and enemy-minded in evil works, ²² **he now** reconciled in the body of his flesh through death, to present you as holy and unblemished and blameless before him...*

Paul often uses the little word "now" to point out a contrast with some previous condition (indicated with words like "once," "at one time" or "then"). It's his way of reminding readers of how much Jesus has changed our lives.

Here are just a few examples: Once you were separate from Christ, but now you who were far off have been brought near (Eph 2:11-13). Once you were enslaved to sin, but now you are set free (Rom 6:20-22). Once your sinful passions bore the fruit of death, but now you serve God through the Spirit (Rom 7:5-6). Once you were disobedient, but now you have received mercy (Rom 11:30). Once you were in darkness, but now you live in the light (Eph 5:8). Paul likely emphasized this contrast because he also experienced such changes. At one time he was a persecutor of the gospel, but now he preaches it (Gal 1:23).

Whenever Jesus enters the picture, dramatic changes happen. Changes happen on a large scale, for instance, as Jesus closes out the old age and inaugurates the dawn of the new age. But here Paul focuses on the more personal changes in those who have come to believe. Perhaps those raised in a godless environment may notice the change more, but even for those who grow up in the atmosphere of the gospel, it is still true that Christ substantially changes their lives. Maybe they did not consciously notice the move from the authority of darkness to the bright kingdom of the Son, but they are in the light nonetheless. Life will never be the same.

Possibly Paul is emphasizing the great change that happened at conversion because the Colossian distortion was de-emphasizing conversion.[69] In such a scenario, the distortionists would agree that conversion was well and good, but what was really important were the next steps, the deeper doctrines, the more difficult spiritual practices, the more mystical rituals. The distortionists were eager to help people move beyond their gospel beginnings. But Paul calls them back to the beginning, for the way forward in the Christian life happens by staying on square one. "Faith never outgrows its beginning. It grows into this beginning."[70] We continue in faith by remaining where we began—in Christ.

Jesus, I'm so thankful that I am not where I would have been in life if it had not been for your grace and mercy to me.

*²¹ And you, once being alienated and enemy-minded in evil works, ²² he now **reconciled in the body** of his flesh through death, to present you as holy and unblemished and blameless before him...*

What brought immense change to the Colossians (and to us) is the reconciling work of God through Christ. Unlike some other religions in which the sinner needs to do what it takes to appease, and thus be reconciled to, a god, the gospel tells us that *God* does the reconciling work.

Paul emphasizes again the sheer physicality of this work. While we might expect reconciliation to be a spiritual exchange of hostile emotions for friendly feelings, Paul paints a very different picture. It happens through the physical body of Jesus, a body that died a bloody death on a cross.

Although our culture associates the physical body with health, beauty, sex, food, and amazing biological processes, the NT mostly thinks of the body in its relationship to death. Not counting the verses which speak of the church as a body, most NT references to bodies are found in the context of death (see, for example, Mt 5:29; Rom 4:19; 7:24; 2 Cor 5:8).

Even more amazing, *every* verse about the body of Jesus (except those that refer to the church) somehow points to death. Jesus called his body a temple that would be destroyed (Jn 2:19-21) and bread that would be given for others (Lk 22:19). The body of Jesus was offered as a sacrifice (Heb 10:5, 10). Jesus bore our sins in his body on a tree (1 Pet 2:24), so that we are "reconciled in the body of his flesh through his death (Col 1:22). His body was anointed for burial, both before (Mt 26:12) and after his death (Lk 23:55). We died to the law through the body of Christ (Rom 7:4). Even the reference to Jesus' resurrection body in Phil 3:21 implies that he had first experienced death.

We might think NT references to the body of Jesus would be more about his coming to earth and taking on human flesh. Instead, *every* NT reference to the physical body of Jesus points to his death.

Much as we might like to think about living in our bodies and extending our life span in these bodies, we cannot get around the fact that our bodies (at least in this fallen world) are mortal, subject to death. Our embodied selves deserve to die, cut off from God. But Jesus offered up his body, so that instead we might be reconciled to God.

What a gift it is, Lord, for you to willingly come to us in a mortal body and embrace death on our behalf, so that death would not have the last word in our lives.

*²¹ And you, once being alienated and enemy-minded in evil works, ²² he now reconciled in the body **of his flesh through death,** to present you as holy and unblemished and blameless before him...*

We are not only reconciled through Jesus' body, but through his body of flesh. The Greek word for flesh is *sarx*. Sometimes *sarx* simply refers to skin and muscle, as when Paul talks about the distinction between animal and human flesh (1 Cor 15:39). Sometimes *sarx* refers to humanity, especially in distinction from what is divine: "This was not revealed to you by flesh and blood, but by my Father in heaven" (Mt 16:17, NIV). Because *sarx* is descriptive of humanity, it also conveys a sense of human weakness as Jesus said at Gethsemane: "The spirit is willing, but the flesh is weak" (Mt 26:41, NIV). And then, because humanity is sinful, the meaning of *sarx* is also extended to include being sinful: "For the mind that is set on the flesh is hostile to God (Rom 8:7, ESV).

Unfortunately, when Paul uses *sarx* in this last way, some Christians fail to notice that this is only one of many meanings for the word, and so they interpret Paul to mean that physical flesh itself is evil and the source of all sin. These Christians have forgotten, however, that Jesus created all flesh (Col 1:16) and that Jesus himself is the Word made flesh (Jn 1:14). To avoid this misunderstanding, some versions translate *sarx* as "sinful nature."

The NT speaks of Jesus' flesh in at least four different ways. First, Jesus' flesh establishes that he is genuinely human, not a spirit-being (Jn 1:14; 1 Tim 3:16; 1 Jn 4:2). Secondly, Jesus' flesh establishes the reality of his resurrection—he's not a ghost (Lk 24:39; Acts 2:31).

Thirdly, Jesus' flesh is something to be taken within: "The bread that I will give for the life of the world is my flesh...Whoever feeds on my flesh and drinks my blood abides in me, and I in him" (Jn 6:51, 56, ESV). Salvation is not found merely in having spiritual ideas about Jesus. The relationship with Jesus must become so close that one could think of it as taking the flesh-and-blood Jesus into oneself, as happens when eating meat.

Finally, Jesus' flesh makes it possible for him to be a sacrifice for sin. Paul boldly states in Rom 8:3-4 that Jesus came "in the likeness of sinful flesh," and thus, he was able to die our death. In this way "he condemned sin in the flesh, in order that the righteous requirement of the law might be fully met in us" (NIV). This is the wonderful reconciling work of Jesus, the physicality of which is celebrated in Col 1:22.

Thank you, Jesus, for not only embracing death on our behalf, but embracing us in our sinful flesh, though you were without sin yourself.

*²¹ And you, once being alienated and enemy-minded in evil works, ²² he now reconciled in the body of his flesh through death, **to present you** as holy and unblemished and blameless before him...*

Many think the goal of reconciliation is to get sins forgiven so that people can go to heaven when they die, admittedly to be with God, but also to see loved ones and spend an eternity doing what they enjoyed on earth, only better. While this picture does contain some elements of truth, it's missing the very goal for reconciliation highlighted here, namely that we appear before God as holy, unblemished, and blameless.

Let's first focus on the idea of being presented (*paristēmi*) before God. This word was mostly used in three different settings: in the temple people presented themselves before God in worship (Dt 18:5); in weddings the bride is presented to the groom (Eph 5:27); and in trials people are presented before the judge (Rom 14:10).

In the NT three different parties do the presenting. Sometimes *we* are to present ourselves to God. The best example of this is Rom 12:1 ("present your bodies as a living sacrifice, holy and acceptable to God"; see also Rom 6:13, 19 and 2 Tim 2:15). Elsewhere we read of *another party* presenting someone to God. Joseph and Mary presented Jesus to God (Lk 2:22), and Paul wanted to present his churches to the Lord as a pure virgin (2 Cor 11:2) or a perfect offering (Col 1:28).

Most relevant to Col 1:22, however, is that *Christ* intends to present us to himself. Instead of us standing *far off*, Jesus will cause us to stand *near* to God (2 Cor 4:14). And instead of us living in shame, Jesus wants to present the church to himself as a pure bride (Eph 5:25-27). Jesus does not want to present us to God merely as people who happened to pray a prayer for salvation, or even as people who have been forgiven. Instead, he wants to present us as holy to the Lord.

While we are called to "make every effort to be found spotless, blameless" (2 Pet 3:14, NIV), this is not ultimately about human effort. Jesus regards it as *his* work to present us as holy, and he delights in that work. As Jude 24 puts it, "For to him who is able to keep you from stumbling and to present you blameless before the presence of his glory *with great joy*" (ESV, emphasis mine). So why should we resist this work that brings so much joy to the Lord by insisting that if he were really gracious he would let us continue in sin?

Lord, if I were only presenting myself before you on Judgment Day, I would not be able to stand. But it's you who will present me. Do your good work in me.

121

[21] And you, once being alienated and enemy-minded in evil works, [22] he now reconciled in the body of his flesh through death, to present you as ***holy and unblemished and blameless before him...***

Oswald Chambers once said that God is not so concerned that we be happy, but that we be holy.[71] Paul would agree. Reconciliation with God reverses the condition of verse 21 so that we no longer think or act as God's enemies, but experience transformation. It is God's goal for our lives that we become holy, unblemished, and blameless before him.

There is a sense, of course, in which we are already holy and blameless in Christ. Jesus took our sins upon himself on the cross, so that "we might become the righteousness of God" (2 Cor 5:21, NIV). But here Paul is speaking of God's further work of not only *counting* us righteous, but *making* us righteous. What God has achieved *for* us on the cross, he also wants to achieve *in* us.[72] This transformation of the human heart may be slow work, but God aims to someday present us to himself—perhaps at the end of our lives or the end of the age—as holy, unblemished, and blameless.

To be *holy* not only means to be set apart as God's treasure to go on God's mission (as mentioned earlier in the devotions on Col 1:2), but also to be set apart to reflect God's character.

Unblemished is associated with OT sacrifices, for only animals without blemishes were acceptable. This changes in the NT. Because Christ himself was a sacrificial lamb without blemish (1 Pet 1:19), there is no more need for us to offer an unblemished *blood* sacrifice. Instead we are called to be unblemished *living* sacrifices, "children of God without blemish in the midst of a crooked and twisted generation" (Phil 2:15, ESV).

Blameless is more of a courtroom word. Jesus intends to present us before the Divine Judge as blameless. Not only is Jesus' blamelessness transferred to us, but God's Spirit also transforms us to live in a blameless way. God "will keep you strong to the end, so that you will be blameless in the day of our Lord Jesus Christ" (1 Cor 1:8, NIV).

So whether we are presented to the Groom as a holy bride, or presented to God as unblemished living sacrifices, or before the divine Judge as blameless, the main point is that Jesus' goal is to transform us through the reconciliation he achieved on the cross. For this goal to happen, Christians must resist the temptation to slip from the celebration of grace to an abuse of grace," as Moo put it.[73] We want God's goal to be our goal.

Lord God, I don't want to become fussy or legalistic about moral matters, but I do want your holy power to transform my life.

*²¹ And you... ²² he now reconciled in the body of his flesh through death, to present you as holy and unblemished and blameless before him, ²³ **if indeed** you remain in the faith*

In verses 21-23 Paul provides a snapshot of our past, present and future. In the *past* we had lived as enemies of God and then were reconciled to him. In the *future* God will present us to himself as his holy people. But in verse 23, we see what is to happen in the *present*: we are to remain in the faith.

Here Paul introduces the important word "if," but it's not because he has doubts about the spiritual condition of the Colossians. He calls them holy ones with a great reputation for spiritual fruitfulness (1:2-6). They have already passed from darkness to light, and are redeemed and forgiven (1:13-14). Already they are filled in Christ, circumcised, buried and raised with him (2:10-14), chosen, holy and loved (3:12).

But even though Paul is confident about their faith, he doesn't want the Colossian distortion to undermine it. So he reminds them of the necessity of remaining in the faith. His words are not intended to make them feel insecure about their standing with God—that's what the distortionists were doing (Col 2:16, 18). Rather, he wants them to remain grounded in what has always given them security: the work of Jesus in their lives.

Security with God is an important part of what it means to be a Christian. Our salvation is not jeopardized by our lapses and failures. Yet our security must be grounded in the right thing. We are not secure because we have faith in our own faith. Nor are we secure because we have faith in some slogan like "once saved, always saved." We are secure because of the Savior in whom we have faith.

It's not that salvation is *dependent* on people remaining in the faith. Instead, salvation *consists of* remaining in the faith. Salvation is not about receiving all kinds of divine goodies in the afterlife. Salvation is about being in an eternal relationship with God; and faith is what we call our side of that eternal relationship. They are two sides of the same coin. So when Paul says "if," he is not adding an extra condition that we must fulfill in order to complete a salvation begun by God. He is only stating the obvious: there is no salvation (which consists of living with Jesus forever) if we fail to remain in the faith (which consists of living with Jesus now). Remaining in the faith *is* what it means to be saved.

Thank you, Lord, for the security of living in you. I can hold on to you because your much stronger hand is holding on to me.

[21] And you....[22] he now reconciled in the body of his flesh through death, to present you as holy and unblemished and blameless before him,[23] **if indeed you remain in the faith**

Many Christians do not like the word "if" in this verse because it implies that there will be negative consequences if the condition of remaining in the faith is not met. "What about unconditional love?" they ask. They would rather follow a popular line that says, "There is nothing you can do to make God love you more, and nothing you can do to make him love you less." We are simply loved by God—no ifs, ands, or buts about it. But in spite of the popularity of the term "unconditional love," it might be a misleading idea.

First, to call his love unconditional implies that God would never say "if" to us. But he has said it to us—often—in both testaments. Moses sets before the people "the blessing *if* you obey...the curse *if* you disobey" (Dt 11:27-28, NIV). Jesus said that *if* we do not abide in Christ we will be thrown like fruitless branches into the fire (Jn 15:6). And this is just a tiny sampling of biblical promises and threats issued with the word "if."

Second, to say God's love is unconditional wrongly implies that there are no real consequences for people's actions as far as God is concerned. Why believe or obey if God loves you regardless? Why did Jesus die on a cross if God loves you without it? And why warn people about hell if there's no way an unconditionally loving God would ever send anyone there? The idea of unconditional love wrongly overlooks the real consequences of sin.

Third, the idea of unconditional love also implies that God is not that concerned about the condition of our relationship with him. On a human level, some might think it's unconditional love to say, "I don't care if you're abusing drugs, I love you anyway" or "It doesn't matter that you're cheating on me, I'll love you anyway." But notice how unconditional love gets associated with phrases of indifference like "I don't care" and "it doesn't matter." God doesn't talk that way. God says, "I do care if you sin—it hurts me deeply, it angers me tremendously, but I will continue to love you."

But if "unconditional love" sounds like a bland blanket of approval, indifferent to the condition of our soul, "conditional" love doesn't sound any better with its implications of God's love being tentative and easily withdrawn from us. Far better would be to speak of God's *steadfast* love—a faithful, enduring, passionate love that cares deeply about the condition of our faith. We do well to surrender unconditionally to this steadfast love.

Jesus, I'm grateful your steadfast love is deeply concerned about the condition of my relationship with you.

*^{21} And you.... ^{22} he now reconciled in the body of his flesh through death, to present you as holy and unblemished and blameless before him, ^{23} **if indeed** you remain in the faith*

When Paul says we will be presented as holy before God on Judgment Day, *if* we remain in the faith, we can't help but wonder, "What happens if we do not remain in the faith?" Can we lose our salvation? Some Christian groups say yes, and others no, and they like to debate each other.

But no matter what conclusion we come to, this is not an abstract issue for Paul. He's talking to real people who are tempted to move away from the gospel. Some of these people regarded themselves as true believers, but later decisions would show otherwise. Whether they actually were true believers or only thought they were, that's not Paul's issue. All Paul knows is that it's possible for people who *think* they trust in Christ to later turn away from Christ, so it's important for him to encourage them all to remain in the faith.

God's Word does not answer abstract questions. When we ask, "Can people lose their salvation?" Jesus' first response would be, "Why do you want to know?" As he does often in the gospels, Jesus answers our questions with his questions to explore the condition of our own soul.

This is why the Bible does not answer our questions about the possibility of losing one's salvation by giving us a slogan, such as "once saved, always saved." The answer really depends on why we want to know. If we want to know because we are afraid of losing our salvation, thinking that it's up to us and our faithful abilities to stay in the faith, then the Lord assures us that no one can snatch us out of his hand. But if our question about losing salvation arises from our desire to walk on the wild side and yet still look forward to heaven, the Lord gives us an entirely different answer, calling us to remain in the faith, or else. This is not a case of situational truth; that would be just as misguided as situational ethics. God's truth is solid, firm, and sure. But God's truth is not solid and firm like an abstract object. It is solid and firm in a living, active, personal way. God's truth moves toward us to speak to the condition of our own heart.

It's important for us to study God's Word, but ultimately, it's not so that we learn to answer abstract questions about salvation. Rather, God's Word always confronts us with the personal question, "Will *you* remain in the faith, continuing to trust Jesus for salvation?"

Jesus, when I'm fearful of the stability of my faith, reassure me. When I'm trying to get away with sin, shake me up. Grant to me the answers I need.

²¹ And you…. ²² he now reconciled in the body of his flesh through death, to present you as holy and unblemished and blameless before him, ²³ if indeed **you remain in the faith**

When some Colossians were tempted to supplement their faith in Christ with other beliefs and practices, Paul urged them (and us) to "remain" in the faith (this word is also translated as "abide"). This phrase "if you remain" (or abide) comes up more often in the NT than you might expect.

For instance, Jesus said in Jn 8:31, "if you abide in my word, you are truly my disciples" (ESV). According to the context, some of the Jews had put their faith in him (8:30), but their faith did not remain. By the end of the chapter, they were ready to stone him (8:59). John is not saying that these Jews were saved for a few brief minutes and then lost their salvation. Rather, he's saying that God's saving purpose is not that we simply believe Jesus, but that we *remain* in that belief. Both responses could be described as a kind of faith, but there's no salvation linked to a faith that does not remain.

In Jn 15:4 Jesus calls us to remain (or abide) in him like a branch on a vine so we can bear good fruit. But Jesus warns of the fatal consequences for those who had some kind of connection to him, but then break away: "*If anyone does not abide in me he is thrown away like a branch and withers; and the branches are gathered, thrown into the fire, and burned*" (Jn 15:6, ESV, emphasis mine).

These "if you remain" verses sound pretty harsh. More mercifully, however, 1 Cor 3:14 says that *if* the work we do as Christians does not *remain* after going through the fires of judgment, we will still be saved—but only after suffering loss. Even more hopeful is the promise of 2 Tim 2:13 that even *if* we are faithless, the Lord will *remain* faithful to us.

The verses just cited clearly tell us—whether we are true Christians or only think we are—that some kind of remaining in the faith is necessary. Salvation is not a magic-moment experience, but an ongoing relationship of placing our trust in Jesus. To paraphrase F. F. Bruce, continuance in faith is the test of its reality.[74]

Remaining in the faith is not a call for us to exercise some inner heroic ability to believe. Instead, remaining in the faith is about relying on the one in whom we believe, the Lord Jesus Christ.[75]

It is my heart's desire to abide in you day by day, Lord Jesus. If I stray, abide in me and draw me back.

*[23] if indeed you remain in the faith, **being foundationed and settled,** and not moving from the hope of the good-message which you heard, which has been proclaimed to every created-being under heaven, of which I, Paul, have become a servant.*

When Paul describes what it means to remain in the faith, he chooses words that convey the idea of staying in one place. Elsewhere Paul will use words that emphasize movement to describe the Christian life (such as walking, following, growing, pressing on, and traveling). But here Paul wants to stress the stability that comes from *not* moving. Although our highly mobile society may prefer words that emphasize movement, if there's nothing but movement, the result is instability. Of course, if there's only stability, there may not be any life either. A full picture of a life of faith includes both stability *and* movement.

Remaining in the faith means "being foundationed." I've turned the English word "foundation" into a verb here because that's what Paul does in the Greek language. God's foundationing activity in the OT is mostly seen in creation and in the establishing of his temple on Mt. Zion. The NT, however, focuses on laying spiritual foundations.

Sometimes *we* are called to lay a good foundation (1 Tim 6:19; Lk 14:29; Mt 7:24-27). But more commonly, it is *God* who lays a foundation for us. "Being foundationed" in Col 1:23 is not an action we do, but an action done for us by God. First Peter 5:10 says that it is *God* who will restore, strengthen, and foundation us. "God's firm foundation stands" (2 Tim 2:19, ESV) because God is the one who lays it. Paul might claim to lay a foundation for the church, but then quickly adds that there is no other true foundation than the one already laid, which is Jesus (1 Cor 3:10-11).

Remaining in faith also means being "settled," which is another architectural word. It refers to being settled in at home, instead of being mobile. Close to the meaning here is 1 Cor 15:58, where Paul told the believers to "be steadfast [this is the same word used for "settled"], immovable, always abounding in the work of the Lord" (ESV). Rather than flitting about from one teaching to another, Paul calls on believers to remain settled upon the solid foundation of the gospel of Jesus. It's their home.

O Lord, my Rock and my Redeemer, whenever my heart gets restless and fidgety, hankering after the latest thing, call me back to your firm foundation.

*²³ if indeed you remain in the faith, being foundationed and settled, **and not moving from the hope of the good-message which you heard,** which has been proclaimed to every created-being under heaven, of which I, Paul, have become a servant.*

Paul adds another phrase to indicate that Christians are not to move or shift from the hope found in the gospel. This idea of not shifting off the foundation is also found in the OT with regards to creation (the established world cannot be moved, Ps 96:10), and Jerusalem (which is like an immoveable tent, Isa 33:20). Many psalms also speak of how good it is not to be shaken or moved. Ps 16:8 declares that because the Lord is "at my right hand, I will not be shaken" (NIV; see also Ps 15:5 and 62:2). The old gospel chorus, "I shall not be, I shall not be moved" is based on these verses.

Even though Paul was a man in motion, always pressing on toward the goal, running the good race, traveling as an apostle sent to the Gentiles, he knew there was one thing a Christian should never move away from, namely, the foundational truth and hope of the gospel of Christ. We can grow in our understanding of this gospel and in our capacity to live out this gospel. But this movement of growth is always based on a settled foundation that never moves.

In case Paul's architectural imagery seems too rigid, stiff, and lifeless for you, you might want to check out his botanical imagery. Christians are also immoveable like plants, rooted in one place, and yet full of life, vitality, and fruitfulness. Paul says in Col 2:7 that we are "rooted [like plants] and being built up [like buildings] in Christ" (see also 1 Cor 3:9; Eph 3:17).

We do not build our lives upon a philosophy, a lifestyle, or a tradition. Rather it is the hope of the *gospel* that is the still point in our turning world. *Without* the hope of the gospel, we would roam like wandering stars in the dark universe (Jude 3), rummaging through the wastelands of our society, searching for something, anything, to give us hope for the future. But *with* the hope of the gospel, we are at home with God—growing and changing, yes, but also content in knowing we are already located at the Source of all that will fulfill any longing we have.

Lord, I want my roots to grow deep and my foundations to be set on solid rock, so that I can never be moved or shaken from your Word.

*^{23} if indeed you remain in the faith, being foundationed and settled, and not moving from the hope of the good-message which you heard, **which has been proclaimed to every created-being under heaven**, of which I, Paul, have become a servant.*

Just as Paul began his letter with references to the spreading of the gospel (Col 1:6), so now he brings this section of the letter to a close by referring to the same things.

The gospel was not proclaimed to only a few select individuals chosen for their great spirituality (which is the method of many false teachers who appeal to people's desire to join an elite group of those "in the know"). Nor was the gospel reserved for only one ethnic group—as some of the early Jewish Christians wanted to do. Rather, says Paul, every created being under heaven is now within earshot of this marvelous message.

On one level, of course, it is not the case that every human being alive when Colossians was written had already heard about Jesus. If that were so, Paul would no longer need to continue his own evangelistic ministry. But on another level, Paul is celebrating the fact that all those for whom the reconciling work on the cross was done (Col 1:20) are in the process of hearing about it. The message is going out and there's no place to get away from it.

To paraphrase Ps 139:7-12, one might ask, "Where can I go from the gospel? Where can I flee from its proclamation? If I go up to the heavens, I hear it there; if I make my bed in the depths, I hear it there. If I rise on the wings of the dawn, if I settle on the far side of the sea, even there the gospel beckons me, your good news will hold my attention fast. If I say, 'Surely the darkness will hide me and the light become night around me,' even in the darkness the gospel rings true so that the night will shine like the day, for darkness is as light when God's word is proclaimed."

The reason Paul speaks so exuberantly here is that he is in the midst of experiencing what Jesus said should and would happen, namely, that his followers would "preach the gospel to all creation" (Mk 16:15, NIV). The Colossians have already heard this word, but they are only the first of many who are hearing and responding.

Today we hear the gospel, and hopefully it is not coming to our ears and running into a dead-end street. We want to be receivers who take this good news and amplify it to a world that's been deafened by bad news.

Jesus, I feel inadequate in proclaiming good news, but I ask that you would use me to make it happen anyway.

[23] *if indeed you remain in the faith, being foundationed and settled, and not moving from the hope of the good-message which you heard, which has been proclaimed to every created-being under heaven, **of which I, Paul, have become a servant.***

Paul transitions to the next part of the letter by identifying himself as a servant of the gospel. He will elaborate on this further in Col 1:24-2:5. Paul is not in charge of the gospel, as if he were its master. Instead, he is its servant, submitting to its call on his heart. Paul does not regard this as an undesirable assignment. Rather, he knows he is "a servant of this gospel by the gift of God's grace given me through the working of his power" (Eph 3:7, NIV).

Paul's assignment is in service to the gospel message, for as he said in 2 Cor 4:5, "For what we proclaim is not ourselves, but Jesus Christ as Lord, with ourselves as your servants for Jesus' sake" (ESV). He is proclaiming himself as a servant because he believes God has given him (and his colleagues) a key role in moving the gospel beyond the confines of the Jewish faith, so the whole world can hear and believe. Just as Jesus submitted himself to the Father's will, and even to the will of those who hated him, so Paul has submitted himself to Jesus' call to proclaim the gospel.

It would be tempting to confine this kind of ministry to Paul and other apostolic figures. But there is a sense in which all Christians are called to be servants of the gospel. We are not to be slaves to our own desires, submissive to our peers, obedient to commercial appeals, or lackeys to some political movement. We are servants of the gospel.

The Lord of the gospel has issued an invitation brimming with good news: "Come to the king's banquet, open the door of your heart, receive free gifts from God." Since the gospel is about God's hospitality, then we who are servants of that gospel are involved in this ministry of hospitality. As servants, we ob-*serve* our Master's indications of what needs to happen for God's guests to feel welcomed. We open doors for the outcast, feed the hungry, befriend the friendless, love the unloved, forgive the unforgiven, and honor those living in shame. When these things are done in the name of Jesus, we are truly servants of the gospel.

My heart is not always so open, Lord. Pry it open with your good news, so that I can join you in your hospitality toward the world.

At One Time We Were Enemies (Colossians 1:21-23)

to the tune of Vox Dilecti: *I Heard the Voice of Jesus Say*
© 2011 David J. Landegent

At one time we were enemies, estranged from Christ the Lord.
We lived as rebels, aliens; with God we were at war.
But now we have been reconciled through Jesus' sacrifice.
Upon the cross in mortal flesh, He paid love's greatest price.

At one time evil thoughts prevailed, indifferent to God's grace.
Our deeds revealed our wicked hearts; our Lord we could not face.
But Jesus will present us all before his Father's throne
As holy, blameless, pure and good, for all has been atoned.

At one time we had built our lives upon the shifting sand;
With no foundation that could hold, we could not take a stand.
But now we're built upon the Rock and grounded in God Word.
Our hearts are settled on His truth; our faith remains secure.

Paul's ministry

Colossians 1:24-29

April 18-May 7

[24] Now I rejoice in sufferings for you, and I fill up that which remains to be completed of the afflictions of Christ in my flesh, for [the sake of] his body, which is the church, [25] of which I have become a servant according to the household-management-plan God has given to me—for you—to fill-out the word of God, [26] the mystery which was being concealed from ages and from generations, but now is revealed to his holy-ones, [27] to whom God willed to make known what are the riches of the glory of this mystery among the nations, which is, Christ in you, the hope of glory; [28] whom we declare, warning every person and teaching every person in all wisdom, so that we may present every person complete in Christ; [29] [a goal] for which I toil, striving by means of his energy, which is energizing me with power.

So far in Colossians, Paul has called himself an apostle (1:1) and a servant of the gospel (1:23). He will continue to talk about his ministry in this section.

When leaders speak of themselves, some might regard their words as arrogant self-praise. However, according to Plutarch's *On Praising Oneself Inoffensively* (written about the same time as Colossians), self-praise will not offend others if speakers: (1) blend their self-praise with praise for their audience, which Paul did in Col 1:3-8; (2) attribute their honorable actions to God or the gods, which Paul does in Col 1:25; (3) mention their weaknesses along with their strengths, which Paul does in other letters; (4) point out that their honorable actions came at the cost of much hardship, as Paul does in Col 1:24; and (5) speak of themselves in order to motivate their listeners to follow them, as may be the case here.

It's doubtful whether Paul is consciously adopting Plutarch's strategies here, but he does exhibit wisdom appropriate to his culture when speaking of himself without offending others.

Although Paul does talk about himself in this section (and the next), the focus on Jesus in Col 1:15-23 is not left behind. Instead, nearly every major phrase here is explicitly tied to Christ.[76] Paul's sufferings are, in some sense, *Christ's* sufferings (verse 24); the church which Paul serves is *Christ's* church, his body (verse 24); the mystery which Paul's message reveals to the nations is "*Christ* in you" (verse 27); Paul's goal is that all people would be complete in *Christ* (verse 28); and Paul works toward that goal empowered by *Christ's* power (verse 29).

Lord Jesus, I pray that when others watch me, they see you; and when others listen to me, they hear you.

^{24} ***Now I rejoice in sufferings for you,*** *and I fill up that which remains to be completed of the afflictions of Christ in my flesh*

Rejoicing was characteristic of Paul. He may have a stern reputation among many, but he often spoke of himself as rejoicing and urged his readers to do the same. In calling on believers to rejoice (Rom 12:12, 15; 2 Cor 13:11; Phil 3:1; 4:4; 1 Thess 5:16), Paul was not asking them to do anything he did not do himself.

According to verse 24, Paul especially rejoiced in his trials. In the midst of a list of his sufferings, he describes himself as "sorrowful, yet always rejoicing" (2 Cor 6:10, NIV). He is glad to know that his sufferings help the church (2 Cor 13:9). Just as parents gladly make sacrifices for their children, so Paul gladly sacrifices for his spiritual children (see Gal 4:19 and 1 Thess 2:7-8). It's a small price to pay.

But there is a price. Paul does not specify here the kinds of suffering he endured (in fact, he doesn't even mention his current imprisonment until Col 4:3), but 2 Cor 6:4-10 and 11:23-29 refer to persecution from both Jews and non-Jews and various kinds of physical deprivation.

Elsewhere, Paul tells us why he rejoices in his sufferings: (1) "The sufferings of this present time are not worthy to be compared with the glory which shall be revealed in us" (Rom 8:18, ESV). (2) The Lord is able to rescue us from them all (2 Tim 3:11). (3) The tidal wave of suffering is met by an even bigger wave of comfort from God (2 Cor 1:5). (4) His suffering will help other believers be strengthened when they suffer (2 Cor 1:7). (5) Suffering for and with Christ is a primary path for growing in faith. According to Phil 3:10 we come to know Christ, not so much by agreeing with teachings about Jesus, but by experiencing the power of his resurrection and *sharing in his suffering*. Paul is not simply rejoicing in generic sufferings, but in sufferings connected to the afflictions of Christ.

Paul's suffering stands in great contrast to the self-imposed suffering advocated by the distortionists. They mistreated their bodies so that sensual indulgence would be restrained and mystical worship experiences be more likely to occur (see Col 2:20-23). Paul would have none of this. Theirs is a kind of suffering that curves in upon the self, performed in vain for their own spiritual benefit. Paul's suffering, however, is not self-centered, but is endured for the benefit of the church, so that the good news could be heard in all the world and Christ could be glorified.

Show me, Lord, that I am not alone in my suffering, but that my own suffering is somehow wrapped up in yours. Help me to see that and rejoice in it.

²⁴ *Now I rejoice in sufferings for you,* **and I fill up that which remains to be completed of the afflictions of Christ in my flesh**

Many Christians are bothered by Paul's wording here, for it seems to contradict Jesus' words on the cross, "It is finished" (Jn 19:30). It sounds as if Paul is making up the difference in what Jesus failed to accomplish on the cross. But that's not at all what Paul means.

First, when Paul says he fills up what "remains to be completed," he's not talking about what is lacking in what Jesus had done. The Greek word used here is never used in the NT to criticize something as deficient. What Jesus suffered on the cross was completely sufficient for atoning for sin.

Second, the Greek word for the afflictions (*thlipsis*) of Christ is never used to refer to Jesus' atoning death on the cross. Instead it refers to Jesus' other forms of last-days suffering, which he still experiences with us (and we with him, see Mt 24:21). Even after he ascended to heaven, Jesus still suffered with his church—which is why he asked Paul in his non-Christian days, "Why are you persecuting me?" (Acts 9:4).

To say we are in Christ and Christ is in us is not just about *being* together. It's also about *suffering* together. To paraphrase 1 Cor 12:26, if one part suffers in the body of Christ, every part suffers with it, including Jesus, the head of the body. For Jesus to share in the "fellowship of suffering" (Phil 3:10, NIV) not only means that he has been through it in the past and so can sympathize with us. The fellowship of suffering also means that Jesus continues to share in our present suffering, and we share in his. It's this kind of suffering, and not redemptive suffering, that Paul fills up.

But still, how does Paul fill up Christ's affliction? What may be creating confusion is that we are not reading the whole phrase correctly. Paul is not filling up what has yet to be completed of "the afflictions of Christ," period. We need to add the last phrase, "in my flesh." To add that phrase, as Houlden argues, means that "it is not Christ's sufferings which are being completed, but Christ's sufferings-*in-Paul*" that need to be completed.⁷⁷

Paul was willing to complete his assignment, to experience the sufferings of Jesus flow into his life (2 Cor 1:5), carrying the death of Jesus in his own body (2 Cor 4:10). But as we've been saying, Paul does not suffer because he's *accomplishing* reconciliation in place of Christ; he suffers because he's *proclaiming* reconciliation through Christ.⁷⁸

Thank you, Jesus, that the sacrifice to overcome sin is completed, and now I can stand forgiven and amazed in your presence.

²⁴ Now I rejoice in sufferings for you, **and I fill up that which remains to be completed of the afflictions of Christ in my flesh**

It's possible Paul chose this unusual way of describing his suffering in order to counteract the Colossian distortion. As noted before, words about fullness are quite common in this letter, often in the context of arguing against the distortion. The distortionists may have been appealing to people's sense that something was yet missing from their lives. They were urging Christians to move beyond simple faith to experience the fullness of God through deeper philosophical teachings, holy days, the worship of angels, and strict regulations about holiness (see Col 2:16-23).

Paul, of course, disagreed strenuously with this and insisted that they already have all the fullness they'll ever need in Christ, who is himself the fullness of God in bodily form (Col 2:9-10). But—with perhaps a touch of sarcasm—Paul may have been willing to concede that for the followers of Jesus there is one thing still incomplete in our lives, namely, our allotted portion of suffering for Christ. All the fullness we need is ours in Christ, but if anyone still thinks something is missing, then Paul would urge them to do as he has done—fill up what's missing by suffering with Jesus.

If this interpretation is correct, it would not be the first time Paul has turned the tables on his opponents by taking one of their favorite terms and applying it to the important role of suffering. For instance, when dealing with false teachers in Corinth who boasted of their visions and miracles, Paul said that he too would boast, but instead of boasting of his spiritual prowess, he promptly began to boast of his sufferings (see 2 Cor 11:16-12:10). In a similar way here in Colossians, Paul concedes that something is missing in his faith, namely, the fullness of suffering with Christ. The distortionists were trying to mistreat their flesh so they could move beyond the flesh to more supernatural experiences in their spirit (see Col 2:18-23). But for Paul, we are not called to escape the flesh, but to suffer in the flesh with Christ. That's the path of true transformation.

Whether this scenario is true or not, Col 1:24 affirms that "the suffering of Jesus on the cross is not the end of all suffering," neither for Christ nor the church.[79] All Christians are "co-heirs with Christ, if indeed we share in his sufferings in order that we may also share in his glory" (Rom 8:17, NIV). Thus, the church or the apostle or the believer who shirks from the path of suffering is shirking from the path of Christ.

Savior, I want to experience your fullness in my life, even if that means walking the path of suffering with you.

*[24] Now I rejoice in sufferings for you, and I fill up that which remains to be completed of the afflictions of Christ in my flesh, **for [the sake of] his body, which is the church***

Paul undergoes suffering not so he can have a solitary mystical experience of being united with Jesus in his trials. Rather, he suffers for the sake of Christ's body, the church.

The NT word "for" (*huper*) often speaks of actions done for the benefit of others. Jesus gave himself *for* us (Gal 2:20) and *for* our sin (Gal 1:4) by laying down his life *for* us (Jn 10:11) to the point of dying *for* us sinners (Rom 5:6) and *for* our sins (1 Cor 15:3). Paul even speaks of Jesus becoming sin *for* us (2 Cor 5:21) and becoming a curse *for* us (Gal 3:13). The risen Jesus then entered heaven *for* us (Heb 6:20) to intercede *for* us (Rom 8:34).

Jesus told Paul from the beginning that he too would suffer much (Acts 9:16), and he did (see especially 2 Cor 11:23-29). Paul spent himself *for* believers (2 Cor 12:15), struggling *for* them (Col 2:1) and suffering *for* them (Eph 3:13; Col 1:24). Anyone who thinks church leadership is a cushy job involving the pleasurable contemplation of divine things has seriously misunderstood the call of Christ to serve his body.

Although the leaders of God's people often suffer (think of Moses and Samuel), in a sense, every believer is called to suffer for the Lord and his people. Believers are counted worthy when they suffer for the Lord (Phil 1:29) and his kingdom (2 Thess 1:5). Peter and John agreed: "For to this you have been called, because Christ also suffered for you, leaving you an example, so that you should follow in his steps" (1 Pet 2:21, NRSV); "By this we know love, that he [Christ] laid down his life for us, and we ought to lay down our lives for the brothers" (1 Jn 3:16, ESV). Unfortunately, few in the Western world think of suffering as a mark of the church, even though the NT speaks more about that than any other church theme.[80]

When Paul suffers for the church, it's not for maintaining an institution. Rather he suffers for the sake of the church's mission to draw others into the family of God. This is the Lord's calling for all believers, and the success of that mission depends on our willingness to suffer. According to John Stott, "the greatest single secret of evangelistic or missionary effectiveness is the willingness to suffer and die. It may be a death to popularity...or to pride...or to racial and national prejudice...or to material comfort... But the servant must suffer if he is to bring light to the nations."[81]

Lord, you suffered for your very flawed people called the church. Overcome my reluctance to follow you in this. Grant me a sacrificial love for your church.

*²⁴ Now I rejoice in sufferings for you, and I fill up that which remains to be completed of the afflictions of Christ in my flesh, for [the sake of] his body, which is the church, ²⁵ **of which I have become a servant***

Being a servant *of the Lord* is a common idea in the Bible, and Paul would certainly qualify as one (2 Cor 6:4; 11:23). And because he was God's servant, Paul was also a servant of God's message, (Col 1:23), God's new covenant (2 Cor 3:6), and God's people, the church (as in today's verse).

Our culture is very familiar with the ideal of leaders being servants of the people—even though it is not often seen in practice. It was Jesus who highlighted this form of service. In the OT, leaders did not think of themselves as servants of the people; rather, the people were their servants (see 1 Sam 12:19). When King Rehoboam was counseled to "be a servant to this people today and serve them" (1 Kgs 12:7, NRSV), he instead decided to get tough with the people. It was rulers like him that Ezekiel criticized as abusive shepherds who didn't take care of the sheep (Ezek 34:3).

But then came Jesus, the Good Shepherd, who leads his flock by serving his sheep (see Mt 20:28; Mk 10:45; Lk 22:27). And Jesus commanded his disciples to lead in the same serving way. If they want to be great among the disciples, they must be servants of those disciples (Mt 20:26; 23:11; Mk 9:35; 10:43). This may account for Paul's sense that he is to serve the church.

Another reason Paul was eager to serve the church is that he regarded Christ and his body (the church) to be in such union together that it was impossible to serve the one without the other. If you serve Christ, you will serve his body, the church.

Today many may feel called to heroically serve Jesus, but are much less interested in the very non-heroic activity of serving the church, with all its quirky people, institutional flaws, slow progress, and petty concerns. To be a servant of Christ sounds adventurous; to be a servant of the church sounds tedious. There's glamor (we think) in being an attendant to the King of kings, but not in attending to the needs of his dowdy partner, the church. But there is no serving the Christ without serving the body of Christ. If we forget this, we will soon echo the complaint of Moses, "What have I done to displease you that you put the burden of all these people on me?" (Num 11:11, NIV). Paul knew this same burden, but he was able to bear it, because serving the church is one of the best ways to serve the Lord.

Lord, I am so thankful that you love the church in a serving way. Give me that same love so I am willing to serve even when it's not very heroic.

*²⁴ Now I rejoice in sufferings for you . . . for [the sake of] his body, which is the church, ²⁵ of which I have become a servant **according to the household-management-plan God has given to me—for you—to fill-out the word of God***

Although Paul serves the church, he does not serve at the whim of the church. Rather, God has given him a specific assignment. He is to serve the church "according to the household-management-plan God has given" him.

The Greek word for household-management-plan is *oikonomia*, which is a compound word made from house (*oikos*) and law (*nomia*). Thus, the *oikonomia* are the "rules of the house." The difficulty of finding an English equivalent is seen in the wide variety of translations of this word: management, plan, stewardship, job, trust, effect, administration, commission, work, position, etc. These are okay, but today many of them sound too much a part of the impersonal business world. In Paul's day, however, businesses were in the home, and those who followed the *oikonomia* were members of the household.

The idea is that God has a management plan for his family—his household—and he has called Paul to play a key role in making these plans come to pass. His role is to fill out the message of God's Word as it applies to the non-Jewish portion of God's estate.[82]

Paul regards his responsibility for carrying out the household-management plan as a gift which God "has given to me." Although we commonly associate gifts with presents or benefits, Paul knows it is also a wonderful gift simply to be entrusted with a responsibility.

Jesus was "given" all authority by the Father (Mt 28:18), not to lord it over others, but to be a servant. And Jesus, in turn, *gave* authority to his disciples to exorcise demons, heal the sick, testify to the gospel, and build up the church. They were "given" power, knowledge, resources, and opportunities. There are too many verses about this to list here, but most of them use this small word "give." Those to whom God has given the privilege of ministry and service also become gifts themselves—God's gift to the church—for "the gifts he gave were that some would be apostles, some prophets, some evangelists, some pastors and teachers" (Eph 4:11, NRSV).

Here, then, Paul is celebrating that his assignment of managing God's household is actually a gift from God. With what responsibilities has the Lord gifted you?

I'm sorry, Lord, that I grumble about my responsibilities. Show me again how they are actually beautiful gifts entrusted to me.

*[25] of which I have become a servant according to the household-management-plan God has given to me—for you—to fill-out the word of God [26] **the mystery** which was being concealed from ages and from generations, but now is revealed to his holy-ones*

When Paul fills out the Word of God, he thinks of this Word as a *mustērion*, from which we get the English word "mystery." Today we think of a mystery as something which cannot (yet) be known or solved: like a crime with few clues or the science of subatomic particles. We assume that with enough hard work and concentrated thinking, these mysteries can be figured out. With spiritual mysteries (like predestination), however, people are often told to just trust God and let mysteries be.

The Bible, however, doesn't follow these contemporary understandings of mystery. Biblical mystery is not something that can be solved by human intelligence and hard work. Nor is a mystery something we should just leave be, beyond our comprehension and hidden in a "cloud of unknowing" (as a mystic once said). Instead, the mysteries of God can be known (at least some of them), but only because God has graciously chosen to reveal them. As Barth said, "We know Him as He gives Himself to be known by us."[83]

In the Bible mysteries are often associated with end-time events and persons (Rev 10:7), such as the resurrection (1 Cor 15:51), the anti-christic lawless one (2 Thess 2:7), Babylon the harlot (Rev 17:5-7), Israel (Rom 11:25), and how the Lord would draw the nations into his kingdom (Eph 3:6, Col 1:27; 2:2). "Mystery," then, is usually a word pointing to the truth that the Last Days have already begun in the coming of Jesus. As Heb 1:2 says, "in these last days he [God] has spoken to us by his Son" (NIV).

This newly-revealed mystery, however, was not completely unknown in the past. The mystery was first declared by the prophets as a promise of things to come, and yet it was a promise "hidden in plain view."[84] Jesus may have "fulfilled" the promises of the Word, but because many did not understand it, Paul (and other apostles) "filled out" the meaning that Word.

Of special concern to Paul is that the "mystery" is about God's "household-management-plan." He puts those two realities together here and also in 1 Cor 4:1; Eph 1:9; 3:2, 9. So if anyone is trying to figure out what God is up to, they only need to look at God's efforts to bring his family together from all around the world, so they find their place in Christ.

Heavenly Father, it's a mystery to me how I came to be included in your family, but I'm thankful it happened.

*[25] of which I have become a servant according to the household-management-plan God has given to me—for you—to fill-out the word of God [26] the mystery **which was being concealed from ages and from generations**, but now is revealed to his holy-ones*

The reason Paul used the word "mystery" to describe the full message of the gospel is that it had earlier been concealed. Some might think it had been concealed by the devil who blinds the minds of people (2 Cor 4:4). But it's more likely that *God* is the one who concealed it in the past. Lk 10:21 uses the same verb to say that God has hidden truths from the wise and revealed them to children. Elsewhere (also using the same verb) Paul refers to a hidden wisdom of God (1 Cor 2:7) and a mystery hidden in God (Eph 3:9). Where did God hide this mystery? In Christ, says Paul in Col 2:3.

But why would God keep such wonderful news hidden? According to Lk 10:21, God hid the message of the kingdom so that those who are wise in their own eyes would come to see their foolishness. First Corinthians 2:7-8 tells us that if the wisdom of the gospel had been revealed earlier, then the rulers of this age would not have crucified Jesus—which would have completely undermined God's plan. If the good news had been let out too early, there would be no news to tell.

This mystery was concealed from "ages" and "generations." Both of these terms have an end-time thrust to them. The current "age" with its worries and sins will soon end (Mt 13:22, 39), and then the Age-to-Come will arrive in its glory (Lk 18:30). Likewise, the past "generations" were marked by wickedness and unbelief, but the generations in the last days have an opportunity to be part of God's kingdom. The gospel may have been hidden in past ages and generations, but it was hidden in anticipation of the end times when the mystery would be revealed.

This is likely the same perspective that shaped Paul's message in Lystra, when he told the crowd, "We bring you good news, that you should turn from these vain things to a living God, who made heaven and the earth and the sea and all that is in them. In past generations, he allowed all the nations to walk in their own ways. Yet he did not leave himself without witness" (Acts 14:15-17, ESV). God had not been silent in the past, but the key to what he had said had not yet been revealed. Now it has been, and Paul proclaims this revealed mystery.

Mysteries may intrigue me, Lord, but I want to be even more intrigued by the truth you have revealed. Show me your way.

^{25} ...to fill-out the word of God ^{26} the mystery which was being concealed
*from ages and from generations, **but now is revealed to his holy-ones***

Back in verses 21-22 Paul used the concept of "now" to contrast the Colossians' former hostility toward God with their current reconciliation with God. Here Paul uses the word "now" to point out another contrast: the mystery of the gospel had at one time been concealed, "but now" it has been revealed. As Witherington reminds us, the "good news" is actually news; something new has happened.[85]

This mystery was revealed *at the cross* when Jesus did his reconciling work. This mystery is revealed *when it is proclaimed* in the preaching of the gospel. And this mystery is revealed *when someone's eyes are opened* and they trust in the reconciling work and message of Christ.

The Greek word for the "revealing" of the mystery is *phaneroō*, a verb used forty-four times in the NT, but only once in the Greek translation of the OT. John and Paul are the writers most drawn to this word. Its meaning leans in the direction of revealing something in a visible way. Most uses of *phaneroō* connect to the end-time realities of (1) Jesus' first coming which ushered in the end times (Heb 9:26); (2) Jesus' resurrection which signaled that the end times had arrived (Jn 21:14); (3) Jesus' second coming (1 Jn 3:2); (4) the end-times exposure of sin and righteousness (1 Cor 4:5); and (5) the proclamation of the gospel in the last days (Titus 1:2-3).

In Eph 3:3 the emphasis is on how God revealed this mystery to *Paul* ("the mystery was made known to me by revelation," NRSV). Here in Colossians, however, Paul emphasizes that this truth was revealed to "all" God's holy-ones.   While it would be possible to interpret this verse to mean that God's people have been set apart only for the *privilege* of receiving a special revelation not given to others, such an interpretation would not fit the missional perspective of the apostle Paul. He believes instead that God's people are set apart not just for the *receiving* of revelation, but for the *proclaiming* of that revelation. The Lord declares in Isa 66:19, "And they [all God's people] shall declare my glory among the nations" (NRSV).

Unlike the mystery religions of Paul's day which appealed to people's elitist desire to know rituals and doctrines unknown to the masses (an appeal which the Colossian distortionists may have also made), Paul preached a mystery that was revealed to God's holy-ones so they would freely proclaim it to all.

Thank you, Lord, for revealing your message of reconciliation to us. Don't let
me ever hoard this good news and keep it to myself.

*[26] the mystery which was being concealed from ages and from generations, but now is revealed to his holy-ones, [27] **to whom God willed to make known** what are the riches of the glory of this mystery among the nations, which is, Christ in you, the hope of glory*

God revealed the mystery of the gospel to his holy ones, because he "willed" to make it known to them.

Perhaps the closest parallel to this is 1 Tim 2:4, which states that God desires/wills "all people to be saved and to come to a knowledge of the truth" (NIV). If God wills for all people to find salvation in the gospel of Christ, this will only happen if God also wills for this gospel to be proclaimed. It's a chain of events similar to what Paul stated in Rom 10:14-15, "How then will they call on him in whom they have not believed? And how are they to believe in him of whom they have never heard? And how are they to hear without someone preaching? And how are they to preach unless they are sent?" (ESV). God willed for Paul to be an apostle who proclaims the gospel (Col 1:1), and he wills for us to do the same.

To will for something to happen often contains a hint of delight in that thing. We direct our wills toward that which we find delightful. In the Greek version of the OT, delighting in and willing something are nearly equivalent ideas. In a sense, when God wills to make the mystery known to the nations, this action is delightful to God. Eph 1:9 draws this connection even more clearly when it says that God "made known to us *the mystery of his will according to his good pleasure*, which he purposed in Christ" (NIV, italics mine). While we might sometimes think of the will of God as a heavy burden imposed upon us, it is instead an expression of what brings joy to God's heart. God rejoices when his truth is made known to us and through us. (The apostle John rejoiced in the same thing in 2 Jn 4.)

The making known of the gospel is not intended by God to be a river of knowledge that flows into a self-contained pool. Just as we love because God first loved us, so we make known the gospel because God first made it known to us. We see this pattern established on Jesus' first night on earth: The angels announced the birth of Jesus to shepherds, who then went to Bethlehem to see this thing which the Lord had made known to them (Lk 2:15). Two verses later, the shepherds began to make known to others what they had seen. God wants us to do the same.

Motivate me, Lord, to make your good news known, for the same reason you have made it known to me—for the sheer delight of passing along good news.

[26] the mystery which was being concealed from ages and from generations, but now is revealed to his holy-ones, [27] to whom God willed to make known **what are the riches of the glory** *of this mystery among the nations, which is, Christ in you, the hope of glory*

Most people think of riches in terms of material goods. Not Paul. For him wealth is about knowing the unsearchable riches of Christ (Eph 3:8-9). He talks about the riches of God's kindness (Rom 2:4), grace (Eph 1:7; 2:7), full assurance (Col 2:2), and glory (Rom 9:22-23; Eph 3:16; Phil 4:19; and Col 1:27). By adding the phrase "of the glory," Paul is referring to the source of this wealth—it flows from God's glorious throne. It's not that Paul is unconcerned with the issues posed by material wealth, but the riches of life in Christ overwhelm Paul so much that he would say, "Money isn't everything, in fact, it's hardly anything at all compared to the surpassing treasure found in Christ." Ordinary riches are barely on his radar.

The Hebrew word for glory signifies God's presence and includes the ideas of brilliant light and a weightiness that makes an impact; heavenly light is "heavy light." The Greek language did not have a word with the same connotations, but the word *doxa* came closest. In regular Greek, *doxa* meant nothing more than an opinion about something's status. As used in the NT, however, *doxa* is more about *having* an exalted status, *acknowledging* that status, or *raising* someone's status, all of which may be applied to either God or people. We give glory to those whom we highly esteem.

God has glory and is to be glorified, but most relevant to Col 1:27 is that God shares his glory with his Son (see Jn 8:54), and then Jesus shares his glory with all those who trust in him. Because we are "in Christ," we not only suffer with him and will be raised with him, but we will also be glorified in him (Rom 8:30; 2 Thess 2:14). This glory not only lies in the future (2 Cor 4:17), but is also experienced now (Jn 17:22). Those who look to Jesus are even now "are being transformed into his image with ever-increasing glory, which comes from the Lord" (2 Cor 3:18, NIV).

The "riches of glory," then, are not some mysterious blessing waiting for us in the future. Rather, these riches are already being revealed in Christ and shared throughout the world whenever the gospel is preached. Jesus did not come merely to provide a salvation ticket to lost people, but to transform those who had been living in darkness, so that the glory of Christ is now reflected in their lives and shining on others who are yet in the dark.

Blessed Lord, the world may not regard me as rich or well-known, but in you I realize how wealthy I am and what a glorious life I live.

²⁶ *the mystery which was being concealed from ages and from generations, but now is revealed to his holy-ones,* ²⁷ *to whom God willed to make known what are the riches of the glory **of this mystery among the nations**, which is, Christ in you, the hope of glory*

"Mystery religions" were very popular in Asia Minor during Paul's lifetime. They were known for their secret rites and teachings which promised eternal life for those who underwent the proper initiation. They naturally attracted those who liked the idea of knowing mysteries unknown to others, and they often appealed to soldiers who sought a mystical basis for their brotherhood. Some mystery religions, such as Mithraism, even used blood rituals to initiate new members.

Whether or not Paul is consciously thinking of these mystery religions when he refers to mystery here, one thing is certain: Christianity is not at all like the other mystery religions, for the mystery of the gospel is to be proclaimed to all the world instead of only to an elite group "in the know." What had been a secret is now being proclaimed to all nations (*ethnos*). While we Christians often wrongly keep the gospel locked up in our hearts or our church buildings, this is not God's design. God wants the message shared with all. If anyone is left out, it should only be because they heard and refused to believe it.

The message of salvation being proclaimed to the nations especially excited Paul. Before he had met Jesus, Paul was fanatical about maintaining the boundaries between Jews and non-Jews, but that completely changed when he met Christ and was called to preach to the nations. Although many Christians would expect Paul to talk a lot about forgiveness or eternal life, these are not nearly as much the focal point of his ministry as the inclusion of the nations in God's kingdom plans. As he said in Eph 3:8, "Although I am the very least of all the saints, this grace was given to me, to bring to the Gentiles [*ethnos*] the news of the boundless riches in Christ" (NRSV).

Although Paul had a special assignment to reach the nations, in a way, every Christian has received this same assignment. Maybe we don't actually leave our homeland for distant mission fields, but we can pray for the nations, support various missions to the nations, and even be a witness when people from other nations come to our part of the world. We are not supposed to be "worldly" Christians, but we are to be "world" Christians.

Open my eyes, Lord, to all the ways that I and my local church can be enthused and active in reaching the nations with your good news.

[27] *to whom God willed to make known what are the riches of the glory of this mystery among the nations, **which is, Christ in you**, the hope of glory*

Here Paul declares that the mystery is not a timetable of future events, a set of hard-to-understand ideas, or a secret ritual. Instead the mystery is a person—a person sent by God named Jesus Christ.[86]

And even better, this person is not far off and distant, but is so close as to live within us. The mystery is Christ *in you*. The presence of Christ within is what determines if a person is a Christian or not. "Test yourselves," says Paul, "Do you not realize that Christ Jesus is in you—unless, of course, you fail the test?" (2 Cor 13:5, NIV). A Christian is not someone who only admires Jesus or imitates him. A Christian has Christ living within. As Paul said in Gal 2:20, "I have been crucified with Christ. It is no longer I who live, but Christ who lives in me" (ESV).

But having Christ within doesn't mean everything is now spiritually settled. When dealing with some wayward Galatians, Paul said he was "again in the pain of childbirth until Christ is formed in you" (Gal 4:19, NRSV). Using a pregnancy metaphor, Paul is saying that Christ is within, but not yet fully formed. The abiding of Christ in believers is not only an accomplished fact, but a growing reality for God's people.

This reality of Christ living within us is a frequent message in the evangelical wing of Christianity. But there's more. Not only is Christ in us, but we are also in Christ. As Jesus said in Jn 15:4, "Abide in me, and I in you" (ESV). Paul also understood both sides of this relationship. In Rom 8:1 he said, "there is therefore now no condemnation for those who are *in Christ Jesus*" (NIV, italics mine), and then a few verses later he declares that we are alive because "Christ is in you" (Rom 8:10). Even as our current verse states that Christ is in us, the next verse (28) will also speak of us being in Christ.

How can we explain this mutual indwelling? Adolf Deissmann offered a physical analogy: "Just as the air of life, which we breathe, is 'in' us and fills us, and yet we at the same time live in this air and breathe it," so it is with Christ and us.[87]

One reason Christ dwells within us is to empower us for mission. Paul saw that happening in his own life when he said God "was pleased to reveal his Son in me so that I might preach him among the Gentiles" (Gal 1:16, ESV). The same is true for us. Jesus lives within us so his light can shine through us.

Thank you, Jesus, for drawing near to me, so near as to live within me. Let your presence shine through me in this very dark world.

[27] *to whom God willed to make known what are the riches of the glory of this mystery among the nations, which is, Christ in you, **the hope of glory***

When I was younger, we would occasionally sing a gospel hymn that seemed unbelievably self-entered: "Glory for Me." Each verse talks about the wonders of heaven, ending with the chorus, "O that will be, glory for me, glory for me, glory for me; when by His grace I shall look on His face, that will be glory, be glory for me."

But I doubt the hymn writer was appealing to our selfish desires for the glories of heaven. More likely, I was misinterpreting the lyrics because of how language changes. Today if we say that something would be "glory for me," it means that I will get all the glory and honor because of that thing. But I think the hymn writer was trying to say instead, "For me, that is, from my perspective, that would be a glorious thing." It's not about the singer's glory, but that which the singer recognizes as glorious. And what is this glorious thing? Seeing Jesus face to face.

That's really not much different from what Paul is saying here. The hope of glory is not some kind of personal reward and recognition that we anticipate receiving in heaven, as if we will be treated like a celestial celebrity. No, Jesus is the hope of glory. There's nothing we hope for beyond him, except for an even greater sense of his presence. There is no glory we long for, other than to be more fully in his presence, seeing him face to face.

But it's not merely Christ himself who is the hope of glory, but "Christ in you" and I who is that hope. Jesus has no desire to be by himself or to have us observe him, worship him, or even follow him from a distance. He wants to be so close as to be in us (and we in him). To have Christ in us now is a present reality that brings us joy and sends us on a mission; to have Christ in us even more fully in the future is our hope of glory. This mystery has been revealed in the gospel and will be revealed even more fully when Jesus returns. And so "we rejoice in hope of the glory of God...And hope does not put us to shame, because God's love has been poured into our hearts through the Holy Spirit who has been given to us" (Rom 5:2, 5, ESV).

I do not long, O Lord, for personal glory and recognition. I only want to see the glory of your face. That, for me, will be glory.

[27] to whom God willed to make known what are the riches of the glory of this mystery among the nations, which is, Christ in you, the hope of glory; [28] **whom we declare, warning every person** *and teaching every person in all wisdom, so that we may present every person complete in Christ*

In order to make the mystery known, God raises up believers like Paul to speak the message. In this verse, Paul uses three verbs about speaking, as if to signal that "the time of obscurity and silence has passed," as Pokorný put it;[88] the mystery is now revealed.

The first verb is the word "declare," followed by verbs for "warning" and "teaching." Today, unfortunately, words are not trusted as much as in the past. Advertisers, government propaganda machines, and biased news sources have made us suspicious of anyone who claims to present words of truth. Because of this prevailing suspicion, some Christians believe we should speak less on Christ's behalf, and act more. It's not uncommon to hear Christians today agree with the following quote (wrongly attributed to St. Francis of Assisi): "Preach Christ, and if necessary use words."

Paul, however, would say it's always necessary to use words. As Litfin reminds us "the gospel is inherently verbal."[89] Litfin goes on to say that while nonverbal communication is effective in conveying attitudes, moods, feelings, and relationships, it is inadequate for telling the story of what God has done through Jesus. Although our contemporary world seems to prefer images and deeds over words, yet God accomplishes great things through the power of his Word, for "it pleased God by the foolishness of *preaching* to save them that believe" (1 Cor 1:21, KJV, emphasis mine).

Although Paul prefers to declare the mystery of Christ in a "good news" manner, not everyone greets the good news with the kind of joyful reception it deserves. Many who are committed to their sinful lifestyle regard the good news as a threat. Thus, Paul finds it necessary not only to announce good news, but also to warn people to leave their sin and find hope and reconciliation in Christ. Not everyone likes to be warned, however. Many cringe at the sound of a siren or alarm. It disrupts the tranquility of the day, and it's just plain annoying if it's a false alarm. But if there is a genuine danger, alarms must be sounded anyway, warnings must be given, and we are fools to ignore them. We will see the importance of these warnings in the last part of Colossians 2.

Jesus, if I am going off in the wrong direction, send people to warn me, and give me a heart willing to accept it.

[27] *to whom God willed to make known what are the riches of the glory of this mystery among the nations, which is, Christ in you, the hope of glory; [28] whom we declare, warning every person **and teaching every person in all wisdom,** so that we may present every person complete in Christ*

Teaching is a common ministry throughout the Scriptures. The OT speaks mostly of teaching God's laws (Dt 6:1; Ps 119:12 and more), but also teaching the fear of God (Ps 34:11), the ways of God (Ps 25:4-5, 9; 51:13; Prov 4:11), the will of God (Ps 143:10), and the deeds of God (Ps 71:17).

Teaching was also an important component in Jesus' ministry (Mt 4:23). After his resurrection, he then charged his followers to carry on this ministry to all nations, "teaching them to obey everything that I have commanded you" (Mt 28:20, NRSV). The apostles, including Paul, did this very thing. Paul specifically says that God appointed him as a teacher in 1 Tim 2:7. And the urgency of this teaching ministry seemed to grow as false teachings kept on cropping up like weeds in the early church.

Preaching the good news and teaching about Jesus went hand-in-hand: the apostles "did not cease teaching and preaching that the Christ is Jesus" (Acts 5:42, ESV); and Paul was "proclaiming the kingdom of God and teaching about the Lord Jesus Christ" (Acts 28:31, NRSV). While we should not distinguish them sharply, preaching and teaching are slightly different. The thrust of preaching is a declaration of what God has done in Christ and an appeal for people to put their trust in Jesus. The thrust of teaching involves drawing out what the good news means, so our thoughts and behavior line up with what God has done and is doing. It is not enough for people to believe the gospel; they need to be taught what it means.

Paul always thinks big. He's not content with only teaching a few people. He wants to change the world. His teaching was not just given to a few wise ones who were spiritually mature enough to learn it (as the false teachers often did). Instead, as he emphasizes in this verse, he warns "every" person and teaches "every" person so that "every" person might be complete in Christ. The teaching of Christ is open to one and all. While it's unlikely that Paul is envisioning the salvation of every single person, he doesn't want to write anyone off. Although Jesus gave permission to shake the dust off our feet and move on whenever someone rejects the gospel (see Mt 10:14; Mk 6:11; Lk 9:5), Paul would rather not do that. Instead, he would press on toward the goal of teaching and presenting *all* people in Christ.

Lord, make me a life-long learner. By your Holy Spirit open my mind and my heart to the fullness of truth in your Word.

*[27]...Christ in you, the hope of glory; [28] whom we declare, warning every person and teaching every person in all wisdom, **so that we may present every person complete in Christ***

The goal for Paul's proclamation is not merely to win souls for Christ. Rather, he preaches the good news so that people's lives are transformed by it, and they develop completely into all that God has called them to be. Conversion is only the first step. In this, Paul's goals follow Jesus' goals. Just as Jesus aims to present us as holy and blameless (verse 22), so Paul aims to present people as completely developed in Christ.

The term "complete" is my attempt to translate a word (*teleios*) which is often translated as "perfect" or "mature." Unfortunately, "perfect" conveys ideals of flawlessness in every area of life (including an immaculate home, a pristine lawn, a trophy spouse, model children, a 4.0 grade average, impeccable manners, a tidy social calendar, and overall precision in every detail of life)—most of which have nothing to do with faith or morality, but drive people crazy trying to achieve them. "Mature" is a better translation, especially for NT verses about those who are further along the road of completion than others. But even "mature" might be setting the bar too low, for it may only signify that we are doing better than someone else. What God seeks is complete wholeness. So I'm using the word "complete" to get at its proper sense here.

Teleios comes from the root noun *telos*, which refers to the end, the goal, the final purpose. Something is complete when it reaches its goal and fulfills its purpose. When I once described something as perfect, my son (who was a child at the time) asked, "perfect for what?" He unknowingly was thinking biblically. Biblical perfection is tied to an end-goal, and the goal is being exactly suited to what God intended for our life in Christ.

Unfortunately, we are often content with only putting out a little effort to be better than most. We see no reason to push ourselves if our efforts will only be imperfect anyway.[90] But that's not Jesus' goal. The key, of course, is that Paul wants to present us as completely developed "in Christ." Apart from Christ we cannot be anything like what God wants us to be, no matter how hard we might try to be righteous or effective in accomplishing things for God. Even the spiritual techniques of the Colossian distortionists were useless without Christ. Our complete development can only be found in an ongoing relationship with Jesus.

Lord, I confess that I can be lazy in being all that you call me to be and do. Put me to work that I may complete your calling on my heart.

[27] *...Christ in you, the hope of glory;* [28] *whom we declare, warning every person and teaching every person in all wisdom, so that we may present every person complete in Christ;* [29] **[a goal] for which I toil, striving by means of his energy, which is energizing me with power.**

Paul's goal of presenting all others as complete in Christ is not merely wishful thinking on his part. He toils and strains, with all the power and energy Jesus provides to reach this goal. In the NT the verbs for toiling and striving are mostly found in Paul's letters. Obviously, "Paul does not go about his work half-heartedly, hoping vaguely that grace will fill the gaps which he is too lazy to work at himself."[91] Instead, he works hard in living for Jesus, and he calls on others to do the same (1 Tim 6:12).

Paul's hard work may be a part of the suffering he mentions in verse 24, the very suffering in which he rejoices. This would mean that Paul's difficult labor and efforts were done with a spirit of joy, which brings glory to God, strength to the church, and light to the nations. Paul's attitude is similar to that of Olympic athlete (and future missionary and martyr) Eric Liddell who told his sister that it's not wrong for him to train so much because, "When I run, I can feel [God's] pleasure."[92]

While some may think that Paul works hard *even though* he lives by grace, Paul would more likely say he works hard *because* he lives by grace. He is not putting out all this effort on his own strength, but is relying on the energizing power of Jesus, which is also a gift of grace. As he said in 1 Cor 15:10, "I worked harder than any of them—though it was not I, but the grace of God that is with me" (NRSV). Paul wants nothing to do with a gift of grace that is merely a ticket to heaven or a prize bestowing spiritual bene-fits. He regards grace as God's empowering gift which equips him to endure, to finish, and to keep the faith (2 Tim 4:7). As Caird said, "The *toil* is Paul's, but the *energy* is Christ's."[93]

All eight of the NT references to energy (*energeia*) are in Paul's writ-ings. This word is made from the preposition for "in" and the word for "work." It signifies an in-working, by which God works not only *upon* a per-son, but *from within* that person. God's energy raised Jesus from the dead (Col 2:12) and will raise us from the dead (Phil 3:21). But in the meantime, God's energy equips the body of Christ to do its work (Eph 4:16; Phil 2:13), especially the work of proclaiming the gospel (Eph 3:7).

Jesus, I do grow weary in well-doing. Please grant me your life-giving energy to be what you've called me to be.

The Mystery of God at One Time Was Concealed

to the tune of Schumann: *We Give Thee But Thine Own*
© 2012 David J. Landegent

The mystery of God at one time was concealed,
But now through Christ the nations know the Word which is revealed.

As servants, we proclaim the riches of God's plan,
And though we suffer for its truth, we gladly take a stand.

What is this joyful Word? What is this wondrous hope?
It's "Christ in you, the hope of glory"—let the nations know!

The Lord empowers us in reaching every soul.
Presenting everyone complete in Christ; this is our goal.

Paul's ministry to the Colossians

Colossians 2:1-5

May 8-20

[1] For I want you to know how great a struggle I have over you and those in Laodicea and as many as have not seen my face in the flesh, [2] in order that their hearts would be encouraged, having been drawn together in love and toward all the riches of the full-assurance of understanding, toward the knowledge of the mystery of God, [which is] Christ, [3] in whom all the treasures of wisdom and knowledge are concealed. [4] This I say so that no one may con you with a convincing word. [5] For even if I am absent in the flesh, yet in spirit I am with you, rejoicing and seeing your orderly-formation and the solidarity of your faith in Christ.

Chapter 1 closed with a reference to the difficult work Paul does on behalf of the church in general. Here he continues that theme, but now emphasizing how his struggle is of direct benefit to the churches in Colossae and the surrounding communities. Paul appears to be following a back-and-forth pattern here, as shown in the following chart:

Col 1:15-20	What Christ has done for all creation
Col 1:21-23	What Christ has done *for the Colossians*
Col 1:24-29	What Paul has done for the church
Col 2:1-5	What Paul has done *for the church in Colossae*

After each paragraph in which Paul speaks of a truth more generally, he follows it up with a paragraph that applies it to the Colossians in particular. Jesus is not only the reconciler of the universe, but also the reconciler of the Colossians. Similarly, Paul is not only the servant of the universal church, but also the servant of the church in Colossae. By bringing this to the attention of the Colossians, he shows why he has a right to speak to the issues he will address later in the chapter.

Because Paul makes this rhetorical move, Col 2:1-5 echoes many of the same themes found in Col 1:24-29. Both sections speak of Paul's struggles (1:24, 29; 2:1), Paul's joys (1:24; 2:5), the purpose of Paul's ministry (1:25, 28; 2:2), and his making known the riches of the mystery of God in Christ (1:26-27; 2:2-3).

Like Paul, it's important for all Christians to do better than live our faith in a generic way in a generalized world. The Lord also calls us to bring it home to the specific location where God has placed us, and among the specific people who live there.

Lord, I pray for the community in which I live, and I pray to be a witness in this place and among its people.

156

*¹ For I want you to know how great a struggle I have over you and those
in Laodicea and as many as have not seen my face in the flesh*

Paul wrote the words "I want you to know" about nine times in his letters. It was a common phrase in ancient Greek letter-writing.[94] Here and in 2 Cor 1:8 he wanted his readers to know about his struggles. While some leaders may want to hide their difficulties (as was true of the false teachers spoken of in 2 Cor 11-13), Paul wants instead for the churches to know that he's a *suffering* apostle, for his sufferings demonstrate that he is true to the gospel of the cross and is not using ministry as a means for personal gain.

Paul does all this, not only for the church at large, but even for churches he has never visited, like Colossae and the nearby cities of Laodicea and Hieropolis. These three cities formed a triangle, with Colossae in the southeast corner, Laodicea lying twelve miles west of Colossae, and Hierapolis six miles north of Laodicea They were located along the Lycus River, east of the coastal city of Ephesus, with Laodicea and Colossae on the south bank and Hierapolis on the north. Hierapolis is mentioned only in Col 4:13. Laodicea, however, is mentioned four times in Colossians (Col 2:1; 4:13, 15-16), as well as being on the receiving end of a stern message from Jesus in Rev 3:14-22. Known for banking, textiles, and a medical school, Laodicea lay along a major road and was more prosperous than Colossae.

So how did churches form in these communities? The best guess is that someone from the area (likely Epaphras) had heard Paul preach while visiting in Ephesus, became a Christian, and brought the gospel back to the Lycus Valley. Paul may not have been the *father* of these churches, but he could be regarded as their *grandfather* in the faith. Although it was not possible for him to visit all the churches that could somehow be traced back to his mission work, he definitely felt a responsibility for them all.

By praying and struggling for believers he had not met, Paul is following in Jesus' footsteps, for Jesus was also aware of people who would later believe in him, even though he never met them face-to-face during his earthly ministry. They would believe because they had heard the gospel message through others. As Jesus prayed in Jn 17:20, "My prayer is not for them alone. I pray also for those who will believe in me through their message" (NIV). It's amazing to realize that our current actions for Christ may impact people that we will never meet.

*Father, thank you for touching my life through people I have never met. I pray
that I would have a similar impact on the lives of others across the planet and
through the upcoming generations.*

*¹ For I want you to know how great a struggle I have over you and those in Laodicea and as many as have not seen my face in the flesh, ² **in order that their hearts would be encouraged***

Some people assume Paul's letter was mostly written in opposition to the Colossian distortion. While that issue does dominate the last part of chapter 2, Paul had a lot more things to say than what *not* to believe. Rather, as he says here, one of his main purposes is to encourage these new believers.

The word translated as "encouraged" is a difficult-to-translate word for calling someone else to act or think differently. In its active form, it is translated with more insistent words (like plead, implore, or urge). In its passive form (as here) it is translated with less-insistent words (like encourage, comfort, and console).

Hearts can easily get discouraged, especially when the initial enthusiasm of new life in Christ fades, and one has to deal with church conflicts, harassment from outsiders, the lure of returning to one's previous lifestyle of sin, or the sense of isolation felt by small churches in small communities. In such situations, one often needs encouragement to press on.

Encouragement comes in many ways in this letter. It is encouraging:

- to know someone is praying for you (Col 1:1-3, 9-12; 4:18).
- to be told you are doing well in living out your faith (Col 1:4-6; 2:7).
- to be reminded of all God has already done for you in Christ (Col 1:13-14, 21-22; 2:11-15).
- to realize afresh that the Lord you trust has power over all things (Col 1:15-20; 2:9-10, 15).
- to know you can face your own difficulties because the Lord has helped others face theirs (Col 1:24-27; 2:1-2; 4:7-9).
- to hear again the great things God has planned for your future (Col 1:27-29; 3:4).
- to be told that those who think your faith is deficient are wrong and that you already have all you need in Christ (Col 2:16-3:3).
- to know you do not have to guess how to live in a God-pleasing way, for the Lord has already told you (Col 3:5-4:1)
- to hear again of the great love God has for you right now (3:12).
- to appreciate the fact that you're not alone in this world, but are surrounded by other supportive Christians (Col 3:9-17; 4:10-17).

Thank you, Lord, for the many ways you have encouraged me. Give me opportunities even today to offer encouragement to others.

¹ For I want you to know how great a struggle I have over you... ² *in order that their hearts would be encouraged,* **having been drawn together in love** *and toward all the riches of the full-assurance of understanding, toward the knowledge of the mystery of God, [which is] Christ*

Paul wants us to be encouraged, but not just in a generic way. He specifies two forms of encouragement in this verse, the first of which is being drawn together in love. Individual encouragement is fine, but what Paul is aiming for is for the whole to church to be encouraged together by mutual love.[95]

The word translated as "drawn together" refers either to drawing together a line of thought or drawing together in unity as a church (see later in Col 2:19 and Eph 4:16).

Here Paul uses his favorite word for love (*agape*), found 75 times in his letters. He also uses the corresponding verb for love 34 times and the adjective for beloved 27 times. These three related words speak of the many relationships of love in Paul's letters (I will only list one Scripture reference for each):

- God the Father's love for Christ (Col 1:13)
- God's love for people (Rom 5:8)
- Christ's love for his church (Eph 5:2)
- Our love for God (Eph 6:24)
- Our love for others (Col 3:14; including spouses, Col 3:19)
- Paul's love for churches and co-workers (Phil 4:1)
- The love of Christians for Paul (Philemon 7)

In our current verse, it is not obvious whether it's God's love for the Colossians or the Colossians' love for one another that will bring encouragement. The latter is more likely, but it's always helpful to remember that we can only love one another because we have first been loved by God (1 Jn 4:19). Paul knows this same truth, for in Eph 5:2 he says, "walk in love, as Christ loved us" (ESV).

Encouraging one another in love is very important, because it's the lack of love in a church which discourages Christians more than anything else. If a Christian experiences love in their church, they can face all kinds of other difficulties in life (illness, persecution, financial problems, and family issues). But when love is in short supply at church, discouragement sets in quickly.

I pray, gracious Lord, that the fire of love would burn so brightly in my church that it would bring encouragement to anyone going through a dark time.

*¹ For I want you to know how great a struggle I have over you... ² in order that their hearts would be encouraged, having been drawn together in love **and toward all the riches of the full-assurance of understanding**, toward the knowledge of the mystery of God, [which is] Christ*

Not only does *love* bring encouragement to the people of God, but *understanding* does as well. When we better understand God, God's plan of salvation, God's way of righteousness, and God's purposes for suffering, we are better equipped and encouraged to walk by faith. Those believers who have little interest in understanding God, but prefer to rely on feelings of intimacy with God or zeal for God instead, will be more likely to succumb to discouragement when the feelings fade.

Love and understanding do not function separately in this work of encouragement. According to Walsh and Keesmaat, when God's love is at work in the life of the church, then the truth proclaimed there becomes even more sure in our minds.[96] On the other hand, if a Christian experiences a profound lack of love in the church, no one should be surprised if that believer begins to wonder about the truthfulness of the gospel. Those who leave the Christian faith mostly do so because of the "internal dissension and lack of compassion they experience in the Christian community," not because of intellectual issues.[97]

But just as love helps understanding to become fully assured, so understanding in turn helps love to find stability, especially in the face of false teaching. In verses 2-3 Paul focuses on words related to the life of the mind (understanding, knowledge, wisdom) because thinking has an important role to play in faith. Paul, of course, is not talking about mental processes which operate on their own in coming to understand God. It's not by our self-generated intellectual capabilities that we can think true thoughts of God. Rather, we can only think rightly of God because God first revealed himself to us. Lining up our thoughts with what God has revealed is a key factor in remaining in the faith (Col 1:23) and becoming complete in Christ (Col 1:28).

This kind of understanding is a thing of great value. The OT says that wisdom and understanding are more valuable than gold or silver (Job 28:17-18; Prov 3:13-14; 8:10-11; 16:16). Paul would agree. Possessions and money quickly depart, but true understanding brings eternal wealth.

Encourage me, Lord, with an understanding heart, a heart that is open to all your truth, and a heart that is closed to every lie.

*¹ For I want you to know how great a struggle I have over you... ² in order that their hearts would be encouraged, having been drawn together in love **and toward all the riches of the full-assurance of understanding**, toward the knowledge of the mystery of God, [which is] Christ*

It's not just understanding which encourages believers; it's the "full-assurance" of understanding. Notice again how fullness is an important theme in Colossians. The word for "full-assurance" is used only three other times in the NT. Heb 6:11 speaks about having the full-assurance of hope until the end, and Heb 10:22 calls us to "approach [God] with a true heart in full assurance of faith" (NIV). According to 1 Thess 1:5, the gospel came to the Thessalonians "not only in word, but also in power and in the Holy Spirit and with full conviction [or assurance]" (ESV).

While the Colossian distortionists may be telling believers that they are missing something—which is a discouraging thought—Paul wants them to understand the fullness that is already theirs, a full-assurance of understanding. The one who is only partially-convinced is all the more likely to doubt, that is, to be double-minded about the truth. Living in doubt is always discouraging, for bad circumstances can then call one's beliefs into question. Living in full-assurance, however, means that no matter what circumstances arise, the rock-solid foundation of faith stands firm. A fully-convinced Christian can withstand any storm.

In today's world, full-assurance or certainty has a bad reputation, for many regard it as a sign of arrogance. This may be true of some forms of certainty, but not all. A certainty shaped by Scripture is a certainty of faith, hope, and love.

- The *certainty of faith* counts on God to be faithful to his promises and avoids an ideological certitude of merely believing right ideas. It's a relational certainty.
- The *certainty of hope* continues to press on toward a growing sense of conviction, rather than an arrogant certitude of thinking we have already arrived at full knowledge. It's a certainty that lives and grows instead of fossilizing behind fortress walls.
- The *certainty of love* humbly carries saving truth to others in need, unlike an intolerant certitude that aims solely at defeating those who are wrong, or a wishy-washy mentality that has no hope to offer.[98]

Encouragement thrives when certainty is based on faith, hope, and love.

Lord Jesus, I do not want to be assured that my opinions are right; I only want to be assured that you are faithful and I can rely on you.

*¹ For I want you to know how great a struggle I have over you... ² in order that their hearts would be encouraged, having been drawn together in love and toward all the riches of the full-assurance of understanding, **toward the knowledge of the mystery of God, [which is] Christ***

What Paul wants the Colossians to know (and be assured of) is the mystery (*mustērion*) of God, which he spoke of earlier (Col 1:27). In our day, we talk about *living out* the mystery or *sensing* the mystery, with the implication that mysteries should remain unknown and be appreciated as such. For Paul, however, mysteries are meant to be known—not *fully* known because of the limitations of our minds—but still known to some degree. It's only in *knowing* the mystery of God that hearts can be encouraged. Discouragement happens when the mysteries of God unfold and we are clueless about them.

Thankfully, the mystery of God has been made known. Of the twenty-eight appearances of *mustērion* in the NT, all but two of them refer to the fact that the mystery has been made known—at least to those with ears to hear. Jesus said, "It is given unto you to know the mysteries of the kingdom of heaven" (Mt 13:11, KJV). Because God has revealed it (Col 1:26-27) and entrusted it to Paul and others (1 Cor 4:1), Paul makes the mystery known in his preaching (Col 4:3). In 1 Tim 3:16, Paul tells us that the mystery of God is great and then explains it as the message of the gospel.

This mystery is not some difficult-to-understand teaching or hard-to-remember ritual, but a person, as the last word of our phrase says. We come to know the mystery of God not by exercising our brains or disciplining our minds, but simply in knowing the person of Jesus Christ. According to N. T. Wright, "Everything we might want to ask about God and his purposes can and must now be answered...with reference to the crucified and risen Jesus, the Messiah."[99] Karl Barth said that neither the ethics, the healings, the end-times teachings, the love for God and neighbor, nor the resurrection "has any value, inner importance, or abstract significance of its own in the New Testament apart from Jesus Christ being the Subject of it all."[100]

Whereas the distortionists had been promoting a knowledge that supposedly moved beyond Christ, Paul says there is no such thing. To move beyond Christ is to move away from him, and to move away from him is to move toward ignorance, not knowledge. Without Christ, we end up with mysteries that leave us in the dark and lure us into deeper darkness. Only as we grow in our knowledge of Jesus do we find true knowledge at all.

Other mysteries sometimes intrigue me, Lord, but lead me away from any dead-end streets to know the mystery of you.

> [2] *...toward the knowledge of the mystery of God, [which is] Christ,* [3] *in* **whom all the treasures of wisdom and knowledge are concealed.**

Isaiah 11:2 described the Messiah as one on whom rests the Spirit of wisdom, understanding, and knowledge. Paul agrees and goes one step further by stating that "all" the treasures of wisdom and knowledge are in Christ, with the strong implication that outside of him there is no true knowledge. When other theories, ideas, doctrines, and philosophies pull us away from Christ, they are also pulling us away from truth.

Something in us wants to protest against Paul's use of the word "all" in this verse. We can easily imagine that all *spiritual* truth is found in Christ— although some even have difficulty with that. But in what sense is "all" knowledge found in Christ, even concerning math, cooking, basketball, or nanotechnology?

We find an answer in the Colossian laudation. Since Jesus is the one in whom all things were created and stand together (Col 1:16-17), then on some level the knowledge of all things traces back to him. While it's certainly possible for non-Christians to have encyclopedic knowledge and to earn advanced degrees in all kinds of fields, without Jesus they are still missing the key component in their understanding of reality. When they do not see Jesus as the one who holds all this together, they cannot see how all knowledge is meant for giving glory to God and serving the purposes of God. The reality of all things (and the knowledge of that reality) flows from Jesus, through Jesus, and toward Jesus, and it is this connection to Christ which fills knowledge with gratitude, love, service, and hope. Just as Jesus alone can unseal the scroll of destiny in Revelation 5, so Jesus alone has the key to all knowledge.[101]

Perhaps today we could word it this way: all truth is relative...to Christ. The world likes to say that all truth is relative, period, which is an easy (and false) way to dismiss the claims of truth upon the soul. For Christians, however, every aspect of truth is relative to Jesus. All truth relates to him, is in relationship with him, flows from him and toward him, and comes under his gravitational pull.

Lord Jesus, show me again how the knowledge I have gained from my workplace and my hobbies is all related to your purposes for this world and for my life.

> [2] *...toward the knowledge of the mystery of God, [which is] Christ,* [3] *in* **whom all the treasures of wisdom and knowledge are concealed.**

According to Paul, the wisdom and knowledge connected to Christ are a "treasure." This is in line with the OT call to search for wisdom like a hidden treasure (Prov 2:4), for wisdom is better than all the treasures of gold and silver (Prov 3:14). In fact, the Greek translation of Prov 2:1-8 refers to wisdom, understanding, treasure, and knowledge—just like our current text. The difference is that in Proverbs we are told to *hide* God's truth within, while Paul declares that God's wisdom is *already hidden*—in Christ.

Jesus said that each of us already possesses internal treasures, and through our daily conduct we are all in the process of bringing these treasures (good and bad) into the open for others to see (Mt 12:35). Colossians 2:3 builds on this idea, declaring that Jesus also has internal treasures to bring out, for in him are hidden all the treasures of wisdom and knowledge. Jesus does not hoard these treasures, but puts them on display in order to draw people to God.

We might expect Paul to say that all the treasures of knowledge and wisdom are *contained* or *revealed* in Christ, but instead he tells us that they are *concealed* or *hidden* in him. This should not alarm us, for Jesus said in Mk 4:22, "Whatever is hidden is meant to be disclosed, and whatever is concealed is meant to be brought out into the open" (NIV). Treasures of wisdom, then, are not concealed in Christ so that they can stay hidden from view, but so that they can be seen. As the apocryphal book *First Enoch* 46:3 said, "the Son of Man...will open all the hidden storerooms." This happens whenever the gospel is preached, as Jesus affirmed in Mt 13:52.

One positive aspect of saying that the treasures of knowledge are "concealed" in Christ is that this reinforces the link between Christ and the treasured knowledge, so that you cannot have one without the other. To paraphrase Schweizer, the knowledge we seek cannot be carted off like goods bought in the marketplace, but can only be found in an ongoing interaction with the living Christ. The treasure chest of Christ is already unlocked—it has been opened by God—and yet the treasures remain inside and are only of value if left in that chest. Apart from Christ, the treasures of knowledge and wisdom lose their value; but in the treasure chest of Christ, they provide the full riches of salvation.[102]

> *I confess, Lord, that it's tempting to focus on the gifts and not the giver, to focus on the wisdom and not on you in whom such treasured wisdom lies. Forgive me.*

*[2] ...toward the knowledge of the mystery of God, [which is] Christ, [3] in whom all the treasures of wisdom and knowledge are concealed. [4] **This I say so that no one may con you with a convincing word.***

For the first time in Colossians, Paul explicitly mentions the threat of false teaching. Because Christ is the treasure chest containing all the riches of knowledge, Paul warns against others who falsely claim to speak the truth.

The problem of deceptive false teachers appears in all of Paul's letters except his brief note to Philemon. He obviously regarded deception as a major threat to the faith of Christians, particularly for new believers who were unfamiliar with the ways of God in the OT. They were very vulnerable to deceivers who could speak all the correct words—Spirit, Christ, grace, righteousness, etc.—but combine them in ways that would lead people away from Christ. Those who think that false teaching is no longer a problem today are themselves deceived. While there may be many different angles from which to perceive God's truth, not all perspectives ring true.

Paul uses a word-play in Greek to make his point, which I've tried to replicate with the words con and con-vincing. Or maybe we could talk about those who trick with rhetoric. In the Greek word-play both words contain the root stem for "word" (*log-*). The term he uses here for deception (*paralogizomai*) likely refers to a spoken word (*logos*) that parallels (*para-*) the truth, but is not itself the truth. It comes alongside the truth; it accompanies the truth; it appears to be a companion of the truth—at least at the moment—but in the end these words move us along a different path.

The importance of using words rightly is also highlighted by the term translated as "convincing word" (*pithanologia*). NT writers often put prefixes in front of *logia* to indicate that words are not just words but reveal the character or purpose of the person who uses them, such as smooth-words, good-words, fitting-words, foolish-words, filthy-words, and mean-ingless-words. Just because preachers are rhetorically effective does not mean they speak the truth. Listeners may be so charmed that they fail to notice that the beautiful arrangement of words is nothing but a gold ring in a pig's snout (see Prov 11:22). This is why clear thinking is important for Christians, especially in watching how words are defined and deployed. While some people criticize biblical controversies as nothing but warring over words, Paul knows that truth is only conveyed when words line up with the reality found in Christ.

Lord, I do not want to be paranoid, but I do want to be on guard against those who misuse words to lead me away from you. Open my eyes to their lies.

*⁴ This I say so that no one may con you with a convincing word. ⁵ **For even if I am absent in the flesh, yet in spirit I am with you,** rejoicing and seeing your orderly-formation and the solidarity of your faith in Christ.*

As a caring Christian leader, Paul felt responsible, not only for the churches and believers who had come to the Lord *directly* through his ministry, but even for those who had come *indirectly*—as was true of the Colossians. It was important to him to maintain contact with these churches through letters, co-workers and personal visits. According to Koskenniemmi, private letters in antiquity had three main purposes: to express a friendly relationship, to continue an ongoing dialogue, and to serve as a way for the sender to be present.[103] In Col 2:5 Paul is focusing on this last purpose.

Since it is impossible to be everywhere at once, Paul is keenly aware of not being physically present with these believers. He longs to see them and makes plans to do so. Every one of his church letters refers in some way to his absence.

In spite of his absence in the flesh, however, Paul does remind the Colossians that he is present with them "in spirit." He made a similar point in the church discipline case of 1 Cor 5:3-5, when he claimed to be present in spirit to pass judgment on the wrongdoer. Here in Colossians, however, Paul is not dealing with a disciplinary case, but he *is* present in spirit to bear witness against the Colossian distortion, and also to assess the spiritual health of the church as it stands against that teaching.

It's hard to know what Paul means by being present in spirit. It's not likely he is thinking about his spirit leaving his body and supernaturally traveling to another location (although he is open to such a possibility when describing his vision of the third heaven in 2 Cor 12:2-4). More likely, Paul believes that because he and the churches are all part of the body of Christ, then they are all linked together by one Spirit who is present throughout the body. By that Spirit, Paul's own spirit is joined together with the other believers in fellowship.

In this way Paul's absent-presence echoes the absent-presence of Jesus in the church. When we gather for worship, Jesus also is absent in the flesh. But the good news is that he is present by the Spirit.

Lord Jesus, sometimes it feels as if you are absent when we gather for worship. We wish you could be here in the flesh. But remind us again that you are truly present no matter what our feelings are telling us.

> *⁴ This I say so that no one may con you with a convincing word. ⁵ For even if I am absent in the flesh, yet in spirit I am with you, **rejoicing and seeing your orderly-formation and the solidarity of your faith in Christ.***

Paul may be concerned about the distorted ideas floating around Colossae, but he is convinced that these lies have not (yet) infiltrated the church too much. Instead he is rejoicing over the good reports about the spiritual condition of the church.

Paul uses two words to describe their faith, both of which may have a military flavor. First, he rejoices in the "orderly-formation" of their faith. He used this same word in 1 Cor 14:40, to say that "all things should be done decently and in order" (NRSV). But here Paul is not talking about orderly worship, but being in an orderly formation, so that they will not succumb to an ambush or frontal attack from false teachers or persecutors.

Secondly, Paul rejoices to see the "solidarity" of the Colossians' faith. Their trust in Christ is not flimsy or fragile, but stands strong and firm, grounded in the truth. Peter uses this same word to command believers to stand *firm* in the faith by resisting the devil (1 Pet 5:9). Hebrews 5:11 and 14 refer to deeper truths as *solid* food. Paul himself warns against wandering from the truth, but instead remaining on God's *solid* foundation (2 Tim 2:18-19). That this same word was used for the ancient military method of forming a solid mass of soldiers who move forward in battle together would fit the Colossian situation even more.[104] Perhaps Paul is acting like a general reviewing the formation of his troops and is satisfied that they will not collapse in the face of an enemy attack.[105]

Many today are wary of using warfare imagery to describe faith, because some Christians with a holy war mentality have resorted to violence in attacking the beliefs of others. Although such wariness is understandable, we cannot avoid the fact that false teachings are an attack upon God's people, and that we must stand together in an orderly way. It simply will not do for our faith to collapse because our beliefs were just a chaotic hodge-podge of ideas we happened to pick up along the way, instead of a well-ordered set of beliefs. Nor will it do if our faith collapses because we do not support each other in the solidarity of truth, but instead break rank when under attack, running in many directions and scurrying for cover. Paul believes the Colossians are ready to face opposition. Are we?

Lord, strengthen your church, that we might stand together in your truth. Send us forth with love for those who oppose you and a firm grip on your Word.

Strengthen our Hearts, Lord
to the tune of Open Our Eyes: *Open Our Eyes, Lord*
© 2012 David J. Landegent

Strengthen our hearts, Lord, that they'd be encouraged
By love drawn together with blessed assurance.
Knowing the riches of full understanding
Strengthen our hearts, Lord, that they'd be encouraged.

Open our eyes to—the myst'ry of Jesus
In Him are all treasures of knowledge and wisdom.
Guard us from lies, Lord, that faith would be grounded.
Open our eyes to—the myst'ry of Jesus

A command and a warning

Colossians 2:6-8

May 21-June 8

[6] As you therefore have received the Christ—Jesus the Lord—walk in him, [7] having been rooted and being built up in him, and being established in the faith just as you were taught, overflowing in thanksgiving. [8] Watch out that no one will be captivating you through philosophy and empty deceit which are according to human tradition, according to the elemental-orders of the world, and not according to Christ;

We've reached a turning point in Colossians. So far, Paul has stated what God has been doing through Christ, what the Colossians have experienced, and what Paul himself has been doing. But one thing has been absent: Paul has not issued a single command. Here he issues two commands: walk in Christ (verse 6) and don't be captivated by false teaching (verse 8).

Of course, giving commands is not the only way to shape the character and actions of others. Paul also uses other methods to do this. For instance, by describing the Colossians as holy ones (Col 1:2) and complimenting them (Col 1:3-8), he gives them a reputation to live up to. Paul also shapes the Colossians by telling them of his hopes and goals for how they will progress in the faith (Col 1:9-12, 28), as well as Jesus' goals for them (Col 1:21-22). The hint that God's good future for the Colossians could be jeopardized if they stray from God's path (see Col 1:23) also has the power to shape character and actions. Finally, when they read of how Paul suffers for them (Col 1:24-2:3), the Colossians will be motivated to follow suit.

But in spite of these other methods, there is still great power in a direct command to shape the character and actions of others. Some may be surprised that it takes Paul this long to give a command, but Paul typically places most of his commands in the second half of his letters. He's not a lawgiver, but a preacher of the gospel. He first wants to establish what God has done for us in Christ, before talking about what we are called to do in response. It is always *God's* actions which take priority. If Paul were to focus instead on *human* actions, we would soon be trapped in the quicksand of moralism, instead of being lifted to the heights of the gospel. The character and actions of Christians can only be an echoing response to the character and actions of God.

The positive command (verses 6-7) and the negative command (verse 8) here will be followed up in the rest of chapter 2 by an extended positive description of what it means to be in and with Christ (Col 2:9-15) and then a negative evaluation of the Colossian distortion (Col 2:16-23).

I thank you, Lord Jesus, for the gift of your commandments. They provide light when I'm walking on a dark path.

⁶ As you therefore have received the Christ—Jesus the Lord—walk in him,
⁷ having been rooted and being built up in him, and being established in the
faith just as you were taught, overflowing in thanksgiving.

Through Christ, God had done much for the Colossians. They, in turn, were not indifferent or unresponsive to Christ. Rather, they "received" him.

North American evangelicals commonly talk about receiving Christ. For those who use this phrase, it's an image of hospitality often associated with the promise of Rev 3:20 about opening a door to Jesus when he knocks on it. Just as a host receives guests, so we open the door and receive Christ into our hearts. There is nothing wrong with this image, but it's not what Paul means here in Col 2:6. If Paul had been referring to the hospitality kind of receiving he would have used a different Greek verb. But the verb here (*paralambanō*) is mostly used by Paul—and rabbis of his day—to refer to "receiving" a teaching or tradition that has been handed down.

The process is similar to passing a baton in a relay race. The first person "passes along" the baton or tradition and the next person "receives" it, only to pass it along to another. The Greek word for *passing it along* is *para-didōmi* (related to the noun *paradosis*, meaning "tradition"), and the word for *receiving* what was passed along is the word used here, *paralambanō*. Elsewhere Paul uses both verbs to describe the complete process: "For I *handed on* to you as of first importance what I in turn had *received*" (1 Cor 15:3, NRSV; see also 1 Cor 11:23). Paul wants believers to continue to believe and practice what they had received from him through his preaching (see 1 Cor 15:1; Gal 1:9; Phil 4:9; 1 Thess 2:13; 4:1; 2 Thess 3:6).

That Paul uses the word "receive" in this sense of "receiving a tradition" is also underlined by two other factors. First, receiving Christ as a kind of tradition will soon be contrasted with those who follow "human traditions" (Col 2:8). Second, since the Hebrew language did not have a word for "tradition," they spoke instead of walking in the way of one's fathers (see 1 Kings 22:43). That's why the Pharisees used the wording they did in their question, "Why do your disciples not *walk* according to the *tradition* of the elders?" (Mk 7:5, ESV; see also 1 Thess 4:1 and 2 Thess 3:6). The ideas of receiving, walking, and tradition all fit together for Paul and for other biblical writers.

Thank you, God, for the generations of believers who have gone before me, so that I could receive the faith they passed along.

> [6] **As you therefore have received the Christ—Jesus the Lord**—*walk in him,* [7] *having been rooted and being built up in him, and being established in the faith just as you were taught, overflowing in thanksgiving.*

Even though Paul uses language about tradition when talking about "receiving," he says it in a way that puts a whole new spin on things. Most traditions are about receiving a body of teachings and practices, but in Col 2:6, we are not receiving some *thing* or *idea*, but a *person*. Paul does not say, "as you have received a tradition about the Christ—Jesus the Lord—so walk in *it.*" Rather we have received Christ and are to walk in *him.* Instead of receiving traditions *about Jesus*, we are receiving Jesus himself as the tradition. And he is a tradition unlike any other tradition that has ever been received.

While some might talk about a "living tradition," meaning that it still has a strong meaning for those who received it, Jesus is even more literally a "living tradition," for he is alive and active in our world. Jesus does not simply pass along the tradition; he *is* the Tradition. Jesus does not only point out the traditional ways of the ancestors; he *is* the Way. Jesus does not only reveal traditional mysteries; he *is* the Mystery of God. Jesus does not only teach traditional wisdom; he *is* the Wisdom of God.

Traditions are often reduced to words, but Jesus himself *is* the Word. Traditions often point to something old, but Jesus makes all things new. Traditions are often followed in an unthinking way and imposed on people, but Jesus sets our minds free to love him. Traditions follow old paths and often settle down in quiet towns called Custom and Habit, but Jesus blazes new trails as we cross the frontier into the kingdom.

Not everyone, of course, receives. Some refuse to do so, for as Jn 1:11 states, "He came to his own, and his own people did not *receive* him" (ESV, emphasis mine to point out that the same Greek word is used here). But the Colossians had received Jesus and their lives were forever changed.

Notice Paul's wording here. They "received Christ—Jesus the Lord." Some translations say they "received Christ Jesus *as* Lord" (NIV, emphasis mine). This is possible, but it gives the impression they could also receive him as something other than Lord, which is impossible. If we have not received the *Lord* Jesus, we have not received Jesus at all.

I thank you, Lord, for not merely passing along traditional doctrines to me, but for giving me your very self.

⁶ *As you therefore have received the Christ—Jesus the Lord—**walk in him**, ⁷ having been rooted and being built up in him, and being established in the faith just as you were taught, overflowing in thanksgiving.*

Here is the first actual command given by Paul in this letter: a call to walk in Christ. What Paul commands in verses 6-7 actually echoes what he prayed for in Col 1:10-12. In both places, Paul uses the word for "walk" followed by four participles (verbs that in English end with -ing) to explain what that walk looks like.[106]

Paul's prayer in Col 1:10-12	Paul's command in Col 2:6-7
to walk worthily (1:10)	walk in Christ (2:6)
fruit-bearing (1:10)	having been rooted (2:7)
growing (1:10)	being built up (2:7)
being empowered (1:11)	being established (2:7)
thanking the Father (1:12)	overflowing in thanksgiving (2:7)

Both prayer and command work together. Paul does not pray and simply wait for God to stir others into action; he commands what he prays for. But neither does Paul command without praying for God to enable the people "to will and to work for his good purpose" (Phil 2:13, NRSV). In this case, he commands us to walk in Christ.

But what does that mean? Recall from two days earlier that the Hebrew language does not have a word for "tradition," but instead talks about walking in the way of one's forefathers. That perspective fits here. To receive the Living Tradition named Jesus means walking in him. Because Christ is alive, he is always on the move, and thus, those who receive him must keep in step with him.

Some may receive Christ and then stop moving, figuring that it is sufficient to "have" him in one's possession. Others may receive Christ and then chase off in other directions. Paul would have none of this, for the only way to reach our destination in our journey of faith is by continuing to walk with Jesus—and not only walk *with* him, but also *in* him. This odd phrase means that as we walk with Jesus, we come to realize that he's not just a walking partner, but he is also the very road we walk on or in. He is the Way (Jn 14:6). We walk *in* him.

Mighty Lord, I do not have what it takes to walk in you, and that's why I'm praying for you to empower me to obey this command and keep in step with you.

> [6] *As you therefore have received the Christ—Jesus the Lord—**walk in him,** [7]*
> *having been rooted and being built up in him, and being established in the*
> *faith just as you were taught, overflowing in thanksgiving.*

Although we might think that the commands of the Bible all focus on morality (like "do not steal"), a surprising number of commands, like the one in verse 6, are more about maintaining and improving the quality of our relationship with the Lord. Perhaps we could think of the latter as faith-commands, and the former as moral-commands. Some examples of faith-commands would be "Put on the Lord Jesus" (Rom 13:14, NRSV), "Be filled with the Spirit" (Eph 5:18, KJV), and "Stand firm in the Lord" (Phil 4:1, NIV). There are many more. Through a faith-command like "walk in Christ," we hear the call for our relationship with Jesus to be ongoing and growing.

Faith-commands and moral-commands belong together, of course. It's not an option to choose which set to obey and which to ignore. When we obey the *faith*-commands and so grow in our relationship with God, then we are thereby empowered to obey the moral-commands. And when we obey the *moral*-commands, we are thereby strengthening our faith-relationship with God. Though they go together, the distinction is important, for the moral-commands alone often lure people into a kind of moralism that overlooks their relationship with God. And faith-commands alone can result in a touchy-feely religion that has no moral backbone.

When Paul calls us to walk in the Lord, he is following an OT reality. In the OT we find a number of references to God walking before *us* or with *us* (see Lev 26:12). And there are also *commands* for God's people to walk with *him* (Micah 6:8). A few OT people were able to do this (like Enoch and Noah), but most ended up going after other gods (who cannot move at all) and walking in the ways of the nations around them (see 2 Kgs 17:8).

Notably, the OT does not speak of walking in God, but only with him, or in his ways or in his name. But Christians not only walk *with* the Lord, but *in* the Lord. And because of that they receive power to stay on the right path. And what a path it is! Walking in Christ means walking in newness of life (Rom 6:4), walking according to the Spirit (Gal 5:16), walking by faith and not sight (2 Cor 5:7), walking in love (Eph 5:2), walking in the light (Eph 5:8), walking in wisdom (Eph 5:15), walking in a God-pleasing way (1 Thess 4:1), walking in manner worthy of God (1 Thess 2:12), and more.

Sometimes, Lord, it's easier to obey your moral-commands than your faith-commands, to do the right thing but not be right with you. I don't want that to be the case in the future. I want to walk in you.

⁶ As you therefore have received the Christ—Jesus the Lord—walk in him, ⁷
having been rooted and being built up in him, *and being established in the*
faith just as you were taught, overflowing in thanksgiving.

Paul has just commanded the Colossians to "walk" in Christ, which conveys
the idea of movement. But this movement is not aimless wandering or
unstable staggering. Rather, it is a movement that is "rooted" in Christ (an
agricultural image) and "built up" in Christ (an architectural image), much
in the same way that Jeremiah was called to build and to plant (Jer 1:9-10).
This mixing of word pictures conveys well that God's church is in motion
(walk), alive in an organic way (rooted) and stable and solid (built up).

The idea of being rooted is found in this verse and also Eph 3:17. In
Ephesians Paul says we are rooted *in love*, while here he states that we are
rooted *in Jesus* himself. This imagery fits with Jn 15:1-6—Jesus is the vine
and we are the branches that abide in him because we are rooted in him.
Branches of the vine may indeed move along the ground for a great
distance, full of life and growth, but this is only possible because they
remain connected to the root. If we are cut off from the root, we will not
only be fruitless, but we will wither away and die. In this way Paul reminds
the Colossians that their journey of faith may take them in many directions,
but only as they remain rooted in Jesus.

But we are not only *rooted* in Christ, indicating a downward direction of
going deeply into him; we are also being *built up* in him. The tense of the
verb emphasizes that we are still "under construction and not yet a finished
product,"[107] and the passive form of the verb means we are not building
ourselves up, but it is the Lord who is doing this. He is the primary contrac-
tor of the church, which is good because "unless the Lord builds the house,
those who build it labor in vain" (Ps 127:1, NRSV).

Paul elaborates on God's construction project in Ephesians: the church
is built on the foundation of Christ, "*in whom* the whole structure...grows
into a holy temple in the Lord" and "*in him* you also are being built together
into a dwelling place for God by the Spirit (Eph 2:21-22, ESV; italics mine).
Against the judgment of the world's builders, the church gladly acknowledges Christ as its only cornerstone (1 Pet 2:7), and he builds up the church
through love (1 Cor 8:1), encouragement (1 Thess 5:11), and the word of
God's grace (Acts 20:32).

Lord Jesus, deepen your church so that we take root in the good soil of your
word, and build up your church to be a holy temple of praise.

> [6] *As you therefore have received the Christ—Jesus the Lord—walk in him,* [7]
> *having been rooted and being built up in him,* **and being established in the**
> **faith just as you were taught***, overflowing in thanksgiving.*

Rooted...built up...and established (*bebaioō*) in the faith — that's what the
Lord seeks to have happen in his church. In the NT when *bebaioō* is applied
to people, they are said to be established in a way that strengthens, sustains
or supports them. According to Heb 13:9, our hearts are established by
grace, not by ceremonial foods. In 2 Cor 1:21, it is God who establishes Paul
and his readers in Christ. According to 1 Cor 1:8, Christ will keep us established (often translated as strong) to the very end. We find the same idea
here about being established in faith.

Paul has already used the word for faith (*pistis*) three times in Colossians (1:4, 23; 2:5) and will do so once more (2:12). These verses together
show that faith is not something limp, wishy-washy, unstable, or spineless.
Instead, faith is "foundationed and settled, and not moving" (Col 1:23), firm
in "solidarity" (Col 2:5), and "established" (Col 2:7). This is important for
Paul to emphasize, because distorted teaching threatens to undermine
people's foundational beliefs, unsettle their minds, move them away from
the truth, weaken their resolve, and break down what they once regarded
as firm. The truth itself cannot be shaken in this way, but a person's faith
that holds to this truth might be. Paul does not think this has happened to
the Colossians, for he knows they have been established in the faith, but he
reminds them of this so that they will remain so.

Paul notes here the role of teaching in establishing people in the faith.
When we personally trust Jesus, this trust is not in some vaguely defined
spiritual presence of a mystical Christ figure. Rather, it is trust in a Jesus
whose person and work are clearly revealed in Scripture and taught to us.
Because we have faith in Jesus, we believe what "the faith" teaches about
him. We do merely guess the truths of the faith or intuitively sense them.
We have been taught them diligently and deliberately by other Christians.
As Paul said in Eph 4:21, "Surely you heard of him and were taught in him in
accordance with the truth that is in Jesus" (NIV; see also Rom 6:17).

Some post-modernists might think Paul is saying here, "Just be quiet
and believe what you're told." But there is no power-grab here. Rather, Paul
wants to make sure that all Christians continue to believe the truth that sets
us free instead of the lies that enslave us.

As you know, Lord, I don't like to be told what to do or what to think. And yet I
need your truth to set me free. Teach me, Lord, through your church.

*⁶ As you therefore have received the Christ—Jesus the Lord—walk in him, ⁷ having been rooted and being built up in him, and being established in the faith just as you were taught, **overflowing in thanksgiving**.*

Although Paul will soon enter into debate against the Colossian distortion, he is not approaching the issue with an irritable, grouchy spirit. Nor does he want the Colossians to do so. Rather, he encourages all those who walk in Jesus and his truth to be overflowing with thanksgiving.

False teachings often gain a foothold whenever Christians become dissatisfied with their faith, looking for something more. That's what happened to the Israelites in the wilderness when they grumbled their way into idolatry (see Ex 32:1 and 1 Cor 10:6-14). To keep the Colossians from walking down that same ungrateful path, Paul urges them to be overflowing with thanks.

The verb for overflowing is a favorite of Paul's; twenty-six of its thirty-nine NT appearances are in Paul's letters. Paul rejoices in overflowing grace (Rom 5:15; 2 Cor 9:8; Eph 1:7-8), overflowing hope (Rom 15:13), and overflowing comfort (2 Cor 1:5). Most relevant to Col 2:7, however, are verses about overflowing thanksgiving prompted by the grace of God (2 Cor 4:15; 9:8, 12). Generous grace causes thanksgiving to overflow. This is not surprising, because as we saw on January 16, the Greek word for grace (*charis*) is part of the word for thanksgiving or gratitude (*eucharisteō*).

We see God's grace even in these few verses. It is only by God's grace that anyone can walk in Christ. It is only by God's grace that anyone can be rooted or built up in Christ. It is only by God's grace that we have been established in the faith and taught the truth in Jesus. In fact, all the acts of God proclaimed in this letter *happened* because of God's grace and *are known* to us by God's grace. Since all this grace (*charis*) is at work, it's only fitting that we overflow with gratitude (*eucharisteō*).

Having a grateful heart surely affects how we deal with those who promote a distorted message. We might be serious and stern in opposing them, but we do not approach them full of anger or with the desire to prove we know better than they do. In that case, we would be planting ourselves squarely in the arena of self-justification. Rather, we come overflowing with gratitude for the grace of God.

Mighty God, when I'm frustrated with all the enemies of grace operating in this world, replace my crankiness with an overflowing gratitude for all you've done.

*⁸ **Watch out that no one will be captivating you** through philosophy and empty deceit which are according to human tradition, according to the elemental-orders of the world, and not according to Christ*

From the first positive command about walking in Christ, we now turn to the letter's first negative command. When walking in Christ, we must watch our step, lest we fall into a trap (see also Eph 5:15).

The Bible often uses the verb for "seeing" to warn us about dangers. We are to watch out for those who would lead us astray (Mt 24:4), persecutors (Mk 13:9), false prophets (Mk 13:22-23), our own unbelieving heart (Heb 3:12; 2 Jn 8), and those who might captivate us.

Although I could have translated this phrase as "Watch out that no one will be *capturing* you," I thought it better to use the word "captivating" instead. When people are *captured*, they are forced into this situation—either by being taken completely unawares (as in an ambush) or by losing the fight against those who would take them. When people are *captivated*, however, they still come under the control of others, but only because they have been cleverly lured into this bondage which they now regret. Something fascinated them so much that they failed to heed the warning signs of danger, and they now bear some of the responsibility for losing their freedom. They were "dragged away and enticed" by their own evil desires (Jms 1:13-15). People are seldom *captured* by false teaching, but rather they are *captivated* by it.

Some are captivated by anything new (see Acts 17:21). Others are drawn to teachings that promise to give them a knowledge unknown to others, appealing to their desire to be "in the know." Some are lured by teachings that promise an easier path to salvation, while others are fascinated by teachings that challenge them to a more rigorous path. Some are seduced when teachings claim to give them greater control of their own lives, while others are captivated by the prospect of submitting their lives to a dynamic leader.

We're not sure what it was about the Colossian distortion that captivated some believers. Since Paul often used "fullness" words in this letter, it may be that some were enamored with a teaching that claimed to provide a greater spiritual fullness or challenge (see Col 2:20-23). Whatever it was, if they continued to be captivated by it, they would be unable to walk in Christ on the journey of faith and freedom.

Holy Redeemer, protect me from any fascination that would take me away from you and your freedom.

*[8] Watch out that no one will be captivating you **through philosophy** and empty deceit which are according to human tradition, according to the elemental-orders of the world, and not according to Christ*

Paul refers to this captivating teaching as a philosophy. On a literal level this word refers to a simple love (*philia*) of wisdom (*sophia*).

Many today regard philosophy as a secular way of thinking, based on logic and reason instead of divine revelation. That distinction did not apply in Paul's day. Any system of thought or religion trying to understand the nature of the universe, humanity, and religion was regarded as a philosophy. This included folk religions, magic, and even the Jewish faith in spite of its conflict with other philosophies. That's because the Jewish faith always encouraged its adherents to love wisdom: "He who loves wisdom, makes his father glad" (Prov 29:3, ESV).

Even though Paul often referred to wisdom (even in this letter; see Col 1:9, 28; 2:3; 4:5), he seems to be wary of the term "philosophy." That's because all the philosophies of his day were missing the main element of wisdom—Christ. Since all wisdom is concealed in Christ (Col 2:3), there can be no true wisdom in philosophies that either omit, ignore, or downgrade Christ. While there may be points of agreement between a given philosophy and the truth found in Jesus, an overall system of thought which is not centered in Christ can only lead one astray.

There are, however, some positive things to be gained from learning about other philosophies. By studying them we can gain a better understanding of our own culture in order to be more effective in our witness. We can also gain a new perspective on God's Word from these philosophies, perhaps noticing something we had previously overlooked. And we can even discover in these philosophies how much of our own thinking has been shaped by our culture instead of the gospel. Yet wariness is in order when looking into philosophies which are not centered on Jesus. Philosophical words and ideas can become so fascinating that they threaten to overwhelm and undermine the gospel's hold on our lives. Philosophical concepts can impose such a strong grid on our minds that we might develop blind spots to the truth in Jesus. I have no axe to grind about philosophy; I majored in it in college. But Christians must first and foremost seek the truth in Christ.

Show me, Lord, how my own thinking has been more influenced by the philosophies of the world than by you.

[8] *Watch out that no one will be captivating you through philosophy* **and** **empty deceit** *which are according to human tradition, according to the elemental-orders of the world, and not according to Christ*

The philosophy being promoted in Colossae, says Paul, is only "empty deceit." Using this same word for deceit, the NT warns us against the deceitfulness of riches (Mt 13:22; Mk 4:19), desires (Eph 4:22), and sin (Heb 3:13). When false teachers come around, these three forms of deception usually come tied together in one package (2 Pet 2:13-14). Beneath all the spiritual talk, false teaching usually brings monetary gain and the gratification of sinful desires for the teachers and sometimes even for the followers—at least for a while. Eventually, though, it shows itself to be only a deceitful lure that promised much, yet delivered nothing but captivity— not only for the followers, but also the teachers.

Because this deceitful philosophy delivers nothing, Paul calls it "empty." Similarly, in Eph 5:6, Paul said, "Let no one deceive you with empty words" (NRSV). The charge of being "empty" would have been particularly galling to the distortionists because they had been claiming to offer a fuller experience of salvation. But you don't need their empty "fullness," says Paul. You already have all the true fullness you need in Christ—the fullness of knowledge and understanding (Col 1:9), the fullness of God in Christ (Col 1:19; 2:9-10), the fullness of God's Word (Col 1:25), and the fullness of assurance (Col 2:2). Since all the treasures of knowledge and wisdom are in Christ (Col 2:3), then any teaching which claims to go beyond Christ will only come up empty-handed.

This empty philosophy actually threatens to undo all the good things the Colossian believers have been experiencing. Christians are walking in Christ (Col 2:6), but the distortionists are captivated and separated from Christ. Christians are rooted, built up, and established in Christ (Col 2:7), but the distortionists—consciously or not—are tearing up roots, toppling faith, and shaking foundations. There is nothing to gain from this philosophy and much to lose.

Paul speaks to every Christian who has said, "There must be more," and goes searching for a deeper religious experience. But if that search leads a person "beyond" Christ or away from Christ, the only "more" they will find is more emptiness.

Sometimes I ache for more in my religious experiences, Lord, but let that ache only keep me focused on you.

*⁸ Watch out that no one will be captivating you through philosophy and empty deceit **which are according to human tradition**, according to the elemental-orders of the world, and not according to Christ*

One reason the Colossian distortion is empty is that it is a philosophy formed "according to human tradition...and not according to Christ." The noun for tradition is *paradosis*, which refers to what has been given over, delivered, or handed down to others.

In the gospels, Jesus always speaks negatively of tradition. He asks the Pharisees, "And why do you break the commandment of God for the sake of your tradition?" (Mt 15:3, NRSV). A few verses later he declares, "for the sake of your tradition you make void the word of God" (Mt 15:6, NRSV).

Paul, the only other NT writer to speak of traditions, refers to both good and bad traditions. Good traditions are the relatively new teachings and practices passed down from Jesus through the apostles to the church: "Maintain the traditions even as I delivered them to you" (1 Cor 11:2, ESV); "Stand firm and hold fast to the traditions that you were taught by us" (2 Thess 2:15, NRSV). He even commands the Thessalonians to "keep away from any brother who is walking in idleness and not in accord with the tradition that you received from us," (2 Thess 3:6, ESV). On the negative side, Paul confesses that he had wrongly persecuted Christians because he had been "extremely zealous for the traditions of my fathers" (Gal 1:14, NIV). This is the kind of zeal which Paul said he now regarded as rubbish in order to know Christ better (Phil 3:4-8).

Tradition in itself is not the problem, for there is nothing wrong with handing over good teachings and practices to other nations and generations, peoples, and institutions. What is objectionable are those traditions which are merely "human" traditions, devised by people, but treated and enforced as if they came from God.

Literally, Col 2:8 warns against the "tradition of men," which is nearly the same phrase used by Jesus when he said, "You leave the commandment of God and hold to the tradition of men" (Mk 7:8, ESV). Paul similarly warns of those who promote circumcision, Jewish myths, and human commands (Titus 1:14), and those who preach a man-made gospel (Gal 1:11). What we need is not man-made tradition, but God-given revelation. Where do your traditions come from?

I thank you, Lord, for the good biblical traditions passed down through the ages, but teach me to be wary of the man-made traditions that creep in.

*8 Watch out that no one will be captivating you through philosophy and empty deceit **which are according to human tradition**, according to the elemental-orders of the world, and not according to Christ*

The distortionists likely agreed with part of Paul's assessment. Yes, their teachings were very traditional. Lohse says, "Tradition, which was distinguished by its antiquity, was universally considered as a proof of the dignity and sacredness of the communicated knowledge."[108] And it's not just the Pharisees who liked tradition; both Jews and pagans appreciated it. According to C. Arnold, "All magical literature is or pretends to be tradition. Recipes, spells and conjurations have been collected and written down from purportedly old and valuable *paradosis* [tradition]."[109] The distortionists probably thought their traditions came from divine sources, but Paul disagreed.

The problem, of course, is that many Christians think their traditions are based on Christ, but they may be mistaken. It is far too easy for people to be fascinated—and captivated—by traditions, partly as a nostalgia for the "good old days" and partly as a way to prove to themselves that they are better believers than others who do not keep to the traditions. Whenever we regard some traditional practice or idea as meaningful for *our* faith, it is tempting for us to assume it should be meaningful for others and we may work to impose it upon them, either through gentle persuasion or by establishing policies. All the while, we fail to notice that our traditions are not required in Scripture and may actually turn people away from Christ. To avoid this, Christians must hold their traditions loosely, always examining whether or not any given tradition is truly necessary for walking in Christ.

It is of more than passing interest that when the noun for tradition (*paradosis*) is used in its verb form (*paradidōmi*), it often refers to handing someone over for a bad end. Occasionally the verb is about handing over a tradition, but 99 of the 119 uses of this verb in the NT are about handing a (usually righteous) person over for imprisonment or death (like John the Baptist, Jesus, and Christians). This predominant meaning of *paradidōmi* should caution us in our attitude toward *paradosis* (tradition). Handing over a tradition may sound innocent enough, but if it is not a tradition based on Christ, then it's like handing someone over to captivity, as Paul warned here in Col 2:8. The very ones who hand over a human tradition may also be the ones who would hand over Jesus or his followers to death.

Lord Jesus, whenever I see a man-made tradition used to squelch the furtherance of the gospel, give me the courage to challenge that tradition.

*[8] Watch out that no one will be captivating you through philosophy and empty deceit which are according to human tradition, **according to the elemental-orders** of the world, and not according to Christ*

The Colossian distortion is also empty because it is based on the world's elemental-orders (*stoicheia,* this is the plural form of the word). Unfortunately, we're unsure what Paul or the distortionists mean by this term. The word itself is open-ended in meaning, for it refers to the basic components that are part of any orderly series. In language, for instance, the *stoicheia* would be the letters of the alphabet. In music the *stoicheia* would be the notes in a scale. Two main contexts may apply in Colossians.

First, in the sphere of knowledge, the *stoicheia* would be the basic starting principles in a given field of study. If we talked about Psychology 101 or the ABCs of chemistry, we'd be referring to the *stoicheia* of those fields. In religion or philosophy, the *stoicheia* would be the basic principles and traditions believed by a wide variety of spiritual people in the world.

Of the seven references to *stoicheia* in the NT, only Heb 5:12 clearly interprets *stoicheia* as basic principles: "For though by this time you ought to be teachers, you need someone to teach you again the basic elements [*stoicheia*] of the oracles of God" (NRSV). The two *stoicheia* references in Galatians might also fit here. According to Gal 4:1-8, until Christ came, both Jews and pagans were enslaved to the basic principles of the world, which was represented by the law for the Jews (Gal 4:3) and various taboos and religious ideas for the pagans (Gal 4:8).

If we apply this same meaning for *stoicheia* to the two references in Colossians, Paul would be warning the believers against a philosophy built according to both man-made traditions and the basic religious principles of the world (Col 2:8). And in Col 2:20 Paul would also be declaring that these basic principles, including the "do not touch or taste" rules of the distortion, have no hold over them, for in Christ they have died to these taboos.

If this is what Paul means, how would the distortionists respond? Two possibilities: (1) If the distortionists embraced this term, thinking it was good to teach basic religious principles, they would have been surprised that Paul criticized it as a religiosity without Christ. (2) If the distortionists thought they were offering deeper knowledge, they would have been insulted to hear Paul critique their teachings as nothing but basic principles. In either case, Paul rejects basic religious ideas that point away from Christ.

Protect your church, Lord Jesus, from a religiosity that has the form of godliness, but denies the power of it that comes from you.

⁸ *Watch out that no one will be captivating you through philosophy and empty deceit which are according to human tradition, **according to the elemental-orders** of the world, and not according to Christ*

But now we must consider a second meaning for *stoicheia*. For many people in Paul's day, the *stoicheia* were the elements of creation (like earth, wind, water, fire, etc.). Peter follows this meaning when he declares that on Jesus' return, "the elements [*stoicheia*] will be dissolved with fire" (2 Pet 3:10). But that meaning doesn't fit with Paul's writing, for in what sense could we be enslaved or deceived by water or air?

A more promising approach would be to think of the *stoicheia* not only as the natural elements, but also as the various gods, goddesses, angels, and demons assigned to those natural elements by pagan religions. Wisdom 13:1-2 criticizes the non-Jewish world because "they supposed that either fire or wind or swift air, or the circle of the stars, or turbulent water, or the luminaries of heaven were the gods that rule the world" (NRSV). Even some Jews believed that God created "the angels of the spirit of fire and the angels of the spirit of the clouds and darkness and snow and hail and frost" (*Jubilees* 2:2). And Revelation also speaks of angels in charge of winds, fire, and water (Rev 7:1; 14:18; 16:5).

If we interpret the *stoicheia* as supernatural powers, this could also help us interpret Gal 4:1-8, for then Paul would be saying that the Jewish law had become an enslaving power similar to the way that demonic powers and idols (*stoicheia*) had enslaved the pagans, which is a very provocative comparison. To view the *stoicheia* as supernatural powers would also fit with the message of Colossians. Since Christ made the powers (Col 1:16) and overcame the powers at the cross (Col 2:15), and since we should not be worshiping angels (Col 2:18), then we should avoid any distorted teaching that comes from these *stoicheia*-powers and/or exalts these powers.

If *this* scenario is correct, again we're not sure how the distortionists would have responded to Paul. Maybe they also regarded the *stoicheia* as evil, and would be surprised to hear Paul say that their teachings were actually demonic in origin. Or more likely, they thought of the *stoicheia* as good supernatural powers who could take believers a step beyond Christ. In either case, Paul would say that no one should base their teachings on any other supernatural power than that of Jesus Christ.

Protect your church, Lord Jesus, from the influence of evil powers who subtly deflect our focus from you.

*[8] Watch out that no one will be captivating you through philosophy and empty deceit which are according to human tradition, **according to the elemental-orders** of the world, and not according to Christ*

Although we might wish to know exactly what Paul meant by the elemental orders (*stoicheia*), certainty eludes us. Is he warning against a philosophy based on basic principles of religion (which are similar to man-made traditions) or a philosophy based on elemental spirits and primal-powers?

I'm not convinced we have to choose. Man-made traditions (especially religious ones) can quickly become demonic, a tool in the hands of spiritual powers who aim to pull us away from Christ. Whenever evil spiritual powers seek to undermine Christians, one of the first things they do is promote religious traditions that put humanity under bondage. These are the "teachings of demons" mentioned by Paul in 1 Tim 4:1. The fact that Paul could use the term *stoicheia* in Gal 4:1-11 to describe both the Jewish understandings of the law and the false demonic gods of the pagans shows that the term can apply both to what is non-personal (basic principles) *and* personal (demonic spirits), for they work in tandem. The same holds true in Colossae. Demons have a keen interest in developing traditions.

It is because the *stoicheia* can mean both elementary principles and primal powers that I translate the word as "elemental-orders." This term conveys meaning in many directions. According to dictionaries, the word "orders" can refer to an arrangement or sequential pattern, a political system, an authoritative command, and various rankings of angelic beings—all of which are a part of how Paul uses the word *stoicheia*. The term "elemental-orders," then, is intended to point to both the impersonal *and* personal aspects of the *stoicheia*—the basic religious principles *and* the spiritual powers who teach them. But even though people can be enslaved to both the powers *and* their teachings, Christ has come to break the chains that bind us to both.

The distortionists may have wanted to "add" the *stoicheia* to the mix of salvation (however they interpreted that word), but, as Moo noted, this "addition means subtraction: one cannot 'add' to Christ without, in effect, subtracting from his exclusive place in creation and in salvation history."[110] No matter how we might define the *stoicheia*, the important thing is that we see our own lives as defined in Christ.

God of wisdom, whenever I feel stuck in trying to interpret the Bible, teach me to look to you to learn what I need to know.

[8] *Watch out that no one will be captivating you through philosophy and empty deceit which are according to human tradition, according to the elemental-orders **of the world**, and not according to Christ*

No matter how we understand the "elemental-orders," Paul says we should avoid them because they are "of the world," a truth repeated in Col 2:20.

Paul uses the word "world" (*kosmos*) forty-seven times to convey many different truths. For instance, God created the world (Rom 1:20), but sin soon entered it (Rom 5:12-13). Yet God had a plan of salvation in mind before the creation of the world (Eph 1:4). This plan did not conform to the world's ideas of salvation, for God chose what is foolish and weak in the world (1 Cor 1:20-21, 27; 3:19). Thus, God sent Jesus into the world to save sinners (1 Tim 1:15), a message which was proclaimed to the world (Rom 1:8; Col 1:6). This message came to sinners who were without God in the world (Eph 2:12), and who walked according to the ways of this world (Eph 2:2). The message was this: God was reconciling the world through Christ (2 Cor 5:19). Thus, many in the world believed on him (1 Tim 3:16), and someday all God's people will inherit the world (1 Cor 3:22). Until then, believers do not leave this world in an effort to avoid its wickedness (1 Cor 5:10), but instead shine as lights in its darkness (Phil 2:15). The world was crucified to them and they to the world (Gal 6:14), so that they were no longer enslaved to it (Gal 4:3). Christians accept the fact that they brought nothing into this world, and can take nothing out (1 Tim 6:7).

The "world" has three basic meanings here, all intertwined: (1) the created universe and the earth in particular; (2) all humanity, created and loved by God; and (3) the network of evil customs and institutions that arose when humanity fell into sin, which has now taken on a life of its own. All three meanings tell us something about the "elemental-orders of the world": (1) The elemental-orders are "of the world" in that they are a part of creation and not its creators. Any philosophy not based on the Creator, but on the created elemental-orders, will only mislead us; (2) The elemental-orders are "of the world" in that people and their man-made tra-ditions are the conduits through which they operate; and (3) The elemental-orders are also "of the world" in the sense that they represent that larger nexus of evil dominated by the spiritual powers.

When we walk in Christ, we do not walk "following the course of the world, following the prince of the power of the air" (Eph 2:2, ESV).

Holy Redeemer, I do not ask to be set free from your created world; it's a beautiful home. But I do ask you to free me from the world of sin.

*8 Watch out that no one will be captivating you through philosophy and empty deceit which are according to human tradition, according to the elemental-orders of the world, **and not according to Christ***

The problem with the philosophy opposed by Paul is that it is based on human tradition and elemental-orders instead of on Christ. There is, however, a philosophy that *is* built on Christ.

Paul would not agree, then, with the assessment of Tertullian, a prominent teacher in the early church, who said that Athens (which was the center of philosophy at that time) has nothing to do with Jerusalem (which could be thought of as a center of the Christian faith). Paul himself brought the gospel to Athens and referred to philosophical issues of the day in his speech there (see Acts 17:22-33). He attempted to build a few bridges by talking about an altar dedicated "to an unknown god" and quoting from the pagan Greek poets Aratus and Epimenides the Cretan (Acts 17:28). He seems to have been aware of other philosophies and ideas.

Because of that, it's likely Paul would not be comfortable with the strong anti-intellectual streak in contemporary American life and in the American church. As David Garland says, too many of us ridicule philosophy as a way of turning "solutions into problems and the simplest things into the most unintelligible."[111] But reasoning and thinking are important for Christian faith, as can be seen in the many references to knowledge, thinking, wisdom, understanding, and teaching scattered throughout this letter (see Col 1:9, 28; 2:2-3, 8; 3:2, 10, 16; 4:5).

Paul's main contrast here is not between a philosophy based on *human* traditions versus one based on *divine* traditions. Rather, the contrast is between a philosophy based on human traditions versus one based on Christ. That's a subtle, but important, distinction, for as noted in the discussion in Col 2:6, even if we think of Jesus as a tradition which must be received, the fact remains that unlike other traditions, he is Tradition personified—a person, not merely a set of true ideas.

Philosophers deal with subjects like God, language, beauty, ethics, politics, and more. Christians need to think through those matters as well. Whether we use the word "philosophy" to describe our thinking doesn't matter. What does matter is thinking through all the implications of Jesus' presence and activity in our lives and our world. We Christians don't have to be intellectuals, but we do have to think...in the presence of Christ.

Lord of knowledge, when I just want to lazily feel my way through life, waken my mind to think before you in a comprehensive and faithful way.

We Have Received Christ Jesus

to the tune of St. Theodolph: *All Glory Laud and Honor*
© 2012 David J. Landegent

We have received Christ Jesus, so let us walk in Him;
He is the Way for pilgrims, adventures now begin.
Both rooted and established, we're built up in the Lord;
With grateful steps we travel, now guided by His Word.

We turn away from teachings that bring captivity;
We shun man-made traditions and vain philosophies.
The elemental spirits, the doctrines of this world
Would only block our journey, our walk with Christ the Lord.

Attached to Christ

Colossians 2:9-15

June 9-July 9

⁹ for in him [that is, in Christ] dwells bodily all the fullness of the deity, ¹⁰ and you have been filled in him, who is the head of all primal-powers and authorities, ¹¹ in whom also you were circumcised with a circumcision made-without-hands, by the stripping of the body of flesh in the circumcision of Christ, ¹² having been jointly-buried with him in baptism, in whom also you were jointly-raised through faith in the energizing-work of God who raised him from the dead ones. ¹³ And you, being dead in the transgressions and the uncircumcision of your flesh, he [God] made you jointly-alive with him [Christ], having granted-grace to us for all transgressions. ¹⁴ Wiping-away the handwritten debt-note against us, which opposed us with its decrees, he [God] has taken it from center-stage, having nailed it to the cross. ¹⁵ Having stripped the primal-powers and the authorities, he [God] exposed them openly, triumphantly-parading them in him [Christ].

Because verse 8 warned against the Colossian distortion, readers might expect Paul to turn immediately to what's wrong with it. Paul will do this in Col 2:16-23, but he would rather counteract falsehood by first celebrating the truth in Jesus once again. Along the same lines as Jesus' parable of the demon (Mt 12:43-45), it does not help to cast an evil teaching out of someone's mind, if you do not replace it with the truth. When that evil teaching returns to an empty mind, it will introduce more false ideas and the person's last state will be worse than the first. So one of the best ways to fend off false teaching is by the establishment of truth.

The discussion of Colossians 2 can be plotted out in the following way:

Col 2:6-7   *positive* command: walk in Christ
Col 2:8   *negative* command: avoid distorted teaching
Col 2:9-15   *positive* portrayal: Christ's effective work in us
Col 2:16-23   *negative* portrayal: the distortion's ineffectiveness

This positive portrayal of the Christian life will, of course, focus on Jesus. In the laudation of Col 1:15-20, many things happened "in," "through," or "toward" Christ. Now, in this section, Paul will frequently refer to being "in" Christ or "with" him. Christians are filled in him (2:10), circumcised in him (2:11), buried with him (2:12), raised with him (2:12), and made alive with him (2:13). But not only is the fate of believers tied to Jesus, but so is the fate of the debt-note against us (2:14) and the primal-powers (2:15).

Lord Jesus, in this fallen world, it's so easy to focus on the negative. Shine your light so that truth, instead of falsehood, takes center stage.

⁹ for in him [that is, in Christ] dwells bodily all the fullness of the deity, ¹⁰ and you have been filled in him, who is the head of all primal-powers and authorities,

Paul has just spoken of the distortion's emptiness (Col 2:8). Now he emphasizes that in Christ there is fullness—the fullness of the deity in Christ himself (verse 9) and the fullness that characterizes those who are in Christ (verse 10). The distortion is empty, but in Christ there is fullness.

The wording here is very similar to what Paul already celebrated in Col 1:19, "for in him all the fullness was pleased to dwell." But there are three main differences.

First, Col 1:19 simply refers to "all the fullness," but never specifies whose fullness this is. Col 2:9, however, says the fullness of *deity* (*theotēs*) was dwelling in Christ. The fullness of deity was not distributed among various powers, but can be found only and fully in Christ. Jesus is not merely god-like, but divine, truly God. Just as God does not *possess* deity (as some kind of quality), but rather *is* deity, so Jesus does not merely *possess* deity, but *is* deity.[112] In this way Paul blocks those who would "lump Christ Jesus with the galaxy of lesser ranking divine beings" as Garland puts it.[113]

But we should not overstate what Paul says. Although *theotēs* has roughly the same meaning as *theos* (which means God), it's also more abstract and less relational in meaning than *theos*. Christians talk to God, but few would say they talk to the deity. Why Paul chose this more abstract word is not clear. Two possibilities seem most likely. Maybe Paul used "deity" because it was part of the vocabulary of the distortionists. If so, Paul is using their words to say that whether we speak of God or deity, the fact remains that all divine fullness is in Christ.

The other possibility is that Paul's upbringing as a Jew, with its emphasis on the oneness of God, caused him to avoid being quite so blunt in talking about Jesus' divinity. Some of the language about the Trinity, which we now take for granted, had not yet been worked out, and so Paul had to feel his way forward in describing how God could be one, and yet Jesus could be the Son of God, equal with the Father. By using "deity" Paul is taking a further step in that direction. Later on, Christians would find no difficulty in saying that the fullness of God dwelt in Christ, or even more explicitly, that Jesus is God.

I confess, Lord, that my heart easily turns into an idol factory. Forgive me. You alone are the one true God—Father, Son, and Holy Spirit.

⁹for in him [that is, in Christ] dwells bodily all the fullness of the deity, ¹⁰ and you have been filled in him, who is the head of all primal-powers and authorities,

A second difference between Col 1:19 and Col 2:9 is the claim that the fullness of the deity dwells in Christ in a "bodily" way. As Col 1:22 said, Jesus did his reconciling work in a "body of flesh." He is not only fully God, but he is fully God in a fully human way. Karl Barth expresses the wonder of this truth: "The Almighty exists and acts and speaks here in the form of One who is weak and impotent, the eternal as One who is temporal and perishing, the Most High in the deepest humility. The Holy One stands in the place and under the accusation of a sinner with other sinners. The glorious One is covered with shame. The One who lives forever has fallen prey to death."[114]

During the first few centuries of the church, many false forms of Christianity arose (now labeled Gnosticism) which thoroughly disagreed with Paul here. Gnostics believed the body and the flesh were so completely corrupted that the pure spirit of God shunned them altogether. Consequentially, many of them also believed that God did not create the body; Jesus did not have a body; and after death believers would not be raised as bodies. For biblical writers, however, even though God is spirit (Jn 4:24), God is not so spiritual that he refuses to be closely associated with the physical body. In fact, the best demonstration of God's attitude toward the body is that God dwells in Christ in a bodily way.

The Colossian distortion leans in this Gnostic direction. They have greater interest in spiritual powers who have no bodies than a Christ who has come in the flesh (Col 2:18). And they regard their own bodies as impediments to faith (Col 2:20-23). But they are wrong, says Paul.

In fact—and here's the third difference between Col 1:19 and this verse—the verb tense for "dwells" implies that the fullness of God is *still* dwelling in Jesus in a bodily way. The embodied Jesus continues to be the one in whom God's fullness is operating in our world. Jesus did not take on flesh at Christmas and then abandon it at the resurrection or the ascension. Rather, Jesus remains embodied, even though his body is no longer subject to death. The fullness of God is now seated at the right hand of the Father in the resurrected human flesh of Christ.

Lord, even though I sometimes long to transcend this body of mine, with all its flaws and limitations, I see my own body differently knowing that you came to this world in a human body and now rule from heaven in a bodily way.

192

⁹ for in him [that is, in Christ] dwells bodily all the fullness of the deity, ¹⁰ **and you have been filled in him**, *who is the head of all primal-powers and authorities*

When we feel empty, it's the nature of the human heart to go searching for something to fill the void—a fact that false teachers and religions are quick to exploit, but are unable to fulfill because their ideas are empty (Col 2:8). But such emptiness does not exist for those who are in Christ. Christ is filled with the fullness of deity, and we are filled in him. Not that Christians never have an empty feeling; they do. But Paul is not talking about "feelings" here, but the truth about our condition. We may sometimes "feel" empty, but we are actually filled in Christ.

That's because Jesus does not hoard his fullness, but freely shares it. The same Jesus who came "from the Father, full of grace and truth" (Jn 1:14, NIV) shares that fullness with those who believe in him: "For from his fullness we have all received, grace upon grace" (Jn 1:16, NRSV).

Paul emphasizes our fullness in Christ in this letter because the distortionists had made the Colossians wonder if their glass of salvation was half-empty, and if they should tap into other sources of spiritual power. But spiritual fullness does not come through rule-keeping, mystical experiences, or other spiritual powers; it only happens in Christ. Because Christ is full and lacks nothing, we also are full and lack nothing in him.[115]

Paul does not specify here what constitutes this fullness. One thing is for sure, however—we do not have the same divine status as Jesus; the fullness *of deity* does not dwell in us. But we *are* filled with Jesus himself so that whatever happened to Christ (such as the circumcision, death, burial, and resurrection of the following verses) also happens to us. "Participation in Christ's death and life is not merely the *means* to possess the fullness, but it actually *constitutes* the fullness," according to Blackwell.[116]

In Christ, we are also being filled with the Holy Spirit (Eph 5:18), the knowledge of God and God's will (Col 1:9), joy and peace (Rom 15:13), the fruit of righteousness (Phil 1:11), and grace (Jn 1:16). This fullness in Christ is not a self-sustaining gift that remains in effect apart from the One who gives it. It is only sustained as we experience Christ's ongoing connection with us, or to use Paul's phrase, as we are in Christ. That's why Paul does not say, "you were filled," but "you have been filled," which implies that the Colossians are full in Christ and find their continued filling in him.

I admit, Lord, that I have my times of feeling spiritually empty and dry. When that happens, show me again that I lack nothing in you.

⁹ for in him [that is, in Christ] dwells bodily all the fullness of the deity, ¹⁰ and you have been filled in him, **who is the head of all primal-powers and authorities,**

Our sense of fullness in Christ would be shaken if there were other spiritual beings who had powers beyond what Christ could offer (as the distortionists may have claimed). That's why Paul is compelled here to put these other powers in their place (as he has done throughout Colossians). He declares that Jesus is the head over all these powers. He created them (Col 1:16), he rescued us from their darkness (Col 1:13), and he publicly exposed them at the cross (Col 2:15).

According to many Jewish writings which focused on the last days, God would not rule over the evil powers until the very end of time, but here Paul tells us that Jesus' authority over these powers is a present reality.[117] It's not only the case that he *will be* their head; he *is* their head. Of course, the future will demonstrate even further how Jesus will exercise his lordship over them, but their subordination has already begun. He is King of kings and Lord of lords, and the Primal-Power of primal-powers.

In Paul's earlier laudation, he referred to Jesus as the head of the body, the church (Col 1:18). Here he uses the same word for "head" to say Jesus is the head of the primal-powers. But that doesn't mean the powers are also the body of Christ. As N. T. Wright says, "the word 'head' was as flexible and evocative in Hebrew or Greek as it is in English, and we should not squeeze all Paul's uses of it into exactly the same mould."[118] The powers-that-be are not the body of Christ, but are rivals to the throne, who will never succeed in capturing the crown.

So instead of us feeling like *we* are under the power of these supernatural beings and fearing how much havoc they can create, it's actually *the powers* themselves that are under Christ's authority. They are also under the authority of all those who are in Christ—that's us.[119] As Jesus said to his disciples, including us, "Behold, I have given you authority...over all the power of the enemy, and nothing shall hurt you" (Lk 10:19).

The Bible may warn us to be wary of demonic powers that prowl like lions on the hunt (1 Pet 5:8), but it also tells us not to fear. "The New Testament places more emphasis on the message that Christ is the head who subjugates the powers...than on the message that Satan and the evil spirits still threaten the faithful."[120]

When I am afraid of powerful forces of evil in our world, remind me again that you are on the throne as King of kings and Lord of lords.

[10] *and you have been filled in him, who is the head of all primal-powers and authorities,* *[11]* ***in whom also you were circumcised*** *with a circumcision made-without-hands, by the stripping of the body of flesh in the circumcision of Christ,* *[12]* ***having been jointly-buried with him*** *in baptism,* ***in whom also you were jointly-raised*** *through faith in the energizing-work of God who raised him from the dead ones.* *[13]* *And you, being dead in the transgressions and the uncircumcision of your flesh, he [God] made you* ***jointly-alive with him*** *[Christ], having granted-grace to us for all transgressions.*

When Paul describes what it means to be filled in Christ in verses 11-13, he uses phrases like "in whom," "in him," and "with him," as well as three compound verbs that all contain the Greek word "with" (translated as "jointly"). When you're filled in Christ, the emphasis is on Christ.

Fullness is not an emotional or mystical union with the divine. Rather, fullness happens through action. Notice the action verbs about being circumcised, stripped, buried, resurrected, and given grace. But it is not we who do these actions. Rather, these actions are done to us in Christ. In fact, they were done first to Jesus, and because we are in him, they are done to us as well. That's because Jesus is not only our *substitute* who undergoes things so that we do not have to, he is also our *representative* who acted on our behalf in such a way as to pull us into that action.[121]

Many today lift up the importance of story or narrative in forming our self-identity as Christians. This section supports that idea, for here Paul is saying, "The story of Jesus is our story."[122] Just as Jews believe every generation was to think of itself as having participated in the Exodus, so all Christians are to see themselves as participating with Christ in his crucifixion and resurrection.

Admittedly, some of the actions done to us do not sound very promising in terms of filling us. On a superficial level, a number of them appear to bring emptiness instead. For instance, circumcision is designed to take something away. Likewise, being stripped or buried also gives the impression of being emptied instead of filled. But it is precisely in the action of emptying us that God is able to fill us. Only those who have been emptied of what is sinful can be filled with what is holy, or even better, with the *One* who is holy. Only those whose flesh has been put to death can be made alive. Only those who have been buried can be raised up.

Lord Jesus, if the only way to experience fullness of life is through being emptied with you, then lead the way.

11 in whom also you were circumcised with a circumcision made-without-hands, by the stripping of the body of flesh in the circumcision of Christ,

Paul begins this mini-section by describing us as being circumcised in Christ. It's unclear why he says this. It's not because the distortionists were requiring circumcision like the false teachers in Galatia, because this is the only reference to circumcision in this letter, and it's a positive one![123] If anything, the distortionists may have promoted a spiritual circumcision of subduing the sinful body of flesh (see Col 2:16-23). If that were the case, Paul would be counter-arguing that the sinful body of flesh has already been removed through a kind of circumcision that all believers have already undergone in Christ. We don't have to strip off the body of flesh; it was already stripped off when we were circumcised with Christ.

Circumcision was practiced by a number of cultures in the ancient Near East, but only among the Jews did it convey a sense of belonging to God. Circumcision started in Israel when God made an everlasting covenant with Abraham. The Lord asked Abraham to *walk* before him, be *blameless*, and *circumcise* all the males in his household as a sign of this covenant (see Gen 17:1-27). Interestingly, Colossians also talks about *walking*, being *blameless*, and being *circumcised*—but all in relationship to Christ (Col 1:22; 2:6, 11).

According to Witherington's take on the apocryphal *Jubilees* 15:25-34, "circumcision is necessary because evil spirits or demons rule the nations. Circumcision removes a person from the evil sphere and into the realm of God and God's presence."[124] According to Col 1:13-14, however, what moves us from the evil sphere into the kingdom of the Son is not circumcision, but the redemption and forgiveness brought by Christ.

In spite of Jewish zeal for it, physical circumcision was not as important in the OT as a circumcision of the heart. In Dt 10:16 the Lord commanded Israel, "Circumcise, then, the foreskin of your heart, and do not be stubborn any longer" (NRSV). He also called them to humble their uncircumcised hearts (Lev 26:40-42). They needed to cut off, that is, circumcise the part of their heart that had become hardened toward God.

Likewise, Jeremiah commanded Israel, "Circumcise yourselves to the Lord; remove the foreskin of your hearts" (Jer 4:4, NRSV; see also Jer 9:25-26; Ezek 44:7, 9). The Dead Sea Scrolls (1 QS V:5) also declared that each man "shall circumcise in the Community the foreskin of evil inclination." Outward conformity to the law did not necessarily bring a changed heart.

I confess, Lord, that even though I look the part of a believer, my heart is not always in line with your will. Change my heart, O God.

[11] **in whom also you were circumcised** *with a circumcision made-without-hands, by the stripping of the body of flesh in the circumcision of Christ,*

After Paul became a Christian, he quickly realized that his own circumcision had not helped him find God's righteousness. Although circumcised as a child (Phil 3:5), his heart had become hardened toward what God was doing through Christ. Paul's eyes were opened when he realized that God had already declared Abraham justified by faith before he ever was circumcised (Rom 4:9-12). From this he learned that God declares us righteous in his sight *only through faith*—whether we are circumcised or not (Rom 3:30).

Paul expressed God's indifference to circumcision three times: "For in Christ Jesus neither circumcision nor uncircumcision counts for anything, but only faith working through love" (Gal 5:6, ESV); "circumcision is nothing and uncircumcision is nothing, but obeying the commandments of God is everything" (1 Cor 7:19, NRSV); "For neither circumcision counts for anything, nor uncircumcision, but a new creation" (Gal 6:15, ESV).

What is needed is a true circumcision, a circumcision of the heart. As Paul argues in Rom 2:25-29, what makes someone a Jew is not a physical circumcision done in accordance with the letter of the law, but the inward circumcision of the heart which is performed by the Spirit. But how does this happen? Most OT texts call on people to circumcise their own hearts, but it appears no one could make this happen. Just as you can't perform open heart surgery on yourself, you can't circumcise your own heart.

Our only real hope for a heart circumcision is revealed in Dt 30:6, "*The LORD your God* will circumcise your hearts and the hearts of your descendants, so that you may love him with all your heart and with all your soul, and live" (NIV, emphasis mine). What God demands, God himself will grant.[125] This idea is repeated in an old Jewish book called the *Odes of Solomon* 11:1-3: "for the Most High circumcised me by his Holy Spirit, then he uncovered my inward being toward him, and filled me with his love. And his circumcising became my salvation."

Paul follows up on this line of thinking in Colossians, but he specifies that our heart circumcision happens in Christ. Through faith in Jesus, those who are physically *circumcised* and those who are physically *uncircumcised* both have their hearts circumcised by the Spirit and so they can say together, "We are the circumcision who worship by the Spirit of God and glory in Christ Jesus and put no confidence in the flesh" (Phil 3:3, ESV).

Lord, I have tried putting my confidence in the flesh and failed miserably.
Thank you for your transforming work in my heart.

> *11 in whom also you were circumcised **with a circumcision made-without-hands**, by the stripping of the body of flesh in the circumcision of Christ,*

Unlike physical circumcision, which is an operation performed by human beings, all those in Christ receive a circumcision "made-without-hands" (a phrase that's one word in Greek). According to the Bible, anything made without hands is something made by God, including a new temple (Mk 14:58), our resurrection bodies (2 Cor 5:1), and a large stone in Nebuchadnezzar's dream that will roll down from heaven and crush an idol representing the kingdoms of the world (Dan 2:34, 45). Stephen adds that God does not live in any houses made by hands (Acts 7:48).

Throughout the Bible, however, the things that *are* said to be made by human hands are associated with false gods. According to the law, for instance, rebellious Israelites will be sent into exile where they "will serve gods of wood and stone, the work of human hands, that neither see, nor hear, nor eat, nor smell" (Dt 4:28, ESV). Ps 115:4 declares, "Their idols are silver and gold, the work of human hands" (NRSV). The prophets said, "Their land is filled with idols; they bow down to the work of their hands, to what their own fingers have made" (Isa 2:8, NRSV). In the book of Acts, Stephen said that those who worshiped the golden calf "reveled in the works of their hands" (Acts 7:41, NRSV). And according to Rev 9:20, people in the last days will "not repent of the works of their hands or give up worshiping demons and idols of gold and silver and bronze and wood, which cannot see or hear or walk" (NRSV).

The circumcision "made-without-hands" in Col 2:11, therefore, is one accomplished by God alone. This stands in great contrast to the physical "circumcision, which is made in the flesh by hands" (Eph 2:11, ESV). By using these loaded phrases, Paul implies that some are treating physical (made-with-hands) circumcision as an idol, an object of human trust. So in spite of the Jews' insistence on the not-made-with-hands character of their God, their continued high regard for made-with-hands circumcision undermined that claim.[126]

To anyone who believes the security of their salvation is based on some human action (even ones commanded by God, like circumcision or baptism), Paul would say instead: salvation is based on what God has done through Christ. A sign of the covenant (like circumcision or baptism) only takes on meaning when it points to the thing signified: the work of God.

I am thankful, Jesus, that you have signified your covenant love for me in baptism, but I pray it never becomes the object of my faith.

[11] *in whom also you were circumcised with a circumcision made-without-hands,* **by the stripping of the body of flesh** *in the circumcision of Christ,*

A circumcision made without hands may sound vague and intangible, but for Paul it was accomplished by the very earthy "stripping of the body of flesh." "True circumcision is not minor physical surgery, but major spiritual surgery," the removal of the whole body of sinful flesh.[127]

The noun used for "stripping" (*apekdusis*) is only used here in the NT, but its verb form is used later in this letter (Col 2:15; 3:9). The related, but less forceful, verb *ekduō* is used for the stripping of Christ at his crucifixion (Mt 27:28, 31; Mk 15:20), the stripping of the victim in the parable of the Good Samaritan (Lk 10:30), and in Paul's discussion of being stripped of the body at death (2 Cor 5:3-4). Nothing is carefully removed from us when we are circumcised in Christ. Rather, the body of flesh is stripped from us in a forceful and probably painful way.

"Flesh" is often associated with circumcision. The Greek translation of the OT speaks of circumcising a *person* (Gen 17:10), circumcising *the foreskin* (Gen 17:23), and circumcising *the flesh of the foreskin* (Gen 17:11, 14, 24-25). In Col 2:11, however, it is no longer a small dispensable piece of flesh being removed. Now it is the whole body of flesh that's being removed, which sounds like another name for death. If a pound of flesh would result in certain death (a key issue in Shakespeare's *The Merchant of Venice*), the circumcision of the whole body of flesh would most certainly be fatal.

The circumcision of the flesh, then, is Paul's way of talking about the death of the flesh. He is not referring to our physical flesh, however, but to that aspect of flesh that is in sinful rebellion against what God desires (see Col 2:13, 18, 23). This is the flesh that is hostile to God (Rom 8:7) and serves the law of sin (Rom 7:25). It is this body of sinful flesh that is stripped from us, so that we are put to death in and with Christ.

Whenever someone is circumcised, something is cut off and dies. When the OT refers to the circumcision of the heart, it's not just a small appendage that needs to be removed, as if it were just a matter of fixing a few flaws. Rather, the entire hardened heart needs to be cut out and removed from the body, which is a fatal act. Even more radically, Paul speaks of cutting out the entire body of flesh. Yet this is where salvation and new life is found. As Karl Barth said, a sin-sick sinner cannot be helped by any medicine or operation, but only by the killing of the patient.[128]

Lord Jesus, thank you for doing more than just fixing a few of my flaws. Thank you for putting my sinful self to death.

[11] *in whom also you were circumcised with a circumcision made-without-hands, **by the stripping of the body of flesh** in the circumcision of Christ,*

Paul's words here fit well with his description of the Christian life in Rom 6:3-11—Christians are united with Christ in his death, and thus we *are* dead to sin and should *consider* ourselves as being dead in that way. The main difference between Romans 6 and Colossians 2 is that the language in Romans of *being crucified with Jesus* is missing in Colossians and has been replaced by the language of *being circumcised with him*. But even though the wording is different, the reality is the same. Christ's circumcision and our circumcision with him represent a kind of death—Jesus' death on the cross, and the death of our sinful body of flesh with him on the cross.

Dietrich Bonhoeffer famously said, "When Christ calls a man, he bids him come and die."[129] By itself this statement could give the wrong impression that dying to sin is completely a matter of human effort, as if Jesus bids us to come and die, and then we have to actually perform what he calls us to do. Colossians 2:11, however, declares that our body of (sinful) flesh has already died in Christ. Just as the flesh of the foreskin dies when it is cut away, so the body of flesh also dies when it is cut away in Christ. God's call then is for us to live out what God has accomplished, namely, being and acting as the people whose sinful selves have been put to death. This does not mean the person who is circumcised by God is a victim of divine violence. Rather, God saves us through this deadly procedure.

Perhaps one of the best allegorical portrayals of this process is found in C. S. Lewis' *The Great Divorce*. He introduces a man who is completely subject to a talkative red lizard on his shoulder. The man claims to dislike the lizard and is glad to hear an angel offer to take care of the problem—but not when the angel declares that the only way to alleviate the problem is to kill the lizard. That's far too drastic for the man. When the man says, "I think the gradual process would be far better than killing it," the angel responds, "The gradual process is of no use at all."[130] Learning new habits and halting old ones might be a gradual process. But gradually conquering sin makes no more sense than gradually becoming faithful to your spouse. Sin can only be conquered when it is put to death.

The shape of who we are in Christ, then, is "carved out" in the circumcision of Christ, a surgical carving that resulted in our death.[131]

Jesus, whenever I launch a new self-help plan to be a better me, take me again to the cross.

¹¹ *in whom also you were circumcised with a circumcision made-without-hands, by the stripping of the body of flesh **in the circumcision of Christ**,*

This stripping of the body of flesh does not happen as an isolated operation apart from Christ, but actually occurs "in the circumcision of Christ." But is this a circumcision he performs on us, or one that was performed on him?

The best reason to go with the first option is to compare Jesus with the OT figure Joshua. Since they share the same name (which is written differently in Hebrew and Greek), it's startling to read in the Greek translation of Josh 5:5 that "Jesus" circumcised all the sons of Israel (this is not found in English Bibles). Joshua is the great Circumciser of the Bible. Perhaps we could say that just as Joshua circumcised the nation when they entered the Promised Land, so Jesus circumcised us when we moved from the authority of darkness to his new kingdom (Col 1:13).

As intriguing as that connection is, however, the grammar suggests that Paul is talking about a circumcision performed on Jesus, which we experience with him. It's not the circumcision that happened when he was eight days old (Lk 2:21), but the stripping of his body of flesh that happened when he was crucified. Rom 8:3 says, "By sending his own Son in the likeness of sinful flesh to be a sin offering...he condemned sin in the flesh" (NIV). So the sequence is: (1) Jesus took on our sinful flesh; (2) that sinful flesh was then stripped from him at the cross as a kind of circumcision; and now (3) since we are in Christ, we too have had the sinful flesh stripped from us, that is, put to death, in the circumcision of Christ. Since being circumcised in Christ and crucified in Christ are nearly interchangeable truths for Paul, it would not be difficult to imagine Paul paraphrasing his own Gal 2:20 (about being crucified with Christ) to say, "I have been circumcised with Christ on the cross. My body of flesh has been stripped away and it is no longer I who live, but Christ who lives in me."

Since the Colossians were concerned about stopping the indulgence of the flesh (as appears to be the case in Col 2:23), from Paul's perspective the only way that can happen is by being circumcised or crucified with Christ. The regulations and spiritual techniques promoted by the distortionists are of no value in this endeavor, for Christians are transformed not by trying, but by dying—dying with Christ. What the distortionists tried to achieve by harshly treating their bodies of flesh, Christ has already achieved for us by the death of his body of flesh on the cross.

I confess, Lord, that my attempts to be holy fail. Transform me by the power of dying with you.

[12] ***having been jointly-buried with him*** *in baptism, in whom also you were jointly-raised through faith in the energizing-work of God who raised him from the dead ones.*

The burial of Jesus was an important part of the gospel message. Notice its inclusion in the summary of the gospel in 1 Cor 15:3-4. Jesus did not simply die and then quickly rise. There was a burial, a time of lying in the grave, a genuine death and not a mere 10-minute heart stoppage.

Here Paul talks about being buried with Christ, which sounds odd to us, but maybe not as much in Paul's day, for some Jews had a custom of burying family members together—in different bones boxes, but in the same cave.

We are buried with Christ because, as noted before, what happened to Christ happens to us. Just as Jesus truly died and was buried, so our sinful selves also truly died and were buried with him. Our sinful selves did not undergo a "near-death" experience, experiencing what seemed like death for only a short period of time, and then reviving. We completely died in Christ and we now live by the miracle of resurrection, not mere resuscitation. As Karl Barth said, "To bury a man is to part with him forever."[132] Cranfield adds, "Burial is the seal set to the fact of death—it is when a man's relatives and friends leave his body in a grave and return home without him that the fact that he no longer shares their life is exposed with inescapable conclusiveness."[133]

We, of course, wonder if our sinful selves have truly died and been buried with Christ, for we are well aware of how persistent our sinful behavior still is. We don't think of our sinful self as dead in Christ, but alive and kicking. Paul recognized this problem in Romans 6, for shortly after he said, "our old self was crucified with him" (Rom 6:6, NRSV)—which sounds like an accomplished fact—then he called on his readers to "consider yourselves dead to sin" and commanded them, "do not let sin exercise dominion in your mortal bodies" (Rom 6:11-12, NRSV). What we learn from this is that even though our sinful selves have truly died with Christ, we need to be reminded to live into this God-made condition.

Although our sinful flesh has died with Christ, it can return like a ghost to haunt us, a ghost that deceives us into thinking it has power over us, even though it does not. It's merely a ghost of ourselves. The only power it has over us is the power we think it has. When it haunts you, send it back to the grave where it belongs and remember who you really are in Christ.

Sometimes I am haunted, Lord, by my sinful past and my present temptations. Return me to the reality of those things being dead and buried in you.

*[12] having been jointly-buried with him **in baptism,** in whom also you were jointly-raised through faith in the energizing-work of God who raised him from the dead ones.*

God signifies our burial with Christ through the action of baptism. When a believer is immersed in water (or comes under water through sprinkling or pouring), God is testifying that their old self, which had lived under the authority of darkness is dead and buried, and the person now belongs to the kingdom of the Father, Son, and Holy Spirit (see Col 1:13).

While we might expect Paul to instruct believers on the meaning of baptism, he seldom talks about it—only 16 times does he use a verb or noun containing the *bapt-* stem. And when he does talk about it, it's mostly about either the unity of the church or being buried with Christ. Surprisingly, he never explicitly links baptism to covenant, evangelism, repentance, forgiveness, or cleansing. When he does talk about cleansing, he doesn't use words with the *bapt-* stem (see 1 Cor 6:11; Eph 5:25-26; Titus 3:5). Maybe he doesn't want to give the impression that baptism does the cleansing. For him, baptism is not about washing away dirt, but lying down in the dirt to be buried with Christ.

Since we participate in Christ's death, burial, and resurrection, we might expect Paul to say we are also baptized in Christ, participating in Jesus' own baptism, but he doesn't. Perhaps that would put too much emphasis on what is supposed to be a sign pointing away from itself to a greater reality. We don't need directional signs that point to themselves in large letters, saying, "This is a sign." What we need are signs that point beyond themselves, which is how Paul would view baptism.

Something would be amiss if a person received a printed love-letter and seemed more enthused about the beauty of the font used instead of the contents of the letter. Yes, a font was needed in order to print the letter, but the font only points toward the love; the font is not the love itself. The same is the case with the baptismal font. Paul does not want the Colossians focusing on their baptism (or even Jesus' baptism), but on their burial with Christ which is signified and sealed by baptism. As Berkouwer noted, "Nothing happens in and through baptism. Rather, baptism is meaningful only through its pointing at another event," and that event is the cross of Jesus where we had earlier died with him.[134]

I thank you, Lord, that the burial of my old self is not merely an interesting idea, but as real as the water that came upon me at my baptism.

*¹² having been jointly-buried with him **in baptism,** in whom also you were jointly-raised through faith in the energizing-work of God who raised him from the dead ones.*

As noted yesterday, baptism for Paul is either about the unity of the church (see 1 Cor 1:10-17; 12:13; Gal 3:27-28; Eph 4:4-6) or burial with Christ (as here). But even here there is a hint of the unity of the church, for Paul is declaring that in Christ all Christians share a common grave. In the grave there is no sense in making divisive comparisons. Dead is dead. The competitive, divisive way of life is buried and gone for Christians because it is not our spiritual accomplishments which bring fullness of salvation, but our participation in the death and resurrection of Christ.

Jesus earlier alluded to this link between baptism and his death. He talked about his own death as a baptism that he would undergo (Lk 12:50). He also hinted that his disciples would also undergo this same baptism of suffering and death (Mk 10:38-39).

Baptism itself is not the point at which we die; rather, baptism is the burial that happens after we die, "a solemn burial as befits the dead."[135] Although a few people have been buried alive and thus die in their tomb, more commonly people die first and then are buried. Thus, baptism does not cause the sinful self to die with Christ. Rather, we died with Christ at Jesus' crucifixion, a reality which dawns on us through faith. And because we've already died with Christ, it is then appropriate to be buried with him.

In Col 2:11 our death with Christ is called being circumcised in him (Rom 6:6 calls it being crucified with him). In either case, our death with Christ on the cross precedes our burial with him in baptism. As Paul said in Rom 6:3-4, "Do you not know that all of us who have been baptized into Christ Jesus were baptized into his death? We were buried therefore with him by baptism into death, in order that, just as Christ was raised from the dead by the glory of the Father, we too might walk in newness of life" (ESV).

The focus of Paul's reference to baptism in Col 2:12 is not on merely *being in* Christ, *forgiven* by Christ, or *belonging to* Christ, but on being in Christ in a particular way, namely, *buried with him.* Baptism does not cause a person to die (or rise) with Christ, but rather it is "the proclamation, the thanks, the praise of that which has already occurred."[136] As Gorman notes, "What really matters is dying with Christ in reality, not in the ritual."[137]

Jesus, whether I remember my baptism or not, I'm thankful that my sinful self died with you and was buried with you.

*¹² having been jointly-buried with him **in baptism,** in whom also you were jointly-raised through faith in the energizing-work of God who raised him from the dead ones.*

Because circumcision and baptism are in close proximity in Col 2:11-12, many have concluded that baptism is an improved NT version of circumcision. There are similarities, of course. "Both are *rites of entry* into the people of God, both *distinguish* the covenant people of God from all others, and both point to a *deeper spiritual transformation.*"[138] They are also both performed by God's command through human hands and are actions done *to* a person, not *by* the person. But one does not replace the other. Early Jewish Christians practiced both circumcision and baptism in obedience to God, which means that they, at least, did not see baptism as the replacement or fulfillment of circumcision; and the same is true among Jewish Christians today.[139]

There are also key differences. Circumcision is performed on males; baptism on both genders. Circumcision incorporates a person into the family of Abraham; baptism incorporates a person into Christ. Circumcision is physically painful; baptism is painless but it sets a person on the road of suffering with Christ. Circumcision leaves a visible mark; baptism leaves no visible mark.

Calvinists (and I'm referring to my own tribe here) have argued for one more similarity between circumcision and baptism: just as infants were circumcised under the old covenant, so infants should be baptized under the new. This fits well into Calvin's theological system, but unfortunately, Col 2:11-12 is the only verse in the Bible that speaks of baptism in proximity to circumcision. Even if circumcision and baptism do have many similarities, nothing in Colossians indicates that the inclusion of infants is one of them. Just because Col 2:11-12 regards circumcision as a form of dying with Christ, and baptism as a form of being buried with Christ, that doesn't mean that baptism is a form of circumcision and must be extended to infants.

This doesn't mean churches should not baptize infants, but it does mean that the biblical case for doing so, based on Col 2:11-12, is not as strong as suggested, and this issue should be approached with more humility than is often the case. Whether we baptize infants or not, the message of our burial in Christ must come through.

Heavenly Father, heal the divisions within your church over the issues surrounding baptism. Show us our place in a common grave with your Son.

*[12] having been jointly-buried with him in baptism, **in whom also you were jointly-raised** through faith in the energizing-work of God who raised him from the dead ones.*

We were not only buried with Christ, but also raised with him in his resurrection. If you were to look up the various words used for resurrection in the NT, you would soon discover Jesus' resurrection is the primary resurrection event. All other forms of resurrection orbit around the central role of Jesus' resurrection.

For example, the NT miracles of people coming back to life may not be full resurrections (so that these people will never die), yet they foreshadow the reality of Jesus' full resurrection. In the glory of these temporary resuscitations, we catch a glimpse of the eternal resurrection of Jesus.

The final resurrection of the last days also orbits around Jesus' resurrection. When Jesus was raised, it was a sign of more resurrections to come, for he is the firstborn from the dead (Col 1:18). As Paul says in Rom 8:11, "If the Spirit of him who raised Jesus from the dead dwells in you, he who raised Christ from the dead will give life to your mortal bodies also through his Spirit that dwells in you" (NRSV; see also 2 Cor 4:14).

And spiritual resurrections (or as I prefer, "heart-resurrections") also flow out of Jesus' resurrection, for already we have been jointly-raised with Christ (Col 2:12). If Jesus had not been raised, we would still be dead in our sins (Col 2:13). But because Jesus *has* been raised, we experience not just renewed spiritual passion, but the resurrection life of Christ himself.

As wonderful as it is, however, a heart-resurrection is not a private experience given for our own sense of well-being. It's a relational event, for we can only be raised *with* Christ. When we are snatched from death and raised to life, we are not to be fascinated with our new selves, but with the One who raised us up.[140] Heart-resurrections are also relational in that we are raised together as the body of Christ. Later in this letter Paul will describe what the new life in Christ looks like when we live it together (see Col 3:5-17).

The good news, then, is that even when we don't "feel" particularly new, we are indeed raised with Christ. Our status before God and the condition of our hearts are transformed because we are in union with the risen Jesus.

It's so easy to take this new life for granted, Lord. But where would I be without your love, joy, peace, and hope that flow from your resurrection into my own heart?

[12] *having been jointly-buried with him in baptism,* **in whom also you were jointly-raised** *through faith in the energizing-work of God who raised him from the dead ones.*

Not only do all forms of resurrection in the NT orbit around Jesus' resurrection, but every one of them is also an end-times resurrection.

Many Jews in Jesus' day believed that resurrection from the dead was a key indicator that the end times had arrived. So when Jesus rose from the dead, the early Christians believed the last days were at hand (see Heb 1:1-2). In Jesus (as seen especially in his resurrection), the future has invaded the present; in him the future last days were already happening. Similarly, when Jesus and his disciples raised people back to life—even though they would die again later—these miracles were also signs indicating that the last days have arrived.

The same holds true for heart-resurrections. When we experience newness of life in Christ, we are already participating in the living power that will be fully unleashed at the end of time. Whenever we are lifted from grief to hope, from shame to forgiveness, from boredom to mission, from anger to love, it's a kind of end-times resurrection we experience in Christ.

Paul, of course, would not claim that the Colossians are so fully raised that there is no need for any other resurrection (an idea he rejects in 2 Tim 2:18). He sees this issue in terms of what scholars call "the already and the not yet." *Already* we are raised with Christ, experiencing newness of life, but *not yet* are we living as fully resurrected people. *Already* we have passed from death to life (see John 5:24), but *not yet* can we avoid dying. *Already* we have power to live in a holy way, but *not yet* are we sinless. When speaking to those who thought they were more advanced than they actually were, Paul emphasized the "not yet" side of the equation. But when speaking to Christians who wondered if they needed something more than Christ (as was the case in Colossae), then Paul emphasized what they "already" had in Christ. This is why Paul speaks so forcefully in Col 2:12 of being already "raised with" Christ.

Though our heart-resurrection *is* incomplete, it's not because Jesus is insufficiently powerful. Rather, it's because we are living between Jesus' resurrection and the end-times resurrection. There is not yet fullness in our heart-resurrection—that awaits the final resurrection—but there *is* fullness in Christ, now and for all eternity.

Thank you, Jesus, that I already have new life in you. Grant me patience as I wait for your return when the fullness of new life arrives.

[12] *having been jointly-buried with him in baptism, in whom also you were jointly-raised **through faith in the energizing-work of God who raised him from the dead ones.***

While it's true that we are circumcised in Christ, buried with him, and risen in him, all this only takes on reality for us "through faith." Without faith, these events occurred for Christ, but we would never know our place with him. But through faith, we ourselves are united with Christ in his work.

Some have attempted to downplay faith by focusing on the distinction between activity and passivity with regards to salvation, as if all the activity belongs to God and we are merely passive recipients of what God is doing. Indeed, it is true that Paul often uses passive verbs to describe Christians as recipients of God's gracious acts of redemption. In Colossians alone, we are on the receiving end of being filled (Col 1:9; 2:10); strengthened (Col 1:11); encouraged and drawn together in love (Col 2:2); rooted, built up, and established in the faith (Col 2:7); circumcised, buried, and raised with Christ (Col 2:11-12; 3:1); supplied and drawn together (Col 2:19); renewed (Col 3:10); loved (Col 3:12); and called as one body (Col 3:15).

Nonetheless, there is more to the Christian life than mere passivity. Thielicke wisely reminds us, "The terms [active and passive] are in order when dealing with objects like the hammer and the anvil but not in personal relations...we are not mere objects of [the Holy Spirit's work] exposed to its activity only as passive recipients. We are caught up into it."[141] It calls forth a response in us; a response of faith. Any stance that downplays faith in order to exalt human passivity actually hinders us from being true recipients of God's blessings.

This does not mean that ultimately it is *our* faith that has the real power to resurrect, as if Jesus and his resurrection were only tools and resources for our faith to use in raising ourselves to new life. When Paul says we are raised with Christ "through faith," it is not a case of *us* using faith to raise ourselves up, but of *God* working through faith to raise us up. Not even Jesus raised himself from the dead, as can be seen in this and many other NT verses (such as Mt 17:23; Acts 5:30; 1 Cor 6:14). And if Jesus needed the Father to raise him up, we certainly do too.

And the Father is up to the task, for he is the one who gives life to the dead (Rom 4:17). In fact, starting with the Jewish book *Joseph and Asenath*, that became a name for God: "The One Who Gives Life to the Dead."[142]

Lord, on my own I cannot muster a faithful or obedient response to you. Yet by Jesus' resurrection power, you have energized me to respond. Thank you.

[13] *And you, being dead in the transgressions and the uncircumcision of your flesh, he [God] made you jointly-alive with him [Christ], having granted-grace to us for all transgressions.*

This is the third time Paul contrasts the Colossians' situation before and after they were in Christ. They had been under the authority of darkness, but now have been relocated to Jesus' kingdom (Col 1:13). They had been alienated from God, but now God has reconciled them to himself (Col 1:21-22). And here, they had been dead in sin—though still walking around like spiritual zombies—but now God has put their lifeless selves to death with Christ on the cross, so they could then be raised with him (Col 2:13).

Paul uses the graphic language of being dead in the transgressions and the uncircumcision of our flesh to convey how dire our situation was (see also Eph 2:1-3). "Sin is more than a moral debt on the pages of a divine ledger...Sin is not merely an affront to God's dignity requiring reparation, or a breaking of God's rules, requiring correction."[143] Sin does not merely make us dirty, so that a good old-fashioned cleansing could purify us. Sin does not simply make us morally ill or spiritually weak—in which case it would still be possible for us to respond to God. No, our problem was far more radical. We were dead.

Just as those who are biologically dead cannot respond to or follow anyone, so those who are spiritually dead cannot respond to or follow Christ. Like the church at Sardis, a person without Christ may have a reputation of being alive, but they are dead to the things of God (Rev 3:1). And when we are dead in sin, only a miracle can bring us to life.

But thanks be to God, this miracle has happened. God has made us alive with Christ. Those who were dead in *transgressions* were made alive with Christ through the grace of forgiveness. Those who were dead in the *uncircumcision of their flesh* were made alive with Christ through a circumcision made without hands (Col 2:11-13).

As you can see, the idea of death can be used in multiple ways in describing the gospel. Sometimes it's *bad* to be dead, as is true when we are dead in sin (Col 2:13). But it can also be *good* to be dead, as is the case when our sinful selves are put to death in Christ (Col 2:11-12a). If we put both truths together, Paul is saying this: we were dead in sin, and then our dead sinful selves died even more fully with Christ, after which we were raised with Christ to new life.

Savior, I confess that I easily forget how bad my situation was without you.
Thank you for raising me from the deadness of sin.

*13 And you, being dead in the transgressions and the uncircumcision of your flesh, he [God] made you jointly-alive with him [Christ], **having granted-grace to us for all transgressions.***

Sin leads to death. Therefore, the only way that those who are dead in sin can experience resurrection is if their sin is dealt with.[144] That's what this last phrase is about. Grace is what makes forgiveness and resurrection happen. We deserved to be left in the deadness of our sin, but God did not let death-dealing sin have the last word in our lives. Instead, God made us alive by showering us with grace to wipe away all the transgressions that had killed us.

Most Bible translations use the verb "forgive" here, but Paul tends to avoid the usual verb for forgiveness. He instead prefers the verb *charizomai*, which is based on the word of grace (*charis*). So I have opted to depart from the standard translation in order to highlight the role of grace. Perhaps I should have gone even further and coined a new verb, *gracify*. God gracifies us when we sin and commands us to gracify those who sin against us (2 Cor 2:7, 10; 12:13; Eph 4:32; Col 3:13).

It's important to emphasize that God meets our transgressions with grace. This would have been astounding, even scandalous, news to the Greek-speaking world. Plato said it would be improper for judges to show grace to wrongdoers: the judge's oath "binds him not to do favours [*charizomai*] according to his pleasure, but to judge according to the laws" (*The Apology* 35c). Their job is to dispense justice, not grace. God, however, dispenses justice by giving grace.

This granting of grace to remove transgressions is an essential part of coming alive with Christ. But it's a grace that does something far more radical than accepting us. God's grace kills us—so that we can rise to new life and walk in Christ. God's grace kills our tendency to trespass into danger zones of death. God's grace kills our fatal attractions and fatal addictions. God's grace smashes our hearts of stone. God's grace cuts away the gangrene that infects our souls.

And it's not just *some* of our transgressions that have been removed by grace, but "all" of them. We are not only forgiven the sins of which we are conscious or from which we have repented. *All* our sins have been overcome by God's grace so that they no longer obstruct our relationship with God.[145]

Lord, I not only sing, "Amazing grace, how sweet the sound," but I also see how sweet is the reality. May I always stand amazed before your love.

¹⁴ Wiping-away the handwritten debt-note against us, which opposed us with its decrees, he [God] has taken it from center-stage, having nailed it to the cross.

Paul here refers to a debt-note (*cheirographon*), similar in function to an IOU. Although many translations ignore it, the word literally means that it's a note written by hand (*cheiros*). This is important because Paul had just spoken of a "circumcision made-without-hands" (Col 2:11), with the implication that those things made *with* hands—whether a circumcision or a debt-note—cannot accomplish God's purposes. The *cheirographon* was a hand-written note written out by the person who took on the debt, not by the person to whom the debt is owed.[146] Thus, the word may be implying that debtors have no one but themselves to blame for their debt load, since the note was written by them.

The problem with this handwritten debt-note is that it stands *against us*. Paul emphasizes this against-ness twice here—it's against us and opposed to us—which many translations drop because it's awkward in English. We signed on for this debt, and when we are unable to repay it, our note testifies against us.

Furthermore, this handwritten debt-note stands against us *with its decrees* (the Greek word is *dogma*). In the few times this word is used in the Bible, it's in the context of conflict. Non-Jewish rulers made decrees against God's people. The Jews in turn refused to give in because they wanted to maintain ancestral decrees (4 Mac 4:23-24). Church leaders issued decrees in order to resolve conflict (Acts 16:4). God even nullified earlier decrees of his that had created conflict between Jews and non-Jews (Eph 2:15).

Finally, this handwritten debt-note which stood against us with its decrees was *wiped away* (*exaleiphō*) by God. God not only wipes away tears (Rev 7:17) and promises not to wipe away our name from the book of life (Rev 3:5), but he also wipes away sins from our record (here and in Acts 3:19, "Repent therefore, and turn to God, that your sins may be wiped out," NRSV). This same word is also used in the Greek translation of the OT, to say that God blots out our transgressions (Isa 43:25; Ps 51:1). When God wipes it away, then our debt-note is nothing but a blank scrap of paper, no longer holding anything over us.[147]

Tomorrow we'll look more closely at what this all means, but for now we rejoice that because God is for us, no debt-note can stand against us.

No matter what comes against me, Jesus, even if it's my own sin, I thank you for standing on my side.

*¹⁴ **Wiping-away the handwritten debt-note against us, which opposed us with its decrees**, he [God] has taken it from center-stage, having nailed it to the cross.*

So what is the debt we owed? To whom did we owe it? And how do the decrees fit into this picture? The common interpretation is this:

We owed a debt to God for our failure to obey his law (decrees) as we had promised, and so Jesus came to pay off this debt on the cross. The idea here, says Moore, is that "man owes God obedience, and every sin, whether of commission or of omission, is a defaulted obligation, a debt."[148] The OT mostly conceived of sin as a weight, and forgiveness as a lifting of the burden.[149] In between the testaments, however, the imagery of sin switched from weight to debt, and Jesus followed suit. In his parables and the Lord's Prayer he talked about having our debts forgiven. In this scenario, the decrees that stand against us are God's laws which testify against us. But then "Jesus paid it all," as the hymn says; and our debt was erased.

Even though this is the most popular way of understanding this verse, there are three problems. (1) The issue of the OT law doesn't come up anywhere else in Colossians; instead Paul talks about the decrees of the elemental-orders of the world (Col 2,20-21). (2) Even though the NT talks about forgiving our debts, it never explicitly says that Jesus paid our debts. And (3) although Jesus talks about sin as a debt, Paul never talks about it that way. If we have been in debt to anything, it was a debt to our sinful nature (see Rom 8:9-13, especially verse 12).

Perhaps Paul avoids the image of sin as a debt because it lends itself to the idea that we can chip away at the debt through good works. According to at least some Jewish writings of the time, "God cancels a debt only when the scales of merits and debts balance."[150] But Paul wants to get away from this talk of merits and debts. Rather, this wiping away of sin is done by God as a free gift of grace (the *charis-grace* which is part of the verb *charizomai* found in Col 2:13).

But even though this interpretation is on shakier ground than we might have expected, it does remind us well that our sins have been thoroughly erased from God's records. People may have a hard time deleting old (and incriminating) Facebook posts, but Jesus can do something far more important and miraculous: erase our sins from God's books.

Forgive my debts, Lord. Blot out my transgressions. Set me free from the foolish sins of my past.

[14] **Wiping-away the handwritten debt-note against us, which opposed us with its decrees,** he [God] has taken it from center-stage, having nailed it to the cross.

As we saw yesterday, there is such a thing as being in debt to God, but Col 2:14 may not be about that kind of debt.

Perhaps we were *in debt to the primal-powers.* At one time we had agreed to obey their decrees of how we should live, but we realized too late that the terms of the loan were not in our favor and actually turned us into the slaves of evil spirits. We were under such a terrible obligation to follow their commands that we needed Jesus to come and erase this bad debt.

This interpretation may fit the context better, for it explains why Paul follows up this verse with the declaration in Col 2:15 that the primal-powers have been defeated by Christ. We are debt-free because those powers to whom we were indebted no longer have any claim upon us. We no longer have to obey their decrees about how to live (see Col 2:20-21).

The handwritten debt-note may also fit well here. An old Jewish book called the *Apocalypse of Zephaniah* said that the devil's angels write down all the sins of men in a hand-written debt note, so the devil has proof for his accusations against us. This same work then speaks of God mercifully wiping away this record of sins, so God's people could cross over from Hades to heaven (see Col 1:13-14). This is not an inspired book, but it shows that Paul could easily have been thinking along the same lines.

On the other hand, maybe this verse means we were *in debt to our own sinful flesh.* This interpretation is based on Rom 8:9-13, where Paul proclaims that Christians are *not* debtors to the flesh, with the implication, however, that at one time we were so indebted and under obligation to obey our sinful nature. Every time we tried to get out from under this debt—making resolutions to do better and following man-made rules of morality (like those promoted by the distortionists)—it only got worse. But now, says Paul, we no longer owe any debt to the flesh, for God wiped it away by having us die with Christ. Once our sinful flesh died with him, then all our debts were canceled, and we were under no more obligation to sin.

Although this verse can be interpreted in many different ways, don't be frustrated by that. Instead, rejoice that no matter how it is interpreted, Jesus has set us free. We are not under a burdensome debt to God's laws, or to primal-powers, or even our own sinful nature. We are free in Christ.

Lord, whenever I'm kicking myself for not living up to expectations—my own, someone else's or even yours—remind me again of what you did at the cross.

^{14} *Wiping-away the handwritten debt-note against us, which opposed us with its decrees, **he [God] has taken it from center-stage, having nailed it to the cross.***

Paul explains further how God has wiped away our debt-note. First, God took (*airō*) it, a seemingly ordinary word, but an interesting choice in light of John the Baptist calling Jesus "the Lamb of God who takes away (*airō*) the sin of the world" (Jn 1:29, NRSV). Indeed, Jesus "appeared so that he might take away (*airō*) our sins" (1 Jn 3:5, NIV).

Where did God take this debt-note? Since it was squawking so loudly about our sins, God took it away from center stage—or more literally, "away from the middle" where it was grabbing all the attention. This phrase may sound odd to us, but it was a Greek way of expressing the desire to get rid of something. When the philosopher Epictetus wanted to say, "away with it!" he would say, "take it from the middle."[151] Since the middle was where accusing witnesses stood in court proceedings[152] (as happened at Jesus' trial in Mk 14:60), then Paul would be saying here that God not only wiped away the accusatory debt-note, but threw it out of court. It's out of order.

And God went a step further in making the debt-note null and void by sending it to the cross to be crucified with Jesus. According to this verse and others, Jesus is not the only one who was nailed to the cross on Good Friday. The other things or people crucified with Christ include: (1) the old sinful self of believers (Rom 6:6; Gal 5:24); (2) the world, meaning the world-system in rebellion against God (Gal 6:14); and (3) the debt-note that stood against us (Col 2:14).

Perhaps Paul is comparing the debt-note to the notice that was fixed on Jesus' cross, informing everyone of his "crime" (see Mk 15:26). Just as the accusation made against Jesus was nailed to the cross, so the debt-note's accusations against us were also nailed with him.[153] This debt-note is not attached to the cross like a garage sale sign on a utility pole. Rather, it's being put to death with Christ. In the words of a Dixie Chicks' song title, it's as if Jesus had said to that debt-note, "If I fall you're going down with me." This note of our indebtedness, then, cannot rise up and make any more demands upon us, for it was put to death with Jesus. God killed it.

Thank you, Lord, that there is now no condemnation for me or anyone else living in you.

^{15} **Having stripped the primal-powers and the authorities, he [God] exposed them openly,** *triumphantly-parading them in him [Christ].*

At first glance, Paul seems to be moving to a new topic, from victory over *sin* to victory over the *powers.* But the two victories are interrelated, for the primal-powers are the ones who tempt us to sin and then accuse us when we fall. So as Lucas notes, "where there is forgiveness of sins there is also freedom from the powers of evil,"[154] and *vice versa.* That's why both Col 1:13-14 and Col 2:14-15 link forgiveness with freedom from the powers.

Although the pagan people of the area worried about the primal-powers bringing misfortune upon them (such as diseases, storms, or accidents), Paul was more concerned about their accusatory role. The primal-powers were speaking through the distortionists to shake the confidence of God's people, making them think they were still missing something, and that Christ was not enough to fill the gap. In other words, the Colossians were not good enough, and Christ was not great enough.

We have already encountered these primal-powers in Colossians, but there is a different mood here. While Col 1:15-20 put a positive spin on them (they were created in Christ and included in the reconciliation brought by Christ), this verse views them more negatively, more in line with his earlier description of the "authority of darkness" (Col 1:13). Jesus may have authority over these powers as their head (Col 2:10), but here he shows how he exercises that authority when they rebel—he strips them.

The primal-powers had wrapped themselves in the mantle of authority over matters which were not theirs to decide. They had put on the robes of judges, acting as if they had the power to decide the eternal destiny of God's people. They were wearing power suits and ties, behaving as if they were God's collection agents, harassing people for their indebtedness to the flesh. They had armed themselves with combat gear to wage war on the people of God, under the pretense of exposing their hypocrisies. Whatever the powers-that-be had clothed themselves in, God stripped them of it so that all their accusations now ring hollow for those who are in Christ.

We needed Christ to do this because, according to Barth, "it is not men, or any one man, who can make the break with these given factors and orders and historical forces."[155] Like a knot that only gets tighter the more it is pulled, so the grip of the powers is only strengthened by human efforts to undo them. God alone can break them in Christ.

Make me aware, Savior, of the spiritual forces that threaten to undo me, and make me even more aware of your power to undo them.

> [15] **Having stripped the primal-powers and the authorities, he [God]**
> **exposed them openly,** *triumphantly-parading them in him [Christ].*

Elsewhere in Colossians Paul talks about how we need to be stripped of the body of flesh in the circumcision of Christ (Col 2:11) and stripped of our old selves (Col 3:9). Here however, it is the primal-powers who are stripped. Although this verb could be translated as "put off," "take off," or "remove," the context suggests something harsher. God is not gently removing the mantle of authority from these powers, but stripping it from them in judgment. Unlike some of the pagans who thought it best to appease the primal-powers, Paul shows instead that Christ came to defeat them.[156]

Many versions of the Bible translate the verb as "disarm" here because it's spoken in the context of spiritual warfare. Yet it's striking that weapons are not mentioned. Rather, Paul is emphasizing that the powers have not only been stripped of weapons, but also of any pretensions to power; they are exposed as powerless. Says König, "Whenever Jesus appears on the scene, the powerlessness of the powers becomes apparent. Even as Jesus approaches they cry out in terror, acknowledge his sovereignty, entreat him not to destroy or hurt them, surrender their victims and make off."[157]

Just as the Roman Empire would humiliate conquered kings by stripping them of their wealth, their authority, their weapons, their dignity, and perhaps even their clothes, so God has stripped the rebellious powers of what they had at one time (or pretended to have). And in the same way that the Lord shamed the gods at his divine council for failing to help the needy in Psalm 82, so here God puts the primal-powers to shame as well. Garland compares them to the Nazi leaders who were tried at Nuremberg. Many people feared their deadly power at one time, but when these men sat in a courtroom looking feeble and weak, we wondered why people were ever afraid of them.[158]

Paul may be engaging in a little word-play here concerning the exposure of the powers. The word for exposed (the exact form used here is *edeigmatisen*) sounds a lot like the word for decrees from verse 14 (the exact form there is *dogmasin*). Thus, Paul is saying that the very powers who used decrees (*dogmasin)* to put God's people to shame will themselves be exposed (*edeigmatisen*) and put to shame.

Lord, you are my light and my salvation, and I have no reason to be afraid.
Though a host of powers surround me, I will be confident in you.

*15 **Having stripped the primal-powers and the authorities, he [God] exposed them openly**, triumphantly-parading them in him [Christ].*

Because the primal-powers were exposed by Christ and his cross, there is no more need to fear them. C. S. Lewis famously said, "There are two equal and opposite errors into which our race can fall about the devils. One is to disbelieve in their existence. The other is to believe, and to feel an excessive and unhealthy interest in them."[159] Living in fear of demonic powers—thinking they have more power than they do—would qualify as believing in them too much.

If the primal-powers have any power left at all, it's the power of the bluff, the ability to fool us into thinking they still have power over us. The primal-powers want us to think that they have tempting goods to fulfill us. They want us to think that we still have a debt (perhaps to God, society, the flesh, or themselves) that we need to work off. They want us to think that they've got the plan to save us or the power to destroy us.

They are like the bank robber who looks as if he has a gun inside of his coat pocket pointing straight at us, even though all he really has in his pocket is his finger. As long as we believe the robber has a gun, we'll do as he says, but once we realize he has no weapon, we can call his bluff. Like-wise, as long as we think the primal-powers do indeed have power, then they can control us. But it's a different story when we realize that God has exposed them. We will not be taken captive by the lies of these primal-powers (Col 2:8) once we realize that they themselves have been taken captive by God. This is why Paul wants the Colossians (and us) to call their bluff. The powers have nothing we want and nothing we fear, for we are in Christ, dead to sin and alive to God.

Of course, the primal-powers have not yet disappeared and are still dangerous to those outside of Christ. But the good news, says König, is this, "Though the powers have been conquered *already*, they will be conquered *again*" in a fuller way yet when Jesus returns.[160]

We do well, therefore, to celebrate Jesus' victory over the powers in bringing us to salvation. Instead of living fearfully and anxiously in a still-hostile world—even striking out against it—God's people can celebrate Jesus' victory over the powers by living in the world with a spirit of love, joy, and peace.

Let your perfect love, O Lord, cast out my fear so that I can live in this hostile world with love, joy, and peace.

217

 15 *Having stripped the primal-powers and the authorities, he [God] exposed them openly, **triumphantly-parading them in him [Christ].***

When the Romans conquered a nation, they would celebrate with a triumphal parade (*thriambos*). Vanquished leaders and soldiers would be stripped of their weapons and dignity and be paraded through the streets of Rome. These captives would be driven in front of the general's chariot to the *jeers* of the crowd, and then the conquering general would follow behind to the *cheers* of the crowd. At the end of the parade some of the enemies would be executed. It was a long-standing custom among the Romans for honoring both the victor and the gods, with over 300 triumphs celebrated between the founding of Rome and the end of the first century AD.[161] Roman orators even claimed that the victories of the emperors were like the mythical victories of the gods over the ancient powers of chaos.[162]

But what was a myth for Rome was reality in Christ. Using the corresponding verb *thriambeuō*, Paul declares that the real victory parade over the powers happened at the cross of Christ. There we see a conqueror completely unlike the Roman emperors. While the emperors used violence against their foes in war, Jesus did not act violently toward the powers, but instead suffered violence himself at their hands. While the emperors rode in the back of the parade, driving their foes ahead of them to their deaths, Jesus led the parade, going to his own death first. While the emperors rode to public acclaim as heroes, Jesus went forth as a loser in the eyes of the world. Jesus has no desire to gloat over the primal-powers, but he wants their reign in the world and in our lives to end.

So then, as Lincoln said, "the powers of evil are defeated not by some overwhelming display of divine power but by the weakness of Christ's death."[163] Jesus did not come to crush his foes like a superpower armed to the teeth. If that had been the case, then Jesus would have only won because he's a bigger bully than the bullies who used to rule the playground of the world. It would be better to look at it from another angle. When the powers wanted to play "king of the hill," Jesus won that game, but—and this is decisive—he simultaneously undermined that game. He not only triumphed over the primal-powers, but he also triumphed over their way of doing business. He won the power game by subverting it. He defeated the powers by giving up power. He became "king of the hill" by dying in weakness on a hill called Mt. Calvary.

Forgive me, Lord, when I have used power-plays to get my way at home, at work, at church. Teach me again the strength of being weak in you.

*15 Having stripped the primal-powers and the authorities, he [God] exposed them openly, **triumphantly-parading them in him [Christ]**.*

Most people in the first century would have regarded Jesus' crucifixion as signaling defeat, and it did. But it was not the defeat of the one hanging on the cross; it was the defeat of the powers who put him there. They thought the cross was their moment of triumph, in which even God's Son had come under their power, but instead they were doing themselves in. Not only did Christ slip from their grasp, but so did everything else formerly under their control. Says N.T. Wright, "The cross was not the defeat of *Christ* at the hands of the *powers*: it was the defeat of the *powers* at the hands—yes, the bleeding hands—of Christ."[164]

"None of the rulers of this age understood this, for if they had, they would not have crucified the Lord of glory" (1 Cor 2:8, NRSV). But as it is, they did crucify him, and in a sense, Jesus pulled them onto the cross with him. In the stripping of Jesus, the powers were stripped. In the mocking of Jesus, they were being mocked. In the parading of Jesus through the streets of Jerusalem, they were being paraded. Although the powers-that-be wanted to give the impression that they are respectable, law-abiding, truthful, peace-loving, honorable, just, and even religious, the cross of Jesus exposed their false claims, their rebellion against God, their lies, violence, and injustice. Their actions against Jesus demonstrated that they had over-reached their authority, and thus lost their authority.

This is true on the political level, of course, for Jesus was crucified "under Pontius Pilate." But Paul is especially thinking of how this is true for all the powers-that-be. According to the Greek translation of Isa 24:21, "God will bring his hand against *the world of heaven* and against *the kings of the earth*" (my translation). And the hand which God brought against these powers was the nail-pierced hand of Jesus on the cross.

In celebrating Jesus' victory, however, there is no justification for the church to adopt a militant, triumphalist spirit. Instead, Jesus' victory reminds us that true Christian victory only happens when we take our place with Jesus in the weakness of the cross. Because the powers have been defeated in Christ, God's people no longer have to fight against the world in the manner of the OT holy wars.[165] Now we deal with the world through the love shown in the weakness of Jesus' cross.

Lead on, O King Eternal, but not with swords' loud clashing nor roll of stirring drums, but with deeds of love and mercy.

Fullness of Deity Dwells in Christ's Body
to the tune of Crusaders' Hymn: *Fairest Lord Jesus*
© 2012 David J. Landegent

Fullness of deity dwells in Christ's body
Now all His people are filled in Him.
Over all powers—and all dominions
Our Lord is head of everything.

In Him we're circumcised, stripped of our wicked life
Buried with Christ, we are dead to sin:
Raised with our Savior, raised by God's power
Forgiven and alive in Him.

God canceled ev'ry debt, which threatened us with death
Our sins were nailed to the cross of wood.
All laws and powers which had accused us
Our Lord exposed them as no good.

Detached from Christ

Colossians 2:16-23

July 10-August 14

16 Therefore, let no one judge you in eating and drinking or in respect to a festival or a new-moon or sabbaths, 17 which are a shadow of coming things, but the body [that cast the shadow is] of Christ. 18 Let nobody disqualify you, insisting on humbling-practices and worship of angels, claiming-access to the things which he has seen, vainly being puffed up by his mind of flesh, 19 and not gripping the head, from whom all the body, being supplied and drawn together through its joints and connecting-tissues, grows with growth from God.

20 If you died with Christ to the elemental-orders of the world, why, as though living in [that] world, would you come under its decrees, 21 "Do not touch; do not taste; do not contact!" 22 all of which goes to decay with use? [Such decrees are] according to the commandments and teachings of men, 23 which indeed are a word having wisdom in self-willed-worship and humbling-practices, the unsparing-treatment of the body, but they are without honor [in going] against the filling-full of the flesh.

In Colossians 2 Paul alternates between positive statements of truth and negative assessments of error. In verses 6-8 he gave a positive command to walk in Christ and a negative warning to avoid distorted teaching. This was followed by a positive portrayal of Christ's effective work in us, and now he presents a negative portrayal of the distortion's ineffectiveness.

Garland helpfully summarizes five dangers that Paul exposes in this section:[166] (1) the danger of a religion that judges and disqualifies others based on its own self-chosen criteria; (2) the danger of do-it-yourself religion which adopts humanly-devised rules and formulas for taming sin; (3) the danger of a religion that wants to walk by visionary sight, instead of by faith; (4) the danger of a religion that fills the gap between ourselves and God with other mediators, like angels; and (5) the danger of a religion that is disconnected from Christ, and thus also from the body of Christ.

Paul gives the strong impression that very few Colossian believers had (yet) fallen for this distortion, for he does not chastise them for being deceived (as he did in Galatians). He does not call them to turn back to the true gospel or warn them that they are nearly beyond hope. Rather, he tells these well-grounded believers (Col 1:3-4; 2:5) not to let these distortionists disturb their faith. This suggests that Paul is trying to nip a problem in the bud before it turns into a crisis.

Lord, show me and my church the little problems that need to be addressed before they turn into full-blown crises.

Read Colossians 2:16-23 once again.

Where did this distortion come from? It does not seem to have come as an organized system of thought taught by outsiders. If it had, Paul would have rebuked them as he did the false teachers in Galatians. Rather, it seems to have arisen from misguided converts within the church.

It's easy to imagine the distortionists as converts from paganism who eagerly searched their new holy book (the OT) for ideas and practices to grow in their newfound faith. They read about fasting, holy days, unclean foods, angels, and visions, but the perspectives of their former pagan mind-set distorted their understanding.

When some of them had supernatural experiences (like visions of heavenly worship and encounters with angels), they were so delighted that they sought spiritual techniques to help them experience these again. As Thompson said, they were "succumbing to the belief—still popular today!—that there is some gimmick, some experience, some secret that will unlock greater depths of insight than have heretofore been attained."[167] Thus, they tried observing special days, fasting, and other forms of humbling oneself in an attempt to subdue the body and experience the spiritual world.

Whatever appeared to be effective in helping them to experience "more" in their faith, they would then share with others, urging them to adopt the same practices and experience the same supernatural visions—and also giving the impression that if others did not follow their advice, then maybe there was something wrong with their faith. Imagine, for instance, a new convert coming across Ezek 44:15-31 with its commands about what garments to wear (17-19), what not to drink (21), who to marry (22), how to observe sabbaths and feasts (24), what not to touch (25), what not to eat (31), and teaching others what is clean and unclean (23)—many issues of which come up in this section of Colossians. If these converts would think, "This is what God is calling me to do," then in their own clumsy, uninformed, but enthusiastic way of imposing their ideas on others, they would quickly create difficulties and hard feelings in the church.

Even today, many Christians are searching for the latest spiritual trends, ideas, and techniques—always looking for something more. We are not immune from this. Maybe you bought this devotional as part of that search. We so easily forget the fullness we already have in Christ.

Jesus, maybe there is such thing as a holy discontentment, but I admit that often it's just plain old discontentment showing up in my faith and in my church. Forgive me; forgive us.

Read Colossians 2:16-23 once again.

The distortionists were tapping into an insecurity that is both ancient and modern. Those who have experienced an inner transformation are often surprised to discover how far they still fall short in their new life. Maybe there's another spiritual power that could help. It is this sense of still lacking the fullness of salvation that false teachers through the ages have exploited to their advantage. If one god only took you so far, they would offer other gods to move you to the next level.[168] Along these same lines, the Colossian distortionists may have taught that the salvation found in Jesus needed to be supplemented by other powers.

The pagan mystery religions provide a prime example of this. In the ancient tale called *Metamorphoses* by Apuleius, a man named Lucius had been changed into a donkey by the goddess Isis because of his bad behavior. She would only transform him back into human form if he went through an extensive initiation into her cult that involved fasting, avoiding certain foods and drinks, ritual washing, and the purchase of costly new garments. Lucius goes through the process, experiencing transformation, only to be told shortly thereafter that now he needed a second costly initiation into the cult of the greater god Osiris. Then yet another initiation is needed, he is told; but not because the first two did not work. Rather, he is to rejoice that he is deemed worthy to be triply blessed.[169]

The distortionists in Colossae were making a similar appeal to the Christians, saying, in effect, there is nothing wrong with first being initiated into Christ, but if anyone wants to move on toward a fuller salvation, then the help of other spiritual beings and the discipline of other spiritual practices are needed. Paul combats this by emphasizing strongly that only in Christ alone can we experience God's fullness.

Although I have summarized my conception of the Colossian distortion, we are still in the dark about exactly what it taught. Frustrating as that may be, the vagueness of what we know may actually be helpful for us. If the content of the distortion were clearer, we might think Paul's response only applied to that one distortion. But because we only have a rough sketch of the distortion, Paul's responses to it can more readily speak against a wide variety of false teachings that have risen through the centuries. Even today, when bits and pieces of the Colossian distortion rise up, Paul's words can help us stay on track.

Protect me, Lord Jesus, from false teachings that exploit my fears. Keep my eyes fixed on you.

*16 **Therefore, let no one judge you** in eating and drinking or in respect to a festival or a new-moon or sabbaths, 17 which are a shadow of coming things, but the body [that cast the shadow is] of Christ.*

The word for judging is used 114 times in the NT, but in Colossians, only in this verse. The action of judging takes on many shades of meaning in the NT, depending on the context, such as (1) the good action of discerning or assessing actions (Lk 7:43; 12:57; Acts 15:19); (2) the wrong action of condemning other people (Rom 2:1); and (3) the rightful action of God (Acts 7:7)—and those designated by God—to decide the fate of others (Jesus in Jn 5:22; the disciples in Mt 19:28; the people of God in 1 Cor 6:2).

Jesus' words about himself show that judging can be both good and bad. In a sense, he did not come to judge, but in another sense, he did: "You judge according to the flesh; I judge no one. Yet even if I do judge, my judgment is true, for it is not I alone who judge, but I and the Father who sent me" (Jn 8:15-16, ESV). Jesus judges in a good way by discerning the truth and even deciding the final fate of people through their reaction to him, but he does not judge in an unjust way.

The verb for judging here is in the form of a command. This is actually only the third command so far in Colossians and it will soon be followed by the similar command, "Let nobody disqualify you" (Col 2:18).

In the NT the most famous command about judging is Mt 7:1 (paralleled by Lk 6:37), "Judge not, that ye be not judged" (KJV). Many people assume this means all notions of discernment are banned, as if there were no such thing as exercising good judgment. The context, however, affirms that there still is a good kind of judging, for we need to be able to discern the planks in our own eyes in order to help others remove the splinters from theirs (Mt 7:3-5). Often forgotten is Jesus' other command about a good kind of judging, "Do not judge by appearances, but judge with right judgment" (Jn 7:24, NRSV). Because of this command, we can call on others to judge what is true (Acts 4:19; 1 Cor 10:15; 11:13).

On the one hand, then, God clearly forbids making condemning judgments of others. But on the other hand, he does want us to use good judgment in assessing the truth and distinguishing right from wrong.

Today, O Lord, when I meet someone, and my instinct is to make negative judgments about them, remind me to thank you for creating them.

> [16] **Therefore, let no one judge you** in eating and drinking or in respect to a festival or a new-moon or sabbaths, [17] which are a shadow of coming things, but the body [that cast the shadow is] of Christ.

In the various NT prohibitions about judging, the rationale varies from text to text. Jesus forbids judging in Mt 7:1 and Lk 6:37, so that his disciples would not act like hypocrites who overlook their own flaws, but would treat others with mercy instead. In Jn 7:24 Jesus forbids judging by appearances because it was keeping people from trusting in him. According to 1 Cor 4:5, judging is a problem because it was undermining the authority of Paul in an unruly church, but in Rom 14:3 and 13 judging was creating divisions in the church based on different practices, and so it had to be stopped.

None of these texts, however, quite fits the situation in Colossae. Here the judging was creating insecurity among the people of God. Believers were shaken, wondering if the judgment calls made by the distortionists were actually true. Maybe, they thought, they *were* missing the mark concerning diets and holy days. To counteract this, Paul tells them to pay no attention to the judgments of the distortionists.

By creating a sense of false guilt in good-hearted Christians, these distortionists were trying to manipulate (or even shame) them into adopting unnecessary practices and false teachings. Paul will argue that it is not submission to rules about holiness which marks one as a Christian. Rather, as Wall notes, "what finally defines the borders of true Christianity is 'being in Christ.'"[170]

So what Paul says here is actually the flip side of Mt 7:1. Not only are we not to judge others, but we are not to let others judge us, at least with respect to the matters mentioned here. It's not that the Colossian church can actually stop the distortionists from *uttering* their judgments, but the church can (and should) stop *listening* to them. Paul wants to strengthen the church's resolve to ignore what the distortionists say. If anyone is casting doubts on the faith of others, says Paul, then take their judgments and cast them into the depths of the sea.

The word "therefore" is significant here because it links this verse with the previous verses. Since the Colossians are forgiven (Col 2:14) and the primal-powers' accusations made against them no longer carry any weight (Col 2:15), "therefore" the accusations made by the distortionists should not carry any weight either (Col 2:16).

Lord, whenever I worry about what others think of me, give me ears to hear what you think of me instead.

*[16] Therefore, let no one judge you **in eating and drinking** or in respect to a festival or a new-moon or sabbaths, [17] which are a shadow of coming things, but the body [that cast the shadow is] of Christ.*

Since Jesus is Lord of all of life, it would make sense that we should be following Christ in our daily living, even with regards to our diet and our calendars. We might assume, however, that the Lord's will on these matters would apply to all Christians the same, but Paul begs to differ. There are some areas of life, says Paul, about which Jesus may exercise his lordship in different ways. He may ask some to fast on certain days, but not others. He may forbid certain foods to one believer, but not to another. With regards to one's diet and observation of holy days, Paul believes it is a matter that should be left between Jesus and each believer (see Rom 14:1-9). Thus, no one has any business judging other Christians in these areas, telling them what God's will is for them.

It was not always this way. For instance, in the OT God gave very specific directions about diet, which applied to all of his people. They were not allowed to eat meat with blood in it (Lev 17:10-14). There was an extensive list of "unclean" animals that were taboo (Lev 11:1-47). Excessive eating and drinking were also forbidden (Prov 23:20). These food laws provided one way for God to separate his people from rest of the world, marking them as holy (Lev 20:25-26). When the Greeks tried to force the Jews to violate these laws, "many in Israel...chose to die rather than be defiled by food" (1 Mac 1:62-62, NRSV).

Sometimes God's people also refrained from food (fasting) for short periods of time in order to express penitence. It is striking, however, that only in the prophet Joel (1:14; 2:12, 15) do we read of God calling for a fast. Otherwise, fasting appears to be humanly-initiated, often by godly people such as Daniel, Ezra, and Nehemiah, but sometimes by evil-doers, such as Jezebel and Ahab (1 Kgs 21:9, 12, 27). Isaiah 58 even has a stunning rebuke of those who fast, but neglect what God really prefers—the practice of justice. Later God promises that days of fasting will be replaced by days of feasting (Zech 8:19).

Given these many OT laws about diet, it's not too surprising that some new believers were trying to figure out how to implement them and perhaps persuade others to follow their lead. But Paul forbids anyone from judging others in this matter.

Jesus, I want to obey you, even in what I eat and drink, but not so I can think I'm better than those who live differently.

*[16] Therefore, let no one judge you **in eating and drinking** or in respect to a festival or a new-moon or sabbaths, [17] which are a shadow of coming things, but the body [that cast the shadow is] of Christ.*

In the NT Jesus had a celebrative attitude toward eating and drinking, even though he also opposed gluttony and drunkenness. And while there are examples of God's people fasting in the NT (Acts 13:2-3), including Jesus himself (Mt 4:2), there is no command to do so. There *is* one command against eating meat with blood in it (Acts 15:19), but we hear little about it.

As for the laws about unclean foods, Jesus undermines them by announcing that it's not what goes into a person's stomach that defiles him, but what comes out of his heart (Mk 7:18-23). "Thus he declared all foods clean" (Mk 7:19, NRSV). Peter learned this same lesson from a heavenly vision of unclean animals, in which a voice said, "What God has made clean, do not call profane" (Acts 10:15, NRSV), a principle that was also extended to the acceptance of non-Jewish people.

Other discussions about food and drink in the NT were not about what to consume or how much, but with whom one should eat. Jesus was known for freely sharing a meal with all kinds of people, even notorious sinners (Lk 5:27-32). The importance of sharing food with the hungry was also taught in Mt 25:42, Lk 12:33, and Jms 2:15-16.

As in Colossians, judging others about food was also a problem in Corinth and Rome, but in those situations, it was not connected to false teaching. The main issue in 1 Cor 8-10 was about eating meat that had been offered to idols, with recriminations flying in all directions. In response Paul urged believers not to eat such meat, not because the idols were real, but to avoid causing formerly idolatrous converts to stumble into old patterns. Love is the rule to follow. In Rom 14:1-23 some Christians were abstaining from meat, while others were not, and each side was judging the other over this issue. Here Paul urges each believer to follow the Lord's calling for them and stop judging others who have a different calling.

Distorted teaching, however, was behind the dietary issues in Colossae, as was also the case in 1 Tim 4:1-5. In that letter, those who regarded creation and the body as hindrances to faith had banned various foods. Paul calls such ideas demonic doctrines because God's creation is good and is to be received with gratitude. It appears the Colossian distortionists were moving in this same demonic direction.

Thank you, Lord, for the bountiful food you have provided. May it not only nourish my body, but also my faith in you as a God who provides.

> [16] *Therefore, let no one judge you **in eating and drinking** or in respect to a festival or a new-moon or sabbaths,* [17] *which are a shadow of coming things, but the body [that cast the shadow is] of Christ.*

Why were the Colossian distortionists judging other believers about food and drink? We don't know for sure, but here are some possibilities:

Perhaps the distortionists regarded themselves as NT versions of the OT priests who were called to help believers "distinguish between the holy and the common, and between the unclean and the clean" (Lev 10:10, NRSV). Paul, however, believes this priestly ministry of distinguishing holy and unholy items is no longer needed. He said in Rom 14:14, "I know and am persuaded in the Lord Jesus that nothing is unclean in itself," and therefore we should not pass judgment on others in these matters (NRSV).

Or even more likely, the distortionists believed that various dietary practices offered spiritual benefits: maybe a sense of spiritual fullness, or a way to overcome evil spiritual powers, or as a preparatory step for receiving heavenly visions (which according to Col 2:18 was a desired goal of the distortionists). They might have said to others, "If you would just avoid meat like I've learned to do, you would be able to concentrate better in your prayers." It's the kind of comment that could be taken either as helpful advice or a subtle criticism smacking of spiritual one-upmanship.

The distortionists could have gotten these ideas about the spiritual benefit of dietary laws from either pagan or Jewish sources. For instance, some pagan mystery religions, like Mithraism, required new initiates to avoid meat for seven days. Others said that if you wanted to summon Apollo the sun god, you needed to avoid sex and fish.[171] Some pagans believed that demons entered the body through food.[172]

Similar thoughts are found in various end-time writings by the Jews (though some of these may have been written after Colossians). Many of them believed that fasting was important for receiving heavenly visions (see *2 Esdras* 5:13, 19; 6:31, 35; *2 Baruch* 9:2; 12:5; 20:5-6; and the *Apocalypse of Abraham* 12:1-2), and for gaining power over demons (*Apocalypse of Elijah* 1:20-21).

In opposition to all these trains of thought, Paul would say, "the kingdom of God is not a matter of eating and drinking but of righteousness, peace and joy in the Holy Spirit" (Rom 14:17, NIV), all of which is found only in Christ.

Savior, when I'm tempted to turn to so-called "effective" techniques in helping my faith to grow, turn me instead to you.

> [16] *Therefore, let no one judge you in eating and drinking **or in respect to a*** ***festival or a new-moon or sabbaths,*** [17] *which are a shadow of coming things, but the body [that cast the shadow is] of Christ.*

The distortionists were also trying to shame other believers into observing special holy days from the OT. All three types of holy days mentioned here are frequently found together in the OT (see 1 Chron 23:31; 2 Chron 2:4; 8:13; 31:3; Neh 10:33; Ezek 45:17; Hos 2:11). These holy days—especially the sabbath—were used by the Jews as an important marker for separating themselves from the rest of the world. When the Greek ruler Antiochus IV tried to ban sabbath observance (1 Mac 1:45), the Jews clung more tightly than ever to it.

Apart from the Day of Atonement, these days were supposed to be for rest and gladness. The apocryphal figure Judith, for instance, fasted all days *except* the sabbath, new moons, and festivals: those were the "days of rejoicing of the house of Israel" (Judith 8:6, NRSV). But by the time of the NT, sabbath observance was becoming a burden instead of delight.

The distortionists, however, likely viewed these days from a pagan perspective. To them these days were not so much for celebrating what God had done in the OT, but for discovering and fitting into the cosmic ordering of time and how that affected their destiny.[173] These days belonged to the elemental-orders who controlled the stars and planets.[174]

For pagans, religion is about rituals, processions, temples, sacrifices, and holy days. So when pagans turned to the Christian faith, with its minimal amount of rituals, it was tempting to observe OT holidays to replace their pagan religious expressions.[175]

But even the OT found fault with the observance of these Jewish holy days. Yes, they were commanded by God, but he hated these festivals if the worshipers were living unjustly: "New moon and Sabbath and the calling of convocations—I cannot endure iniquity and solemn assembly. Your new moons and your appointed feasts my soul hates; they have become a burden to me; I am weary of bearing them" (Isa 1:13b-14, ESV; see also Amos 5:21). God even threatened to turn them into occasions for mourning instead (Amos 8:10) and to end them completely: "I will put an end to all her mirth, her festivals, her new moons, her sabbaths, and all her appointed festivals" (Hos 2:11, NRSV).

Thank you, Lord, for holy days and holidays, days of rest and days of work.
Teach me always to observe them as you see fit.

*16 Therefore, let no one judge you in eating and drinking **or in respect to a
festival or a new-moon or sabbaths,** 17 which are a shadow of coming
things, but the body [that cast the shadow is] of Christ.*

When Jesus came, the Jewish religious leaders were working hard to
determine exactly what activities were forbidden on the sabbath. He was
constantly in trouble for violating their sense of what was appropriate on
the sabbath, especially by healing people (Mt 12:10-12). For Jesus, the sabbath question was not, "What work do I need to stop doing?" but "What
good work can I do on this day?" He taught that "the Sabbath was made for
man, not man for the Sabbath," and referred to himself as the Lord of the
sabbath (Mk 2:27-28, NIV).

It is striking that, of the Ten Commandments, only the law to remember
the sabbath day is not repeated in the NT. The only thing Paul said specifically about the sabbath day is here in Col 2:16, about not letting anyone
judge others with regards to the sabbath. This fits well with two other
verses, which do not mention the sabbath by name, but do refer to special
times and days: Rom 14:5 ("Some judge one day to be better than another,
while others judge all days to be alike. Let all be fully convinced in their own
minds," NRSV) and Gal 4:9-11 ("Now that you have come to know God...how
can you turn back again to the weak and worthless elementary principles
[*stoicheia*, used also in Col 2:8, 20] of the world...You observed days and
months and seasons and years! I am afraid I may have labored over you in
vain," ESV). The observation of holy days, as decreed by the *stoicheia*, will
not bring holy order into the chaos of life. Only Christ can do that, says Paul.

Paul is wary of the spiritual dangers of holy days. Observing them can
cause a person to stray away from salvation in Jesus (as he saw happening
in the Galatian church), or it can cause Christians to quarrel amongst themselves (as he saw happening in the Roman church). In Colossae he saw both
results happening due to the distortionists' interest in holy days; they were
pulling away from Christ *and* dividing the church. The solution, says Paul, is
for people to work it out with God whether and in what way they will
observe various holy days, and no one—including the distortionists—
should judge others concerning that decision. It is surprising how often
Christians through the ages have ignored Paul's words in their debates
about the sabbath. It's only Jesus who is Lord of the sabbath, not us.

*Show me, Lord, how you want me to observe the sabbath, and restrain me
from judging those who hear differently from you.*

231

*¹⁶ Therefore, let no one judge you in eating and drinking or in respect to a festival or a new-moon or sabbaths, ¹⁷ **which are a shadow of coming things,** but the body [that cast the shadow is] of Christ.*

Here Paul describes food and festival practices as mere shadows of what was coming (and has now come in Christ). By calling them shadows, Paul is not saying that all the practices and rules of the distortionists are thoroughly evil and have never been of any value (see Col 2:23). But he is saying that whatever value they had is now obsolete.

The book of Hebrews echoes this idea, for it describes the OT temple as "a copy and shadow [*skia*] of the heavenly things" (Heb 8:5, ESV). In fact, says Heb 10:1, the whole OT law is a shadow of what was to come. Paul is making the same claim about OT laws concerning holy days and diets.

Some biblical nuances of shadows help us understand Paul's point. Just as the shadows of plants can protect us from heat (Isa 4:6), so the OT laws served as guardians to protect God's people from moral chaos, but now they are no longer needed (Gal 4:1-11). Similarly, just as shadows quickly pass (Job 8:9), so the rules about diets and days were just a fleeting reality, whose time has come and gone. And just as shadows ominously point towards death (Ps 23:4), so these OT rules will ultimately lead to death if we put our trust in them instead of Christ. Now that Jesus has come, there's no need to focus on the shadows that signified his approach.

Paul does not specify how the dietary and holy day laws foreshadowed Christ. Perhaps the laws about clean foods point to the necessity of a heart cleansed by God. Maybe the feasts involving food point to the Lord's Supper, or remind us of the great joy that is yet to come when Christ returns, or point to the day when there would be no more need to separate Jews from non-Jews. As for the laws about sabbaths, these might foreshadow the rest that Jesus came to give (Mt 11:28) or the great sabbath rest that awaits the people of God (see Heb 3:7-4:11), or the importance of resting in God's grace instead of striving to measure up to a certain standard.

However we view it, we must not lose sight of Paul's main concern. He is not trying to explain how exactly these laws foreshadowed the end-time realities that began arriving with Christ—that would only increase our interest in these laws. Rather, Paul emphasizes that these laws are *only* shadows and no longer deserve much attention. In the last days we must focus on the One who was foreshadowed, not the shadows themselves.

Thank you, Lord, for inspiring the Old Testament so that we can understand better who Jesus is and what he came to do.

*[16] Therefore, let no one judge you in eating and drinking or in respect to a festival or a new-moon or sabbaths, [17] which are a shadow of coming things, **but the body [that cast the shadow is] of Christ.***

Although Paul dismisses OT rules as shadows, they are not free-floating shadows. Like all shadows, they are shadows of something. Sometimes shadows follow an object and sometimes they precede an object, depending on where the source of light is. The imagery here implies that the shadow came first, followed by the person or object that cast the shadow. It's a "foreshadow" of coming things that arrive with the Coming One. The laws foreshadow the whole gamut of end-times realities—including judgment, resurrection, eternal life, and the new creation—things that arrive with Christ in his first and second comings.

Christ is the body (*sōma*) who cast the shadow. The Greek here is very terse, almost to the point of being unclear (literally it only says, "but the body of Christ"). In the interest of clarity, many versions opt to translate "body" with other words like substance (ESV, NRSV) or reality (NIV). Such translations are perfectly acceptable, but given the importance of the word "body" in dealing with the Colossian distortion (1:18, 22, 24; 2:11, 17, 19, 23; 3:15), it's better to keep it in this verse.

All the laws promoted by the distortionists are concerned with what a person does with their body—what foods or drink they put in their body, and when they are to rest or celebrate with their bodies. But Paul will argue that such laws, which supposedly keep the body in check through harsh discipline, do not actually do what is claimed. We do not become holy by focusing on *our* bodies, trying to get them under control through various laws. Rather, we become holy by focusing on a different body, the one that belongs to Christ. It is only through *his* body—a body that was crucified, buried, and then raised (Col 2:11-12)—that holiness can be found.

Thus, the "body" of laws promoted by the distortionists have no "body" at all, for the true body is that of Christ, the one who came in bodily form in the Last Days, ushering in all the coming things. The body belongs to Christ, and the laws about diet and holy days are only a shadow cast by his body. Before the body comes, we might look at the shadow to see what is coming, but once the body arrives, there is no reason to focus on the shadow anymore.

Teach me, Lord Jesus, to find your presence and promise throughout the Scriptures, so that I encounter you whenever I read them.

> ¹⁸ **Let nobody disqualify you,** *insisting on humbling-practices and worship of angels, claiming-access to the things which he has seen, vainly being puffed up by his mind of flesh,* ¹⁹ *and not gripping the head*

Verse 16 began with a command not to let anyone *judge* the believers over food or festival laws. Verse 18 begins with a similar command, only this time they are not to let anyone *disqualify* them. These two commands oppose the distortionists who are playing on the Colossians' fear of missing out on all that God has for them. The distortionists tell the Colossian believers that their supposedly substandard beliefs and practices disqualify them from experiencing God's fullness, with the hope that these believers will follow their advice on how to meet the qualifications.

As for those who attempt to disqualify others, verses 18-19 use four participles (verbs ending with -ing) to describe them. They are: (1) *insisting* on humbling-practices and the worship of angels, (2) *claiming-access* into the visions they have seen, (3) *being puffed up* vainly, and (4) *not gripping* Christ as the Head of the body. The distortionists may have agreed that the first two were accurate descriptions of themselves, but the last two are Paul's evaluation of what they were really about.

The verb for disqualify is used only here in the Bible. Scholars have found only three uses of this verb prior to Colossians, and two of them are about wrongfully robbing people of their property or inheritance.[176] The distortionists may have been claiming that others were not qualified for their share of God's inheritance (see Col 1:12).

The distortionists regarded themselves as judges who were not only authorized to decide what qualifications were needed to experience the fullness of faith, but also to determine who met those qualifications. But Paul would argue that if *anyone* is unqualified, it is these very distortionists. The Colossians should therefore pay no heed to their opinions.

Here we see a great contrast between how Paul treats the Colossian believers and how the distortionists treat them.[177] Whereas the distortionists "disqualify" the believers, increasing their insecurity, Paul assures them that God has been at work "qualifying you for a share of the inheritance of the holy-ones in the light" (Col 1:12). While the distortionists glory in their private visions of heaven and look down on those poor souls who have not been so blessed, Paul suffers for all believers in order to build them up (Col 1:24, 29; 2:1-2).

Father, I know I'm not worthy to belong to your family, and others probably agree, but I thank you for qualifying me anyway by grace.

> *¹⁸ Let nobody disqualify you, **insisting on humbling-practices** and worship of angels, claiming-access to the things which he has seen, vainly being puffed up by his mind of flesh, ¹⁹ and not gripping the head*

Two things which the distortionists regarded as necessary for living in God's fullness were humbling-practices and the worship of angels.

It is surprising to hear Paul criticize the distortionists for their humbling-practices (*tapeinophrosunē*), for this is the same word that means "humility" in the rest of the NT. In nearly every other NT instance of this noun (and other words using the *tapein-* root), humility is regarded as a good thing. Paul, for instance, tells the believers to act "with all humility" (Eph 4:2) and "in humility to count others more significant than yourselves" (Phil 2:3, ESV). Even later in Colossians Paul will command us to clothe ourselves with humility (Col 3:12). So it's surprising to see Paul regard it as a negative quality of the distortionists, here and in Col 2:23. Perhaps he means to say it's only a false humility (as the NIV puts it), but the word "false" is not in the text.

More likely Paul uses this term because the distortionists were using it to describe their own practices.[178] They may have picked this up from the Greek translation of the OT, which uses *tapein-* words in reference to self-affliction. Lev. 16:29 says that on the Day of Atonement, "you shall afflict [*tapeinoō*] yourselves and shall do no work" (ESV). Sometimes fasting was specified as a particularly appropriate way of humbling oneself before God. According to Ps 35:13, when others were sick, "I afflicted [*tapeinoō*] myself with fasting" (NRSV).

Lots of Jewish writings in Paul's day used *tapein-* words to refer to religious self-affliction, which might include weeping, brooding, beating the breast, fasting for seven days, wearing a black tunic, removing all jewelry, putting on sackcloth, lying in ashes, sighing, screaming, grinding idols to dust, throwing food to the dogs, and pulling out hair (all cited as forms of humility in the apocryphal book *Joseph and Asenath*). Put this together with Col 2:23's reference to the distortionists' "harsh treatment of the body," and you can sense the kind of "humility" Paul is talking about here. Thus, I have translated it as "humbling-practices" to avoid confusion with the good quality of humility.

I pray to be humble, O Lord, but I also pray that I will not notice when you have answered that prayer.

¹⁸ *Let nobody disqualify you, **insisting on humbling-practices** and worship of angels, claiming-access to the things which he has seen, vainly being puffed up by his mind of flesh,* ¹⁹ *and not gripping the head*

Since Paul criticizes this self-afflicted humility, we cannot help but wonder what's wrong with it? Didn't Jesus call his disciples to take up the cross and deny themselves (Mk 8:34)?

We should recall, however, that it's possible to act humbly in a very proud manner. F. F. Bruce calls this "a show of superior humility."[179] It's possible to deny oneself in order to focus on or call attention to oneself. It's possible to fast in a way that feeds one's ego. It's possible to work too hard at sabbath resting.

Words about humility and affliction with a *tapein-* root are featured throughout the discussion of fasting in Isa 58:3-10. The people wonder why God is not impressed with the way they have humbled (*tapeinoō*) themselves through fasting (Isa 58:3). God retorts that real fasting is not about *self-affliction* (*tapeinoō*), but about helping those who have been *afflicted* (*tapeinoō*) by others (see Isa 58:4-5, 10). Likewise, the apocryphal book Sirach 34:31 asks, "So if one fasts for his sins, and goes again and does the same things, who will listen to his prayer? And what has he gained by humbling [*tapeinoō*] himself?" (NRSV). Jesus also lashed out against the religious people of his day who humbled themselves through fasting, tithing, and sabbath observance, but their hearts were far from God (see Mt 6:1-6, 16-18). All they were doing was using humbling practices to achieve the opposite effect of increasing their status.[180]

Those involved in self-humiliation, then, are not necessarily the friends of God or his people, but may well be their enemies. It's about such people that Sirach 12:11 said, "Even if he humbles [*tapeinoō*] himself and walks bowed down, take care to be on your guard against him" (NRSV).

Faith, then, involves humility. But, as Barth said, "Faith is not a self-chosen humility, like the Colossian error (Col 2:23). It is not the humility of pessimism, skepticism, defeatism, misanthropy, a weariness with the world and oneself and life."[181] Rather, true humility conveys joy, not the proud adoption of a posture of deprivation. This is why Paul does not praise the self-humiliating actions of the distortionists, but criticizes them.

I pray, Lord Jesus, for those who have been humiliated and mistreated by religious people and for those who have been humiliated and mistreated by me.

[18] *Let nobody disqualify you, insisting on humbling-practices **and worship** **of angels,** claiming-access to the things which he has seen, vainly being puffed up by his mind of flesh, [19] and not gripping the head*

The distortionists also promoted some kind of angel worship. The word translated "worship" is fairly uncommon. In the apocryphal book Wisdom of Solomon it is associated with worshiping idols, animals, and rulers (Wisdom 11:15; 14:17-18, 27). Idolatry is a factor in Colossians as well.

The word "angel" simply means messenger, but in the majority of biblical references it refers to supernatural messengers from God who often appear in human form. In both the OT and NT, angels do the following actions (I will provide only one reference of many from each testament):

- Angels worship God (Ps 148:2; Heb 12:22).
- Angels provide sustenance in the wilderness (1 Kgs 19:7; Mt 4:11).
- Angels protect God's people from danger (Ps 91:11; Acts 5:19).
- Angels bring judgment on the wicked (Ps 78:49; Mt 13:41).
- Angels go to war against God's enemies (Dan 10:5-14; Rev 12:7).
- Angels bring messages from God (Gen 22:11-12; Acts 8:26).
- Angels announce God's saving actions (Judg 6:11-12; Mt 28:5-7).
- Angels announce the births of saviors (Judg 13:3-21; Lk 1:26-33).
- Angels guide prophets in end-time visions (Zech 1:9; Rev 21:9).

But Karl Barth also points out what angels cannot do. They cannot speak God's Word as if it were their own; they cannot save, redeem, forgive, reconcile, judge the world, create, establish covenants with humanity, rule history, or overcome death. They do not act on their own. They'd be demons, not angels, if they directed attention to themselves instead of to God.[182]

Paul is leery of paying too much attention to angels. He often speaks negatively of them. The old covenant is inferior to the new because it came through angels (Gal 3:19). God's people will judge angels (1 Cor 6:3) and to speak their language without love is worthless (1 Cor 13:1). No angels can separate us from God's love (Rom 8:38). We should be especially cautious of angelic messages because even Satan disguises himself as an angel of light (2 Cor 11:14). Paul also issues a solemn curse, "But even if we or an angel from heaven should proclaim to you a gospel contrary to the what we proclaimed to you, let that one be accursed" (Gal 1:8, NRSV). For Paul, the distortionists' worship of angels is just another satanic trick.

Lord, whenever I get fascinated by something supernatural, like the angels, draw my eyes back to you.

> [18] *Let nobody disqualify you, insisting on humbling-practices **and worship of angels,** claiming-access to the things which he has seen, vainly being puffed up by his mind of flesh,* [19] *and not gripping the head*

We might assume that when the distortionists were trying to persuade people to join them in the worship of angels, it was a case of blatant idolatry. But they may have been subtler than that—yet still wrong.

For instance, the distortionists might have been calling people to experience heavenly visions of worshiping with the angels (similar to what is found in Revelation 4-5). Jewish writers from this time, including the Dead Sea Scrolls, were very fascinated by visions of angels worshiping God. Various Jewish mystics suggested the rigorous spiritual disciplines of prayer and fasting would be necessary to receive these heavenly visions (there's an example of that in Dan 10:2-9).[183] The *Apocalypse of Abraham*, for instance, portrays Abraham as fasting while with an angel who led him to heaven to join the angelic congregation in praise. Such scenarios fit well with this verse's references to angels, visions, and humbling practices.

But all this is objectionable to Paul. Visions are fine—Paul had his own share of them—and angels are glorious, but the attempt to worship *with* the angels will quickly turn into the worship *of* the angels themselves. For instance, in the *Songs of the Sabbath Sacrifice* (a Dead Sea Scroll document which depicts angels in worship), all the attention is on the angels and very little on God.[184] It's an easy line to cross, for even the apostle John was tempted to worship his angelic guide in Rev 22:8-9. If you truly want to join the angels in worship, don't concentrate on seeing them in action, rather concentrate on the one they are worshiping—Christ the Lord.

Or perhaps the distortionists were only telling people to call on angels for help. They might say, "If it's not idolatrous for Christians to ask other *people* for help, why would it be idolatrous to ask angels for help?" According to archaeological inscriptions, prayers to angels were very common in the area of Colossae. Pagans and Jews alike wanted angelic help in the form of protection, guidance, the cursing of enemies, and finding love. For example, in the Jewish apocryphal *Testament of Levi* 5:5, "Levi" says to an angel, "I beg you, Lord, teach me your name, so that I may call on you in the day of tribulation."[185] Christians were also falling into this error.

But as we said yesterday, any angel that draws attention to itself as a source of help is acting like a demon who blinds us to the reality of Jesus.

I'm thankful, Lord, to be part of a vast congregation in heaven and on earth in worshiping you. May all the glory be yours.

*^{18} Let nobody disqualify you, insisting on humbling-practices and worship of angels, **claiming-access to the things which he has seen**, vainly being puffed up by his mind of flesh, ^{19} and not gripping the head*

While Paul urges the Colossians to keep their eyes on Christ alone, the distortionists had their eyes elsewhere. They were seeing heavenly visions. Visions, of course, are found throughout the Bible and can be given by God's Spirit (Acts 2:17), but caution must be exercised. Some "speak visions of their own minds, not from the mouth of the Lord (Jer 23:16, NRSV). Thus, we should not believe every vision, but test it (see 1 Jn 4:1).

The Colossian distortionists were claiming to see visions, perhaps of angels in heavenly worship services. They were entering or "claiming-access" to these supernatural realities. Jewish visionary writings of that day often talked about entering into heaven after much fasting. For instance, the Dead Sea Scrolls document, *Songs of the Sabbath Sacrifice*, highlights the doorways the angels used to enter God's presence, and Ezekiel's vision of the New Temple focuses a lot on the thresholds and gates (Ezek 40:5-16, 20-38; 41:1-4, 15-26; 43:11; 44:1-5).

Perhaps the distortionists claimed to be priests of the new covenant who had found an access point into heaven (through various humbling practices) and were wondering why others were not following them. If so, Paul would counter that entering into the heavenly kingdom is not something we achieve through human techniques. Providing entrance is God's work, and he has already accomplished this when he "relocated [us] to the kingdom of his loved Son" (Col 1:13), thus giving us a share in the Father's inheritance (Col 1:12). In some sense, then, we are already in the heavens with Christ, but in a hidden way to be revealed later (Col 3:3-4).

In those few times that God's people were granted a heavenly vision— as was Paul—they did not "claim access" to it, as if by their efforts of stepping forth or stepping up they could reach its heights. Rather, they could only be "caught up" into heaven, brought there by God's power (2 Cor 12:1-4). According to Lincoln, the verb for being "caught up" means that "Paul's experience was an involuntary one in which God took the initiative rather than one brought about by preparation or special techniques."[186] Unlike the distortionists who are puffed up by their efforts to reach heaven, Paul can only boast of his weaknesses with respect to heavenly visions. All the glory belongs to Christ (2 Cor 12:5-10).

"Be Thou my Vision, O Lord of my heart. Nought be all else to me save that Thou art. Thou and thou only be first."

*[18] Let nobody disqualify you, insisting on humbling-practices and worship of angels, claiming-access to the things which he has seen, **vainly being puffed up by his mind of flesh**, [19] and not gripping the head*

Paul does not comment on whether the distortionists' visions were a hoax, or a demonic illusion. Instead he rejects the visions because they bore bad fruit—pride (verse 18). The verb for "being puffed up" is *phusioō*, a term that conveys its own meaning because in saying it aloud it sounds like a puff of air, similar in English to the slang word "phooey."

It's ironic that these distortionists are very arrogant about how well they perform various "humbling practices" concerning diet and holy days. If these humbling practices actually worked, you would think they would be humbler. Instead, Paul describes them as "vainly" puffed up. "Vainly" is a good translation because the English word "vain" is associated with both pride and futility. The distortionists' visions puff them up with pride and also fail to accomplish anything important.

Grammatically, it's not the visions themselves that puff up the false prophets, but how their own "mind of flesh" interpreted them. "Mind of flesh" is an unusual phrase because it joins two opposites in Greek culture. It's as if Paul called their visions high-minded sewage or intellectual trash. The distortionists may think they are overcoming the sinful flesh through heavenly visions, spiritual powers, and practices aimed against the very fleshly act of eating, but actually their minds are more immersed in the flesh than ever. In trying to be less fleshly, they are acting more and more according to the flesh. In trying to be so spiritual, they work in opposition to the Spirit of God.

Oddly enough, it is not the physical flesh which Paul condemns as "fleshly"; instead it's the "spiritual" attempt to escape the physicality of our flesh which is "fleshly." It is an attempt to escape our created reality by out-spiritualizing God. When Adam and Eve, for instance, wanted to move beyond their created flesh and become like God (Gen 3:5), that's when they became the least like God. They were the most spiritual when they were content with being in the flesh. They became the most fleshly when they tried to become more spiritual than they were.

The pride of the distortionists, then, means that their words can be dismissed. Their teaching could well be summarized as "emotionally elating, ego inflating, and worst of all, brother berating."[187]

I confess, Lord, that I have been proud of my faith and obedience. I thought I was holy, but I was only haughty.

¹⁸ Let nobody disqualify you… vainly being puffed up by his mind of flesh, ¹⁹ **and not gripping the head,** *from whom all the body, being supplied and drawn together through its joints and connecting-tissues, grows with growth from God.*

We usually associate the mind with the head. If you're exercising your mind, you're using your head. To separate a mind from a head would be similar to the fatal act of separating a brain from a skull. But this, according to Paul, is what the Colossian distortionists are doing. They are using their *minds* (albeit a mind of flesh), but they are disconnecting them from the *head*, which is Christ (Col 1:18; 2:10).

Our society engages in many controversies over the separation of church and state, but Paul saw a far worse problem: the separation of church and Head. It's not a Headless Horseman that should horrify us (as it did in *The Legend of Sleepy Hollow*), but a Headless Churchman. That's what the distortionists were. But the Christian life involves holding onto, or gripping, Jesus as our Head.

But what does it mean to "grip" Christ as the Head? Normally we don't think of a mind or neck or any other body part gripping the head. We know it's necessary for them to be attached, but the attachment just seems to happen, apart from any conscious effort. But Paul's word choice reminds us that faith is not a carefree, "along for the ride" lifestyle, but one in which we hold tightly to Jesus. Ultimately, of course, it is Christ's grasp of us that provides the true security, for no one can snatch us out of his hand (Jn 10:28-29). In fact, all things are held together in Christ (Col 1:17). But this vital truth does not negate the importance of our own gripping action. We hold onto him because he first holds onto us.

In the Apocrypha we are called to grip God's wisdom (Sirach 4:13), the fear of the Lord (Sirach 27:3), and God's law (Baruch 4:1). In the NT we are to hold on to our confession (Heb 4:14), our hope in the Lord (Heb 6:18), the name of the Lord (Rev 2:13), and what we already have in Christ (Rev 2:25; 3:11). Here we grip Christ himself.

Unfortunately, some grip the wrong thing, like false teachings (Rev 2:14-15) and traditions (Mk 7:3-4, 8)—both of which the distortionists were doing. And in doing so, they were letting go of Christ. They may have thought their teachings were an improvement on Paul's "Christ alone" message, but they ended up with an aloneness without Christ.[188]

Sometimes, Jesus, I have tried to live out my Christian faith in a self-reliant way. Remind me again of how disastrous that is. I need you.

*[18] Let nobody disqualify you…vainly being puffed up by his mind of flesh, [19] and not gripping the head, **from whom all the body, being supplied and drawn together through its joints and connecting-tissues,** grows with growth from God.*

In our individualistic culture, we might assume Paul is only calling on individual Christians to grip Christ as the Head of their lives. But Paul's point is different. *Together as the church* we are to grip Christ as our Head, for it is only through that Head that we are the church. We are not merely a body of believers; we are the body of Christ, belonging to him who is the Head. If the church loses its grip on Jesus, it ceases to be the church.[189]

From Christ the Head, the whole body/church is "supplied and drawn together." The Head is not only involved in ruling (emphasized in Col 2:10), but it is especially involved in giving life and strength to the body. The Roman orator Seneca hoped (in vain) that Nero would be a life-giving head of the body of the Roman Empire when he said, "It is from the head that comes the health of the body" (*On Mercy* 2.2.1). He was looking to the wrong head. It is Christ who supplies what the body needs to thrive.

Paul does not specify what those supplies might be. We could easily imagine such things as God's commands, promises, strength, faith, love, and the Holy Spirit as part of the supply line. Paul's main point, however, is that if Christians fail to grip the head, they cut themselves off from the very source of the church's life. If the church were to follow the distortionists' interest in visions, angels, and rules involving humbling practices, we would soon be competing and squabbling over different loyalties. Only in Christ, who is the Head, can the body thrive.

By neglecting the Head, the distortionists were also demonstrating their lack of concern for the health of the greater body, the church. As Sumney says, "Defining spirituality as something that benefits only, or primarily, the individual rather than the community was common in the ancient world."[190] It's still a problem today. But if we care more about our own spiritual health than the health of Christ's body, we are on the path blazed by the Colossian distortion. Koester said, "The test of orthodoxy is whether it is able to build a *church* rather than a club or school or a sect, or merely a series of concerned religious individuals."[191] The distortionists failed that test. The fullness of Christ is only found in the wholeness of the church, where the Lord connects his people to himself through one another.

Lord, I pray for the church I attend, and ask that you would supply it today with what it needs. You know even better than we do what that is.

> [18] *Let nobody disqualify you...vainly being puffed up by his mind of flesh,* [19] *and not gripping the head, **from whom all the body, being supplied and drawn together through its joints and connecting-tissues,** grows with growth from God.*

The second verb here, drawn together, is the same word used earlier in Col 2:2 to speak of Christians drawing together in love. But this drawing together can only happen because the Head is working through the joints and connecting tissues of the body. The most obvious parallel to this is Eph 4:16, which states that from Christ the whole body is "joined and held together by every joint with which it is equipped" (ESV).

The message of the distortionists, however, will not draw the body together, but only pull it apart. Instead of building relationships, the distortionists pursue their own spirituality through private angelic visions, avoidance of certain foods, the observation of holy days, and their criticism of those who do not follow the same path. Instead of feasting together, they are fasting alone. None of this was building up the body of Christ.

Some may dismiss Paul's reference to the joints and connecting tissue as a word picture that has gotten out of hand, but these terms play an important role in Paul's depiction of the church. The body of Christ thrives not because each part has its own private connection to the Head. Rather, Jesus supplies and draws his body together through the many connections formed within the body. To change the imagery, we are not to think of each Christian as a separate strand of fabric, but as strands intricately woven together with others. Nor are we to imagine that only a few select leaders serve as important connecting joints, and the rest of us hang on them. Since we are all bound together, with no free-floating body parts hanging loosely from the rest, then every Christian is used by Jesus as a connecting tissue or joint. The body of Christ, then, is not a well-oiled machine, but an organic whole.

Interestingly enough, the same Greek word for joints can also mean a skin outbreak or wound (see Lev 13:2-6 and 2 Sam 7:14). And the word for "connecting-tissues" is related to the word for chains or bonds (which is almost always a negative thing). Yet it's the wounded ones and the ones in bondage who especially serve as the joints and connecting-tissues that hold the church together. We are connected by our mutual caring for the weak.

When I'm tempted to pull away from the messiness of life together in the church, show me again how much you've connected me to others in the body.

> [18] *Let nobody disqualify you...vainly being puffed up by his mind of flesh,* [19] *and not gripping the head, from whom all the body, being supplied and drawn together through its joints and connecting-tissues,* **grows with growth from God.**

The Lord's purpose in nourishing his body is not that we could nestle together or learn the wonder of being interdependent.[192] Rather, the Lord nourishes his body so that it would grow with a growth that comes from God. Some forms of growth do not come from God; these are only cancerous growths that bring death. Growth from God, however, brings life.

In the OT the verb and noun used here for growing almost always referred to the biological growth of bodies and families. But NT references are overwhelmingly about spiritual growth. In Jesus' teaching we learn about the kingdom from the growth of lilies (Mt 6:28; Lk 12:27), mustard seeds (Mt 13:32; Lk 13:19), and other seeds (Mk 4:8). As a child Jesus "grew and became strong in spirit" (Lk 1:80, NRSV; see also Lk 2:40), and later John the Baptist said that Jesus must grow, or increase, and he must decrease (Jn 3:30). As the Word of God grew in its impact (Acts 6:7; 12:24; 19:20; Col 1:6), God gave growth to the church (1 Cor 3:6-7). God grows a harvest of righteousness (2 Cor 9:10), so that God's people grow in faith (2 Cor 10:15), grace and knowledge (Col 1:10; 2 Pet 3:18), into salvation (1 Pet 2:2), and even into Christ the Head (Eph 4:15). When all the parts of the body are working together, it "makes the body grow so that it builds itself up in love" (Eph 4:16, ESV). In this way, God's household "grows into a holy temple in the Lord" (Eph 2:21, NRSV).

If we only relied on the OT usage of the "grow" words, we might conclude that Paul is talking in Col 2:19 about the numerical growth of the church through successful evangelism. While we should not exclude that aspect of the growth of the body of Christ, spiritual growth is the main thing here. But it's not merely an *individual* or *private* spiritual growth; that kind of growth would have been more of a concern of the distortionists. Instead Paul points to God granting spiritual growth to the *whole* church. The body of Christ *together* grows in its faith and love. To focus on one's own spiritual experiences, as the distortionists do, ruins true spiritual growth, prevents the growth of church unity, and undercuts missional growth as well.[193] The only kind of growth that happens with the distortionists is the swelling of their heads (Col 2:18).[194]

Lord, I pray for my church—your church—to grow, not in a cancerous way, but in a way that comes from you.

[20] *If you died with Christ to the elemental-orders of the world,* why, as though living in [that] world, would you come under its decrees, [21] *"Do not touch; do not taste; do not contact!"*

Paul goes on to question those who have been intrigued by the distortion. First, he reminds them of their identity as those who have died with Christ. Paul had earlier proclaimed their death with Christ (Col 2:11-12), and he will return to this in his discussion of how Christians live (Col 3:3, 5).

By beginning with the word "if," Paul is not casting doubt on whether the true believers have died with Christ, but "he is inviting us to consider whether, indeed," we are true believers who have died with Christ.[195]

Because of this truth, "those who believe in Jesus can no longer look at their death as though it were in front of them. It is behind them," as Barth said.[196] Physical death may yet lie in the future, but the death that really changes everything has already happened and we are now risen in Christ.

In dying with Christ, we also die to many things. First, we die to sin (Rom 6:2) and are thus set free from it (Rom 6:7). Secondly, by dying with Christ, we also die to the law, the written code that held us captive (Rom 7:6; Gal 2:19). Thirdly—and this is highlighted here—by dying with Christ, we die to "the elemental-orders of the world," the very same powers who use moral traditions and principles (both Jewish and pagan) to pull people away from God (Col 2:8).

Just as physical death puts us in a different realm where we are no longer affected by this life, so when we die with Christ, we are transferred to another realm, no longer living under the powers that once held sway over us (Col 1:13). We are thus out of their sphere of influence, beyond their reach or jurisdiction.[197] Christians, of course, still live in the world understood as God's creation. They do not, however, live in the world understood as a system of sin under the authority of the elemental-orders.

Notice again that Paul does not say the *elemental-orders* have died. It is *we* who have died and thus are free from the control of these other powers. Jesus may have vanquished these powers (Col 2:15), but they continue to operate. Yet their rules no longer apply to us. Just as the physically dead no longer have to obey traffic laws or zoning ordinances, so those who have died in Christ can ignore the decrees of the elemental-orders. We no longer need fear that breaking from them or their rules will bring repercussions. We are free.

Thank you, Lord, for delivering me from all the man-made taboos, customs, and expectations that the world tries to lay on me.

[20] *If you died with Christ to the elemental-orders of the world, **why, as though living in [that] world, would you come under its decrees,*** [21] *"Do not touch; do not taste; do not contact!"*

Much to Paul's consternation, Christians often act as if they were still living in the world of the elemental-orders and subject to their decrees. This might be understandable if being a Christian were *only* a matter of moving from one realm to another. Then we would explain our continued sin by calling it spiritual jet lag; we haven't yet gotten accustomed to our new environment. It would be like a person from England sometimes driving on the left side after they had moved to the United States.

But our situation is much more radical than that. Christians have not only been *transferred* out of the world's old kingdom (Col 1:13), they have *died* to that old world. They have not only adopted new loves and loyalties, they have died to old decrees and commitments.

This is why Paul is so stunned when old ways flare up. Just as he asked in Rom 6:2, "How can we who died to sin go on living in it?" (NRSV), here he asks a similar question, "How can we who died to the world of the elemental-orders still live in that world?" It makes no sense. If the best the distortionists have to offer is rules about diets and days, with promises of visions, it's not much compared to what we already have in Christ. [198]

But that's the nature of sin. It always causes us to turn our backs on God's best so that we settle for something less, like mere morality. Jacques Ellul said that "Morality is the means whereby the Christian dodges death in Christ and fashions a living way of his own. As such it is the worst of all illusions. For under the pretext of letting us live as good Christians," morality robs us of life and freedom in Christ.[199] Paul brings us to our senses by asking us the pointed question of Col 2:20.

Paul has no objection to Christians being commanded—he issues many commands himself. But if the commands come from the world to which Christians no longer belong, there is no reason to obey them.

So while the distortionists believe that these decrees will lead people into deeper truths and fuller experiences of God, Paul recognizes that they only represent basic principles (one of the meanings of *stoicheia*). They are elementary commands for immature children, not for those who are adopted as full-grown and liberated sons and daughters of God (see Gal 4:1-7). These decrees are a sign of an immature faith, not a mature one.[200]

Protect me, Lord Jesus, from settling for something as meager as morality. Open my heart to all the wonders of life in you.

> [20] *If you died with Christ to the elemental-orders of the world, why, as though living in [that] world, would you come under its decrees,* [21] **"Do not touch; do not taste; do not contact!"**

What kind of decrees were the elemental-orders issuing? Since they work in opposition to God, we might assume they would be commanding their adherents to live wildly—indulging in sexual immorality, greed, drunkenness, and violence. But that's not the case at all. The elemental-orders were very "puritanical" in their decrees, filled with moralistic "thou shalt nots" designed to protect a person from impurity. As Seitz says, they were creating a "climate of regulatory impulses that interfere with the work of Christ."[201]

Karl Barth made a similar point in discussing the serpent's temptation in Eden: "What the serpent has in mind is the establishment of ethics."[202] In wanting to know good and evil apart from God, humanity showed "pathetic earnestness, an outward air of the most serious responsibility, the most stringent sense of duty, the most militant virtue. As judge of good and evil, man wants to stand at God's side."[203] But when moralism wins the day, the devil wins the victory. That's why Paul opposes the distortion.

Paul does not enter into a discussion of whether the distortionists were sincerely hoping to build a moral kingdom with their decrees, or whether they were deceitfully presenting themselves as angels of light (2 Cor 11:14), using a pietistic veneer to lure God's people into a fruitless path of Christless moralism. Most likely the distortionists were sincere (though wrong), but the elemental-orders standing behind them were operating deceptively.

According to the distortionists, the decrees that would help one experience and maintain the fullness of salvation involved avoiding the impurities of the world as much as possible, neither handling, tasting nor touching various items. Even among the creation-affirming Jews, there were some for whom it was the avoidance of many created things that marked the path of holiness. According to the Jewish *Epistle of Aristeas* 142, "[God] hedged us in on all sides with strict observances [literally "purities"] connected with meat and drink and touch and hearing and sight."

But Paul disagrees. We do not, he says, become less worldly by avoiding the things which God created as good (see 1 Tim 4:1-5). According to Lucas, since Christ has created all things (Col 1:16), "it would be a strange road to Christlikeness to refuse the blessings that Christ had made."[204]

Holy Lord, in the face of all the moral issues in our world, show me how to avoid the temptation to know good and evil apart from you.

[20] *If you died with Christ to the elemental-orders of the world, why, as though living in [that] world, would you come under its decrees,* [21] **"Do not touch; do not taste; do not contact!"**

Paul summarized the distortionist decrees as "Do not touch; do not taste; do not contact." Paul is probably not quoting them exactly, but may be reducing their rules to these simple prohibitions in order to point out how hollow they are.

The first prohibition against touching (*haptō*) uses a verb found 113 times in the Greek OT. The vast majority of these references describe illicit kinds of touching. For instance, God's people should not touch what was unclean (such as a corpse, certain foods, or a person with an unclean disease). Nor should they touch the holy things that belonged to God alone, any woman who was not one's wife, or another person in order to harm them. We could also include here Eve's explanation that she should not touch the forbidden tree (Gen 3:3) and the proud assertions of pagan rulers about touching the clouds or stars (2 Macc 9:10). In the OT this word is not used for compassionate human touch.

The OT's predominant perspective on touching, then, is that the world contains dangerous things which people must not touch. Some things are so *unholy* that they could contaminate God's people, and on the opposite extreme, some things are so *holy* that it would be dangerous for God's people to touch them.

With the NT use of the word *haptō*, however, there is a stunning change of mood. Instead of refraining from touch, we encounter a Jesus who freely touches and allows himself to be touched, all with saving and healing effect. He is not worried about being defiled through touch, but instead his touch exudes a holy power to bless sinners, the diseased, and even the dead. Apart from the command to "touch no unclean thing" (2 Cor 6:17, NIV), the overwhelming message of the NT is that those who are in Christ need not be worried about what they touch, for the holy power of Jesus in them has greater power than anything that might be regarded as defiling. Instead of taking up the motto, "Everything the unclean one touches shall be unclean" (Num 19:21, NETS), those who are in Christ can say, "Everything the Clean One touches shall be clean." The same applies to what can be tasted or contacted.

We rejoice, O Lord, that this is your world, full of good things for us to taste and touch.

[20] *If you died with Christ to the elemental-orders of the world, why, as though living in [that] world, would you come under its decrees,* [21] **"Do not touch; do not taste; do not contact!"**

The distortionists thought holiness meant *not* touching or tasting, as if the problem of sin could be located out there in the objects that had defiling power. But according to Jesus, "There is nothing outside a person that by going into him can defile him, but the things that come out of a person are what defile him," things like sexual impurity, greed, pride, slander, and more (Mk 7:15, 21-23, ESV). That's what defiles a person.

So if the problem does not come from external *objects*, but from within the evil human heart and the evil external actions that proceed from it, then all the "do not touch" commands of the elemental-orders will have no effective power in bringing the fullness of salvation (see Col 2:23). What's needed instead is for the heart to die and rise with Christ, so that the sins of the heart listed in Mark 7 would wither away. Then we who are in Christ can touch others with grace.

Paul is not against prohibitions. He has his own list of attitudes and actions to avoid in Col 3:5-11. What he opposes are prohibitions that (1) locate the problem outside the human heart, (2) overlook the absolute necessity of being in Christ for walking in obedience and holiness (Col 2:19), and (3) originate in either man-made ideas (Col 2:22) or in OT laws that were only a shadow of what has now come (Col 2:17).

When the distortionists add their own man-made prohibitions, they sound like Eve, who not only knew God's command against eating from the forbidden tree, but also added her own command about not touching the tree (see Gen 3:1-3). When we add our own prohibitions, we play right into the hands of Satan.

We do well to remember the words of C. S. Lewis: "There is no good trying to be more spiritual than God. God never meant for man to be a purely spiritual being. That is why he uses material things like bread and wine to put the new life into us. We may think this rather rude and unspiritual. God does not: he invented eating. He likes matter. He invented it."[205] Paul's poem of praise in Col 1:15-20 would say the same about Christ: Jesus likes matter; he invented it; he took it upon himself and became flesh among us and for us.

Righteous Father, forgive the mess that can be found in my heart. Continue your holy work of cleansing me from the inside.

[20] If you died with Christ to the elemental-orders of the world, why, as though living in [that] world, would you come under its decrees, [21] "Do not touch; do not taste; do not contact!" [22] **all of which goes to decay with use?**

The decrees of the elemental-orders focus on "perishables"—things that do not last. Once you use them, they are used up. They have no lasting value, but quickly decay and perish. Jesus said a similar thing in Mk 7:18-19 when discussing the issue of unclean foods, "Do you not see that whatever goes into a person from outside cannot defile, since it enters, not the heart but the stomach, and goes into the sewer?" (NRSV). F. F. Bruce said that these "are things which come to an end in the very act of being used. Handling or eating them, or the like involves their destruction. Food, once eaten, ceases to be food."[206]

To make this same point here, Paul uses a noun that can mean both physical and moral decay (or corruption). Physical decay is associated with death and destruction; it's what happens when a living thing dies and decomposes. Moral decay refers to a destructive rottenness in the soul.

Although many today associate the term "decadent" with excessively sweet desserts, it more rightly describes a soul or society in decay. Because of human sin, all creation has been in "bondage to decay" (Rom 8:21, NRSV), but this will change with the resurrection. Paul applies this on a moral level as well, when he says "the one who sows to his own flesh will from the flesh reap corruption" (Gal 6:8, ESV). Peter also describes Christians as having "escaped the corruption in the world caused by evil desires" (2 Pet 1:4, NIV), and so we must not listen to false teachers who are "slaves of corruption" (2 Pet 2:19, NRSV). Since one word can signify both physical and moral decay it's likely that the two types of decay work together. Just as the wages of sin is death, so the wages of moral decay is physical decay.

Perhaps the distortionists would say to Paul. "You're right Paul. Certain foods and items are subject to decay and that's why we should avoid touching them, lest they bring their corrupting power into our lives." If so, Paul would counter them by saying, "You are spending far too much time and energy on avoiding what is only temporary anyway. Whether we touch or taste such temporary things is not worth our attention. Rather, we should focus on Christ who has the power to bring real change to our hearts, changes that will last forever."

There is something rotten to the core in our society, Lord, but we look to you to overcome this decay with your holy touch.

*[20] If you died with Christ to the elemental-orders of the world, why, as though living in [that] world, would you come under its decrees... [22] all of which goes to decay with use? **[Such decrees are] according to the commandments and teachings of men***

The distortionists may have claimed that their commands came from their heavenly visions, but Paul knew they came from demonic powers (verse 20) and man-made ideas (verse 22). Paul likely believed the primal-powers worked through human beings to promote their agenda, often using long-standing human ideas and ideals to do so. These commandments, then, do not bring *heavenly* wisdom, but only *human* wisdom—or worse.

In the nearly 300 biblical texts that refer to commands, about 90% of them specify in some way that the commands come *from the Lord*. That's what makes the reference in Col 2:22 to *human* commandments so striking.

The closest parallel to this verse is Isa 29:13, where the Lord says, "in vain do they worship me, teaching human precepts [commandments] and teachings" (NETS), an accusation also quoted by Jesus in Mt 15:9 and Mk 7:7. This rebuke is directed against those who appear to be very religious. Unfortunately, their commands represent humanity's attempt to reach God, but consciously or not, they also represent a rejection of God's efforts to reach humanity. God's commands can transform humanity, but human commandments only keep us locked into a system of self-serving religiosity.

The temptation to make our own commands is an ancient one. It was the prospect of being able to form their own morality that lured Adam and Eve into eating from the Tree of the Knowledge of Good and Evil. They wondered why they should rely on God for knowing good and evil when they could decide it for themselves. Even when Eve was defending God's command not to eat from the tree, she added her own extra command, "nor shall you touch it" (Gen 3:3, NRSV). Boulton comments, "As if to certify and make a show of their impeccable orthodoxy and obedience, humans over-state the divine prohibition. They manufacture an amendment...With this lie they have added merely human words to the divine Word."[207]

Paul has caught the distortionists in the same compromising position. Says Boulton once more: "The religious urge to justify ourselves through some new (or fashionably old) religious reform persists, a permanent temptation to claim and supposedly carry out the work of salvation as though it were the work of the people," and not the work of God.[208]

My Lord and Redeemer, speak your royal law of liberty that I may be set free from the bondage of human commands.

²⁰ If you died with Christ to the elemental-orders of the world, why, as though living in [that] world, would you come under its decrees... ²² all of which goes to decay with use? **[Such decrees are] according to the commandments and teachings of men**

The decrees not only contain human *commandments*, but also merely human *teachings*. This same word is also used in the three other parallel texts cited above: Isa 29:13, Mt 15:9, and Mk 7:7.

Although we could highlight possible differences between "commandments" and "teachings"—the former being more practical and ethical in nature and the latter more theoretical and abstract—Paul would see them as functioning together. Teachings, even those that are quite theoretical, always point (explicitly or not) toward how one ought to live. True teaching "accords with godliness" (1 Tim 6:3, ESV), while false teaching does not (see 1 Tim 1:9-10).

Most of the time Paul speaks of the good teaching that is based on Scripture (Rom 15:4; 2 Tim 3:16) and taught in the churches (Rom 12:7; 1 Tim 4:13; 5:17; 6:1; Titus 1:9; 2:10), especially by himself (2 Tim 3:10) and his associates (1 Tim 4:6; Titus 2:1, 7). But "teaching" is also used often in contexts where sound teaching is contrasted with false teaching, as is true in Col 2:22. God's people should not be tossed around by "every wind of doctrine, by human cunning, by craftiness in deceitful schemes" (Eph 4:14, ESV), for they would then fall into all kinds of sins that are "contrary to sound teaching" (1 Tim 1:9-10, NRSV). These are the "teachings of demons," which the Spirit says will draw people from Christ in the last days (1 Tim 4:1, NRSV). "People will not put up with sound doctrine, but having itching ears, they will accumulate for themselves teachers to suit their own desires" (2 Tim 4:3, NRSV). They will want to hear "different doctrine" that "does not agree with the sound words of our Lord Jesus Christ and the teaching that accords with godliness" (1 Tim 6:3, ESV). Paul was concerned about teaching the true gospel of Christ in nearly every letter he wrote (see especially Gal 1:6-9).

While this verse in Colossians rejects false teaching, the positive side of teaching is also prominent in Colossians: (1) Paul is involved in teaching God's wisdom in Christ (Col 1:28); (2) the Colossians themselves were established in the faith through this teaching (Col 2:7); and (3) they should continue to teach one another in all wisdom (Col 3:16).

Give me ears, Lord, to discern true teaching from false, and give me lips to teach others your truth.

> [22] ...*[Such decrees are] according to the commandments and teachings of men,* [23] ***which indeed are a word having wisdom*** *in self-willed-worship and humbling-practices, the unsparing-treatment of the body, but they are without honor [in going] against the filling-full of the flesh.*

With regard to the commandments and teachings of men, Paul admits that they contain a grain of truth—or as he puts it "a word having wisdom" (I'm not following those translations that say the distortionists only have "an appearance of wisdom"). Perhaps Paul is being sarcastic, but more likely he recognizes there is some wisdom in these man-made commandments.

For example, if alcohol causes so many problems, doesn't it make sense to stay away from it? In a society plagued by self-satisfaction and gluttony, wouldn't it be sensible to encourage people to deny themselves these pleasures and train their souls for God's better things? Where sexual immorality is rampant, wouldn't it be wise not to touch those of the opposite sex? Even Paul himself said he treated his body harshly for the sake of his mission: "But I discipline my body and keep it under control, lest after preaching to others I myself should be disqualified" (1 Cor 9:27, ESV). He also believed that God's grace is "training us to renounce impiety and worldly passions, and in the present age to live lives that are self-controlled, upright, and godly" (Titus 2:11-12, NRSV).

But even though a set of teachings could be called a "word having wisdom," for Paul this does not necessarily make it worth following. The content may be good, but it accomplishes little and weakens faith.[209] Most of the verses in the NT that join "word" (*logos*) with "wisdom" (*sophia*) point out that the words of wisdom from the world are inferior to the word of wisdom from God (1 Cor 1:17; 2:1, 4, 13). What people need are not human words containing a measure of wisdom, but words from Christ that contain all wisdom: "Let the word [*logos*] of Christ dwell in you richly, teaching and admonishing one another in all wisdom [*sophia*]" (Col 3:16).

Wisdom without Christ is ultimately no wisdom at all.

Lord, I have learned things from the world, even some helpful things, but I pray that the things I've learned would be pulled into your gravitational force and revolve around you.

*²² ... [Such decrees are] according to the commandments and teachings of men, ²³ which indeed are a word having wisdom **in self-willed-worship** and humbling-practices, the unsparing-treatment of the body, but they are without honor [in going] against the filling-full of the flesh.*

Human commandments and teachings often pull us in the direction of "self-willed worship" (*ethelothrēskia*). Since this is the first recorded use of the term anywhere (and its only use in the Bible), Paul may be coining a word. It is a compound noun formed from *thelō* (a verb meaning "to will something") and *thrēskeia* (a noun meaning "worship" or "religion," which Paul used in Col 2:18 in reference to the worship of angels). As noted earlier, *thrēskeia* is often used in contexts of idolatrous worship.

It's not completely clear what Paul means by this term. The ESV translates it as "self-made religion," that is, a religion that conforms to one's own will instead of God's. Another possible translation is "self-imposed piety" (NRSV) or "self-imposed worship" (NIV), implying that it's a spirituality for cultivating one's will-power. In any case, it refers to a worship somehow driven by human will-power.

But any kind of worship which focuses on the human will (that is, human desire and determination) eventually becomes a worship of one's own will and one's own self. Christ fades into the background as the worshipers concentrate on gaining spiritual experiences and the fullness of salvation for themselves alone, as well as a sense of pride and accomplishment for any success achieved in this.

Another problem is that the church as the people of God becomes less and less important when a religion is all about fulfilling one's own will, one's own experiences, and one's own spiritual yearnings (see Col 2:19).[210]

Self-willed-worship, then, is really nothing but "would-be worship."[211] This verdict is fitting because the English "would" comes from the word "will." Would-be worshipers (or put it in slang terms, "wanna-be" worshipers) might think they are worshiping God, but they are not. By focusing on human will-power, they bring glory to themselves instead of God. As Peterson said, "It is an odd phenomenon to observe followers of Jesus, suddenly obsessed with their wonderfully saved souls, setting about busily cultivating their own spiritualities."[212]

Forgive me, Lord Jesus, for all the times I've evaluated a worship service by how well it fits my wants and wishes, instead of yours.

[22] ...*[Such decrees are] according to the commandments and teachings of men,* [23] *which indeed are a word having wisdom in self-willed-worship **and humbling-practices, the unsparing-treatment of the body**, but they are without honor [in going] against the filling-full of the flesh.*

This "self-willed-worship" being promoted in Colossae also involved "humbling-practices," which Paul just mentioned in Col 2:18. As noted there, these humbling practices called for forms of self-denial, such as fasting. Paul further defines these humbling practices as the "unsparing-treatment of the body." Such a person does not pamper their body, but is willing to put it through difficult distress.

It's not immediately clear what's wrong with this. The Bible says that the wicked should not be spared, including Canaanites (Dt 7:16), idolaters (Dt 13:8), or murderers (Dt 19:13). The guilty were not to be spared (Dt 19:21; 25:12). So if other sinners are not to be spared with regards to harsh treatment, it's not too much of a stretch to think we should also be unsparing toward our own body with regards to sin. That's why the apocryphal figure of Sirach calls upon the Lord to set whips over his thoughts and not spare him when he falls (Sirach 23:2-3).

An even harsher treatment of the body is commanded by Jesus, "And if your hand or your foot causes you to sin, cut it off and throw it away. It is better for you to enter life crippled or lame than with two hands or two feet to be thrown into the eternal fire." (Mt 18:8, ESV). What Jesus said and what Paul practiced (in 1 Cor 9:27), then, indicate that true disciples will treat their body harshly in the conflict with sin.

So what's the difference between the harsh treatment of the body that is proper for disciples and the distortionists' unsparing-treatment of the body which is criticized by Paul? Christ is the difference. For the distortionists the body is the source of evil. For them, a harsh treatment of the body will solve the sin problem.

For Christians, however, the body only reflects the sin that's in the heart (Mk 7:23). You can treat the body harshly, but the sin in the heart still keeps festering and coming out. Something more radical is needed—death. Both the heart and the body of flesh must be put to death, an act we cannot accomplish on our own, but has been accomplished through Jesus. In our union with Christ our body of flesh is stripped off in his circumcision, that is to say, in his crucifixion (Col 2:11).

Lord Jesus, all my little acts of self-discipline and self-denial have not yet transformed my life. For that I'm looking to you.

[22] *...[Such decrees are] according to the commandments and teachings of men,* [23] *which indeed are a word having wisdom in self-willed-worship and humbling-practices, the unsparing-treatment of the body,* **but they are without honor [in going] against the filling-full of the flesh.**

The commandments and teachings of men may have a word of wisdom, but they have no value in resisting the lure of sin. That's what Paul is saying here, even though the way he says it is difficult to translate.

The filling-full of the flesh is yet one more "fullness" word in this letter. This is its only appearance in the NT, but its appearances in the Greek OT signify an abundance, usually of food, but sometimes it's about an excessive, decadent abundance (Ex 16:3; Prov 27:7; Sirach 18:25), which leads to sin (Ezek 16:49; Hos 13:6; Hab 2:16) and may even be a form of God's judgment (Ex 16:8; Ps 106:15; Ezek 39:19). Perhaps the distortionists were promoting a spiritual fullness in opposition to a sinful fullness, but Paul says their methods are completely ineffective.

The word "honor" is the same word used in the Greek OT for honoring one's parents. It could also be translated as "value," for we value the things that we honor; but I have gone with "honor" to indicate that in the battle against sin, the distortionist message gains no honor because it consistently fails. Its battle plans are a fiasco.

Paul and the distortionists, then, both stand against the "filling-full of the flesh." Their main disagreement is how this is accomplished. The heart is not changed simply because a person abides by certain rules not to touch or taste forbidden items. Karl Barth observed that a person can be a vegetarian and abstain from alcohol and tobacco, and yet go by the name of Adolph Hitler.[213] Much evil can be done by those who deny themselves. Perhaps the sinful desires can be contained for a while, and even a long while, in much the same way that an alligator can be kept in a cage, but the heart of the beast is still raging. "Passions are never tamed by rules against them."[214] The only hope, as we noted before, is for the sinful flesh to be put to death in Christ (see Col 2:11 and the upcoming discussion in Col 3:5-11).

Some have even contended that the distortion is not only ineffective in stopping fleshly indulgence, but that it actually *increases* fleshly indulgence. "Far from 'freeing' people from the flesh, these teachers are 'feeding' the flesh."[215] Or to put it another way, by starving the *physical* flesh, they end up feeding the *sinful* flesh.[216] That may be true, but it's not Paul's main point.

Lord, I have tried many things to resist sinful indulgences, but nothing has been helpful except looking to you for deliverance.

Let No One Condemn You

to the tune of Gordon: *My Jesus, I Love Thee*
© 2013 David J. Landegent

Let no one condemn you based on what you eat
Or what times you worship, which days of the week.
These are but a shadow, such things do not last.
It's Christ that we worship, to Him we hold fast.

Let no one insist you must follow their lead.
Resist all their rules, and their man-made decrees.
They boast of their visions, their angels and fasts,
But what's found in Jesus cannot be surpassed.

When holding to Jesus, not losing our grip,
We grow as His body, a graced fellowship.
By dying with Jesus, the die has been cast:
We're now in His Kingdom, the world's in our past.

Seek the things above

Colossians 3:1-4

August 15-31

[1] *If therefore you were jointly-raised with Christ, seek the things above, where Christ is, sitting at the right-hand of God.* [2] *Think the things above, not the things on the earth.* [3] *For you died and your life is hidden with Christ in God;* [4] *when Christ (your life) is revealed, then also you—with him—will be revealed in glory.*

Paul continues to alternate between positive truths to embrace (Col 2:9-15) and negative lies to avoid (Col 2:16-23). At this point, Paul moves us beyond the rejected falsehoods to the truth of what it means to walk in Christ in terms of our thinking (Col 3:1-4) and our actions (Col 3:5-4:6).

As is often the case for Paul, the imperatives (commands) are based on indicatives (statements of truth). Thus, the two commands to seek and think the things above (Col 3:1-2) are sandwiched between three statements of truth: we have died and were jointly raised with Christ in the past (Col 3:1, 3); we are presently hidden with Christ (Col 3:3); and in the future we will be revealed with Christ (Col 3:4).[217] In all this, says Thompson, we do not merely "*imitate* Christ's path, but rather *participate* in his death, resurrection, and ultimate revelation in glory."[218]

Both the previous paragraph (Col 2:20-23) and this one begin with "if" statements.

Col 2:20   "If you died with Christ"
Col 3:1   "If therefore you were jointly-raised with Christ"

Dying with Christ to this world means there is no need to obey the distortionists' rules. *Being raised* with Christ means we have moved from the realm of this world into the realm of heaven, and thus are called to seek and think about what is above this earth. This paired reality of dying and rising with Christ was also highlighted earlier in Col 2:11-12.

Our identity with Christ is the key reality for this whole paragraph. The name or title "Christ" is used four times in as many verses, with an additional pronoun that refers to Christ in verse 4. Even more notable, however, is that Christ is not portrayed as a solitary figure, but as one with whom believers are identified: we are jointly raised with him (verse 1a); we have died with him (verse 3a); our life is hidden with him (verse 3b); and we will be revealed with him in the last day (verse 4).[219]

Thank you, Lord, for not just serving as a far-off model for me to imitate, but as a very present Savior with whom I can participate.

¹ If therefore you were jointly-raised with Christ, seek the things above, where Christ is, sitting at the right-hand of God.

Just as in Col 2:20, Paul uses the Greek word for "if" here. Many are quick to point out that this "if" does not indicate uncertainty about whether the readers were jointly-raised with Christ, and so could just as easily be translated as "since." But according to Moo, we should keep the word "if," not because Paul wants to make his readers feel insecure, but because the term "if" causes the readers to really think through where they stand with Christ, instead of just making assumptions.[220]

Paul would never say that Christians are raised to new life, period. They are only jointly-raised *with Christ*, which is the same truth expressed earlier in Col 2:12 (see also Eph 2:6). Being "with" Christ or "in" Christ is not only important for our understanding of ourselves, but also for our understanding of Christ. When we speak of Jesus in his humanity, we not only are to think of him as human in himself; he is also and especially human *with us.*[221]

Because we have died with Christ, we can ignore the authority of darkness and its decrees. And on the positive side, because we have been raised with Christ, we can gladly acknowledge his authority over us. Rather than regarding earthly foods and calendars as spiritually significant, we can instead pay attention to what is important in the realm of heaven; we can seek the things above.

The command here is "seek," a very common word in the Bible. We must clarify three things, however. First, by using this word Paul is not encouraging us to live in a kind of seeking that never find or even intends to find. He is not advocating fruitless wandering and searching—characteristic of many in today's society. His emphasis is not on the seeking but on that which is sought.[222]

Second, to seek does not mean to search for what is absent and unknown, but to "pursue more deeply and fully" what we already know and have in Christ.[223]

Third, even though fruit-*less* seeking is not our calling, we should not regard seeking as a short-term assignment, so that once we find, we can stop looking further. The command is given in the present tense, implying that this seeking is an ongoing activity, always fruitful, always full of discovery and delight, but ongoing—at least until Christ returns—and perhaps even into eternity.

Lord Jesus, thank you for your promise that those who seek will find.

> ¹ *If therefore you were jointly-raised with Christ, seek* the things above, where Christ is, sitting at the right-hand of God.

So what is it we are to seek? Especially prominent in the OT are verses about people seeking God or God's face. There are also many *commands* in the OT to do so (such as Isa 55:6). We might expect Paul to build on this common OT call to seek the Lord, by calling us to "seek Christ." But he does not. In fact, the NT as a whole says little about seeking God or Christ. It's only mentioned four times in the NT (only once by Paul, and then to say that *no one* seeks after God, Rom 3:11).

If there's any seeking after *Christ* in the NT, it is mostly negative. Sometimes the seeking is fueled by misunderstanding, as happened with crowds seeking free bread (Jn 6:26), or the women seeking Jesus' body on Easter morning (Mt 28:5). Even worse are those who seek Jesus to undermine him, arrest him, and kill him (multiple references fit here). Most of those who are seeking Jesus in the NT, then, were either trying to kill him, arrest him, trap him, or use him for their own purposes.

Perhaps the NT virtually ignores the OT call to seek God because it is more pessimistic about the human ability to do so. As Paul said, "no one seeks God" (Rom 3:11, ESV). But fortunately for us, God is seeking humanity. Unlike the ancient *Corpus Hermeticum* X: 25, which states, "None of the heavenly gods will leave heaven and come down to earth," the Bible proclaims that the true God has done just that.[224] Jesus fulfilled the prophecy of Ezekiel 34:11-16 by seeking the lost sheep of Israel (Lk 19:10). And unlike the declaration of Wisdom 6:16, that God's wisdom "goes about seeking those worthy of her" (NETS), Jesus intentionally seeks those who are lost and *unworthy* of being found.

While there may be appropriate ways to speak of us seeking God (as the OT testifies), Paul never referred to them, perhaps because of a conviction that Christians are people whom God has already sought and found. Paul's own experience would back this conviction. When he was heading toward Damascus, the only seeking Paul had in mind was his search-and-destroy mission against Christians. But Jesus was seeking him and turned his life around. There is no need to seek for the One who has found you. Salvation only happens when God seeks us, not when we seek God.

Thank you, Lord, for seeking me when I was lost and needed to be found. I may have thought I was doing the seeking, but it was really you.

¹ If therefore you were jointly-raised with Christ, seek the things above, where Christ is, sitting at the right-hand of God.

In the Bible, the search for God is often counter-productive, for we end up finding a god of our choosing instead of the true God. Duguid said that many people today are spiritual seekers "but only on their own terms...[they] assume that God can be found whenever and wherever they choose to seek him. For them 'seeking' is another word for 'shopping.' But...God is not a cosmic merchandiser, for whom 'the customer is always right.'"[225]

Among the many bad things that people seek, false gods could be added to the list. Moses warned the people about the nations around them, "you shall not seek their gods" (Dt 12:30, NETS). Various kings are condemned in the OT for seeking the help of false gods as well. Most people who seek for God don't even realize they are missing the mark. Not only is seeking after God often counter-productive, but it's often the case that God is found instead by those who were *not* seeking him: "I was found by those who did not seek me; I revealed myself to those who did not ask for me" (Rom 10:20, NIV, quoting Isa 65:1). Again we have to say, salvation happens because God seeks us, not because we seek God.

It's always tempting to devise our own paths to God. In the OT God had already said that he would be found by those who came to worship him at the temple in Jerusalem. But the people of the northern kingdom refused to do that and made their own temple for God at Bethel, which contained a calf-idol. The Lord rebuked this man-made religiosity through the prophet Amos, "Seek me and live; but do not seek Bethel" (Amos 5:4-5).

This truth is what the distortionists in Colossae missed. They thought they could experience a fuller salvation by seeking the Lord through their man-made rules about fasting and holy days, but this was only leading them into idolatry. They had overlooked the fact that the Christian faith was not about them seeking God, but about *God* seeking *them*, and God already finding them in Christ. Because they thought it was still necessary to search for God, they were unknowingly walking right past the Lord Jesus who had found them. They did not realize that "if the life of the believer is already joined to the risen Christ, then no further initiation into the heavenly realm is either required or available."[226]

Forgive me, Lord, when I insist on seeking you in my own time and on my own terms. I want to rejoice instead that you have already found me.

*¹ If therefore you were jointly-raised with Christ, seek **the things above,** where Christ is, sitting at the right-hand of God.*

Even though Paul doesn't talk about seeking the *Lord*, he *does* speak about seeking things *associated* with the Lord. There is no need to seek the Lord, for we already know where the Lord is: ruling in heaven (the next phrase of this verse), nourishing the church (Col 2:19) and abiding in our hearts (Col 1:27). There is, however, a need for seeking the things of the Lord. Just because we have already been found by the Lord does not mean we have uncovered all the treasures hidden in him (Col 2:3). This is why Paul calls us in Col 3:1 to seek the things above, the further treasures of the risen and ascended Christ.

This distinction between seeking God and seeking the things of God may be subtle, and it's not found everywhere in Scripture. For instance, Amos says "Seek the Lord and live" and then "Seek good...that you may live" (Amos 5:6, 14, NIV), as if they were nearly the same thing. But Paul seems to recognize a distinction.

Some of the heavenly things we are called to seek include: the priceless pearl of the kingdom (Mt 6:33; Lk 12:29, 31); entrance through the narrow door into the kingdom (Lk 13:24); glory, honor, and immortality (Rom 2:7); the good of our neighbors instead of ourselves (1 Cor 13:5; 10:33; 2 Cor 12:14); justification through Christ (Gal 2:17); and a second covenant because the first one was not effective (Heb 8:7). Even Jesus was seeking— seeking his Father's will (Jn 5:30) and his Father's glory (Jn 7:18; 8:50).

Especially relevant are NT *commands* to seek things associated with God. Jesus commanded us to seek and we would find (Mt 7:7-8; Lk 11:9-10), and more specifically he instructed us to seek first the kingdom of God and not to seek what we are to eat and drink (Mt 6:33; Lk 12:29, 31). Paul also commanded Christians to seek the good of their neighbors (1 Cor 10:24) and the building up of the church (1 Cor 14:12). Peter quoted Ps 34:14 in telling Christians to seek peace with others (1 Pet 3:11). In most of these verses (except for 1 Cor 10:24 and 1 Pet 3:11), the grammatical form of the command to "seek" is exactly the same as found in Col 3:1.

Lord, I have heard your call to seek first your kingdom. Forgive me when I've sought other things first instead.

*¹ If therefore you were jointly-raised with Christ, seek **the things above,** where Christ is, sitting at the right-hand of God.*

Paul says we are to seek "the things above" (*anō*), a word that mostly refers to heaven in the NT. Jesus claimed that he was from above (Jn 8:23), and Christians can also think of the Jerusalem above as their homeland (Gal 4:26). Paul's goal was to reach this homeland, to "press on toward the goal for the prize of the upward [*anō*] call of God in Christ Jesus" (Phil 3:14, ESV).

This seeking what is above is very different from the seeking of the distortionists. One difference between them is that Paul never moves beyond Christ in seeking the things above, for it is in Christ that all the treasures of wisdom are hidden (Col 2:3). The distortionists, however, are looking beyond Christ—a vain effort if ever there was one—in an attempt to get their fill of other heavenly things, like angels and visions. But by looking at the angels, they are missing Jesus on the throne. Only by focusing on the Christ will anyone be able to think truly on the things above.

Another difference is that the distortionists' version of seeking the things above was all about having private experiences of angels in heavenly worship that would have little impact on others. But for Paul, seeking the things above does not mean leaving this world behind, but seeking the things that Jesus on the throne is attending to. And what is the heavenly Jesus paying attention to? He is focused upon the world, seeking to save those who are lost, building up the church, and interceding on its behalf. It is not a true praise of God—either on the part of angels or people—which ignores what is on God's heart, namely, humanity and creation.

So in an odd way, it's by keeping our eyes on the things above that we truly focus on what's needed here on earth. An odd fish called the anableps (from the Greek words for "above" [*anō*] and "see") may illustrate what Paul is calling Christians to do. The anableps' two eyes are each divided into two parts. The lower part of each eye is intended for viewing what is underwater. The upper part is mostly kept above the surface of the water for finding insects to eat. Both sets of eyes are important, but the fish is only able to find nourishment because of the eyes set on the things above. Like this fish, Christians operate with two different sets of eyes. On the one hand, we need eyes to notice what's going on around us here below. On the other hand, we also need eyes to focus on things above, our primary source of spiritual sustenance.

Give me eyes, O Lord, not only to look to you, but also to the things that are on your heart.

[1] If therefore you were jointly-raised with Christ, seek the things above, **where Christ is,** *sitting at the right-hand of God.*

When Paul speaks of things "above," some might reject such talk as remnants of an ancient understanding of the universe, consisting of a flat earth with a heaven hovering over it (as if Paul were giving us a lesson in cosmic geography). They may prefer to think of heaven as an ideal, a word-picture, or a state of mind.

But heaven is a place, even though we cannot locate it on a map. "When the Lord's Prayer speaks of God, it locates God [as the Father who is in heaven]. God is not some mushy, generalized pantheistic presence always and everywhere, therefore not now and nowhere."[227] God locates himself in a place. Even with our modern understanding of a round earth, "above" still makes sense. It represents what is beyond all the things found on this planet. When we look up and away from the earth, we are seeing the larger realm of God, the not-yet-visible kingdom that encompasses the universe.

But the "things above" are not merely items located in the heavenly place. They are "where Christ is." It is the *presence of Jesus* in the heavens above which causes the "things above" to be available to us and have any value for us. Without Jesus, these other heavenly realities—such as love, faith, hope, joy, life, grace, mercy, peace, the kingdom—either disappear, move beyond our grasp, lose their value, or lose that which makes them what they are. Apart from Christ, they become mere human ideals. But through Christ these realities take their true form and become something we can seek and find. So it's critical that we do not merely seek the things above, but the things above *where Christ is.*

Of course, Paul also rejoices in the truth of "Christ in you" (Col 1:27), yet we dare not think of him as being our own personal deity or household god. Christ is more than in our hearts; he is also in heaven—with God the Father. That was Christ's place from all eternity, the place he left when he came to earth, and to which he returned and now reigns in glory. This same pattern of descending and ascending is portrayed in Phil 2:5-11, which states that Jesus did not consider equality with God something to be grasped, but emptied himself to take the form of a servant and die on the cross, and because of this, "God exalted him to the highest places and gave him the name that is above every name" (Phil 2:9, NIV).

Lord, sometimes I look forward to heaven because of all the awesome things that will be there. But the most awesome aspect of heaven will be you.

*¹ If therefore you were jointly-raised with Christ, seek the things above, where Christ is, **sitting at the right-hand of God.***

Paul is not so much concerned with how Jesus returned to heaven, but that he is there, and that he is there with authority, sitting at God's right-hand.

In the OT God's right hand signifies his power to create (Isa 48:13) and his power to save. On the shores of the Red Sea, the Israelites celebrate with the words, "Your right hand, O Lord, glorious in power, your right hand, O Lord, shatters the enemy" (Ex 15:6, ESV). With his right hand, God works salvation (Ps 60:5; 98:1) and upholds his people (Ps 63:8; Isa 41:10).

To be seated at the king's right-hand was a high honor, one that Solomon accorded to his mother (1 Kgs 2:19). Ps 110:1 speaks of a greater honor, that of being seated at the right hand of the Lord. This Messianic psalm is quoted in the NT more than any other OT passage (some count at least 33 references, including Mt 22:44; Acts 2:34; Heb 1:3).[228]

Of particular interest—in light of the distortionists' interest in angels—are texts that contrast Jesus' position to that of the angels. Angels might bow before or stand around the throne, but only the Son *sits* at God's right hand (Heb 1:13; see also 1 Kgs 22:19).[229] Because Jesus has "gone into heaven and is at the right hand of God," then all "angels, authorities and powers" have been placed under his authority (1 Pet 3:22, NRSV).

And Jesus is not only seated at God's right-hand; he is seated *on a throne* (Mt 19:28; 25:31; Rev 3:21; 7:17; 22:1, 3). The throne is not a place of rest, but a place from which Christ rules over all things.[230] He acts with steadfast authority instead of frantic anxiety.

Unlike the divine claims of authority being made by the Roman emperors, however, the Lord Jesus does not have the authority of a tyrant, but the authority of a Savior. His is not the authority of one who is mighty to kill, but of one who is mighty to save. His is not the authority of one who inflicts suffering and death, but of one who endured suffering and death on behalf of his people. It's because Jesus has this authority that we are called to seek the things above, the place from which he rules over all.

From above is where Christ has done much. From above he created (Col 1:16). From above he came to bring reconciliation on the cross (Col 1:22). From above he is the head over all powers (Col 2:10) and over the church (Col 2:19). From above he will return (Col 3:4). And right now, from above Jesus reigns on the throne (Col 3:1).

I praise you, Lord Jesus, for ruling over this world, and my life, with righteousness, mercy, and grace.

*¹ If therefore you were jointly-raised with Christ, seek the things above, where Christ is, sitting at the right-hand of God. ² **Think the things above, not the things on the earth.***

Here Paul builds on his earlier command to *seek* the things above by now commanding the Colossians to *think* the things above. Just as in English, there are many Greek and Hebrew words about thought-processes, often with subtle differences. The following continuums will help us understand better what is involved in thinking the things above.

From random daydreaming to intentional investigating. Good and important thoughts may arise when we daydream, but the sinful mind will often run toward the gutter if undirected. Paul is calling on believers to direct their minds along a certain path, pointing their thoughts in a heavenly direction.

From an ongoing process of learning to reaching comprehensive conclusions. While there is a place for the latter, here Paul is not asking us to come to final conclusions about the things above. Rather, he wants believers to continually reflect on what the Lord on the throne is doing and has done.

From ruminating on the past to planning for the future. It's probably fitting that Christians think in all three directions of time, especially concerning how it *was* that Jesus came to rule in heaven, how he *is* ruling now, and how the Lord wants us to fit into his plans for the future.

From abstract theorizing to practical thinking. For the biblical writers, thinking never remains in the sphere of abstraction, but is always tied to practical action. Faith is not just depositing beliefs in our brains, but living out constructive ideas.[231] Those who are truly heavenly-minded are always of earthly good.

From developing a mind-set to devising a solution. Even though thinking on things above does have practical implications, it's not a problem-solving kind of thinking. It's more about meditating and pondering the ways of God in such a manner that your character is transformed and a mindset is developed.

From relational knowing to mastering information. One of the main biblical purposes of thinking is the building of relationships with God and others. Biblical thinking is not an individual quest to come up with new ideas that can enter into debate with competing ideas, but for forming community. We will consider this last one even more tomorrow.

Capture all my thoughts, Lord, so that they line up with your heavenly thoughts instead of slogging around in the gutter.

*¹ If therefore you were jointly-raised with Christ, seek the things above, where Christ is, sitting at the right-hand of God. ² **Think the things above, not the things on the earth.***

The verb for "think" used in this verse is *phroneō*. It's a word that often serves a unifying and relational role in the NT. When Rom 15:5 says "to live in such harmony" (ESV), it literally says to "think [*phroneō*] with one another." This same phrase is found in 2 Cor 13:11. In his appeal for unity in Phil 2:1-5, Paul uses *phroneō* three times, asking the church to think the same, thinking as one, followed by a command to think among themselves the thoughts that were in Christ Jesus.

Thinking the same does not mean Paul is encouraging mindless group-think. Rather, he wants people to think in ways that discourage competition or over-against-ness. God created us to be thinkers so we might develop the kind of mindset needed for loving God and one another.

"Thinking things above," then, does not mean thinking in an "uppity" way. Using the same verb *phroneō* and the related word *huperphroneō* (a kind of "hyper-thinking"), Paul warned believers, "I say to everyone among you not to think of yourself more highly than you ought to think, but to think with sober judgment, each according to the measure of faith that God has assigned" (Rom 12:3, NRSV). Thinking is also mentioned twice in Rom 12:16a, which says we are to be "thinking the same things with one another, not thinking uppity, but associating with the humble" (my translation).

Since Paul had earlier accused the false teachers of being puffed up with self-importance based on visions (Col 2:18), it would be fair to say they were thinking on "uppity" things instead of the things above. Perhaps the distortionists believed that "thinking the things above" meant learning higher truths that would make them superior to others in terms of knowledge or morality. If so, they would have completely missed the mark. To think the things *above* means that our thoughts foster fellowship with the risen Christ and his church. By contrast, to think the things *of the earth* means that our thoughts hinder our fellowship with Christ and others.[232]

So when false teachers create divisions by encouraging the kind of thinking that fosters pride, rivalry, selfish boasting, and competition, Paul speaks against such thoughts. "For those living according to the flesh think [*phroneō*] the things of the flesh, but those [living] according to the Spirit [think the things] of the Spirit" (Rom 8:5, my translation).

Lord, I confess that I have often used my mind to be critical of others. Teach me to use my mind for more loving purposes.

*¹ If therefore you were jointly-raised with I, seek the things above, where I is, sitting at the right-hand of God. ² Think the things above, **not the things on the earth.***

Paul not only calls on Christians to think about things above, but also *not* to think about things on the earth. The Lord, of course, is present in both places: "the LORD is God in heaven above and on the earth beneath; there is no other" (Dt 4:39, NRSV). Heaven and earth together were created by God, join in the worship of God, serve as witnesses to God's judgment, will be reconciled to God, and will be made new. A few verses (like this one), however, do point to a *contrast* between what is above and the earth below.

For instance, Jesus implied that heaven is further advanced than earth in the doing of God's will when he taught us to pray, "your will be done, on earth as it is in heaven" (Mt 6:10, NRSV). A greater contrast between what is above and below is portrayed in Jms 3:15, which highlights the difference between wisdom which is from above and demonic wisdom that is earthly. Paul also makes a sharp contrast in Phil 3:19-20 between the false teachers who operate "with minds set on earthly things" and the Philippian believers whose "citizenship is in heaven" (ESV).

While the Philippian opponents, however, sought to satisfy their physical desires (for "their god is their belly"), the Colossian distortionists were squelching physical desires and yearning instead for heavenly "goodies." But it was all done in an earthly way. Instead of their god being their belly, their god became their *empty* belly. They replaced their physical lusts with "spiritual" lusts and were none the better for it. Though their eyes were filled with visions of angels instead of appetizers, they were still overlooking the only One worthy of filling the horizons of the mind, thus cutting themselves off from Christ (Col 2:18-19). Once that was done, they lost heaven altogether and set their minds on the earth.[233]

Unfortunately, Paul's words have often been misused to say that Christians should ignore the earth, as if spirituality is an otherworldly matter, having nothing to do with creation. This cannot, however, be Paul's message, for he has been keen to affirm the role of creation in God's work (Col 1:15-20). Seeking and thinking the things above instead of the things of the earth does not mean, in Karl Barth's words, having "a warm love for the eternal and a cool contempt for the temporal."[234] Rather, we have the same warm love and concern for what is earthly that our Lord in heaven has.

I confess, Lord, that I have often operated on the basis of earthly wisdom, even when I thought I was acting spiritually.

*¹ If therefore you were jointly-raised with I, seek the things above, where I is, sitting at the right-hand of God. ² Think the things above, **not the things on the earth.***

Most likely Paul uses "earth" here in the same way that biblical writers sometimes used the word "world." On the one hand, "world" can refer to the good planet created by God and the people God created in his image. On the other hand, the "world" also can be defined as the system of evil in operation on this planet. This sinful aspect of the world is especially highlighted by the English adjective "worldly." Both good and bad aspects of the world are well-represented in the NT.

With the word "earth," however, the dominant reference is to the good place that God created. Usually the "earth" is not seen as evil in the same way that "world" is. For instance, when 1 John 2:15 says, "Do not love the world or the things in the world" (NRSV), we would be surprised if it said, "Do not love the earth or the things of the earth." Yet here and in Col 3:5, Paul does use the word "earth" in this negative sense.

By calling us to think of things above instead of things of the earth, Paul is saying we should set our minds on the holy actions of heaven instead of on the sins that happen on the earth. Thus, instead of contemplating sexual immorality and impurity, we focus on the purity of God. Rather than being passionate about earthly projects, we become passionate about God's purposes. While some might concentrate on satisfying evil desires, those who think on things above will meditate on God's desires. Whereas idolatrous greed worships at the altar of earthly wealth, the heavenly-minded person worships God alone. And it's not just the "degenerate" sins which are earthly. We are also thinking along earthly lines when we—like the distortionists—pursue spiritualities that overlook Jesus.

But however we interpret verses 1-2, the commands to seek and think the things above only make sense in the light of being raised with Christ. If we have not already been raised with Christ, then seeking and thinking on things above would be nothing but running after our own fantasies and projections of the after-life (which may be more like what the distortionists were doing in Col 2:18). But because we have been raised with Christ, we have already been transferred to the heavenly kingdom of the Son, even though we are still walking upon the earth (see Col 1:13), and so can pursue a life that reflects our new location.

Heavenly Father, may your will be done on earth as it is in heaven, and may it be done in my life as well.

*¹ If therefore you were jointly-raised with Christ, seek the things above, where Christ is, sitting at the right-hand of God. ² Think the things above, not the things on the earth. ³ **For you died** and your life is hidden with Christ in God*

As indicated by the word "for," this verse supplies the reason we can (and should) seek and think on the things above. It's because our earthly life has (in some sense) died and our new life is already with Christ in heaven, though in a hidden form. We can seek and think the things above because in Christ that is already the location from which we operate (see Eph 2:6 for an even stronger way of stating this).

Paul highlights our death with Christ because he does not want us to think that being raised with Christ (Col 3:1) means we walk about as "divine men and women," always victorious, healthy, wealthy, and wise. Being jointly-raised with Christ does not mean God's glory is already shining through us in its fullness, obvious to one and all. Instead, he wants us to know that even though we are raised with Christ, we also remain dead.[235] We died to sin and the elemental-powers (Col 2:20), and we're still dead to them; ours is a life-style that could be called a death-style. Our new life is filled with victory—not because it's devoid of suffering—but precisely because this new life is cross-shaped.[236]

There is, then, no being raised with Christ unless there is also a dying with him. While the tense of the verb here indicates that our death with Christ is completed (rather than being an ongoing, drawn-out process), the next section (Col 3:5-11) will remind us that this completed death continues to have ongoing repercussions for daily living (or should we say "daily dying"). So, odd as it may sound, our *resurrection* life with Christ is not so much characterized by daily triumphs, but by daily dying with him. As Karl Barth noted, "To know Easter means...to be implicated in the events of Good Friday."[237] To paraphrase Brueggemann, a feel-good, triumphalist, or therapeutic gospel might allow Easter Sunday to obliterate Good Friday, but in an honest reading of the NT, the negative aspects of Good Friday continue to make their claims.[238]

The death and resurrection life of Jesus do not happen to us in succession, but simultaneously and interactively. In Christ, we rise as we die, and we die as we rise. We experience resurrection as a kind of dying, and dying as a kind of resurrection.

Shape my life, Lord, by your cross, and fill my suffering with the power of your resurrection.

*¹ If therefore you were jointly-raised with Christ, seek the things above, where Christ is, sitting at the right-hand of God. ² Think the things above, not the things on the earth. ³ For you died **and your life is hidden with Christ in God***

Our resurrection life—though very present and real—is nonetheless present and real in a *hidden* way, for it is hidden with Christ. The fullness of this new life will not be obvious to anyone, not even ourselves, until it is revealed with Christ in his future glorious return.

This new life is given (Rom 2:7), received (Mk 10:30), and even inherited (Mt 19:29). We are not merely passive recipients, however, for God calls us to take hold of this new life (1 Tim 6:12, 19) and enter into it (Mt 19:16-17) by taking a hard path (Mt 7:14). What is most important to the NT writers is that our life is linked to that of Jesus, who said, "Because I live, you also will live" (Jn 14:19, NRSV).

According to John's emphasis, people receive this life by *believing in* Jesus (Jn 3:15-16), but this is not merely some mental acknowledgement of Jesus. Rather, *believing* in Jesus somehow involves *being* in Jesus. "The free gift of God is eternal life *in* Christ Jesus our Lord" (Rom 6:23b, ESV, emphasis mine). Jesus is essential for life, not only because he *has* life and *gives* life, but because he himself *is* "the way, the truth, and the life" (Jn 14:6, NRSV). Since Jesus is life, then eternal life is not something one can "have" apart from him. To paraphrase Eugene Peterson, eternal life is not merely perpetual future, but the perpetual presence of Jesus.[239]

But when does this eternal life begin for believers? Can we have eternal life now, or is it granted to us after death (or even after Jesus' return)? The answer is "yes"; we experience life now *and* later. On the one hand, Christians already have eternal life: "Truly, truly, I say to you, whoever hears my word and believes him who sent me has [a verb in the present tense] eternal life. He does not come into judgment, but has passed from death to life" (Jn 5:24, ESV). On the other hand, the full reality of eternal life has not yet happened (Rom 6:22). But this is no contradiction. Eternal life is a present reality as well as a future hope.

Paul is saying something similar in Col 3:1-4. In one sense, we already have eternal life, for we are jointly-raised with Christ. In another sense, we still await the full reality of this eternal life, for the life we have in Christ currently is hidden with Christ, still waiting to be revealed in the last day.

Thank you, Lord, for the new life I experience even now because I experience you day by day.

³ *For you died **and your life is hidden with Christ in God***

When talking about hiddenness, Paul is *not* saying that the true church is an invisible reality, distinct and better than the visible institutional church. Any church that tries to downplay or overcome its visible reality is trying to separate itself from the God who took on visible reality in Christ.[240] So what does it mean to be hidden in Christ? Here are some possibilities.

Hiddenness as Protection. Just as God hid people to protect them from their foes (Ps 27:5), so God hides our lives in Christ to protect us from hostile spiritual powers. In dying with Christ, we are beyond their reach.

Hiddenness as an indication of being treasured. According to Col 2:3, "all the treasures of wisdom and knowledge are concealed," that is, hidden in Christ. If wisdom and knowledge are valuable treasures hidden in him, then our own hiddenness in the Lord means that he also treasures us.

Hiddenness as a burial. The Greeks referred to those who were buried as being "hidden in the earth." By contrast, Christians are not hidden in the earth, thinking earthly things. We are buried and hidden in Christ to think on what is above.[241]

Hiddenness as an explanation (but not an excuse) for our failures. Although we are a raised to new life in Christ, we often don't look very new. Our new selves—though very real—are as yet hidden in Christ. This truth should not function, however, as an excuse for moral sloppiness, as if to say, "If the new self won't be revealed until Jesus returns anyway, there's no need to have it make an early appearance." Our life is hidden in *Christ*, not hidden and obscured by *sin*.[242]

Hiddenness as characteristic of Christian suffering. While some might expect Christian living to be one victory after another, we are actually jars of clay, subject to all kinds of suffering. Few people can yet tell that we are more than conquerors. But even though our suffering is obvious to all, our hidden inner nature is being renewed daily in Christ (2 Cor 4:7-18).[243]

Hiddenness as a mark of humility—God's and ours. Not only are *we* hidden in Christ, but Christ and the Father are also hidden. In contrast to visible idols, God is one who hides himself (Isa 45:15). Jesus and his power to rule are also hidden from the eyes of the world. And since Jesus is hidden, then we who are in him are also hidden. In contrast to the distortionists who put their humbling-practices on display, we live in the true humility of hiddenness. We let our light shine, yes, but not as a spotlight on ourselves.

When destructive forces rage, when showy temptations rise, when I feel exposed and alone, hide me, Lord, as a treasure held close to your heart.

*³ For you died and your life is hidden with Christ in God; ⁴ **when Christ (your life) is revealed, then also you—with him—will be revealed in glory.***

Although Paul has been speaking of things above, he knows these things are not located there in a settled kind of way; the things above are on the move, coming to our world, accompanying Christ in his return.

When Paul speaks of concealing and revealing here, he uses nearly the same verbs he used in Col 1:26 concerning the mystery of the gospel, but there is a difference in timing. The mystery of the gospel *had been concealed in the past*, but *is revealed now*. Our life in Christ, however, *is concealed now* and *will be revealed later*. We live between the time of the past revelation of the gospel and our future revelation of being in Christ.

But that future revelation is coming. As we noted under Col 2:11-13, whatever happens to Christ in some sense happens (or will happen) to us. Our lives narrate the same story line as Jesus' life.[244] Since Christ died, we died with him. Since Christ was buried, we were buried with him. Since Christ was raised, we are raised with him. And here we see that when Christ is revealed at the end of time, we will be revealed with him. So there is not only present *participation* in Christ's death and resurrection; there is also present *anticipation* of what lies ahead for Christ and us.[245]

We can say this because Jesus is not only our peace (Eph 2:14), our hope (1 Tim 1:1), our wisdom, righteousness, sanctification, and redemption (1 Cor 1:30); he is also our life, as our current verse says.[246] Since this is so, we can never again speak of our life as something that exists on its own, apart from Christ.[247] Any efforts of ours to form our own self-identity, instead of finding our identity in Christ, is to miss the point of what a Christian is.[248] When Christ returns we will be revealed to the world, and also to ourselves, for we do not yet fully know what we shall become (see 1 Jn 3:2). As Barth said, "As he discloses Himself to us, He also discloses us to ourselves."[249]

Of course, our being revealed in glory only happens "with Christ." The end of time is not for bringing our human potential to glorious light, so all can see what a wonderful person we really are. Rather, it is only in the revelation of Christ that our own full identity is revealed.

You can see then all three tenses of salvation in this section. We were raised with Christ in the past (Col 3:1), are hidden with Christ in the present (Col 3:3), and will be revealed with Christ in the future (Col 3:4).[250]

Lord, I look forward to seeing you in the full revelation of your glory when you return, and also truly knowing myself as I look into your eyes.

If You Have Been Raised with Christ

to the tune of St. George's Windsor: *Come, Ye Thankful People, Come*
© 2013 David J. Landegent

If you have been raised with Christ,
Lifted up and given life,
Seek the things of heav'n above,
Where now rules the Lord of love.
Think of things above the earth,
Things of value, things of worth.
Love and justice, truth and peace –
Set your mind on things like these.

You have died with Jesus Christ;
You've been raised and given life;
Yet that life is hidden now,
Hidden with the Lord somehow.
But when Jesus is revealed,
You will no more be concealed.
All that you were made to be
Will be shown most gloriously.

Commands for life in the church

Colossians 3:5-17

September 1-October 28

⁵ *Necrotize, therefore, the parts [of you which are] of the earth: sexual-sin, impurity, passion, bad desire, and greed (which is idolatry)—* ⁶ *because of these the wrath of God comes.* ⁷ *In these you also once walked when you were living in them;* ⁸ *but now, you, throw-off all these: wrath, anger, bad things, slander, filthy-talk from your mouth.* ⁹ *Lie not to each other, having stripped off the old man with his practices,* ¹⁰ *and having clothed [yourself] with the new [man], which is being renewed in knowledge according to the image of the one who created him.* ¹¹ *Here there is not Greek and Jew, circumcision and uncircumcision, barbarian, Scythian, slave, free, but all and in all is Christ.*

¹² *Clothe [yourselves], therefore—as God's chosen-ones, holy and being loved—with the heart of compassion, kindness, humility, gentleness, patience,* ¹³ *bearing with one another and granting-grace to each other if ever anyone has a grievance. Just as the Lord has granted-grace to you, so should you [grant-grace to others].* ¹⁴ *Over all these things, [put on] love, which is the connecting-tissue of completeness.*

¹⁵ *And let the peace of Christ, to which you were called in one body, arbitrate in your hearts; and be thankful.* ¹⁶ *Let the word of Christ dwell in you richly, teaching and warning each other in all wisdom with psalms, hymns and Spirit-oriented songs, singing by grace in your hearts to God.* ¹⁷ *And in all of whatever you do—in word or in work—[do] all things in the name of the Lord Jesus, giving-thanks to God the Father through him.*

While the church is to include people without regard to their ethnicity or social position (see Col 3:11), this does not mean that any and all moral behavior is to be included and tolerated. As Gill said, "Every person is welcome in the community of God's grace, but not every behavior or attitude is welcome."[251] Thus Paul includes this section of commands.

And please note that these commands are for Christians *as they live in relationship with others*. According to Witherington, "One of the major mistakes in handling the ethical material in [Paul's letters] is to assume that this is primarily advice by Paul to individual Christians, rather than to communities about communal life."[252] It's not about personal self-improvement, but about the improvement of the community of God.

Teach me, Lord, through these commands so that my participation in your
church would make it a more loving place.

Read again Colossians 3:5-17.

Paul was not one to begin his letters with commands. He did not talk about what *we* are to do in Christ until he first established what *God* has done for us in Christ and who we *are* in Christ. What we are to do flows out of: who we are (new creations in Christ), where we live (in Christ), and who lives in us (Christ). By making a strong connection between morality and our relationship with Christ, Paul is instructing God's people in what could be called a "relational ethic."[253]

And this is not a relationship that doesn't go anywhere. Rather, it's a relationship involving movement, a storyline, a narrative of what God has done in Christ and how we became involved in that storyline (which is summarized in Col 2:9-15). The *story* of God with his people and the *commands* of God for his people dance together. In Paul's letters, the gospel story may take the lead in the dance, but the story never dances alone. (We find a similar thing in the books of Moses, where blocks of narrative and blocks of commands are joined together.)[254]

Because God's commands follow the storyline of the gospel, Christians live in the light of the past (what Christ has done for us and in us) and also in light of the future (what Christ will do when we are revealed with him in glory). As Moo said, "Christians are not only to 'become what we are'; we are also to 'become what we one day will be.'"[255]

In the first part of this letter (Col 1:1-2:5), Paul had focused on important truths about the identity of Christ and our identity in him, and he only gave a few commands. But Paul is not content to leave it at that, for the reality of Christ cannot help but be shaping the lives of those who trust in him. The story of Jesus gives us a reason to transform our behavior, as well as the power to do so.

Some might wonder if Paul is using these commands as part of a power-play to gain or sustain control over the Colossian church. But the actual commands given are not designed to boost Paul's status, authorize a church power-structure, enhance the church's domination in society, or make money. The only power found in Paul's big picture story and its follow-up commands is the power of Christ's sacrificial love, not the power of oppression.[256]

Thank you, Lord, for including me in your story of salvation and commanding me into that story as well.

Read again Colossians 3:5-17.

So far Paul's commands have come in pairs: walk in Christ and avoid false teachings (Col 2: 6, 8); let no one judge you or disqualify you (Col 2:16, 18); and seek and think the things above (Col 3:1-2). Now, however, commands begin to appear more frequently. Paul is in command-mode in this section (as well as in the next two sections of Col 3:18-4:1 and 4:2-6).

Paul commands the Colossians in order to remind them that the life given in Christ has to be lived. Paul is not calling on Christians to merely *attempt* obedience; rather, they are called to actually obey. Nor is Paul giving us a list of good things to choose from, but is calling us to obey in all things.[257] Through the bluntness of this ethical list, says N.T. Wright, "Paul sets a clear standard for the church both ancient and modern" without lapsing into legalistic rules.[258] So even though this section is dominated by commands, according to Pokorný, it "is not moralizing at all; instead, it is a vehicle for the proclamation of the rule of Christ."[259]

Unfortunately, as Turner observes, many people regard commands as "unpleasant, even destructive, limitations on the lives of *individuals* that diminish the diversity of societies, constrain the freedom of *persons*, and inhibit the development of *selves*."[260] But it's this individualistically-minded world that especially needs God's community-building commands.

Many refer to this section as a list of vices and virtues, as found in other ancient philosophers. But the philosophers treated virtues as purely human dispositions and actions. In fact, the word "virtue" (Latin *virtus*) stems from the Latin word for man, *vir*. Virtues defined manliness and were for producing good soldiers.[261] A virtue, then, could be thought of as a quality of human origin and strength, which is very different from what we might think of as the fruit of the Spirit. For many people, virtues and vices can be discussed, debated, and practiced irrespective of one's relationship with God, but Paul cannot imagine such a thing. For Paul, everything moral is dependent on life being transformed by one's relationship with God through Christ.

So even though some of Paul's moral commands seem similar to the moral advice of other religious approaches and philosophies, it's a superficial similarity. For Paul, it's the motivation and empowerment for moral living provided by the triune God which sets his lists of sins and good qualities and actions apart from all others.

Lord, I have attempted to obey your commands, but often it has only been a feeble attempt. Send your Spirit to empower me to obey.

Read again Colossians 3:5-17.

In the NT there are at least 26 lists of sins to avoid and good qualities and actions to live out. There has been much discussion over the sources of these lists, ranging from the Ten Commandments and other Jewish writings to non-Christian philosophies like Stoicism. Most likely, however, the NT lists arose from the natural need for any group to categorize ethical matters when trying to teach them in an easy-to-understand fashion.[262]

The lists of the NT use at least 123 different words to talk about sins to avoid, and 48 different words to speak of good things to live out. There is surprisingly little overlap from one list to the next: 83 of the 123 sin-words are used only once, and only 11 terms are used more than three times (sexual sin, sexual sinner, impurity, desire, lewdness, idolater, malice, slander, strife, murder, envy). As for the 48 good qualities, 31 terms are used only once, and only two more than twice (love and faithfulness).

These NT lists serve a variety of purposes. Sometimes they describe the immoral quality of life without God, often with an additional purpose of warning Christians not to return to these sins or to fellowship with those who have. Some lists also help believers distinguish true leaders of the church from false ones. Most often, however, these lists are written to direct believers in the way of Christ, which is true of this text.

Among these lists, the greatest overlap of sin-words are sexual sins, idolatry, and the sins of anger (all of which are emphasized in Colossians 3). Why these?

Sexual sins and *idolatry* were emphasized because pagan society approved and encouraged these things, and the NT was retraining converts to act otherwise.

Sins of anger received a lot of attention for the opposite reason—not because the NT had to counteract pagan moral standards (even pagans agreed that anger was unwise). Rather these sins were highlighted because church life placed new believers in a new social situation where conflict could easily emerge. Churches uniquely brought together people from a wide variety of social and economic classes so there was great potential for misunderstanding and taking offense.

Other sins did not receive as much attention in these lists because even the pagan culture agreed they were wrong. Thus there was little reason to argue for moral standards that the new converts already subscribed to.

Lord, I appreciate these biblical lists of commands, but let me never confuse following a list with heart-felt obedience.

Read again Colossians 3:5-17.

We have spent many days on the overall picture of these moral commands. But why is this section about sin and good qualities and actions even in Colossians? Perhaps it's because Paul commonly moves from teaching-mode to command-mode in his letters, wanting to give his churches not only good news to celebrate, but also words to live by.

But it could also have something to do with Paul's opposition to the distortion. If so, however, it's not clear how these commands relate to the distortion. Here are some possible scenarios.

Perhaps the distortionists believed moral living in the body was unimportant once a person had tapped into heavenly power. But if this scenario were true, we would expect Paul to do as he does in other letters, namely, to accuse the distortionists of moral corruption.

Or in an opposite sense, maybe the distortionists thought of themselves as the party of morality, while it appeared to them that Paul was negligent in this matter. But nothing here indicates the distortionists had been attacking Paul or his teaching, so that he needed to defend himself.

Most likely the distortionists thought they were in line with Paul's gospel and his call to holiness, but they didn't realize Paul would not at all agree with their concept of holiness and how it is lived out. The distortionists' concept of holiness focuses on an individual piety caught up in private heavenly visions and rules for treating the body harshly, while Paul's concept of holiness focuses on a transformed way of loving others through Christ. Paul also believes their methods of attaining holiness are flawed because they flow from merely human ideals (Col 2:22); are ineffective and superficial in dealing with sin (Col 2:23); and cause people to pull away from Christ (Col 2:18-19).

For Paul, holiness can only be found by participating in Christ. Because we have died with Jesus (Col 2:11, 20; 3:3), we put our sins to death, stripping them out of our lives (Col 3:5-9). Because we have risen with Jesus (Col 2:12-13; 3:1), we put on the new man and clothe ourselves in the qualities of Christ (Col 3:10-14). This seems to be the most likely scenario and best fits the rest of the letter.

Whether or not we figure out the exact situation in Colossae, we need to hear and obey the Lord's commands in this section.

Lord Jesus, if I've been too careless or too scrupulous in my moral living, call me back with your commanding voice, so that my obedience is grounded in you.

*⁵ **Necrotize, therefore, the parts [of you which are] of the earth**: sexual-sin, impurity, passion, bad desire, and greed (which is idolatry)*

Not only are we to avoid *thinking* "the things on the earth" (Col 3:2), but we are also called to *put to death* those parts of us still attached to the earth. Instead of just *considering* ourselves dead to sin (as Paul said in Rom 6:11), now we are to be actually involved in its demise. The fight against sin is not just about finding our *identity* in Christ, but also taking *action* in Christ.[263]

But why is action needed? Because even though the Colossians have already died with Christ (Col 3:3-4), there's a sense in which the old sinful self is still active and kicking, creating havoc by casting a large shadow. Perhaps we could think of it as a zombie (simultaneously dead and alive) or a ghost (haunting us even though it's dead). Even this haunting presence, however, needs to be eliminated. What has already died in Christ must still be put to death. This is in contrast to the solution of the distortionists, who sought to correct human behavior through rules. But as N. T. Wright notes, "The old taboos put the wild animals of lust and hatred...into cages: there they remain, alive and dangerous, a constant threat to their captor. Paul's solution is more drastic: the animals are to be killed."[264]

Many versions opt to translate the active verb here (*nekroō*) as "put to death," but I was looking for a single word to convey its meaning. "Kill" or "slaughter" sounded too brutal, "execute" sounded too formal, "murder" implied a wrongful death, and the old-fashioned word "mortify" is now mostly used in contexts of embarrassment. So I coined a new verb based on the Greek, "necrotize." An advantage of this word is that it calls to mind a contemporary medical condition known as "necrosis" (also based on the same Greek term), which refers to the death of most or all the cells in an organ or tissue. A "necrotizing" infection, for instance, is one that kills off cells. The patient is alive, but the cells in some of his body parts are dying.

Even here, however, we must remember Barth's words that "dying, destruction, putting off the old man, being dead, this too is obviously outside the range of our own possibilities...it never means a work which it is in our hands to fulfill."[265] Any activity on our part in bringing death to our sinful selves can only happen as we are caught up in the death of Christ. It is "by the Spirit"—not by our own strength—that we "put to death the deeds of the body" (Rom 8:13, NRSV).

I am still haunted by the ghost of my sinful self, Lord, so I call on you to give me the determination and energy to put to death what is already dead through you.

> [5] **Necrotize, therefore, the parts [of you which are] of the earth**: *sexual-sin, impurity, passion, bad desire, and greed (which is idolatry)*

"Necrotize" is a fitting translation because Paul is not talking about putting to death the whole sinful self—that's already been accomplished in Christ. Instead, Paul speaks of putting resistant "parts" of the self to death. Just as a necrotizing infection kills off *parts* of the whole body, so here Paul wants us to "necrotize" *parts* of our whole selves.

Most translations overlook this idea of putting "parts" of the body to death. Instead, they speak vaguely of putting to death "whatever" is earthly. But the word here is *melos,* which literally refers to a body part. So Paul says in Rom 6:13, "Do not present your members [*melos*] to sin as instruments for unrighteousness, but present...your members [*melos*] to God as instruments for righteousness" (ESV). Jesus even talked about cutting off body parts that caused us to sin (Mt 5:29-30).

It may sound odd to speak of sin as if it were located in parts of the body, but we commonly associate various sins with body parts. We steal with our hands, lust with our eyes, and use our tongues to gossip. Our feet take the wrong path and the rumblings of our bellies pull us toward gluttony (see Prov 6:16-18). When the biblical writers make these associations, they are not saying the body parts themselves are to blame for the sin; the whole person is responsible.

But if the whole person is responsible, why does Paul tell us to necrotize only *parts* of the body. Why not the whole self? Why this seemingly half-hearted measure in dealing with sin? Because there is no need to kill off the whole self; that has already happened in Christ. Yet parts of us have been resistant to the death of the whole. Thus God calls us to finish up the death of the sinful self by necrotizing these remnants of resistance.

Chicken farmers know that when they chop off the head of a hen, and it's dead, it still takes a while for all the parts of the body to realize that the whole has died. After its head is chopped off, the body of the chicken will continue to scamper around erratically for a while, even though the chicken as a whole has died. Similarly, sinful parts of our selves continue to run loose, even though the whole has died in Christ. It's these sinful parts that need to be necrotized, so the whole self and all the parts with it are thoroughly dead in Christ.

I confess, Lord, that there are remnants of resistance in my own life. When they continue to run loose, let them also die with you.

⁵ Necrotize, therefore, the parts [of you which are] of the earth: sexual-
sin, impurity, passion, bad desire, and greed (which is idolatry)

Some might misinterpret Paul to be saying that righteousness can be
obtained by literally lopping off a body part or subduing it. But this line of
thinking would take us straight to the distortionist techniques condemned
in Col 2:20-23, which assume that the sinful flesh can be controlled by
harshly treating the body and following rules about what to touch and taste.
This can't be what Paul means.

Garland compares this superficial way of dealing with sin to painting
over wooden siding that has been damaged by termites.[266] It may look on
the outside as if things have improved, but the conditions of the house continue to deteriorate. What's needed is an exterminator. It's the same with
sin. What we need are not more rules, but an exterminator. Jesus is our
exterminator (*and* "resurrectionizer").

And here we must note a huge difference between the modern medical
meaning of necrosis and Paul's meaning here. In the medical world, the
patient is alive, but parts of the body have died (become necrotized), and
the doctors try to prevent death from spreading to the rest of the body. In
Paul's word picture, however, it's just the opposite. We (the patients, if you
will) are already dead in Christ, but some of the parts of the body are still
functioning, and so what's needed is to extend death to these resistant parts
so that everything dies. In the medical world, life is the goal; but in Paul's
word picture—at this point anyway—the goal is the full death of the self
and all its sinful parts. This is not to be a gradual approach to sin management, but the death of it all.

Paul chooses the relatively rare *nekroō*, then, because he is not talking
about the normal kind of putting to death. If he had wanted to say that,
there were at least seven other Greek verbs for this that were available (and
used elsewhere by Paul). But Paul wanted to focus on putting only resistant
parts of the self to death to join the rest of the body in being dead in Christ,
an idea for which *nekroō* was better suited. Even the other two uses of
nekroō in the NT (Rom 4:19 and Heb 11:12) both refer to someone who is
simultaneously alive and not alive, for Abraham lived in this border zone
between life and death, with a body "as good as dead," as many translations
put it.

I am in this border zone between life and death, Lord—dead to sin but not yet
fully dead, alive to you but not yet fully alive. Draw me, Lord, across the
border.

⁵ *Necrotize, therefore, the parts [of you which are] of the earth:* **sexual-sin,
impurity, passion, bad desire,** *and greed (which is idolatry)*

Paul could have listed some body parts which needed to be necrotized (like
the eye or ear), but instead he lists sins which "dwell" in those body parts.
Although Paul uses general words instead of itemizing specific sins here,
this does not mean we are permitted to do what's not on the list or that
these are only suggestions. They are God-given commands.[267]

The first four items in this list are associated with sexual sins, but that
doesn't mean they are the worst sins. More likely sexual sins are listed first
because they involve body parts in an obvious way—the genital organs, the
lustful eyes, the groping hands, and the fantasizing brain.

The first item is sexual-sin (*porneia*), the same word used in 1 Cor 6:18
("flee from sexual sin"). It's also the first work of the flesh listed in Gal 5:19-
21. This word appears in all the main OT genres, but in the prophets Hosea,
Jeremiah, and Ezekiel it often served as an image for Israel's unfaithfulness
to God. Sexual sin and idolatry often went hand-in-hand.

Sexual sin is not evil because it involves the body or the sexual organs,
but because it's a perversion of God's good creation, as well as destructive
of our relationships with God and others. Although the biblical warnings
against sexual sin are widely ignored today, the fact remains that it is not to
be overlooked, condoned, or rationalized. Only through necrotization will
there be a true sexual revolution.

The second item listed, impurity, especially focuses on *sexual* impurity.
Paul speaks against the impurity of same-sex relations (Rom 1:24); mourns
those who have not repented of impurity and sexual immorality (2 Cor
12:21; Eph 4:19); calls us to abstain from sexual immorality and impurity (1
Thess 4:3-7; Eph 5:3); and lists sexual immorality and impurity together in
the works of the flesh (Gal 5:19).

Some might dismiss purity issues as irrelevant as the OT laws about
unclean foods, or as misleading as the distortion's fussiness about what to
touch and eat (Col 2:21). Yet it's an important word. What makes sexual sin
impure, is not that it puts people in contact with genital organs and body
fluids, but that the person is using their body (which belongs to God) for a
purpose God never intended, namely to have sex with someone besides a
marriage partner. Sex that is pure is unadulterated; it's a sex which is not
mixed together with inappropriate partners or attitudes.

*Lord, I celebrate your good gift of pure sex, but I also ask that you cleanse me
from the perversions of my sex-saturated world.*

> [5] *Necrotize, therefore, the parts [of you which are] of the earth:* **sexual-sin, impurity, passion, bad desire**, *and greed (which is idolatry)*

The third item here is passion. The *English* word has both good and bad meanings, all involving intensity. Sometimes it refers to intense suffering, as in the passion of Jesus on the cross. In other contexts, passion refers to intense sexual feelings and actions, usually sinful ones. Today, however, many use it in reference to intense enthusiasm. A passionate baseball fan or a passionate Christian is fervent and enthusiastic in his or her devotion.

The Greek word for passion (*pathos*) is only used by Paul in the NT. In all three of its appearances, it refers to *sinful* sexual desire. Rom 1:26 refers to same-sex behavior as rooted in "dishonorable passions." In 1 Thess 4:4-5 Paul urges every believer "to control your own body in holiness and honor, not with lustful passion, like the Gentiles who do not know God" (NRSV). Col 3:5 is the other reference.

In the book of 4 Maccabees, passion is bad because it is irrational. What's needed is for passion to be controlled by reason. Paul, however, believed that both passion *and* reason were sinful. Minds can be hardened (2 Cor 3:14) blinded (2 Cor 4:4), debased (Rom 1:28), hostile to God (Col 1:21), depraved (1 Tim 6:5), corrupted (2 Tim 3:8) and defiled (Titus 1:15). The way forward is not for the mind to rule over the passions, but for Christ to transform the mind (Rom 12:2; Eph 4:23). Only then can sinful passions be overcome, and even necrotized.

For the fourth item Paul combines the common noun for desire (*epithumia*) with the adjective for bad. Paul recognizes that some desires (including sexual ones) are good. But bad desires also plague the human heart. Of the thirty-eight uses of this noun in the NT, thirty-five refer to bad desires which are impure (Rom 1:24), sinful (Rom 6:12), deceitful (Eph 4:22), passionate (1 Thess 4:5), harmful (1 Tim 6:9), self-centered (2 Tim 4:3), worldly (Titus 2:12), tempting (Jms 1:14-15), corrupting (2 Pet 1:4), and defiling (2 Pet 2:10)—to name just a few.

Paul does not advocate re-channeling these desires or using our minds to tame them. Rather, they are to be necrotized, for they are already dead in Christ. The immediate context of Colossians 3 suggests that God's people are to necrotize sexual and monetary desires, but even the *spiritual* desires of the distortionists—to gain deeper knowledge, or follow human traditions, or be better than others—these also must die.

Lord, make my passions and desires holy to you and pleasing in your sight.

> [5] *Necrotize, therefore, the parts [of you which are] of the earth: sexual-sin, impurity, passion, bad desire,* **and greed** *(which is idolatry)*

God also calls us to necrotize greed (*pleonexia*), which literally means "more having." Greed is the desire for possessions and money, a way of seeking the things below, rather than the things above (see Col 3:1). Unlike the thankful ones who have been filled in Christ (Col 2:10), the greedy person is the dissatisfied one who thinks more is needed in order to find fullness.

In the NT greed is often included in lists which warn against various sins. It is one of many sins that come from within a man's heart to defile him (Mk 7:20-23). It's a sin that people fall into when they exchange their worship of God for idols (Rom 1:28-31; see also Eph 4:19). In Lk 12:15 Jesus warned, "Take care! Be on your guard against all kinds of greed, for one's life does not consist in the abundance of possessions" (NRSV).

The reference to "all" *pleonexia* implies that the grasping nature of greed takes many forms, including a desire for money, food, attention, power, and sex. A sexual greed is seen in the tenth commandment against coveting a neighbor's spouse, in the false prophets who "have hearts trained in greed" and "eyes full of adultery" (2 Pet 2:14, NRSV), and in the sinners who are "greedy to practice every kind of impurity" (Eph 4:19, NRSV).

Because there is such a thing as sexual greed, some attempt to interpret all five sins in this verse as sexual in nature. But this is unnecessary and actually misses the important connection between economic sins and sexual sins. "Why end a list of sexual sins with an economic sin?" ask Walsh and Keesmaat—"Because sexual sin is fundamentally a matter of covetousness."[268] Individuals and cultures which give free rein to materialistic greed are also in hot pursuit of sexual pleasures—and vice versa. The *Fifty Shades of Gray* in the sexual realm, as the title of a popular pornographic book put it, are matched by Fifty Shades of Greed. Sexual immorality and financial greed are two sides of the same coin. Both of them undercut community by turning people into those who grasp and grope for more.

Necrotizing greed might mean plucking out the eyes that lust after the hottest consumer goods. Or cutting off the hand that reaches out to grab a bigger slice of the pie. Or slicing off the tongue which has acquired a taste for the "finer things in life." Some may defend greed as the combustion engine powering today's economy, but it is not fitting for those who have died with Christ.

Point out to me, Lord, the different forms of greed that live in my heart, that I might evict them and be thankful instead.

⁵ Necrotize, therefore, the parts [of you which are] of the earth: sexual-sin, impurity, passion, bad desire, and greed **(which is idolatry)**

There may be a sense in which all sins are forms of idolatry. In rebelling against God's ways and going our own way, it's evident that we worship our selves, as if we were the highest authority for our lives.

Paul, however, sees a particularly strong connection between idolatry and greed, even to the point of making them nearly identical. Eph 5:5 makes the same connection: "No...greedy person—such a person is an idolater—has any inheritance in the kingdom of Christ and of God" (NIV).

Brian Rosner spells out the implications of this equation. On one level Paul is saying that *greed is as bad as idolatry*. For those who think greed is an acceptable sin, Paul grabs their attention by equating it with idolatry. Paul also means that *greed leads to idolatry*. As it says in the Jewish book, the *Testament of Judah* 19:1, "My little children, love of money leads to idolatry; because when led astray through money, men name as gods those who are not gods." But Paul goes further by *equating greed with idolatry*, for the greedy are giving to wealth the same service, love, and trust which they should be giving to God.[269] Even if no one is actually bowing down to their money, they are treating it as if it were a god, following its directions, displaying their affections for it, and finding their security in it.

A true Christian must not *serve* money: "You cannot serve both God and money" (Mt 6:24, NIV). A true Christian must not *love* money: "Keep your life free from the love of money" (Heb 13:5, NRSV; see also 1 Tim 6:10). A true Christian must not *trust* money or find security in it: "those who trust in their riches will fall" (Prov 11:28, NIV; see also Ps 52:7; 1 Tim 6:17).

So in order to wake up believers who make excuses for their greed, the ones who think it's the "lack" of money that is the root of all evil,[270] Paul exposes its true character: greed is idolatry. In making this charge, Paul does us a great service, for "in the fight against greed there is no more effective weapon in Christian ethics than the recognition that greed is idolatry."[271] Therefore, greed needs to be necrotized, not only because it deprives the poor, harms God's creation, and makes our lives shallow, but also because it is an act of unfaithfulness which pulls us away from the true God toward lesser gods. Just as the greedy pursuit of visions makes us lose our grip on Christ (Col 2:19), so our greedy economic pursuits sever that connection as well. Faith and greed pull our lives in opposite directions.

Break down every idol, cast out every foe; now wash me and I shall be whiter than snow.

⁵ *Necrotize, therefore, the parts [of you which are] of the earth: sexual-sin, impurity, passion, bad desire, and greed (which is idolatry)—* ⁶ **because of these the wrath of God comes.**

Because the sins of verse 5 are flourishing in the world rather than being necrotized, Paul warns that the wrath of God is coming.

Philosophical lists of vices and virtues did not ever mention the wrath of God, but it's often in NT lists. Rom 1:32 concludes a lengthy catalog of sins with reference to "God's decree, that those who practice such things deserve to die" (NRSV). Gal 5:21 and 1 Cor 6:10 declares that those who sin in the ways listed will not inherit the kingdom of God. Speaking of God's wrath, then, brings the discussion "to a whole new level of seriousness."[272]

Of all the angry ones in the Scripture, God is the angriest of them all. More than three-quarters of the 298 OT references to wrath concern *God's* wrath. Sometimes God seems angry with the whole world: "For the LORD is enraged against all the nations, and furious against all their host; he has devoted them to destruction, has given them over for slaughter" (Isa 34:2, ESV). Surprisingly, however, the dominant recipients of wrath are God's own chosen people.

An awareness of God's wrath, though, should not blind us to the fact that God is "merciful and gracious, slow to anger, and abounding in stead-fast love and faithfulness" (Ex 34:6, ESV). God does not always execute his wrath, but often restrains it (Ps 78:38; Isa 60:10; Hos 11:9; Mic 7:18).

In the NT 32 of the 36 references to wrath are about *God's* wrath. Human wrath is regarded as an evil, but God's wrath is not. According to Jn 3:36, "whoever does not obey the Son shall not see life, but the wrath of God remains on him" (ESV). Paul speaks of both the present and future wrath of God. *In the present,* "the wrath of God is being revealed from heaven against all godlessness and wickedness of people, who suppress the truth by their wickedness" (Rom 1:18, NIV). God shows his wrath through disasters, but even worse is when God shows his wrath by giving people over to their sins; he lets them self-destruct (Rom 1:24-32). It's not only a dreadful thing to fall *into* the hands of the living God (as Heb 10:31 says), but it's even more dreadful to fall *out of* God's hands and be given over to sin. And as for God's *future* wrath, Paul says that those who harden their hearts are only "storing up wrath for [themselves] on the day of wrath when God's right-eous judgment will be revealed" (Rom 2:5, NRSV).

Lord, our world would rather not hear about your wrath. I'd rather not hear about it either, but I pray to see how your wrath is a part of your love.

*[5] Necrotize, therefore, the parts [of you which are] of the earth: sexual-sin, impurity, passion, bad desire, and greed (which is idolatry)— [6] **because of these the wrath of God comes.***

Many people today prefer a God who would not be too hard on sin. But we must resist constructing our own god and instead remain faithful to what God has revealed about himself in the Scripture. God is displeased with evil and passionately resists every will which is set against his.[273]

God's wrath is especially difficult to understand if we think of God as merely a larger version of ourselves. Since it would be wrong for *us* to burn with wrath toward those who cross us, we expect it would be wrong for God too. But God is not like us, nor is his anger like ours. God is holy, so infinitely holy that we do not realize what an affront it is for us to reject him and his Word. Nor do we realize that God, as our Creator, has complete rights to do with us as he wishes, even taking our life. You and I do not have such authority over the lives of others, but God does.

We must not forget, however, that God's wrath against sin comes under the larger umbrella of his moves to reconcile all things in Christ (Col 1:20). Because God is just, it's easy to assume that God's wrath will always end in punishment. But justice also works toward reconciliation.

Here we see a big difference between the OT and the NT. God's wrath burned against his people Israel in the OT, but it does not burn against his people in the NT—the church as a whole. (We do, however, see God's wrath against individual churches, as in Revelation 2-3.) This is not because the NT church lives more righteously; it too is plagued with moral failure. The real reason why God's wrath is not directed at Christians is because they are "in Christ"—the very Christ who already absorbed the wrath of God on the cross. Since he took the wrath upon himself, there's none left over for believers to receive: "There is therefore now no condemnation for those who are in Christ Jesus" (Rom 8:1, ESV).

The wrath of God does come upon the disobedient (Eph 5:6), but for those "justified by [Jesus'] blood, much more shall we be saved by him from the wrath of God" (Rom 5:9, ESV), for Jesus "rescues us from the wrath that is coming" (1 Thess 1:10, NRSV). In fact, "God has destined us not for wrath but for obtaining salvation through our Lord Jesus Christ" (1 Thess 5:9, NRSV). We should not, then, gloat about our rescue or take it for granted. Instead, our awareness of and rescue from God's wrath compels us to walk in God's way and extend the gospel to those who are perishing.

Thank you, Lord Jesus, for delivering me from wrath and condemnation.

⁵ Necrotize, therefore, the parts [of you which are] of the earth: sexual-sin, impurity, passion, bad desire, and greed (which is idolatry)— ⁶ because of these the wrath of God comes. ⁷ **In these you also once walked when you were living in them;** *⁸ but now, you, throw-off all these: wrath, anger, bad things, slander, filthy-talk from your mouth.*

As he did earlier in Col 1:21, Paul helpfully reminds the Colossians of what they were like before Christ came to them. These former pagans didn't merely dabble in sexual sin or experiment with impurity and passion. They did not occasionally succumb to bad desires or greed. Rather, they "walked" in the well-worn path of the sins listed in verse 5. These sins provided the daily environment in which they lived.

In Col 1:10 and 2:6, Paul talked about a good kind of walking, but here he warns them against walking in evil ways, which is a common NT theme. The writings of John frequently contrast walking in the light with walking in darkness (Jn 8:12; 11:9-10; 12:35; 1 Jn 1:6-7; 2:11). Paul warns against walking in sexual sins, drunkenness, and quarreling in Rom 13:13. Elsewhere Paul contrasts walking according to the Spirit with walking according to the flesh (Rom 8:4; Gal 5:16). In 2 Cor 5:7 Paul contrasts walking by faith (which is good) with walking by sight (which, if not evil, is less than good). There is also a difference between walking as wise or unwise (Eph 5:15) and walking in idleness or with a work ethic (2 Thess 3:11).

The verses paralleling Col 3:7 most closely are found in Ephesians. In Eph 2:1-3 Paul describes his readers as at one time being "dead in the trespasses and sins in which you once walked, following the course of this world, following the prince of the power of the air, the spirit that is now at work in the sons of disobedience—among whom we all once lived in the passions of our flesh, carrying out the desires of the body and the mind, and were by nature children of wrath, like the rest of mankind" (ESV). In Eph 4:17 Paul bids his readers to "no longer walk as the Gentiles do, in the futility of their minds" (ESV).

By describing their past lives, Paul is not merely reminding the Colossians of how their lives have changed. Rather, he is calling them to continue to live out those changes. His intent is not to rub their nose in their former way of life, but to increase their resolve never to return to that life again. Any remnants of these old sins need to be necrotized.

Lord, lead me always in your new paths of righteousness, so that I never return to the ruts of my old ways.

*⁷ In these you also once walked when you were living in them; ⁸ **but now, you, throw-off all these***: wrath, anger, bad things, slander, filthy-talk from your mouth.*

Once again Paul paints a contrast between then and now. He had done this earlier in the letter, when Paul pointed out that the Colossians were once alienated, but are now reconciled to God (Col 1:21-22). Here, however, Paul puts this pattern to a different use. They have not merely been moved by God from one condition to another, but are now summoned to *act* differently: once you walked in sin, but now throw that off. Paul made a similar move in Rom 6:19, "just as you once presented your members as slaves to impurity…so now present your members as slaves to righteousness for sanctification" (NRSV). People are not only passively transferred to the kingdom of the Son (Col 1:13), but are also called to active duty in that kingdom.[274] Their new situation demands new behavior.

Paul switches his imagery here. In addition to *necrotizing* sins, we are to *throw them off* (*apotithēmi*), treating them like rotting clothes and stinky old shoes. Throwing them off means more than merely abstaining from them. It also "entails more of a deliberate, active renunciation" of something we had been doing.[275]

Heb 12:1 uses this same verb to describe what the followers of Jesus do: "Therefore, since we are surrounded by such a great cloud of witnesses, let us also throw off [*apotithēmi*] everything that hinders and the sin that so easily entangles. And let us run with perseverance the race marked out for us" (NIV). Other NT texts use this verb to call us to throw off the works of darkness (Rom 13:12), the old self (Eph 4:22), and all wickedness (Jms 1:21), including falsehood (Eph 4:25), malice, hypocrisy, envy, and slander (1 Pet 2:1).

We do not throw off sins only because Paul said so. Most of these texts about "throwing off" supply a reason for doing so. We throw off works of darkness *because* the day of God's kingdom is at hand (Rom 13:12). We throw off falsehood *because* we have learned the truth in Jesus (Eph 4:21-25). We cast off weights and sins in the race of faith *because* Jesus is going before us (Heb 12:1-4). Here in Col 3:8 we throw off sins because they deserve God's wrath.

My sins stink, O Lord, so strip them from me. I want to run the race you've set before me without being burdened by their weight.

*[7] In these you also once walked when you were living in them; [8] but now, you, throw-off all these: **wrath, anger, bad things, slander, filthy-talk from your mouth.***

Here we find a different batch of sins that must be dispensed with. The previous list in verse 5 focused on the sins of desire (ranging from sexual desire to materialistic desires and every evil desire between them). Such sins can remain hidden for a long time (although eventually they get acted upon). Like a cancer or infection, they fester in the heart, and that's why they need to be necrotized before they move into the open.

The sins listed in verse 8, however—most of which involve angry speech—are more likely to be seen and heard in public settings. Perhaps this explains why Paul shifts from the action of necrotizing sins to that of throwing them off. Sins of conflict and anger are not like hidden infections, but more like offensive in-your-face garments (similar to some of today's t-shirts). Thus it would make more sense for these sins to be thrown off instead of necrotized. What sins of desire and sins of anger have in common, however, is that both have a negative impact on the community.

Nothing in this letter indicated that the Colossians were struggling particularly with the sins listed in verse 5. The same cannot be said, however, about the sins listed here in verse 8. With the distortionists judging other Christians as spiritually unfit (see Col 2: 16, 18), the tension in the church would create plenty of opportunities for expressions of wrath, anger, and slander. A similar thing happened with the false teaching in Galatia (see Gal 5:15, 19-21). Throwing off these sins, then, is not done for the purpose of making an isolated soul more holy. Rather, these sins are removed in order to transform the community life of the body of Christ, and thus enhance its witness to a watching and listening world.

It would not do, however, to simply remove what's evil without putting on what's good. Neither would it be fitting for us to put righteous garments over top of our sinful rags, as if it were only a cover-up. As Garland notes, "Paul does not tell us to put on new clothes over the old; the old must be stripped off and thrown away."[276] Of course, we should not take Paul's imagery too far by concluding that it's impossible to do anything good until all the sins within us are first removed. The removal of the bad and the putting on of the good are happening simultaneously. The important thing is that both activities are happening in our lives.

Although I don't always notice it, Lord, my sins adversely affect my family, my church, my community, and nation. Forgive and transform me.

*[7] In these you also once walked when you were living in them; [8] but now, you, throw-off all these: **wrath, anger, bad things, slander, filthy-talk from your mouth.***

The first two sins listed here are nearly equivalent. Wrath and anger are found together in one hundred verses in the OT and six in the NT, often in a phrase like "the wrath of his anger" or "the anger of his wrath." *God's* anger or wrath accounts for over 70% of these biblical references. Some might conclude from this that God's anger gives us license to show anger as well, but what is appropriate for God is not always appropriate for God's people. Divine wrath is a fitting response to human sin (Col 3:6), but human wrath is usually sinful. Even so-called righteous wrath is tainted.

There are small hints that anger can be appropriate, such as "Be angry but do not sin; do not let the sun go down on your anger" (Eph 4:26, NRSV). But this is a minority voice. The predominant word about human anger is this: "the anger of man does not produce the righteousness of God" (Jms 1:19-20, ESV). We are to forsake the works of the flesh like anger (Gal 5:20), put away all wrath and anger (Eph 4:31), and leave things instead to the wrath of God (Rom 12:19). According to the Greek OT, we should "cease from wrath and forsake anger" (Ps 37:8).

While some believe that anger is just an emotion and thus cannot be sinful, can we really claim that emotions are somehow exempt from the corrupting power of sin? The emotion of anger, like every other emotion, is also tainted by the Fall. Some *suppress* their anger, pretending they are not angry, and maybe even fooling themselves, only to see it come out in other ways later on. To avoid this, others believe it's best to freely *express* their anger, but this doesn't work out very well either. It would be better if people learned instead to *confess* their anger, that is, acknowledge it before God, and seek to have it not only forgiven but also thrown out of their lives.

According to 4 Maccabees 3:3, "No one of you can eradicate anger from the soul, but reason can help to deal with anger" (NETS). Paul would agree with the first half of the statement (sinners cannot eliminate anger), and he might give a qualified assent to the second half (reason can "deal with" anger). But "dealing with" anger is not the goal of the Christian. Rather, we must throw it off completely, a task only made possible by our dying to sin with Christ and eradicating the remnants of evil through God's power.

Forgive me, Lord, for all the times I have tried to justify my anger, even though it was not producing your righteousness.

*⁷ In these you also once walked when you were living in them; ⁸ but now, you, throw-off all these: **wrath, anger, bad things, slander, filthy-talk from your mouth.***

Three more sins need to be thrown off: bad things, slander and filthy talk.

The noun "bad things," often translated as "malice," is a plural noun (*kakia*) based on the adjective for bad (*kakos*). In the Greek OT (where it is used 142 times), it mostly functions as a general term for human evil, but it can also refer to disasters brought on by the Lord ("Because they forsook the Lord…therefore the Lord has brought this evil [*kakia*] upon them," 1 Kgs 9:9, ESV). So just as wrath and anger are permissible for God but not humanity, the same could be said about "bad things." Here, however, *kakia* refers to bad things that sinners do (see Titus 3:3). Generic words like *kakia* may sound humdrum in a list of sins, but they are important. For those who think their sin is allowable because it's not specified in a list, the use of the general term *kakia* means that even unspecified sins need to be removed.

"Slander" is my translation of *blasphēmia*, which of course is the root of the English term "blasphemy." Although the English word is almost always confined to the vertical dimension (against God), the people of the NT also used it for "horizontal slander" against other humans (see Mt 15:19; Mk 7:22; Eph 4:31; 1 Tim 6:4-5). Slanderous words and actions do not fit the Christian wardrobe and need to be removed.

The last item, filthy-talk, refers to words about shameful matters. To speak a shameful word is like throwing excrement on others, so that everyone present experiences shame. When filthy words are spoken, the minds of those who hear it are quickly brought into the gutter from which they came. As Paul stated in Eph 5:12, "it is shameful even to mention what the disobedient do in secret" (NIV). In the same vein, Paul said, "Let there be no filthiness nor foolish talk nor crude joking, which are out of place, but instead let there be thanksgiving" (Eph 5:4, ESV). Some may think it's silly to frown on "dirty words," as if it were just a case of prudishness about the body and sexuality. But if we truly appreciate and respect God's beautiful gifts of the body and sexuality, then our words about them also need to be tender and respectful, not crude and lewd. When our tongues are shrouded in shameful words, the light of Christ cannot shine from our hearts as it should. Whether we call it corrupting talk or filthy-talk, it must be extracted from our mouths like a rotten tooth.

May the words of my mouth and the meditations of my heart be acceptable in your sight, O Lord.

> [9] **Lie not to each other,** *having stripped off the old man with his practices,* [10] *and having clothed [yourself] with the new [man], which is being renewed in knowledge according to the image of the one who created him.*

Back in verse 5, Paul listed five sins to necrotize and then added a sixth explanatory sin, idolatry. In verse 8 Paul lists five sins to throw off, but now adds another one, lying. Falsehood is a problem in society, with enemies lying to us or about us. But lying especially makes life difficult in church, which is Paul's main concern here, for he warns against lying *to each other.* Citing Ananias and Sapphira as an example (from Acts 5:1-11), Smedes states, "It should come as no surprise, then, that it was lying which first spoiled the life of the blossoming Christian community."[277] True community only grows where there is truthful communication. But as N. T. Wright said, the "truth is often inconvenient, untidy or embarrassing, and we are constantly tempted to bend it into a less awkward shape."[278]

Lying to each other can happen in many ways. Teachers or prophets might share their own delusions instead of the true Word of God. Some might lie to God, as did Ananias and Sapphira. Others may give the impression they are in fellowship with God when they are actually walking in darkness (1 Jn 1:6). Still others may spread false rumors. If there is mistrust in the church, it is difficult for the body of Christ to function well. As Paul said in a similar context, "So then, putting away falsehood, let all of us speak the truth to our neighbors, for we are members of one another" (Eph 4:25, NRSV).

Paul frequently writes about doing good things for or to "each other," such as loving (1 Thess 3:12), showing honor (Rom 12:10), living in harmony (Rom 12:16), welcoming (Rom 15:7), caring (1 Cor 12:25), serving (Gal 5:13), bearing burdens (Gal 6:2), forgiving (Eph 4:32), submitting (Eph 5:21), encouraging (1 Thess 4:18), edifying (1 Thess 5:11), and doing good (1 Thess 5:15). But Paul also warns against actions that Christians should *not* do to each other, such as sexual sins (Rom 1:27), judging (Rom 14:13), devouring (Gal 5:15), provoking (Gal 5:26), and hating (Titus 3:3); Col 3:9 adds lying to this list.

If we wrap ourselves in falsehoods, we will eventually be exposed. But if we are truly in Christ, we will throw off the lies and live out the truth—for Jesus is the truth (Jn 14:6; Eph 4:21) and cannot lie (Heb 6:18).

I confess, Lord, to lying. I even lie to myself about how often lies come from my mouth. Forgive me. Purify me by your truth.

297

*⁹ Lie not to each other, **having stripped off the old man with his practices,***
¹⁰ and having clothed [yourself] with the new [man], which is being
renewed in knowledge according to the image of the one who created him.

We conquer sin by stripping off the old man with his practices. The verb here is stronger than verse 8's "throw-off." Paul used the noun form of this verb in Col 2:11 for the "stripping of the body of flesh in the circumcision of Christ." He's not talking about "the removal of an insignificant scrap of bodily tissue, as the old circumcision was, but the stripping off of the whole 'body of flesh,'"[279] that is, our death with Christ.

It's not a case, then, of us saying, "I can do it myself." We strip off the remnants of our old selves because the deed is already done. Christ has already stripped our sinful flesh from us, and we are merely living out what has been done to us. To stick with the imagery of clothing, our filthy and inappropriate garments have been removed by Christ, and now he's empowering us to rip off any tattered fabric left behind.

Notice that Paul does *not* say we have stripped off our old *sins*. Instead what has been stripped off is the "old man." It's the same idea found in Rom 6:6 that our old man "was crucified with him in order that the body of sin might be brought to nothing, so that we would no longer be enslaved to sin" (ESV). To be more gender-inclusive, modern versions translate "old man" as "old self," but this sounds too psychological and individualistic, as if conversion were only a matter of turning over a new leaf.

But Paul is not talking about a change of personality.[280] Rather, it's our former solidarity with the fallen old man named Adam which is to be stripped, so that instead we are raised to new life in the new man named Jesus (see Rom 5:12-21 for more on this). The old man is not merely being fixed up; rather it has been put to death and stripped off with Christ. The remnants of the old are still dying and being removed, but it's misleading to say that old and new coexist. One replaces the other.[281] "Renewal may be a process, but it's a process that can only move forward because the end result is already complete in Christ."[282]

This truth is not an abstract illusion but affects our "practices" as well. The death of the old man in Christ is not a theory to be believed, but a life to be lived. As this verse says, when we truly know Christ, not just our sinful *nature* is stripped away, but so are our sinful *practices*. Since the old man is deceased, the old lifestyles need to die off as well.

Strip away, Lord, everything that's left of my sinful self, so that I can be
clothed in your righteousness.

⁹ Lie not to each other, having stripped off the old man with his practices, ¹⁰ **and having clothed [yourself] with the new [man],** *which is being renewed in knowledge according to the image of the one who created him.*

It would not be fitting to be stripped of the old (verse 9) and left naked. We remove the old *and* put on the new. Just as clothes often identify a person's social or marital status (especially in Paul's day), so we put on new "clothing" which conforms to our new identity in Christ.

A few other ancient writers said something similar. The Jewish philosopher Philo said, "Come, let us cast off this showy tunic and put on the sacred one inwoven with the varied embroidery of virtues."[283] The Greek writer Philostratus tells of a young man who stripped off the garments of frivolity and put on the cloak of the philosophers.[284] Biblical texts about clothing also resonate with what Paul is saying here:

• When fig leaves failed to adequately cover Adam and Eve's sin-caused shame, God mercifully provided animal skins for clothes (Gen 3:21). In the same way, when we were living in sinful shame, God mercifully clothed us with the new man in Christ.

• Jacob wore his brother's clothes in order to deceptively steal his brother's blessing (Gen 27:15, 27). In Col 3:9-10, however, Paul calls us to strip off deception and instead put on our new selves created by God.

• Status was often conferred on people through clothes, as happened to Joseph (Gen 37:3; 41:42), Daniel (Dan 5:29), and the prodigal son who returned home (Lk 15:22). In a similar way, humanity's original position as the crown of creation is restored when we put on the new man.

• The high priest was not allowed to come before the Lord unless properly attired. He would be stripped of his regular clothes and then garbed in white linen (the holy garments of Lev 16:4). Similarly, in Zech 3:3-5, the Lord says to a high priest, "Remove the filthy garments from him," and "Behold, I have taken your iniquity away from you, and I will clothe you with pure vestments" (ESV). The Lord does the same for us.

• Priests were required to wear linen in the temple and not wool (Ezek 44:17), which may explain the OT laws about not wearing clothes that blend wool and linen (Dt 22:11). It is unfitting to mix what is holy (linen) with what is common (wool). In a similar way, it would not do for Christians to mix holiness with what is common or unclean.

If "clothes make the man," then clothe me, Lord, in your righteousness and holiness that I may live in your presence.

⁹ *Lie not to each other, having stripped off the old man with his practices,* ¹⁰ **and having clothed [yourself] with the new [man],** *which is being renewed in knowledge according to the image of the one who created him.*

Here are some more biblical references to clothing that may help us understand what Paul is getting at in this verse.

•   Occasionally the OT speaks of hoping for enemies to be clothed with shame and disgrace (Ps 35:26). The Roman empire also liked to portray those they had conquered as naked and put to shame. In Colossians, however, God reconciles himself to those who had been enemy-minded toward him (Col 1:21-22) and provides them with new garments of love.

•   Various good qualities are also depicted as articles of clothing in other Bible verses, which are close to the spirit of Col 3:10. Some are clothed with salvation (2 Chron 6:41), righteousness (Ps 132:9), and justice (Job 29:14). The apocryphal books also refer to being clothed with revelation, truth, justice, wisdom, and holiness. Most important for Christians is that the One who is anointed by the Spirit of the Lord (which is Jesus) will be clothed in a garment of salvation and joy (Isa 61:10). Now that we are in Christ, we also will wear the qualities he wore.

•   In Eph 6:11 Paul calls believers to "put on the whole armor of God, so that you may be able to stand against the wiles of the devil" (NRSV; see also Rom 13:12 and 1 Thess 5:8). We can be so clothed because God himself is clothed in battle armor. He is dressed in power and majesty (Ps 93:1), and has also put on the armor of righteousness and justice (Isa 59:17).

•   God's Holy Spirit also comes upon people like a garment. In the OT the Spirit clothed Gideon (Judg 6:34), the military leader Amasai (1 Chron 12:18), and the priest Zechariah (2 Chron 24:20). In the NT God's people are likewise clothed with the Spirit. Jesus said on Ascension Day, "I am going to send you what my Father has promised, but stay in the city until you have been clothed with power from on high" (Lk 24:49, NIV).

•   Perhaps closest in spirit to Col 3:10 is that of putting on Jesus like a garment. Rom 13:14 states, "Clothe yourselves with the Lord Jesus Christ, and do not think about how to gratify the desires of the flesh" (NIV), and Gal 3:27 adds, "For as many of you as were baptized into Christ have clothed yourselves with Christ" (NRSV). When we wear clothing, we are in a sense inside those clothes (especially if we're bundled up for a blizzard). Likewise, when we wear Christ, we are in him.

Some may wear clothes to make a fashion statement. I want to be dressed in you, Lord, to make a faith statement.

⁹ Lie not to each other, having stripped off the old man with his practices, ¹⁰ **and having clothed [yourself] with the new [man],** *which is being renewed in knowledge according to the image of the one who created him.*

What garment, then, are we to put on? The Greek only says we are being clothed with the new. The identity of this new thing is not specified, but Paul is probably contrasting the "old man" which was stripped off in verse 9 with a "new man" that is put on. God is not clothing us with various good qualities (that will come up in verse 12). Nor is God clothing us with a new being, as if we become angelic or divine. Rather, we become new humans, new men and women.[285]

Again, many versions translate this as the "new self," but as with the previous verse, this psychologizes the text too much. Just as the "old man" points us in the direction of the first man named Adam, so the "new man" points us in the direction of the "last Adam" named Jesus (see 1 Cor 15:42-49). We have stripped off the image of the sinful old man (Adam), and now we are wearing the image of the righteous new man (Jesus).

It is tempting to extend this thought even further to say that the new man we put on is Jesus himself (not merely his image), and Paul does speak of this elsewhere (see yesterday's meditation). It does not appear, however, that Col 3:10 takes the imagery in this direction, for in the next phrase Paul will say that this new man is being renewed, an odd thought if the new man is Jesus. Still the connection between Jesus and the new man is important to maintain for we are not merely clothed in an improved version of our selves. Rather, we have put on the new man, that is, one made in the image of Christ (who is, in turn, the image of God). This thought is also found in Eph 4:21-24: "you were taught in [Jesus] to put off your old [man] ...and to put on the new [man], created after the likeness of God in true righteousness and holiness" (ESV). And even though we call this the "new" man, it's the image God intended for humanity to be from the very start.

Notice that Paul is not giving a command in this phrase, ordering the Colossians to clothe themselves with the new man. Rather he is reminding them that this has already happened. As Barth says, "The Word of grace does not say that man will be this new man, but that he already is" [this new man.[286] Later on (in verse 12), Paul will command his readers to clothe themselves with various items, but here in verse 10 he points out that they are already wearing the new man.

Lord, I don't want to be an angel or some other divine creature. I want to be who you made me to be, a new human being in the image of Jesus.

> [9] *Lie not to each other, having stripped off the old man with his practices,* [10] *and having clothed [yourself] with the new [man], **which is being renewed in knowledge** according to the image of the one who created him.*

This "new man" that believers are wearing already is not something that will later become old. Rather, it is always "being renewed." Unlike the necrotizing of verse 5 (written in a tense that suggests sudden, decisive action), the verb for being renewed is in the present tense, which here implies that this renewal is an ongoing process.

In addition, because Paul uses the passive form of the verb for renewal, *we* are not the ones doing the renewing work. Rather, the new man we wear is being renewed by another, presumably by God. This word is used only one other time in the NT (2 Cor 4:16) and there it is also passive: "Though outwardly we are wasting away, yet inwardly we are being renewed day by day" (NIV). We are the recipients, not the producers, of renewal.

Being "renewed *in knowledge*" does not mean that Christian transformation is nothing more than adding Christian ideas and concepts to the brain's storehouse of information. Even though Paul uses at least eight different words in Colossians about thinking and the mind, he does not believe for a minute that education and right thinking alone will bring renewal to a person's life. Knowledge that renews will include true ideas and concepts about God, yes, but it will also include personal knowledge of Jesus that flows into action. Without the knowledge of Jesus, any knowledge-based efforts toward moral living flounder in a sea of self-effort. In fact, this kind of knowledge would be nothing but a return to the Tree of the Knowledge of Good and Evil, which had such bad consequences for humanity in Genesis 3. It would be an attempt to be good without God, which is another name for evil.[287]

The knowledge that *does* transform the human heart is "the light of the *knowledge* of the glory of God in the face of Jesus Christ" (2 Cor 4:6, NRSV, emphasis mine). Since sin is connected to a deficient knowledge of God— "For although they knew God, they did not honor him as God or give thanks to him, but they became futile in their thinking" (Rom 1:21, ESV)—then what is needed is that we "be transformed by the renewing of [our] minds" in Christ (Rom 12:2, NRSV), so that we live in obedience and gratitude.

Without you, Lord, my thoughts get old and stale and travel along jagged ruts of the mind. I need you to renew my mind.

*⁹ Lie not to each other, having stripped off the old man with his practices, ¹⁰ and having clothed [yourself] with the new [man], which is being renewed in knowledge **according to the image of the one who created him.***

Some might think we will be renewed when we line up our lives according to our own sense of what feels right. But then we would only be modeling ourselves after an image we had constructed, which is a form of idolatry rejected in verse 5. Instead, our renewal is to be in accordance with "the image of the one who created him."

Idolatry not only throws off our ideas of what God is like, but it also throws off our ideas of what humanity—made in God's image—is supposed to be like. That's why Dt 4:16 forbids making idols in the likeness of men or women. If we model our lives on any man-made images of what humans should be, we quickly fall into idolatry. To avoid these "man-made" images of an ideal humanity, Paul insists that the new man must line up with the image which God the Creator had in mind. According to Thielicke, "Divine likeness is not just that from which I come. It is also that to which—through the gift and claim of God—I go."[288] Through Christ we not only become more godly, but also more fully human.

It's not enough for us to become like the image of God that Adam bore before the Fall. The greater goal is to see humanity in the image of God that is Christ himself (as noted in Col 1:15). In a way that surpasses Adam, Jesus is the true image of God. As the *eternal* Son of God, Jesus is the image of God who perfectly reflects God the Father; and as the *in-the-flesh* Son of God, Jesus is also the image of God who perfectly reflects what humanity was created to be. The Cynic philosopher Diogenes said that "good men are images of God,"[289] but he did not know what Paul knew—there are no good human beings except for Jesus, the Son of God in human flesh.

The point of being in the image of the Creator is not that we are created to *live*, but that we are created to *live out* our relationship with God and the good qualities found in God (many of which are listed here in Col 3:5-17). We are like mirrors reflecting God and his goodness. But if we "mirrors" refuse to reflect the Lord's glory and only want to radiate our own glory, we'll have no glory at all. When you put a mirror in a dark room, it reflects nothing but darkness. In the same way, if we turn from the light of Christ, we only reflect darkness.[290]

Lord, I admit that it's sometimes difficult to see your image in hard-to-love people. But I pray that, by the way I live, those hard-to-love people always see your image in me.[291]

[11] Here there is not Greek and Jew, circumcision and uncircumcision, barbarian, Scythian, slave, free, but all and in all is Christ.

Up to this point we might think Paul was only speaking of being *individually* clothed with the "new man." But Paul believed that it's not in isolation, but together, that we are clothed with the new man and renewed in the image of God. All the commands in Colossians are, in fact, plural commands, as if Paul were saying, "All of you together, walk in Christ, be wary of deception," etc. We will be able to keep these commands more fully if we are doing them together. If one is walking in Christ, but another is not, the church gets out of step. If one is wary of false teaching, but the other is gullible, heresy still spreads. If one necrotizes his or her sin, but another lets it fester, the infection still grows. Things go best if we put on the new man together.

Each of the ethnic and social groups mentioned in this verse would wear clothing that identified them as such when out in public. But within God's family, the identifying function of their outward clothing has been superseded by their new clothing, which is the new man in Christ. In this one new man together, all the distinctions emphasized by the world no longer matter. "Here," that is, in the one new man, the divisive categories used by the world have no place.

Of course, there still are individual Greeks and Jews in the church, as well as slaves and non-slaves. Ethnicity and economic classes have not disappeared. But the categories by which we might be tempted to divide up the body of Christ are irrelevant in him. Says Caird, "We are not asked to envisage a monochrome society, whose members are devoid of individual qualities, but one in which such differences are no longer grounds for discrimination or division."[292] These worldly categories have no place in the church because they represent a denial of the new creation in Christ.

The Roman Empire was also trying to bring all people together. But there was a big difference. In the empire, one ethnic group (the Romans) saw themselves as superior, and thus absorbing all other groups, often forcibly so, with plenty of disdain shown toward these others.[293] In the church, however, it's not the case of one superior ethnic group (like the Jews, or even the Jewish-Christians) absorbing all the others. Rather, all ethnic groups (and other categories of people) are brought together as one in Christ, and it happens by love, not force.

Thank you, Lord Jesus, for the wide diversity in the church, and even more that we are all brothers and sisters in you.

[11] *Here there is not Greek and Jew, circumcision and uncircumcision, barbarian, Scythian, slave, free,* but all and in all is Christ.

One worldly division that is irrelevant in Christ is the divide between Greek and Jew. In Paul's day this divisive gap was immense and the hostility was intense. The Jews interpreted their laws as a call to live separately from the rest of humanity, and non-Jews took offense at this.[294] But "here" in Christ, the gap is closed, the hostility is gone, and the categories are irrelevant. Even though "Jews and Gentiles alike are all under the power of sin" (Rom 3:9, NIV), the gospel is "the power of God for salvation to everyone who believes, to the Jew first and also the Greek" (Rom 1:16, ESV). Jesus is Lord of both the Jews and the non-Jews (Rom 10:12).

And it's not just the Greek and Jewish categories which have disappeared in Christ; so have other divisions. For instance, in the new man in Christ, it doesn't matter if you're circumcised or not either. What matters is a relationship of faith through Christ: "God is one—who will justify the circumcised by faith and the uncircumcised through faith" (Rom 3:30, ESV). At one time, some may have been far from God and others nearer, but now they both have access to the Father (Eph 2:17-18).

Others made divisions based on culture. Those within the Roman empire (including the Jews) disparaged those outside the empire as being crude and uncultured barbarians. And the Scythians (who lived just north of the Black Sea) were regarded as the worst of the worst—no better than wild beasts, said the Jewish historian Josephus. Yet for Paul, even this division disappears in Christ, for he was "under obligation both to Greeks and to barbarians" to preach the gospel (Rom 1:14, ESV).

One's economic class—whether as a slave or a free person—also did not matter in the body of Christ, but this will be considered more closely when we get to Col 3:22-4:1.

The irrelevance of these societal differences also was emphasized in two other letters by Paul. To the believers in Galatia who were tempted to adopt Jewish ways, he declared, "There is neither Jew nor Gentile, neither slave nor free, nor is there male and female, for you are all one in Christ Jesus" (Gal 3:28, NIV). Similarly, when addressing the Corinthian church, deeply divided over many issues, Paul said, "For in one Spirit we were all baptized into one body—Jews or Greeks, slaves or free—and all were made to drink of one Spirit" (1 Cor 12:13, ESV).

Lord, if I'm unconsciously allowing ethnic, social, and economic differences to block me from fully loving others, show me my sin and change me within.

^{11} *Here there is not Greek and Jew, circumcision and uncircumcision, barbarian, Scythian, slave, free, **but all and in all is Christ.***

Here Paul highlights the important role of Christ in defining the people of God. He specifically rejects any attempt to define the church by *racial, ethnic, economic,* or *social* barriers. Nor will he allow *ritual* boundaries to determine who belongs to the people of God (such as circumcision). Some might argue that in this whole section (Col 3:5-17) Paul instead establishes *moral* boundaries for who belongs to the people of God,[295] but this overlooks the fact that the morality itself is based on being in Christ.

Thus we are left with the truth that it is *Jesus* who is the boundary marker of who belongs to the people of God, or even better Jesus is the *center* of what constitutes the people of God. Jesus erases divisions and brings unity, if not yet to the world, at least to the church. So when we are gathered with the people of God, the main thought in our mind should not be, "Here's a Jew and there's a Greek, and over there is a slave." Rather, as you look from face to face, you see Christ in them all.

Most of Col 3:11 spells out the answer to the phrase "Here there is no..." But the last word of the verse points out what *is* here: "here there is...Christ." The unity of the church is not based on common polity, actions, or even a confession, but on a common relationship with Jesus. As Thompson said, "What the diverse members of the church share is not a 'common humanity,' but a common human being, namely, Jesus of Nazareth, the crucified and risen Lord."[296]

For Paul to refer to Christ as "all and in all" demonstrates again Jesus' exalted status, for these are nearly the same words used in 1 Cor 15:28 to describe God the Father. Some might mistake this phrase as endorsing a vague and mystical pantheism, a belief system in which God is everything and everything is God. But Paul is not thinking of Jesus in a speculative, pantheistic way anymore than a pop singer crooning, "You are everything and everything is you," is intending to proclaim a pantheism based upon his lover. Instead of teaching pantheism, such words express wonder at how all reality revolves around and is encompassed by the one we praise. The apocryphal book Sirach said similarly about God, "By his word all things hold together. We could say more but could never say enough; let the final word be: 'He is the all'" (Sirach 43:26-27, NRSV).

I may use the phrase "my reality," Lord, but I recognize that—either willingly or unwillingly—all of reality revolves around you; it's your reality.

*[11] Here there is not Greek and Jew, circumcision and uncircumcision, barbarian, Scythian, slave, free, **but all and in all is Christ.***

For Jesus to be all and in all means that he is not a partial solution to sin (as the distortionists taught); he is the whole solution. And Jesus not only *brings* the whole salvation; he *is* the whole salvation.

Everything in our human situation that could be considered good stems from the work of Christ. It's good we were created and now live; Christ is the one who created us (Col 1:16). It's good that we are no longer under the dominion of hostile forces; Christ is the one who rescued us from them (Col 1:13-14; 2:15, 20). It's good that suffering does not tear us to pieces; Christ is the one who holds us together (Col 1:17). It's good that we belong to the family of God, the body of believers; Christ is the head who holds us together and sustains us (Col 1:18; 2:19). It's good that we have hope for the future; Christ gave us this hope through his resurrection from the dead (Col 1:4-5, 18, 23, 27; 2:12-13; 3:1-4). It's good that we are not left in the dark about God, but actually know him; Christ is the one who revealed God to us (Col 1:10, 19, 25-28; 2:2-3, 6-8). It's good that our sins are forgiven and we are reconciled to God; Christ is the one who forgave us through the cross (Col 1:13-14, 20-22; 2:11-14). It's good that we are growing in faith and bearing good fruit instead of being empty and unfulfilled; that also is the work of Christ in our lives (Col 1:3-6, 10-12, 22, 28; 2:10; 3:5-17).

No matter how you think of salvation—creation, victory, belonging, hope, knowledge, forgiveness, growth, mission, etc.—Christ is all of it, the all-encompassing totality of salvation. Schweizer said, "Christ is the measure by which everything is to be defined,"[297] even the concept of the new man. From every angle by which you view this new man, you are not looking at admirable human spiritualities, high moral values, or favored ethnic groups; rather, you are looking at Jesus Christ.

But when Paul says Christ is in all things (including all people), he is not saying everyone is a Christian, but that Christ overcomes all human distinctions (as noted earlier in this verse). He dwells within all categories of people. So if you were to look at the members of the Colossian church, your main response should not be, "What a diverse group of people!" Rather, it should be, "Christ is in all of them!" In spite of the enormity of humanity's sin-problem, this problem has met its match in the massive salvation brought by the infinite greatness of the Triune God.

Thank you, Jesus, for being the totality of our salvation. All of it we find in you.

[12] *Clothe [yourselves], therefore*—*as God's chosen-ones, holy and being loved*—*with the heart of compassion, kindness, humility, gentleness, patience,*

Not only do sins need to be stripped off (as noted in verses 8-9), but good things need to be put on in their place. Unlike the distortionists who defined holiness primarily in terms of prohibitions (Col 2:21), Paul knew that holiness was not truly whole unless the evil is replaced by what is good. As Gill said, "If we only say no, we are only half holy, which is unholy."[298]

The particular good qualities and actions emphasized in verses 12-17 are those that foster a sense of belonging together as believers, rather than the solitary forms of religiosity found in the distortion.[299] It is not only individual Christians who need to be clothed as Paul commands; rather, it is the whole body of Christ—the church—that needs this clothing.

According to verse 10, we are already clothed in the new man (which is the image of Christ), but now Paul commands us to clothe ourselves with various good qualities and actions. So are we already clothed with what's new or not? Yes. We are both already clothed in the new man, and not yet completely clothed in some traits that belong in the new man's wardrobe. Just as we are already dead with Christ (Col 3:3), but still need to put sins to death (Col 3:5), so here we are already clothed in the new man (Col 3:10), and need to be further clothed (Col 3:12). We need a full wardrobe.

Some may think this word picture gives a bad impression, as if being a Christian is something you "put on" in a fake manner: you put on compassion and kindness in some settings and take them off in others. But this is not what Paul means here. According to Barth, "The figure of the new garment...does not mean...that what is given him is no true Christian being but only something external, not to speak of a mere Christian appearance, a hood which is pulled over him and under the concealment of which he can be the same as he always was."[300] Perhaps it would be helpful to contemplate an interesting English phrase used about clothing. When a person wears some fine clothing, others might remark, "it's very becoming," or "that dress becomes you." When Christians wear the qualities of Jesus, such as kindness or humility, "it becomes us." It's no longer outer wear, but becomes who we really are in Christ.

I confess, Lord, that it's tempting to fake it with regards to living the Christian life. Make me real so that on both the inside and the outside I reflect your new work.

*¹² Clothe [yourselves], therefore—**as God's chosen-ones, holy and being loved**—with the heart of compassion, kindness, humility, gentleness, patience,*

Paul makes his appeal to the Colossian Christians on the basis of who they are in the sight of God. The world will still label them with the categories listed in Col 3:11 (Jews, Greeks, barbarians, slave, free, etc.), but God sees them instead as his "chosen-ones [*eklektos*], holy [*hagios*] and being loved [*agapaō*]." This is important because perceiving ourselves as God does, rather than as the world does, goes a long way toward changing behavior.[301] Paul summons us, then, to new behaviors, not so that we become chosen, holy, and loved, but because we are already chosen, holy and loved.

Before these three words were ever used to describe Christians, they were used in the OT to describe Israel. In fact, all three terms (or closely related words) are used in Dt 7:6-8 (NETS) to describe the Israelites: "For you are a people holy [*hagios*] to the Lord your God...It was not because you are more numerous than all nations that the Lord chose you and picked [*eklegomai*, the verb form of *eklektos*] you...Rather, because the Lord loved [*agapaō*] you..." Now, amazingly enough, these same terms can apply to Greeks and barbarians through faith in Christ.

But not only were these three terms used to describe Israel; they are also used in the NT to describe Jesus. Before all others, *Jesus is the chosen one*, the "living stone rejected by men but in the sight of God chosen and precious" (1 Pet 2:4, ESV). Above all others, *Jesus is the "Holy One of God"* (Jn 6:69). And prior to all others, *Jesus is the one loved by God*, the one God called "my Beloved Son" at his baptism (Mt 3:17) and transfiguration (Mt 17:5). Jesus was chosen, holy, and loved *before* all others. But he was also chosen, holy, and loved *for the sake of* all others.

The fact that we are chosen, holy, and loved is true only because we are in Christ. It's not merely *the breadth of God's mercy* that includes non-Jews in God's kingdom; it's *Jesus* who makes that inclusion happen. The good news is not only that former outsiders are now insiders, but that Christ is the insider, living inside of his people, and they are insiders in him: "Christ, all and in all" (Col 3:11). Therefore, we are chosen, holy, and loved because *we are in Christ and Christ is in us*.

Lord, I will probably not be very obedient if I perceive myself to be worthless. Shape my obedience by a renewed perception of how you have chosen and loved me.

¹² *Clothe [yourselves], therefore—**as God's chosen-ones, holy and being loved**—with the heart of compassion, kindness, humility, gentleness, patience,*

The word translated as "chosen-ones" is the adjective *eklektos*, which is also related to two verbs for choosing (*eklegomai* and *eklegō*) and the noun for choice (*eklogē*). The English terms "elect" and "election" are rooted in this Greek word. Most people today think electing and elections are about humans choosing by popular vote, but this is not how the word is used in the Bible. In Col 3:12 the focus is on God having chosen us for himself.

The Bible, of course, contains many other kinds of choosing. Sometimes *humans* do the choosing. They choose things (like livestock), people (to be soldiers), and spiritual and ethical options—like choosing life (Dt 30:19). More commonly, however, when people make "spiritual" choices in the Bible, they choose their own idolatrous ways: "These have chosen their own ways, and in their abominations they take delight" (Isa 66:3, NRSV). But "the gods whom you have chosen" are unable to save (Judg 10:14, NRSV). Only once in the Bible is it said that people choose God: "Then Joshua said to the people, 'You are witnesses against yourselves that you have chosen the LORD, to serve him'" (Josh 24:22, ESV). But even this sole case of people choosing God is undermined by verses just prior to this, for Joshua warned the people: "You are not able to serve the Lord" (Josh 24:19, ESV).

Far more important in the Bible are *God's* choices. God chose both the city of Jerusalem and the temple built there, but primarily God chooses people. He chose individuals like Abraham, Moses, Aaron, and David. In the NT Jesus chose other individuals, most importantly the Twelve disciples and later Paul who "is my chosen instrument to proclaim my name to the Gentiles" (Acts 9:15, NIV). All these individuals, however, were not chosen for their own private salvation or blessings. Rather, they were chosen to represent and lead the rest of God's chosen people.

But the most important Chosen One in the Bible is Jesus. Although the mockers who stood at the foot of the cross could not believe this dying man was God's chosen one (Lk 23:35), Peter regarded him as the "living Stone—rejected by humans but chosen by God and precious to him" (1 Pet 2:4, NIV). At his transfiguration, God said of Jesus, "This is my Son, my Chosen One" (Lk 9:35, ESV). He too was chosen not for privileges, but for the sake of blessing his people.

I sometimes act, Lord, as if my choices were determining the direction of my life. But in my better days, I realize it's your choices that make the difference.

¹² *Clothe [yourselves], therefore—**as God's chosen-ones, holy and being loved**—with the heart of compassion, kindness, humility, gentleness, patience,*

Although God chose Jesus above all others, it was a choice made for our sake. God's purpose all along was to choose, not just individuals, but a people to love. In the OT this people is Israel, a truth often expressed in the Bible. Israel was not chosen because it was deserving of such an honor, but simply because it was God's choice to love (Dt 7:7-8).

The NT acknowledges God's choice of Israel, but of more interest is that God has also chosen to include non-Jews among his people. Peter said, "Brothers, you know that in the early days God made a choice among you, that by my mouth the Gentiles should hear the word of the gospel and believe" (Acts 15:7, ESV). Thus, most of the NT references to those chosen by God refer to Jews *and* Gentiles who are now in Christ: "But you are a chosen race, a royal priesthood, a holy nation, God's own people" (1 Pet 2:9, NRSV). But as with Israel, the church was not chosen because of its loveable qualities. Rather, God purposely chose those whom the world regarded as foolish, weak, lowly, and despised (1 Cor 1:27-28).

Like the OT, the NT also downplays human choosing. Jesus said pointedly, "You did not choose me, but I chose you" (Jn 15:16, ESV). Our human choices were dismissed: "You did not choose me." Instead, all the glory goes to God who has chosen us.

And God makes this choice not only to bless and save us, but also that we might fulfill his mission and exhibit the qualities which are characteristic of God. This purpose is shown in how Jesus completed the just cited words from Jn 15:16, "You did not choose me, but I chose you *and appointed you that you should go and bear fruit and that your fruit should abide*" (ESV, emphasis mine).

Paul is saying a similar thing in Col 3:12-17. God has chosen his people, not so they can bask in God's favor, but so they can extend God's favor to others through their way of life. We have been chosen for mission, and this mission, according to the next few verses, can happen because God has chosen us to put on compassion, kindness, humility, gentleness, patience, and love. God has chosen us to freely forgive, to express gratitude, and to do everything in the name of the Lord Jesus.

Thank you, Lord, for choosing me in Christ to extend your love and mercy to others as it has been extended to me.

*¹² Clothe [yourselves], therefore—**as God's chosen-ones, holy and being loved**—with the heart of compassion, kindness, humility, gentleness, patience,*

God's chosen-ones are also called "holy." When God's people are chosen that means they are holy to the Lord. All three aspects of holiness mentioned under the devotion on Col 1:2 probably come into play here. We are *possessionally* holy, treasured by God and thus chosen and loved. We are *morally* holy, and that's why we can clothe ourselves with compassion, kindness, and more. We are *missionally* holy, set apart for the mission of bringing glory to God.

In addition, God's people are also *being loved.* My translation could have just said we are loved or beloved, but I wanted to emphasize that we are on the receiving end of this love. In the OT God's people were frequently said to be loved by God (see 1 Kgs 10:9). Likewise, in the NT Christians are loved by God (1 Thess 1:4) and "beloved in God the Father" (Jude 1, NRSV).

The three key terms here in Col 3:12 are not only found by themselves elsewhere in the Bible, but also in various combinations. *We are holy and chosen*: "For you are a people holy [*hagios*] to the Lord your God, and it is you the Lord your God has chosen [*eklegomai*] to be an exceptional people" (Dt 14:2, NETS). *We are chosen and loved*: "For we know, brothers loved [*agapaō*] by God, that he has chosen [*eklogē*] you" (1 Thess 1:4, ESV). *We are holy, chosen, and loved*: God "chose [*eklegomai*] us in Christ before the foundation of the world to be holy [*hagios*] and blameless before him in love [*agape*]" (Eph 1:4, NRSV; see also Dt 7:6-8; Rom 1:7; 2 Thess 2:13).

All three terms belong together. Without being *chosen*, we might think we deserved God's love because of our holiness. Without being *holy*, we might think being chosen and loved gives us a license for moral carelessness. Without being *loved*, we might only think of ourselves as chosen to follow a stern moral code. All three terms are necessary.

And not only do we treat other Christians well because *we ourselves* are chosen, holy, and loved; we also treat them well because *they* are chosen, holy, and loved. How can we dare to withdraw compassion from someone who is *holy* to God? How can we fail to be gentle toward someone who is *chosen* by God? How can we show impatience toward someone who is *loved* by God? It is God's assessment of those around us which further motivates us to love them.

Lord, forgive me for mistreating those around me who are chosen by you, holy to you, and loved by you.

312

*¹² Clothe [yourselves], therefore—as God's chosen-ones, holy and being loved—**with the heart of compassion,** kindness, humility, gentleness, patience,*

Now that Paul has reminded us once again of who we are in Christ, he goes on to describe the qualities we should clothe ourselves in. Wearing these qualities does not cause God to choose us, love us, or regard us as holy—it would be impossible for sinners like us to successfully put them on anyway. Rather, we wear these qualities because God has already chosen us, loved us, and regarded us as holy in Christ.

Since these qualities are part of putting on the new man in the image of Christ, it's no surprise that they especially reflect the character of Jesus.[302]

Some call these qualities virtues, but the four cardinal virtues of the Greek culture (wisdom, bravery, self-control, and fairness) are noticeably missing here.[303] That's because the Greek virtues are mostly "personal qualities that bring honor to their possessor," as Sumney notes.[304] Paul instead highlights interpersonal qualities that draw the people of God together in love. His main concern is not strengthening the private virtues of individuals, but building up of the body of Christ.

The first item to be worn is the heart of compassion. To have compassion does not merely mean to have feelings of pity from a distance, but to move toward the person in need.[305] The nouns, verbs, and adjectives related to compassion are chiefly used in the Bible to describe *God* and *God's* actions, and only secondarily *human* actions. Of the 77 OT uses of "compassion" words, only 18 refer to human compassion (and three of these are about the *lack* of human compassion). Compassion is far more characteristic of God than of people.

We find the same thing in the NT. God is the Father of compassion (2 Cor 1:3; see also Lk 6:36 and Jms 5:11). In the three verses about *human* compassion, it is always based on *God's* prior compassion. For example, in Lk 6:36 Jesus told his followers to "be compassionate even as your Father is compassionate" (my translation). Given the God-centeredness of compassion, we must conclude that when Paul urges us to put on compassion, it's not just because it's the nice thing to do. We do it because when we are in Christ, then his compassionate character and actions will be reflected in us.

Clothe me with your compassion, Lord, not only on this day, but every day.

*¹² Clothe [yourselves], therefore—as God's chosen-ones, holy and being loved—with the heart of compassion, **kindness,** humility, gentleness, patience,*

The second quality to be worn by those who are in Christ is kindness (*chrēstotēs*, which is often translated as "goodness"). As was true of compassion, kindness is also mostly characteristic of God and not humanity. God *is* kind and God *shows* kindness (Ps 119:68).

The coming of Jesus especially demonstrates God's kindness toward those who do not deserve it: "But when the kindness [*chrēstotēs*] and love of God our Savior appeared, he saved us, not because of righteous things we had done, but because of his mercy" (Titus 3:4-5, NIV). In Eph 2:7 Paul adds that God saved us "so that in the ages to come he might show the immeasurable riches of his grace in kindness toward us in Christ Jesus" (NRSV).

God's great kindness stands in marked contrast to the lack of human kindness. Ps 14:3 declares of humanity, especially those who disbelieve in God, "There is no one practicing kindness [*chrēstotēs*]; there is not even one" (NETS, listed as Ps 13:3 in the Septuagint, this verse is also quoted in Rom 3:12). The apocryphal Sol 5:13-15 admits that there is such a thing as human kindness, but emphasizes how different it is from God's kindness: "The kindness [*chrēstotēs*] of man is stinginess, and if [the kindness] were repeated tomorrow without grumbling, it would be a wonder. But your gift [O Lord] is abundant with kindness and rich, and he whose hope is in you will not be stingy with a gift. Your mercy, Lord, is on all the earth in kindness [*chrēstotēs*]" (translation mine). True kindness does not come naturally to people, but must be empowered by God

The NT expands upon this. Paul urges the believers to "be kind [*chrēstos*] to one another, tenderhearted, forgiving one another, as God in Christ forgave you" (Eph 4:32, ESV). It would not be a stretch to hear Paul similarly say, "be kind to one another...as God in Christ was kind to you." This ability to be kind does not come from our own human resources, but is a fruit of the Spirit within us (Gal 5:22). So when Col 3:12 calls us to put on kindness, it's not telling us to work harder at being a good person. Rather, it is calling us to wear a quality that can only be regarded as characteristic of God. It dares to call us to this because God himself is working in us through Christ and by his Spirit.

Thank you for your abundant kindness to me, Lord Jesus. I pray that your kindness would flow through me into this very unkind world.

> *¹² Clothe [yourselves], therefore—as God's chosen-ones, holy and being loved—with the heart of compassion, kindness, **humility**, gentleness, patience,*

The noun for humility is *tapeinophrosunē*, a term which the Greek culture usually regarded as a negative thing, a slavish self-humiliation unworthy of human life. The Stoic philosopher Epictetus even said that the best way to learn wisdom is by *not* seeking it with humility.

The Jews, however, had a more positive assessment of humility (see Ps 51:17). The Greeks may have thought the free and powerful person was ideal, says Sumney, "but in Judaism, humans recognize their dependence upon God and live as God's servants."[306] Both Paul and the Colossian distortionists regarded humility as a positive quality, but differed markedly on what it was. As noted before in Col 2:18 and 23, Paul used *tapeinophrosunē* to criticize the distortionists for a brand of humility that puffed them up with pride about their visions, and the harsh treatment of the body.

But even though the distortionists used the term wrongly, Paul was not ready to concede the word to them. For Paul, there is also a right kind of humility which should characterize all Christians. This true form of humility is associated with compassion and kindness (just mentioned in Col 3:12) and comes from Christ. With man-made humility, the distortionists' end-goal was to be a step above others in terms of humility. But Christ-like humility aims to stoop down to a lower level in service to others, especially to those who have been oppressed and humiliated (as noted in Isa 58:1-12).

The ancient world might have reluctantly agreed that humility *toward the gods* was a good thing, but they did not think humility was a good thing to have *toward other humans*.[307] In their honor and shame culture, they would rather humiliate others than be humble themselves. From their perspective, the only way to attain honor was by taking it from someone else. But according to the NT, humble service is to be given to both God (Acts 20:19) and others: "clothe yourselves with humility toward one another" (1 Pet 5:5, NIV; see also Eph 4:2 and Phil 2:2-3).

Although there is no talk in the OT of God being humble, in the NT we do see the humble heart of God in the face of Jesus. He not only claimed to be humble (Mt 11:29), but he demonstrated it by taking up the towel (Jn 13:3-16) and the cross to serve us (Phil 2:6-8). Those who have put on the new man in Christ will do the same.

You have not taught me, Lord, to look down upon myself, but instead to humbly look beyond myself by serving you and people in need.

*¹² Clothe [yourselves], therefore—as God's chosen-ones, holy and being loved—with the heart of compassion, kindness, humility, **gentleness,** patience,*

The Greeks and Romans of Paul's day appreciated gentleness (often translated as meekness). Gentleness was seen as far better than uncontrolled anger,[308] especially when exhibited by those who had power over others.[309] The Jews and Christians agreed. God intends for his people to be characterized by gentleness: "On that day...I will remove from your midst your proudly exultant ones...But I will leave in your midst a people humble [gentle] and lowly" (Zeph 3:11-12, ESV).

But as was true with humility, the Bible does not say that God is gentle or meek. It does, however, say that God helps those who are gentle. God "rose up to establish judgment, to save all the meek of the earth" (Ps 76:9, NETS), for "the meek he will guide in justice; the meek he will teach his ways" (Ps 25:9, NETS). Because of God, the meek and gentle will inherit the earth (Ps 37:11), a truth quoted by Jesus in the Beatitudes (Mt 5:5).

One OT verse, however, points toward the gentleness of God. Zech 9:9 announces the good news of a gentle king who comes to Jerusalem riding a donkey. Jesus, the Son of God, later fulfilled this prophecy on Palm Sunday (see Mt 21:5). Jesus even described himself as gentle: "Take my yoke upon you, and learn from me; for I am gentle and humble in heart, and you will find rest for your souls" (Mt 11:29, NRSV).

Since Jesus is gentle, it is no surprise that he instills gentleness in those who walk in him. Thus, Paul appeals to wayward believers "by the meekness and gentleness of Christ" (2 Cor 10:1, ESV). He also includes gentleness as part of the fruit of the Spirit (Gal 5:22-23) and urges the believers to treat each other with gentleness (Eph 4:2). This gentleness is especially needed when restoring someone who has been trapped by a sin (Gal 6:1) or whose teaching needs to be corrected (2 Tim 2:25).

If we have a strong desire to be in control in life, it will be tempting to bully others to bend to our will. But those who have learned to "let go and let God" are much more able to treat others gently.[310] As we have seen with the other good traits, gentleness is not a man-made virtue, but a quality of Christ, which he then instills within us. We are gentle because we were first treated gently by Jesus.

Lord, in this pushy world, teach me again the way of gentleness in dealing with other people.

¹² Clothe [yourselves], therefore—as God's chosen-ones, holy and being loved—with the heart of compassion, kindness, humility, gentleness, **patience***,*

Earlier in Colossians, Paul used the word for patience (*makrothumia*) to tell the church that he was praying for them to have "endurance and patience with joy." Again, the main thing to emphasize is that patience—like compassion and kindness—is, above all, a characteristic of God and Christ. And this means we are only able to wear patience because we are in Christ, and Christ is in us (Gal 5:22; Eph 4:2; Col 1:11; 2 Tim 3:10; 4:2; Jms 5:10).

Patience is an important component of the five qualities listed in verse 12. It flavors the other qualities in a good way. For instance, if we lack patience, our compassion and kindness will soon develop fatigue, because many of those we help will not respond well. When we give financial assistance to someone in need and they squander it, we will need patience to keep on being compassionate. When we spend precious time and energy to help someone conquer an addiction, only to see them fall into old patterns, it will take patience to continue in our kindness.

Patience is also needed in being humble and gentle. When people realize that we're humble people who don't demand attention, it will be easy for them to ignore us and our needs. Once they see that we're gentle and don't snarl at them, they'll be tempted to just run right over us. They might be cautious about crossing a nasty, grumpy person, but they don't mind stepping on a gentle person. Scenarios like these will tempt us to forsake the way of humility and gentleness. But that's precisely when we need the patience it takes to press on in the way of Christ.

When considering the five good qualities listed in verse 12 together, someone might think that Paul is encouraging people to be weak doormats for others to take advantage of. But the qualities listed are actually signs of strength, not weakness, for they strengthen the relational bonds that hold God's people together.[311] The body of Christ is not strengthened, but weakened, when its members push and shove or boast and brag to get their way. All our collective energy is sapped when people are jockeying for power and maneuvering for position. We can as powerful as bodybuilders, but if we don't lift a finger to help someone in need, we're actually weak. It is only through compassion, kindness, humility, gentleness, and patience that we are actually strong enough to do what Jesus created us to do.

Make me strong, Lord, in the only ways that count—strong enough to serve and care for others.

> [12] *Clothe [yourselves], therefore—as God's chosen-ones, holy and being loved—with the heart of compassion, kindness, humility, gentleness, patience,* [13] **bearing with one another** *and granting-grace to each other if ever anyone has a grievance. Just as the Lord has granted-grace to you, so should you [grant-grace to others].*

Even if everyone in church wears the wonderful qualities listed in verse 12, Paul is realistic enough to know that the body of Christ will still experience difficulties. We must bear with one another, even when we have sinned or merely acted in an "immature and tiresome" way.[312] This is not easy. Even God had trouble bearing with hypocritical worshipers (Isa 1:13-14), and Jesus could hardly bear the faithlessness of people around him (Mt 17:17).

Yet God continues to bear with us and calls us to do the same. Rather than bearing grudges, we will be bearing with one another. Superficially this may sound similar to tolerance, but it is actually quite different from modern conceptions of tolerance.

Universal tolerance means setting aside all sense of right and wrong, and giving everyone a "free pass" to do as they please. But biblical tolerance means continuing to love even though we recognize sin as sin.

In *distant tolerance* people live by the motto, "You go your way and I'll go mine," but this doesn't build relationships. Biblical tolerance, however, means being firmly committed to a relationship in spite of differences.

With *contractual tolerance*, we informally agree that "if you don't point out my flaws, I won't point out yours." But in biblical tolerance we form a covenant to challenge each other to be all that God has made us to be.

Finally, in p*olitically-correct tolerance,* everything is tolerated except for whatever is currently regarded as evil, which in our day includes smoking in restaurants, the sexual abuse of children, and (ironically enough) the belief in moral absolutes. But biblical tolerance does not depend on moral fads, for we are to bear with even the worst of the worst.

According to Peterson, "We no longer stand around as amused or disapproving spectators of the sins or troubles of others but become fellow-sufferers and participants in the sacrificial life of Jesus" as he bears our sins; "sin is not rejected, it is *borne,* carried in an act of intercession."[313]

This biblical tolerance is to be directed toward the world, but it's especially needed in the church, where the closeness of our fellowship means we are more often exposed to each other's sinfulness.

I must confess, Lord, that there are people in my church who are hard for me to tolerate. Change my heart toward them even now.

> ¹³ *bearing with one another* **and granting-grace to each other if ever anyone has a grievance.** *Just as the Lord has granted-grace to you, so should you [grant-grace to others].*

We not only are to bear with one another, but also grant grace (*charizomai*) to each other. Most versions translate this verb as "forgive," but as we saw in Col 2:13, that translation loses the link between grace (*charis*) and forgiveness (*charizomai*).

Earlier, Col 2:13 focused on how *God* responds to *our sin* with the gift of grace. Here Paul is emphasizing how *we* also are to respond to *the sins of others* with the gift of grace—not with our own grace, but with God's grace. What is called for is more than uttering words, like "I forgive you," but a rich outpouring of grace toward others who have hurt us, so that they experience blessings, kindness, and acts of compassion through us.

There are, of course, other pastoral issues involved when the hurt has been deep, as happens with emotional, physical, or sexual abuse. Plenty of wise books offer counsel in these matters. But for the many little ways that we hurt each other, we should not be looking for reasons to withhold grace from others, but instead seize every opportunity we can to give it.

Even in situations where there has been a grievance, grace is the proper response. Although we often focus on what the offender should do to correct a problem they created (such as apologizing or making amends), Paul focuses on the responsibility of the one who has been offended. The offended party is to show grace.[314]

Paul is under no illusion that Christianity produces faultless people in this age; rather it produces people who know how to deal graciously with their own faults and the faults of others.[315] As Smedes said, when Paul describes love in 1 Corinthians 13, he is not describing what love will be like in a perfect world, but rather what love is to be like in our very imperfect world.[316]

This kind of forgiveness is not only needed by the person who caused the hurt, but also by those who experienced it. An aggrieved person once said, "The greatest damage of an offence—often greater than the offense itself—is that it destroys my freedom to be me, for I will find myself involuntarily dominated by the inner rage and resentment—a type of spiritual poison which permeates throughout all my being"; only forgiveness provides the antidote.[317]

Lord, a man once prayed to you, "I believe, help me in my unbelief." I want to pray today, "I forgive, help me in my unforgiveness."

*13 bearing with one another and granting-grace to each other if ever anyone has a grievance. **Just as the Lord has granted-grace to you, so should you [grant-grace to others].***

The reason we are called to respond with grace, as well as the reason we are *able* to respond with grace, is because that is how the Lord has responded to us. Although the Lord could have plenty of things to list as grievances or complaints against us, he instead pours on us grace upon grace (John 1:16). It would only be fitting for us to do the same for others.

This thought is not original to Paul, for Jesus said the same thing, even though he used a different word for forgiveness. Using the verb *aphiēmi* for "forgive," (which Paul also used in Col 1:14), Jesus taught his disciples to pray, "Forgive us our debts as we also have forgiven our debtors" (Mt 6:12, EVS). He then went on to say, "For if you forgive others their trespasses, your heavenly Father will also forgive you, but if you do not forgive others their trespasses, neither will your Father forgive your trespasses" (Mt 6:14-15, EVS).

Later Jesus told a parable of a king who forgave an enormous debt only to retract it when the forgiven debtor refused to show the same forgiving spirit to someone who owed him a much smaller amount (Mt 18:23-35). It's because God has forgiven us that we are to forgive others and not even bother counting how often this is needed (Mt 18:21-22).

This follows a pattern summarized in 1 Jn 4:19, "We love because [God] first loved us" (ESV). Likewise, we forgive because God first forgave us, and we show grace because God first showed grace to us. We would not be in error if we were to extend this to the other truths of Col 3:12-13 as well: we show compassion, kindness, patience, and forbearance, because God first showed these to us. We also act humbly and gently toward others because Christ acted humbly and meekly toward us. Significantly for us, there is one dimension of God's action that believers are expressly *forbidden* to imitate—namely, God's role as avenger and judge."[318]

It's important to realize that ours is not a *distant* imitation of Jesus (as if we were only copying things Jesus did long ago), nor is it a *reciprocal* imitation (as if we were merely paying Jesus back for the favors he has shown us). Rather, this is a *participatory* imitation. As Jesus interacts with us, he empowers us to extend grace to others.

Lord, I can think of someone right now who has hurt me in the past. I pray that they would experience blessings of grace from you—and from me.

*¹⁴ **Over all these things, [put on] love,** which is the connecting-tissue of completeness.*

Paul began this paragraph by describing Christians as those who are loved by God (Col 3:12). Now he brings this paragraph to a close by calling on Christians to clothe themselves with love.

We are indeed channels of God's love, but not *only* channels, as if we did not participate at all in the act of loving. Karl Barth said, "It is not the work of the Holy Spirit to take from man his own proper activity, or to make it simply a function of his own overpowering control."[319] We are active, involved channels of God's love.

There are two ways to envision what Paul is saying here. On the one hand, love could be the outer garment that we put on over all the multiple layers of other qualities we wear in Christ. Perhaps wearing so many layers of clothing sounds odd, but it might help to know that in Paul's day people initiated into the cult of Isis would wear twelve robes in the ceremony.[320]

On the other hand, love might be like a belt in the Christian's wardrobe, that we put on last to tie everything else together. In favor of this is that the word I have translated as "connecting-tissue" could also be translated as band or belt.[321] But however we picture it, Paul wants to highlight the importance of love. Whether placed first in a list (as in Gal 5:22-23) or last (as here and 2 Pet 1:5-7), love is supreme and holds everything together.

The noun for love here is *agape.* In the Greek OT this word and the corresponding verb were mostly used in reference to God's love for his people (Jer 31:3) or the people's love for God (Dt 6:5). Very few OT texts speak of people loving other people. But while few in number, they are mighty in importance, for we are to love our neighbors as ourselves (Lev 19:18) and even love strangers and sojourners (Lev 19:34; Dt 10:18-19).

But if *agapē* love is not often directed toward other people in the OT, it's the opposite case in the NT. There the predominant message from Jesus and the NT writers is that we are to love others, especially other Christians (Jn 13:34-35; 1 Pet 4:8), but also our neighbors (Mt 19:19; Jms 2:8), those who do not return our love (Mt 5:46), and even our enemies (Mt 5:43-44).

Paul will highlight elsewhere the importance of loving others in that it fulfills the law (Rom 13:10), is a debt that we owe everyone (Rom 13:8), sets an example for others (1 Tim 4:12), and pleases God (1 Thess 1:3).

Lord, without love, all my other claims to be your follower would only ring hollow. So fill me today, Lord Jesus, with love for the people I meet.

[14] *Over all these things, [put on] love, **which is the connecting-tissue of completeness.***

Paul had been rolling with his clothing imagery for a few verses, but now he changes the picture. Love may be like an outer garment, but it is not merely an external fashion accessory. Love is also the living tissue woven into the fabric of all the other good qualities of Christ, drawing them together in the heart of the believer. When love is this organic connecting tissue, it's not external to us, but "becomes us." This love from Christ is what holds the church together, and even the whole creation together (Col 1:17).[322]

Paul had earlier used this same word to describe the church as a body which is "supplied and drawn together through its joints and connecting-tissues" (Col 2:19). The ancient preacher Chrysostom said that a body without love is like a body without any connecting tissues.[323] The bones and organs may be healthy, but without the connecting tissues, the body would just collapse on the floor like a big blob.

Here Paul is not thinking of love as something worn by individual Christians, but as something that pulls together the whole church. Love is the living tissue that connects Christians to Christ as our Head (see Col 2:19) and to all the rest of the body of Christ. This would fit Paul's earlier desire for the hearts of the Colossian believers to be "drawn together in love" (Col 2:2).

When this connecting tissue is in operation, the result is completeness. Earlier Paul said that his goal was to present everyone complete in Christ (Col 1:28). Here we see that this completeness is not about individual self-fulfillment, but about finding fulfillment together through love. God's end-goal is for his people to be completely inter-connected by love. That is to be our goal too.

Churches might pledge themselves to all kinds of vision and mission statements, but if loving one another is not happening in all its mission-driven activity, these churches will actually fail to complete the mission assigned to them by the Lord. Only love can bring completion to the body of Christ and the mission of Christ. The distortionists may have been seeking completion through heavenly visions, but as the Christian mystic Meister Eikhart once said, "If a man were in rapture like Saint Paul, and knew a sick man who needed some soup from him, I should think it far better if you abandoned rapture for love."[324]

"Lord Jesus, I long to be perfectly whole," as the hymn-writer said, but I'm praying also for your church to be perfectly whole—through love.

[15] *And let the peace of Christ, to which you were called in one body, arbitrate in your hearts; and be thankful.*

Although Paul is well aware that our relationship with God and our relationships with others are woven together, up to this point in Col 3:5-17 Paul has been focusing on how Christians live in their horizontal relationships with other people. In these last three verses, however, Paul shines the spotlight on our vertical relationship with God. As Garland said, "The new creation enables the new morality, which, in turn leads to the new worship in 3:15-17."[325]

But this new worship is not so much about a private relationship with God. Rather, God's people *together* relate to God in the three ways described here, each of which is centered on Christ: the peace of Christ (verse 15), the word of Christ (verse 16), and doing all in the name of Christ (verse 17).

We begin with the peace of Christ. Paul referred to peace in his greetings (Col 1:2) and the related verb for peace-making in Col 1:20. Paul's letters portray peace from four different angles: (1) a general peace that comes from God, (2) peace within the heart, (3) peace with others, and (4) peace with God. Although we make such distinctions, each provides a different perspective on the same peace. None of these forms of peace can be sustained alone; each form of peace stands with the others. Even in Col 3:15, all four perspectives are found in varying degrees, as we'll see today and tomorrow.

Peace from God. Col 3:15 highlights the divine origin of peace; it is the "peace *of* Christ." This is a peace that Christ experiences himself, a peace he has created (or "made" on the cross, as Col 1:20 puts it), a peace that belongs to him, and a peace that he eagerly gives to others. Jesus affirmed this last point in Jn 14:27, "Peace I leave with you; my peace I give to you" (NRSV). According to Eph 2:14, Jesus himself is our peace. However conceived, this peace is not produced by human effort, but can only come as a gift from God.

Notice how Paul does not call on church leaders to impose the peace of Christ; instead the peace of Christ is already at work in the church. We may have some role in "letting" it arbitrate for us, but it's actually Christ's peace that is the active agent here. Christ's peace is making a "peaceful invasion" and our role is to submit to its benevolent rule.

Lord, I have tried to find peace from so many other sources—all in vain.
Today, Lord, and each day, I seek your peace.

¹⁵ **And let the peace of Christ, to which you were called in one body, arbitrate in your hearts;** *and be thankful.*

Peace within the Heart. Without the peace of Christ, our hearts can be tossed around like a restless wave, surging back and forth in a chaos of emotions. The distortionists, with their words of judgment, had likely put the hearts of some believers in turmoil, making them wonder about the quality of their faith (see Col 2:16, 18). And when the heart is troubled, it is less likely to notice and respond to the needs of others. But when Christ says, "peace, be still," to the stormy heart, then our lives can be ordered with compassion and patience for others.

The rare verb translated "arbitrate" is an athletic term for the actions of a referee in deciding if someone was qualified to enter or win a race. So when our thoughts throw the heart into turmoil, then the peace of Christ intervenes by calling them "out," if you will, so they can't even get to first base in our lives. Phil 4:7 echoes this: "the peace of God, which surpasses all understanding, will guard your hearts and your minds in Christ Jesus" (NRSV). Paul's point, then, is not merely that Christ's peace be present with us, but that it holds sway and exerts authority in and among us.[326]

Peace with Others. The peace of Christ not only brings inner tranquility; it also establishes peace with others, especially within the church. We are called to this peace of Christ not only "in your hearts," but also "in one body." The peace of Christ is not just for isolated individuals, but for the church to experience together. Whereas the distortionists had disqualified other Christians, the peace of Christ will decide in their favor, bringing people into the family of God instead of pushing them out.[327]

Just as we are called to eternal life (1 Tim 6:12), fellowship with Christ (1 Cor 1:9), holiness (1 Thess 4:7), freedom (Gal 5:13), and hope (Eph 4:4), so we are also called to live in peace with one another. Christians have not been called to be an assembly of warring factions, a debate club, or a dysfunctional family. Rather, we have been called to be one body in peace (Rom 12:18; 14:19; 2 Cor 13:11; 1 Thess 5:13).

Peace with God. Col 3:15 doesn't speak of this directly, but it must be acknowledged that the only reason the peace of Christ can arbitrate in our hearts is because Jesus reconciled us to God in the first place, making peace at the cross (Col 1:20). Without this peace with God, there is no peace within or peace among believers.

Lord, even though the song says, "let there be peace on earth and let it begin with me," I know it really begins with you. Thank you!

¹⁵ *And let the peace of Christ, to which you were called in one body, arbitrate in your hearts; **and be thankful.***

This verse concludes with a short command to "be thankful" (or perhaps "become thankful"). Paul could have used the verb for thanking (*eucharisteō*) at this point (as he had earlier used it in Col 1:3 and 12, and will use it in 3:17). But instead he used the word for being or becoming and put it with the adjective for "thankful" (*eucharistos*).

This is the only use of this adjective in the NT, and its only use in the Greek OT is Prov 11:15, which is about a thankful wife. It may be only a stylistic change, but it does remind us that gratitude is not only something one does, but it's also a way of *being*. Someone who only intermittently gives thanks would be obeying the call to *give* thanks. But only those who cultivate an ongoing thankful spirit are obeying the call to *be* thankful.

Some may wonder if Paul just adds this command as an after-thought, as if he were saying, "Oh yeah, I nearly forgot, but thankfulness is a good thing too." But thankfulness is more important than that. A heart that is thankful *to God* for his saving love is a heart motivated to put aside all the grasping and angry sins of verses 5 and 8. When you are not thankful for what you have in terms of relationships or possessions, you will wrongly desire other people and things. And when you are not thankful for the people around you, you will lash out at them in anger, wishing they would get out of your way.

And on the positive side, a heart that is thankful for other people is a heart motivated to show love and all the other good qualities mentioned in verses 12-14. It's hard to love people about whom you grumble. If you are always noticing their faults and even wishing they would go away—maybe moving to a different job or community—you will not be able to truly love them. But if you see the people around you as gifts of God to you, so that you thank the Lord for their presence in your life, you will find reason to love. Perhaps we could even say that learning to love others begins by being thankful for them.

So rather than just an after-thought to verses 5-15, thankfulness is what provides the motivation to break through the "culture of perpetual dissatisfaction."[328] as Walsh and Keesmaat call it, and instead do what Paul commands here.

Lord, I've said thanks to you and others many times, but I don't want to just say it now and then; I want you to make me be a thankful person.

[16] **Let the word of Christ dwell in you richly,** *teaching and warning each other in all wisdom with psalms, hymns and Spirit-oriented songs, singing by grace in your hearts to God.*

It's not only the *peace* of Christ that operates in our hearts; so does the *word* of Christ. These are two interrelated realities. The *peace* of Christ is not a vague spiritual feeling, but is given direction and substance by the *word* of Christ. And the word of Christ is not a burdensome list of commands given to increase anxiety or competitiveness. Instead, this word is spoken to create peace in the body of Christ.

This word of Christ is to be heard and read. It is also to be celebrated and obeyed. But even beyond that, this word is to "dwell" in us. In the OT the issue of *where God's people will dwell* was of primary importance. This concern was transformed in the NT, however, so that now the issue is *who or what will dwell in the people of God.* According to Paul's usage of the word "dwell," what dwells within us is the Holy Spirit (2 Tim 1:14; Rom 8:11), God himself (2 Cor 6:16), faith (2 Tim 1:15), and the word of Christ (here).

Without using the word for "dwell," the OT also speaks of God's Word being in our hearts: "You shall therefore lay up these words of mine in your heart and in your soul" (Dt 11:18, ESV; see also Dt 30:14; 32:46; Job 22:22; Ps 37:31; 119: 11; Prov 4:4; Ezek 3:10).

The NT also refers to taking God's Word within. Jesus' parable of the soils describes those "who, hearing the word, hold it fast in an honest and good heart, and bear fruit with patience" (Lk 8:15, ESV). In Rom 10:8 Paul quoted Dt 30:14 to say that God's Word is in our heart and mouth. Jms 1:21 refers to "the word planted in you, which can save you" (NIV).

God's indwelling Word empowers and guides our obedience. As the later rabbis said: "he who dwells in a house is the master of the house, not just a passing guest."[329] If we apply this truth to Col 3:16, we would conclude that when God's Word truly dwells within us—individually and as a church—then the Word is the master of our lives, and not just a passing guest.

This word of Christ, then, does not *barely* dwell within us, as if we could confine it to some small corner of our church, or merely regard it as a meager supplement to the total intake of our minds. Rather, the word of Christ is to dwell "richly" within us. God is richly pouring out this word in us and we are enriched by it.

Pour out your Word, O Lord, so that it fills my heart and mind to overflowing.

 [16] *Let the word of Christ dwell in you richly, **teaching and warning each other in all wisdom** with psalms, hymns and Spirit-oriented songs, singing by grace in your hearts to God.*

One of the primary means by which the word of Christ dwells in a church is through teaching and warning. Paul is echoing the words he used earlier to describe his own ministry as one of "warning every person and teaching every person in all wisdom" (Col 1:28).

Here, however, he expands this teaching ministry. Paul does not limit this ministry to the apostles or those specially appointed to teach. In fact, Paul does not mention anyone in Colossians being specifically designated as a teacher (as he does in Eph 4:11). Rather, he calls on *all* Christians—men and women, young and old—to be involved in this ministry of teaching and warning. Using a different verb Paul said a similar thing in Rom 15:14, "I myself feel confident about you, my brothers and sisters, that you are...able to instruct one another" (NRSV).

Teaching in the church is not to be a top-down enterprise in which the enlightened ones inform the ignorant ones. Rather, the truth in Jesus flows so abundantly in the church that every believer has something to teach the others.

Paul's words are surprising, because in all likelihood the distortion originated with some members who were doing just what Paul says: they had some ideas of how to advance in the Christian faith and began to share them with others. Nothing in Colossians suggests that these distortionists were official teachers of the church. Instead, they were members of the church who were willing to give voice to their experiences and beliefs.

If this is the case, we might expect Paul to put a stop to such out-of-bounds teaching by appointing (or endorsing) official teachers who alone would instruct others in what is correct. But instead, after he discredits the distortion, Paul calls on the rest of the church to get involved in this ministry of teaching one another. What's needed in the church is not fewer (approved) sources of teaching, but *more* sources of teaching by those in whom the word of Christ is dwelling richly. Perhaps when the distortionists began promoting their ideas, the other Colossian Christians cut back on their own ministries of teaching and turned into passive listeners. Now Paul calls them to rise up and fill the assembly with teachings and warnings flowing from the word of Christ.

Lord Jesus, you have given me some kind of teaching ministry. Show me who it is that you want me to teach, and how.

*[16] Let the word of Christ dwell in you richly, teaching and warning each other in all wisdom **with psalms, hymns and Spirit-oriented songs,** singing by grace in your hearts to God.*

One appealing element of the distortion was its emphasis on heavenly worship (Col 2:18). The impression given, however, is that this was a private spiritual experience which often made its recipients feel superior to others. Paul, however, contrasts this private experience with the true worship that involves all the believers singing and teaching together.[330]

The grammar here contains the surprising truth that Paul regards singing as an important form of teaching. The believers not only are singing "to God" (as the latter part of the verse states), but their songs also speak truth to the congregation. With the same lyrics, they both praise the Lord *and* teach (and learn from) one another. It might seem unusual to us to address both God and one another, but the Psalms frequently go back and forth (even within the same verse) between addressing God and addressing the people (as can be seen in Psalms 30, 32, 66, 104 and 116).[331]

Because singing is for letting the word of Christ dwell richly within, then it's important that the songs not be mere expressions of feelings, but very Word-oriented. A song with an emotionally moving melody but short on biblical truth would not correspond to what Paul is talking about here.[332] Christian singing is not about self-expression, but about having one's heart formed by biblical truth set to music. Perhaps we could even say that the truthfulness and importance of a given teaching is questionable if it cannot be sung to God in worship.

Songs of worship are an important component in living out the commands of Colossians 3. It is through worship that the people of God seek and think the things above (Col 3:1-2), throwing off their sins and entering into the reality of being made in the image of Christ (Col 3:8-10). And it is also through worship that they unite together as a church. According to Peterson, worship songs "provide the primary language for embracing and savoring what God does and who God is in all matters of salvation," so that the history of our world and of our lives is "salvation-defined" instead of "sin-defined."[333] And as Barth adds, any church which "does not really sing but sighs and mumbles spasmodically...can be at best only a troubled community which is not sure of its cause and of whose ministry and witness there can be no great expectation."[334]

Put a song in my heart, O Lord, that I might worship you, and that my heart and mind would be shaped by your saving goodness.

*¹⁶ Let the word of Christ dwell in you richly, teaching and warning each other in all wisdom **with psalms, hymns and Spirit-oriented songs,** singing by grace in your hearts to God.*

The musical terms used in Col 3:16 and the parallel in Eph 5:19 are the same words in the same order: psalms, hymns, and Spirit-oriented songs. It's popular to regard "psalms" as originating only from the book of Psalms, "hymns" as musical expressions of biblical themes, and "Spirit-oriented songs" as spontaneous tunes given by the Spirit during worship. There is not much to back up these distinctions. In fact, in Greek "psalms" can refer to any music, secular or sacred, accompanied by strumming.

Perhaps the three terms are intended to convey a sense of the variety and richness of music that could and should be a part of worship.[335] We might think boredom is a modern phenomenon, but the fourth century church father Basil the Great said, "I think it is useful to have diversity and variety in the prayer and psalmody at these appointed times, because somehow the soul is frequently bored and distracted by routine."[336]

Paul does not want the churches merely to write or compile or listen to songs of worship, as if their primary function is to be an audience. Rather, songs of worship are meant to be sung by the people of God.

Many verses in the Bible directly command God's people to sing—not just to listen, but to join in the singing. Here are just a few of the over one hundred commands to sing: "Sing praises to the Lord" (Ps 9:11, NRSV); "Sing to the Lord a new song" (Isa 42:10, NIV); "Sing to the Lord, all the earth" (1 Chron 16:23, ESV). In the case of Col 3:16, singing is how one obeys the command to let the word of Christ dwell richly in the church.

Since we often associate commands with ethical concerns, some might wonder why singing would be commanded. Here we need to remember the distinction between moral-commands and faith-commands (see the May 25 devotional on Col 2:6). The command to sing is a faith-command, calling on God's people to draw near to God through praise. And by drawing near to God in song, we are then better able to obey the moral-commands. Through musical worship, we are being instructed to remember who we are (God's chosen-ones, holy and loved, who have died and risen with Christ) and what behaviors line up with that identity (all the ethical matters listed in Col 3:5-15).

Lord, sometimes I resist obeying your commands, but the command to sing is one that brings delight to my own heart as well as yours.

[16] *Let the word of Christ dwell in you richly, teaching and warning each other in all wisdom with psalms, hymns and Spirit-oriented songs, **singing by grace in your hearts to God.***

The connection between musical worship and obedient living is not an automatic given. People often sing to God and yet remain deaf to the implications of what they're singing. They might think they are pleasing God with their beautiful music, but the fact that their lives remain in a sinful state shows they are not paying attention to the lyrics coming out of their mouths or entering their ears.

This gives no pleasure to God. As God declared through the prophet Amos: "Take away from me the noise of your songs; to the melody of your harps I will not listen. But let justice roll down like waters, and righteousness like an ever-flowing stream" (Amos 5:23-24, ESV). God calls us to resist this tendency to separate worship from morality.

But just as musical worship disconnected from one's actions is a travesty, so is musical worship disconnected from one's heart. That's why Paul adds the last phrase, "singing by grace in your hearts to God." Far too often "worshipers" merely mouth the words without a heart-felt expression of awe and love for God. They are the kind of worshipers criticized in Isa 29:13, "These people draw near with their mouths and honor me with the lips, while their hearts are far from me" (NRSV, quoted also by Jesus in Mt 15:8; Mk 7:6). As Claudius said in Shakespeare's *Hamlet* (Act 4, Scene 3), "My words fly up, my thoughts remain below, words without thoughts never to heaven go." It is vital that worshipers sing with their hearts, and not only their vocal cords. If a musician plays what is technically correct but has no heart for it, the audience can quickly tell. Likewise, the Lord is disappointed if we sing true words with perfect pitch, but our heart is not in it.

Another mark of worshipful singing is that it is to be done "by grace." This is often translated as "with thanksgiving," a closely related idea. Yet the word here almost always means "grace." Our singing is not merely fueled by our own humanly-generated sense of gratitude, which we may or may not feel at any given moment. Rather, our singing is fueled by the grace God has poured into our hearts. Our worshipful singing is ultimately grounded in *God's* grace, not in the quality or quantity of *our* gratitude.

Lord, on my own, my worship is weak, so please pour out your grace that I might worship you with all my heart and all my life.

> *[17] And in all of whatever you do—in word or in work—[do] all things in the name of the Lord Jesus,* giving-thanks to God the Father through him.

Some, like the distortionists, believe it's important to formulate and obey detailed codes of conduct to cover all kinds of situations (see Col 2:21). While such rules served a purpose before Jesus came, now that he has come, it's usually best to cover the totality of life with general commands, such as, do everything in the name of Jesus.[337] All-encompassing commands may strike some people as a totalitarian attempt to control everything, but Paul sees it as a liberation from slavery to the law.

Nearly all ethical systems basically agree about desirable and undesirable behaviors, but this verse points out a truly unique element in Christian ethics: the motivation to do everything for the sake of Jesus.[338]

It's important to observe that the previous verse about worship is immediately followed by this verse. Worship is not about having private, ecstatic experiences of the supernatural, unrelated to daily life (as the distortionists thought). Rather, worship is about the people of God coming together to focus on the Lord (Col 3:16), and then moving out together to act in the name of the Lord (Col 3:17). We are not in Christ only when we are in a worship service.[339]

Paul relies heavily on the common Greek adjective for "all" (*pas*) in conveying his message in Colossians; he uses it thirty-seven times. And "all" is not only a *frequent* word in this letter, it's also an *important* word. Jesus creates all, is Head over all, and reconciles all. Paul also saw his own ministry wrapped up in these all-encompassing concerns, for he warns and teaches *all* people in *all* wisdom that he might present them *all* complete in Christ (Col 1:28).

But it would be a mistake to think that only Jesus or a Paul can do all-encompassing things. Even for ordinary Christians in their everyday living, the word "all" is fitting. For here Paul reminds believers that living in Christ—necrotizing our sinful members, and being clothed with the image of the new man and all the good qualities of Christ—this is not just something done now and then as the occasion fits. Rather, we live for Christ and in Christ in "all" that we do—and Paul uses the word "all" twice in this verse to emphasize that (many translations hide one of the two "alls"). There is no part-time Christianity.

Lord, when I want to compartmentalize my faith, confining my life of faith to only some places and times, I want you to knock down the walls so that my life is wholly lived before you and for you.

[17] And in all of whatever you do—in word or in work—[do] all things in the name of the Lord Jesus, giving-thanks to God the Father through him.

With the word "do," Paul serves notice that new life in Christ always affects our actions. We might be thinking the things above (Col 3:2), but we are not living in the clouds. Our feet are planted firmly on earth, and our whole bodies are actively involved in living out our faith.

But what does it mean to do something in the name of another?

(1) Acting in the name of someone means we are representing them. They have sent us to do what they would have done if they were present. Thus, we might think of ourselves as representing God to the world and to one another. Although God is always invisibly present by the Holy Spirit, he sends us as his visible representatives, his ambassadors (2 Cor 5:20).

(2) Acting in the name of the Lord also means that our actions affect the reputation of God's name in the world. If we act dishonorably, we cause God's name to be profaned among the nations (see Ezek 36:21). But if we act righteously, as Paul is encouraging here, God's reputation is enhanced and people bless his name.

(3) Finally, by doing things in the name of another, we are empowered to act with their authorization. Accordingly, when we act in the name of Jesus, it means we are not acting alone but are authorized and empowered to do so by Christ through the Holy Spirit. By ourselves, we would be unable to do anything; but in the name of Jesus, we can act boldly for the Lord.

Putting these components together means that when we do things in the name of Jesus, we are acting as his empowered representatives to enhance God's reputation. And when we do this, as 1 Cor 10:31 says, God will be glorified: "So whether you eat or drink, or whatever you do, do everything for the glory of God" (NRSV).

In all this we must remember that our human actions of glorifying God only echo the far more powerful action of God glorifying his own name. The line from the Lord's Prayer, "Hallowed be thy name," is not a call for *us* to hallow God's name (as important as that is), but a prayer for God to hallow his own name. If we glorify God's name in our own strength, we are really only glorifying our own name. According to Barth, "We are to play our part but not try to play his [God's]."[340]

I confess, Lord Jesus, that I have not always represented you well in my workplace or in my family. Awaken me to my responsibility in these matters.

¹⁷ And in all of whatever you do—in word or in work—[do] all things in the name of the Lord Jesus, giving-thanks to God the Father through him.

The call to do *all things* in Jesus' name is a marvelous call. Rather than separating spiritual and secular activities, we can joyfully discover that all kinds of activities can be a form of worship and service. One can imagine kayaking in the name of the Lord Jesus, making love in the name of the Lord Jesus, watching a movie in the name of the Lord Jesus. But while it's true that these activities can and should be included here, it would not be wise to let our pleasure-oriented culture determine the focus of Col 3:17. Paul would be disappointed if we believed that doing pleasurable things alone in the name of Jesus was a sufficient form of obedience to verse 17.

It might be helpful to look at activities done in the Lord's name in the Bible. Most of them fit in the following categories (and I'm providing only a couple scriptural citations—one from each testament—for each category):

- We worship and pray in the name of the Lord (Ps 89:16; Eph 5:20).
- We speak in the name of the Lord (1 Kgs 22:16; Acts 9:28).
- We do miracles in the name of the Lord (2 Kgs 5:11; Acts 3:6).
- We battle in the name of the Lord (1 Sam 17:45; Acts 16:18)—the OT speaks of human enemies, but the NT focuses on demonic foes.
- We bless others and show kindness in the name of the Lord (2 Sam 6:18; Mk 9:41).

Some of these categories are found in the immediate context of Colossians. Verses 15-17 point to actions of worship: giving thanks and singing in the name of Jesus. Verse 16 highlights actions associated with God's word: teaching and warning in the name of Jesus. And verses 12-14 are about deeds of kindness done in the name of Jesus. So while verse 17 joyfully includes the fullness of life in its embrace, it is not encouraging us to do whatever pleasurable thing we feel like doing in the name of the Lord, and then counting it as a great act of obedience on our part.

Of special note is that while most of the actions in the OT are done in the name of *the Lord* or the name of *God*, most of the NT actions are done in the name of *the Lord Jesus*. Given the high status accorded to Jesus throughout Colossians, it's no surprise that Col 3:17 fits this same pattern of focusing on Jesus.

Lord, give me eyes to see that whatever I do today, except for my sin, can be done as a form of worship and service to you.

*[17] And in all of whatever you do—in word or in work—[do] all things in the name of the Lord Jesus, **giving-thanks to God the Father through him.***

Here is yet another call to give thanks. Since this phrase comes on the heels of his command to do *all* in the name of Christ, we are not to do *all* in the Lord's name with a grudging spirit, but a grateful heart. That's why Paul elsewhere calls us to "give thanks in all circumstances" (1 Thess 5:18, NIV).

This call to give thanks has similarities to what was known as the benefaction system in ancient Greece and Rome. In those cultures thankfulness was the expected response to the giving of a gift. Talbot explains, "Benefaction started a relationship. A gift was given. The beneficiary reciprocated. A gift was returned...The relationship continued as the circle of gift-giving and gift-reciprocating continued"[341] —perhaps in the form of an inscription that honored the benefactor and with words of gratitude and pledges of loyalty. Garland adds, "Accepting gifts in the ancient world placed one under a social obligation to show gratitude."[342] If Paul was following this societal understanding, then God would be the benefactor who has blessed us tremendously, and now it's up to us to return the favor by being thankful.

But in spite of similarities between this ancient social practice and our relationship with God, there are at least two ways in which the gospel message is greater.[343] First, the benefaction system sounds more like a business transaction than the genuine giving of a gift. But God is under no obligation to give a gift in the first place, nor is he obligated by our response to continue giving. The gifts of God are genuine gifts, freely given. As the Jewish philosopher Philo said, "God is no salesman, hawking his goods in the market, but a free giver of all things, pouring forth eternal fountains of free bounties, and seeking no return. For He has no needs Himself and no created being is able to repay his gift" (*On the Cherubim* 123).

Second, because God's gifts are genuine gifts, that means God acts as a benefactor even when no one responds with gratitude. According to Lk 6:35, God is "kind to the ungrateful and the wicked" (NRSV). So even though sinful humanity is characterized by ingratitude toward God (Rom 1:21), God nevertheless sent the greatest gift, his Son, to do what we were incapable of doing, namely, offering up the right response to God. This is why our thanks can only be offered to God "through" Christ. With Christ as our worship leader, if you will, we can truly give thanks.

On my own, Lord Jesus, my gratitude is often half-hearted, even manipulative. So I'm glad that I can be thankful through you.

Lord, You Are All in All

to the tune of *You Are My All In All* 344
© 2013 David J. Landegent

Putting to death our sin and shame
Throwing off evils that remain
Lord, You are all in all
Clothing us with a life that's new
Made in the image found in You
Lord, You are all in all
Lord, may all we do—be done in Your name
Lord, may all we do—be done in Your name

Here there is no divisiveness
Everyone's chosen, loved and blessed
Lord, You are all in all
All of us clothed with love and grace
Following You, we run the race
Lord, You are all in all
Lord, may all we do—be done in Your name
Lord, may all we do—be done in Your name

Giving Your peace to rule our lives
Letting Your Word dwell deep inside
Lord, You are all in all
Joyfully singing hymns and songs
We are so thankful we belong
Lord, You are all in all
Lord, may all we do—be done in Your name
Lord, may all we do—be done in Your name.

Commands for life in the home

Colossians 3:18-4:1

October 29-November 27

[18] Women, submit to [your] men as fitting in the Lord. [19] Men, love [your] women, and do not be embittered against them.

[20] Children, obey [your] parents in all things, for this is well-pleasing in the Lord. [21] Fathers, do not provoke your children, lest they become dispirited.

[22] Slaves, obey in all things [your] lords according to the flesh, not by way of "only-when-watched service," as people-pleasers, but in sincerity of heart, fearing the Lord. [23] In whatever you do, work from the soul, as for the Lord and not for men, [24] knowing that from the Lord you will receive the reward of the inheritance. Slave for the Lord Christ, [25] for the one doing wrong will receive-back what he did wrong—and there is no partiality. [4:1] Lords, give justice and equal-treatment to [your] slaves, knowing that you also have a Lord in heaven.

This section is known among scholars as *Haustafeln* (a German word meaning "house-table"), but we'll refer to it as household-instructions.

Households vary tremendously from culture to culture, and Paul cannot help but speak to his own culture. He would have no conception of the modern nuclear family, our mobility, feminism, cohabitation, or an economy not based on slavery. But this does not mean that Paul has nothing to say to us. That Paul can speak to different cultures was even true in his day, for households then (as now) did not all fit the same cookie-cutter pattern. There were (and are) many different household cultures in every community. For instance, not every adult is married or has children.

It's the wide variety of family-types, then and now, which always makes it difficult for preachers (including Paul) to speak to family issues without making someone feel left out or having their situation misunderstood. Yet Paul was not paralyzed by the variety in family situations. He thought it better to say something than nothing. But instead of offering detailed counsel like an advice columnist,[345] he focuses on general principles for those household relationships that were characterized by authority and submission. In this way people could see how Christ's authority changed the dynamics of the typical authority structures in the ancient world.[346]

While some think Paul wrongly reinforces bad cultural patterns here (an issue we'll look at later), it's better to explore how God did speak through Paul's words to the Colossians (and to us).

Jesus, you are Lord of my family, so I pray that I would be open to hearing how you would direct us to live together.

Read Colossians 3:18-4:1 again.

The responsibilities of household members were frequent subjects of Greek, Roman, and Jewish writings during Paul's day and even earlier. The philosopher Epictetus, for instance, wanted "to know what my duty is towards the gods, towards parents, towards brothers, towards my country, towards strangers" (*Discourses* 2.17.31). On a very general level there are some resemblances between NT household-instructions and these other writings, but any so-called parallels are vastly overrated. In terms of form and content, nothing else is like the household-instructions of the NT.[347]

Paul instructs three relational pairings typically found in a household (wives and husbands, children and fathers, slaves and masters). Other writers mentioned the same three pairs, but that's not very significant because if you asked anyone on the street to name the basic relationships found in a household, most would give the same three pairings.

Most ancient writers only described how families should operate, but Paul addresses the household members with commands. Philosophers thought their job was to describe reality and then once people see it, they will act accordingly. But for Paul, the status quo without Christ is wrong and needs to be changed.[348]

Some Jewish household-instructions *did* give commands, but these were only issued to the husband/father/master, who in turn could inform those dependent upon him. As the Jewish philosopher Philo said, "The husband seems competent to transmit knowledge of the laws to his wife, the father to his children, the master to his slaves" (*Hypothetica* 7.14). In most household-instructions, "the idea that women, children and slaves could also act in an ethically responsible way is scarcely considered."[349] Paul, however, shows his respect for wives, children, and slaves by speaking to them as responsible people. In doing this he is establishing that their ultimate identity is in Christ, not in their human status.[350]

One reason Paul can speak directly to them is that he knew his letters would be read to the whole congregation when wives, children, and slaves would be present to hear it. According to Hering, "The context of the public reading, the fellowship meeting, allows for all members to 'overhear' the instruction directed to others, a critical element in understanding the moral force of the letter."[351] Pagan philosophical writings, however, would be less likely to have been read in the presence of wives, children, or slaves.

Thank you, Lord, that no matter what role society assigns to me, you value me and hold me in your love.

Read Colossians 3:18-4:1 again.

Another feature of the Colossian household-instructions is the emphasis on the mutual responsibilities of each paired group toward one another. Not only do the wives, children, and slaves have responsibilities toward the husband/father/master, but he also has responsibilities toward them. Because of this emphasis on mutual responsibilities, it's important to remember that the commands given to each group in the pairing should not be interpreted separately, but together.[352]

Also characteristic of the Colossian household-instructions is that the "weaker" party in each pair is spoken to first (and by "weaker," I mean the person who had less social power in Paul's day). This is highly unusual, but its significance is not clear. Perhaps Paul believes that if he were to address the husbands/fathers/masters first, they would get defensive, so he speaks to the "weaker" members first in order to catch the men off-guard.

A very important characteristic of the Colossian household-instructions is their frequent references to the Lord. It's as if Paul took the thought of Col 3:17 ("do all things in the name of the Lord Jesus") and used it to point out all the things that can be done in the name of the Lord in the family.[353] Of the fourteen references to the Lord (*kurios*) in Colossians, seven of them are found in the household-instructions. While the philosophers talked about what is "fitting" (as Paul does in verse 18) and what is "pleasing" (as in verse 20), Paul emphasizes that these actions are fitting and pleasing "in the Lord."[354] Unlike the moral philosophers of his day, Paul says nothing here about conforming to natural law or reason, but instead remains centered on the Lord.[355] Some may dismiss this difference as a superficial addition aimed to "christianize" what is basically a pagan code, but this would not "fit" with how Paul perceived reality. The aim of believers is not to fit into society, but to fit into God's kingdom.

When Paul refers to the "Lord" here, he is not speaking of a generic deity, but of Jesus Christ. This Lord is not a divine power-figure who rules distantly from the top of an organizational chart. This is the Lord who does have all power, but who uses this power to love, to give, and to submit himself to the Father by laying down his life for us. Submission and obedience is fitting and pleasing to the Lord, because this is the kind of Lord who knows by experience what it means to submit and obey in love.

I praise you, Lord Jesus, for demonstrating to me and my family what love, submission, and obedience actually look like.

Read Colossians 3:18-4:1 again.

Some people today are disappointed that Paul wrote these household-instructions. How can the one who said that in Christ there is no Greek or Jew, slave or free (Col 3:11) or even male and female (Gal 3:27-29), now turn around and talk about obedience and submission.[356] It sounds like he's caving in to social pressure so that he doesn't upset those who held power.

Not at all. Paul is not concerned here about whether our Christian behavior conforms to the world, but whether it conforms to the *Lord*. Although some may think the ideas of submission and obedience are problematic, Paul does not, for they characterize what it means to live in God's kingdom. Even the Lord Jesus himself was submissive to the Father and will be in the Last Day as well (1 Cor 15:28). God's kingdom will definitely eliminate the power arrangement of today's world, but it will not eliminate submission and obedience.

So why did Paul write these household-instructions? Here are four contextual clues.

(1) These instructions keep our faith firmly planted in the ground of daily life. We may be called to seek and think the things above (Col 3:1-2), but not by abandoning or neglecting our families. [357]

(2) These instructions help us obey the commands given in Col 3:5-14. If you wonder why households need rules, you would do well to listen to C. S. Lewis's words, "If the home is to be a means of grace it must be a place of *rules*...the alternative to rules is not freedom but the unconstitutional (and often unconscious) tyranny of the most selfish member."[358]

(3) These household-instructions help the church. If anyone wonders why Paul would jump from the worship concerns of Col 3:15-16 to household matters, we need to remember that churches at that time met in homes. If there was trouble in the household, it could not help but affect the church. "A harmonious, well-regulated household promised a harmonious well-regulated church," noted Garland.[359]

(4) These instructions teach us to do everything in the name of the Lord Jesus (Col 3:17), including what we do at home. Whether or not we are truly clothed in the image of Christ (Col 3:9-10) is best seen in how we treat others in our household. Many people know how to show a "pretend" love in the sporadic encounters of the marketplace and the church, but in the ongoing interactions of the home one's true colors are shown.

In my life, in my home, in my church, and in my workplace, may your name be glorified, O Lord.

[18] **Women, submit to [your] men as fitting in the Lord.** [19] *Men, love [your] women, and do not be embittered against them.*

The first individuals addressed in Paul's household-instructions are the married women (There was no separate word for "w ife" in Greek). With respect to the marriage relationship, Paul urges the wives to submit [*hupotassō*]. The word "submit" is hard for our contemporary society to hear without thinking of various forms of unjust sexism and abuse, but at least Paul doesn't follow the Jewish philosopher Philo who said "wives must be in servitude to their husbands" (*Hypothetica* 7.3).

The compound verb *hupotassō* is formed from the preposition *hupo* (meaning "from" or "under") and the verb *tassō* (meaning "to set or appoint"). Thus when people are appointed (*tassō*) to a position, they are under (*hupo*) the authority of the one who appointed them, and thus they submit (*hupotassō*). This is most evident in Lk 7:8, where a centurion informs Jesus, "I too am a man set [*tassō*] under [*hupo*] authority" (ESV), with the expectation that he will submit to his commanders, just as his own soldiers submit to him. Even the prefix "sub" in the English word "submit" points in this direction of coming under (as in the word submarine).

Coming under a task and bearing it need not be demeaning if we realize God is honoring us by appointing us to do it. We are under a task or position which God has laid upon us. *Hupotassō* does not necessarily mean we are submitting to someone above us. We can also submit to an equal or subordinate, as seen in the mutual submission commanded in Eph 5:21.[360]

With the verb *hupotassō*, it makes a big difference whether it's used in the active or middle/passive sense. The active sense means "to make someone else submit." In the NT human beings are never called to make others submit to them. Rather, the focus is on God causing all things to submit to Christ—a thought taken from Ps 8:6 ("you have put [*hupotassō*] all things under his feet") and often applied to Jesus in the NT (1 Cor 15:27-28; Eph 1:22; Phil 3:21; and Heb 2:5, 8).

We must state very emphatically, then, that husbands who think it is their responsibility (or right) to make their wives submit have not at all interpreted this verse correctly. Even though the Bible speaks approvingly of submission in general, it's not anyone's job to make someone else submit. That's not our role at all.

Lord, there is a part of me that wants to make others—even family members—submit to my will. Instead Lord, I want to submit to your will.

*¹⁸ **Women, submit to [your] men as fitting in the Lord.** ¹⁹ Men, love [your] women, and do not be embittered against them.*

When we submit ourselves to another person, sometimes this might be an unwilling submission, as happens when we give in to the demands of a tyrant. Here, however, Paul speaks of a willing submission.

It would be possible to interpret these words in the worst way—and many have. But if we listen closely, we realize these words are not spoken to oppress women, but to undermine oppression.

First, it's an amazing thing that Paul addresses the women at all, which of itself is a challenge to the dominant position of the men.³⁶¹ Rather than only dealing with the husbands, Paul gives dignity to the women by speaking to them directly, treating them as people made in the image of God and remade in the image of Christ. As this verse says, submission is fitting for someone who is "in the Lord." Women are not possessions or objects of desire. They are royal daughters of the King, sisters in God's family.

Secondly, submission here is not something forced on the women. Rather, it's God's call for the women to offer it as a gift of love. An outside observer may think that such a gift only perpetuates the unjust oppression of women (a very real possibility), but submission could also be thought of as a way to gain power over oppression. Instead of being a victim of a husband's tyrannical rule, the wife will see herself as a participant in Jesus' revolution of love. No longer does she submit because she has no choice in the matter. Now she submits because she has freely chosen to show love in this way.

No longer is the woman on the losing end of a power game. Instead, she is initiating a new game that has no losers because both partners are on the same team. It may take the husband a long time to notice the game has changed (and it's possible he may never realize it), but for the woman, she's no longer playing the victim, but is an overcomer who is transforming marriage through the submissive spirit of Jesus.

Is it possible for a woman to be hurt while living out this revolutionary subordination, so that oppression only increases because she doesn't fight back? Yes. That's why, when safety is at stake for herself or her children, she should move out, but not because she is staging an angry revolt. Rather, all her actions are fueled by irrepressible love.

Lord, I pray for women who have been oppressed by men in society and even the men in their own families. Set them free, Lord, by the power of your love.

¹⁸ **Women, submit to [your] men as fitting in the Lord.** *¹⁹* *Men, love [your] women, and do not be embittered against them.*

We should take notice that Paul is placing Christ in the center of the marriage dynamics. Psychologists may advise against "triangulating" in a marriage (using a third party as an ally against one's spouse), but there is a kind of holy triangulation going on here. No longer is the woman alone in her relationship with her husband, and thus overpowered by his position in a patriarchal society. Rather, her relationship with her husband is shaped by the presence of Jesus in the home. She lives in the *Lord's* domain, not in her *husband's* domain. She does not compartmentalize her love, with some reserved for Jesus and some for her family members. Rather, she loves the Lord so fully that it overflows into all her other relationships. To paraphrase 1 Jn 4:20, because she lovingly submits to the Lord whom she cannot see, she will also lovingly submit to the husband whom she can see.

Actually, Paul is not asking anything from the women that he is not asking from the men, indeed from all Christians. Submission in marriage is not about being a doormat for a power-hungry person's desire to dominate. According to Atkins, many "think of the submissive wife as quiet, domestic, passive, and—dare we say it?—rather dull. Yet no qualities could be more irrelevant to true submission. Who was more obedient to God than Elijah or John the Baptist? Who was more submissive to Christ than Paul? Indeed, who has ever submitted more humbly than Jesus himself? These people should be our models for submission; yet they were tough, outspoken, unconventional, and courageous in the extreme."[362] Submission is about doing all the things mentioned in the previous section: wearing compassion, kindness, humility, meekness, and patience in the home, bearing with one another and granting grace to each other when hurts happen, clothing everything in the marriage with love, letting the peace of Christ arbitrate in one's heart and being thankful. (Col 3:12-16).

There will always be marriage partners who take unfair advantage of a Christian who wears these good qualities, but the disciple of Christ cannot use that as an excuse to throw away the wardrobe God has chosen for them. If we are only wearing God's holy garments in superficial social relationships, that's not saying much. It's especially in the thick of marital conflict that the Christian must reflect the character of the Lord who dwells in them. There is no marital exemption from bearing the fruit of the Spirit.

Lord Jesus, teach me to be a submissive person with the same tough, outspoken, courageous love shown by you.

[18] **Women, submit to [your] men as fitting in the Lord.** *[19]* Men, love [your] women, and do not be embittered against them.

Even though contemporary society resists the idea of submission, the truth is that the human heart has been resisting submission since the Garden of Eden. As sinners, we want what we want when we want it, and we only care about the desires of others if doing so advances our own agenda. Although our society understands life as a matter of asserting rights, no marriage can survive long in that environment. Those who think submitting is a terrible model for marriage should take note that contemporary submission-less models of marriage appear to be even less workable.[363]

Submitting, according to verse 18, "is fitting in the Lord." It's unclear how "fitting in the Lord" qualifies the submitting. Either it means that the act of submitting itself is what is fitting in the Lord,[364] or that we are only to submit to those demands which are fitting in the Lord, implying that a woman could disobey what is unfitting, such as a husband's demands to worship idols.[365] The first option explains *why* we submit (because it fits the Lord's own actions), while the second explains *what* we submit to (human demands that fit with what God demands). Most likely Paul is focusing on the former, but he'd agree with the concerns of the latter.

Notice what Paul is not saying. Paul does not say Christian wives are to submit so they can fit better into their culture and thus not make any waves that could sink the progress of the gospel. Nor does he say that wives are to submit in order to fit into their proper role in creation (although he may be saying that in 1 Tim 2:13-14 and 1 Cor 11:8-9). Rather, he says that wives submit because this corresponds to the character and activity of Jesus himself, who "did not count equality with God a thing to be grasped, but emptied himself, by taking the form of a servant" (Phil 2:6-7, ESV). Just as Jesus submitted to the Father, so the followers of Jesus submit to God and one another, even in their marriages.

Christians submit in this way because Jesus himself dwells within them, and they dwell in Jesus. Their lives are characterized by Christ-like submitting because Jesus is the atmosphere and domain in which they live, as well as the empowering presence of God within them. Thus it would be totally unfitting for those who are "in the Lord" (including husbands and wives) to try to dominate others by using sex, anger, money, or deceit to get their way. That path is not available to those who are in Christ (Col 3:5-9).

Rise up, O Lord, so that your Spirit of submission might fill my heart, my home, and my church.

*¹⁸ Women, submit to [your] men as fitting in the Lord. ¹⁹ **Men, love [your] women,** and do not be embittered against them.*

Here Paul addresses the husbands (since there is no Greek word for husbands, he used the term "men"). Rather than speaking of their rights, which was of concern to the philosophers, Paul focuses on their primary responsibility, which is to love their wives—and here the verb for love corresponds to the Greek noun for love in 1 Cor 13.[366]

Although many contemporary readers might wish Paul had said, "Husbands, likewise submit to your wives," Paul has chosen to express himself differently. Some might think his own cultural blinders prevented him from offering such a radical word, but more likely our own cultural blinders have kept us from seeing the radical message he does bring. Paul is not merely asking husbands to feel affection for their wives and act nicely toward them. Rather, he commands them to love their wives in the way demonstrated in the life of Jesus. This is far better than the philosophers who said that good husbands know how to control their wives, or as Dionysius of Halicarnassus put it, ""to rule their wives as necessary and inseparable possessions" (*Roman Antiquities* 2.25.4). It's not that love and affection were absent from pagan marriages, but it was not expected.

When Paul commands husbands to love, he is not talking about husbands running a benevolent dictatorship or being friends with their wives. Paul is commanding the kind of love that forsakes the attitude of asserting one's own rights and is instead focused on meeting the needs of the one who is loved. Paul brings this out even more clearly in Eph 5:25 "Husbands, love your wives, just as Christ loved the church and gave himself up for her" (NRSV).

Any husband who thinks this command is fulfilled by occasionally bringing flowers to his wife and saying "I love you" is not understanding the sacrifices Paul is expecting. Such a husband has been taken in by our culture's cheap and sentimental notions of love instead of truly understanding what God's love is like. To love as the Lord loves is not only to submit, but to go beyond what the loved one might ever ask or expect, actively finding ways to build up and sacrifice for the loved one. Yet this kind of love is possible for husbands (and wives, Titus 2:4) to live out because Jesus himself is the empowering source of this love. We love because he first loved us (1 Jn 4:19).

Lord, I confess that my ideas about love are mostly focused on sentimental emotions. Teach me your path of sacrificial love.

*¹⁸ Women, submit to [your] men as fitting in the Lord. ¹⁹ Men, love [your] women, **and do not be embittered against them.***

Paul adds here that men should not be embittered against their wives. Bitterness happens when we suffer at the hand of someone else and learn to resent them. Bitterness often creates a cycle in which bitter suffering leads to bitter resentment, which lashes out at its first opportunity to make their oppressor suffer bitterly in return. Someone has to stop the cycle, and here Paul calls on husbands to do just that.

When a husband is loving his wife, he may experience periods of frustration. He may feel his efforts are not appreciated or noticed. Perhaps he thinks she doesn't deserve his kindness, because she seems crabby or bossy, or nags and complains. A husband who lives from a strongly patriarchal perspective might even be irritated when his wife is not submitting in a way he believes is fitting in the Lord. It is very tempting in these situations for a husband to become embittered and resentful toward his wife, and thus less loving. But even if a husband's negative assessment of his wife were accurate, Paul would say in no uncertain terms that love must prevail anyway—and any resentful bitterness must not be allowed to take root in his heart. "Any defiance or insolence on the wife's part does not cancel the husband's absolute obligation to love her," says Garland.[367] Even the philosophers agreed with Paul. Plutarch criticized angry men who show how weak they are when they "rage bitterly against women" (*On the Control of Anger* 457A).

Many translations of verse 19 avoid the idea of being embittered. Instead, they focus on harshness: "do not be harsh with them" (ESV, NIV) and "never treat them harshly" (NRSV). These translations are attractive because they speak out more directly against any kind of abusive behavior by husbands. But such a translation would be more fitting if the verb were in the active mode; then it could be translated "Do not embitter your wives." But the passive mode is used here, and so it warns husbands against becoming embittered toward their wives. This angle is actually more helpful in the long run because it points out that the root of outward abuse is an inward bitterness in the man's own heart toward his wife (or maybe even toward women in general). Thus, Paul is saying more than "be nice to your wife." Rather, he's getting at the (bitter) root of the problem.

If I have become embittered toward a family member, Lord, reveal that to me, and replace my bitterness with love.

²⁰ **Children, obey [your] parents** in all things, for this is well-pleasing in the Lord. ²¹ Fathers, do not provoke your children, lest they become dispirited.

Next Paul addresses the children of the household. Although Paul may be referring to non-adult children, his words could also be directed toward any adult who still has a parent living. The Bible never speaks of outgrowing God's requirement of respecting and obeying one's parents.

Children are commanded to "obey" their parents. We might wish Paul had told children to love their parents, but as Smedes said, "A hug or a kiss on the cheek is very pleasant, but nothing suits honor better than doing what your father tells you to do...Honor is the moral fiber that holds the family together so that all the warm and loving, cold and hateful feelings between parents and child can be enjoyed and endured in a structure of loyalty and respect."[368]

Obedience to parents was also the expectation of Greek and Roman culture. The philosopher Epictetus said of a father that a son is "to be obedient to him in all things, never to speak ill of him to anyone else, nor to say or do anything that will harm him, to give way to him in everything and yield him precedence, helping him as far as is within his power" (*Discourses* 2.10.7). Obedience to parents was required in Jewish families also.

The word for obey is a compound verb formed from the preposition *hupo* (under) and *akouō* (the ordinary verb for hearing or listening). The connection between *akouō* and *hupakouō* is a close one. Even in English we talk about "listening" to one's parents as a form of obedience. When we obey, we listen in a way that places us under the words of another.

In the vast majority of biblical references to obedience, it is God we are called to obey. As for obedience to humans, the Bible seems fairly skittish about the idea. In fact, *hupakouō* is only used once in reference to obeying a ruler (1 Chron 29:23). The Greek version of Prov 28:17 even adds an extra line that says, "You shall *not* obey a lawless nation" (NETS, emphasis mine).

That's why the main form of obedience to another human doesn't happen in the political sphere, but in the household. Ten times in the book of Proverbs, children are commanded to listen in an obedient way to their parents. Jesus agreed with the Ten Commandments about honoring parents (Mt 19:19; Mk 10:19; Lk 18:20) and even rebuked religious people who found a pious loophole to avoid helping their parents financially (see Mt 15:4-5; Mk 7:10-12).

Lord, since my youth there have been times it was difficult to obey my parents. Grant to me a compliant heart instead of a rebellious one.

*[20] Children, obey [your] parents **in all things, for this is well-pleasing in the Lord.** [21] Fathers, do not provoke your children, lest they become dispirited.*

In our culture, where ethical issues are often decided based on unusual case studies and borderline situations, the line about obeying one's parents in *all* things is startling. Most of us can readily think of situations in which a child should not obey their parents. Would Paul want children to obey parents who use them to satisfy the parents' sick desires for power and sex? Or by getting them to run drugs, tell lies, or shoot someone? And certainly Paul would not want children to obey their parents in worshiping false gods.

No, Paul would not. After all, even Jesus did not regard the parent/child relationship as having ultimate significance. He often mentioned that disciples might have to forsake their parents in order to follow him (Mt 10:35, 37). Even non-Christians in Paul's day and earlier allowed for exceptions to obeying one's parents if they became insane or commanded something evil, unjust, or shameful.[369] So why does Paul speak so broadly here about obeying in *all* things? Two things can be said.

First, the focus of "in all things" is probably not so much about including evil actions, but it does include actions that that are unpleasant or tedious. We should *not* obey parents if they command something sinful, but we *should* obey them even if they command something we don't enjoy doing.[370]

Secondly, Paul is not approaching this moral issue from the margins, the borderline cases, and the unusual exceptions. Rather, he approaches it from the center. In normal life, when ordinary parents are aiming to do what's best for their children, then it is only right for the children to obey. We cannot allow unusual situations and exceptions to provide us with loopholes for neglecting this obedience and giving ourselves a free pass to ignore what God calls us to do.

The reason for obeying parents is that this is "well-pleasing in the Lord." While there may be a sense in which obedience would be well-pleasing to the parents, or to society, or even to Paul, the focus of this verse is how it is well-pleasing *to the Lord*. The Lord's concerns—not our concerns—form the proper center of all biblical commands. Obeying parents, then, is one way to fulfill Paul's prayer for us "to walk worthily of the Lord in every form of pleasing" (Col 1:10).

Lord, it's so easy for me to find loopholes and excuses for avoiding what you expect of me. Teach me instead the simplicity of obedience.

> ²⁰ *Children, obey [your] parents in all things, for this is well-pleasing in the Lord.* ²¹ **Fathers, do not provoke your children,** *lest they become dispirited.*

It's not only children who are called to obey, so are the parents: they must obey this command not to provoke their children. Although mothers were also involved in training the children, in Paul's day it was mostly regarded as the father's responsibility (see Heb 12:7-11).

While the OT focuses on earthly fathers with an occasional reference to God being a Father (Isa 63:16; 64:8; Mal 2:10), it's just the opposite in the NT. Yet we do find NT verses like this which address earthly fathers.

Paul does *not* follow most household-instructions of his day, which called on fathers to rule or govern their children.[371] Ancient Roman law gave fathers a lot of leeway in punishing their sons in any way they chose, including prison, scourging, and even death. It's doubtful, however, that first century Roman fathers used the extreme forms of this power. Public opinion was against unnecessary strictness.[372] Roman fathers wanted to build a sense of dignity in their sons, so they avoided whipping, which was regarded as deeply humiliating—a punishment fit only for slaves.[373] *Slaves* might be punished with a whipping (Latin *verbera*), but *sons* were mostly reprimanded with words (Latin *verba*).[374] The main environments in which a free Roman citizen might receive a beating or flogging was in the military or at school, but not so much at home.[375]

Paul would agree with these non-Christian writers, for he tells fathers not to provoke their children. There are many ways fathers can provoke children: harsh words, being unwilling to forgive, imposing excessive punishments, verbal or physical abuse, being critical about minor matters, treating them as less mature than they actually are, being inconsistent with moral standards or discipline, giving the silent treatment, never encouraging, expecting too much, etc. Paul instead calls on fathers to remove wrath and anger (Col 3:8) and put on compassion, kindness, humility, patience, forgiveness and love (Col 3:12-14).

Paul brings this up because he knows that those in positions of authority, like fathers, can easily be tempted to abuse their position by failing to show love, perhaps withholding it when a child disobeys. But as N. T. Wright says, "obedience must never be made the condition of parental 'love.'"[376]

Just as you disciplined me in love, Lord Jesus, I pray that I would be able to do the same with anyone I am responsible to discipline in my life.

> [20] *Children, obey [your] parents in all things, for this is well-pleasing in the Lord.* [21] *Fathers, do not provoke your children, **lest they become dispirited.***

While most of his contemporaries were worried about how children might possibly disgrace their parents, Paul was more concerned about how parents might possibly discourage their children.[377] This concern could be traced back to Jesus' own love for children (Mt 18:2-5).

Karl Barth notes that the failures of parents can be dangerous to a child in three ways: (1) the child might learn his or her lessons too well and imitate the parents' failures; (2) the child might think he or she knows better and assumes an attitude of superiority over the parents; and (3) a child "might transfer the disillusionment which he has experienced in his parents to the God whose witnesses they should have been for him."[378] Paul is focusing on this last problem.

We might expect children who have been provoked by their fathers to grow up to be surly and hot-tempered. That's possible, but instead, Paul is also concerned that they become dispirited, as if the wind was taken out of their sails. On a literal level, the word for dispirited (*athumeō*) means without anger or passion, and can also be translated as discouraged, despondent, or disheartened. It describes the kind of person who, having been mistreated, becomes listless, without any drive or zeal for life.

For fathers to gain such domination over their children that they become resentfully compliant is not a good thing. Obedience and submission does not mean passive, dispirited compliance. Even pagan philosophers in Paul's day would have agreed. Pseudo-Plutarch said, "children ought to be led to honorable practices by means of encouragement and reasoning, and most certainly not by blows or ill-treatment" (*Education of Children*, 8F). He added, "Our friends' shortcomings we bear with: why should it be surprising that we bear with our children's?" (13D-E). The Jewish writer Pseudo-Phocylides echoed these words, "Do not apply your hand violently to tender children," and, "Do not be harsh with your children, but be gentle" (*Sentences* 150, 207).

This is how God treats his own children. He wants us to be obedient, but he also wants us to be fully alive and full of heart, for God is "a shelter to all who are dispirited" (Isa 25:4, NETS). The task of Christian parents, then, is not primarily to attest to the Law to their children (through harsh discipline), but instead to attest to the gospel.[379]

Lord, I pray that you would use me to enliven and give heart to those you have placed in my care.

*²² **Slaves,** obey in all things [your] lords according to the flesh, not by way of "only-when-watched service," as people-pleasers, but in sincerity of heart, fearing the Lord.*

First century slaves could be found in many work situations, but they often worked in homes. So when Paul addresses the members of the house, he also speaks to the slaves. The quality of master-slave relationships was as varied as those between husbands and wives. Some masters were cruel; others kind. Some slaves were hard-working, others lazy. Some slaves were loved like family members, while others were regarded as nothing but living property. Paul is not able to address all the different circumstances, but he does give these general commands.

In contrast to his short directives to the other household members, Paul speaks at length to slaves. This may be due to the situation that had arisen earlier between the Colossian Christian slave owner (Philemon) and his runaway slave (Onesimus)—which is the subject of Paul's letter to Philemon.[380] This remains, however, a guess. In any case, the fact that Paul addressed the slaves at all is a good thing because some Greek philosophers, notably Aristotle (*Politics* 1260a), taught that slaves are incapable of deliberation.[381] Paul knows otherwise.

Many people today are repulsed by Paul's words. We have such an instinctive aversion to the idea of slavery—and rightly so—that we wonder how it could have been tolerated for so long. Why doesn't Paul cry out against this very unjust system, especially since only a few verses earlier he had declared that there is no slave or free in Christ (Col 3:11)? How could he even say things that could be interpreted as a blessing on the status quo of people being held in bondage?

It's because of how Paul looks at life in Christ. For him, every person's situation, including that of the slave, is "the stage upon which allegiance to Christ is proven."[382] We can still have our questions about these matters, but what can minimally be said in Paul's defense is that, even though his words may not sound very revolutionary, he does not endorse slavery,[383] and actually speaks truths which will eventually undermine the institution of slavery. Nonetheless, these truths still took a long time to bear fruit (a thought we will return to later).

Lord, it is hard to comprehend how the biblical writers could tolerate slavery, but I pray you would teach me through Paul's words.

*²² **Slaves,** obey in all things [your] lords according to the flesh, not by way of "only-when-watched service," as people-pleasers, but in sincerity of heart, fearing the Lord.*

It's easy for us to read these words from the perspective of early American slavery, but there are some differences. For one thing, American slavery was based on African ethnicity and thus tainted by cruel racism, but first century slavery extended to all ethnic groups. In Paul's day people were slaves because they were conquered during a war, or they were driven by indebtedness to sell themselves into slavery, or were born to enslaved parents.[384] But even if first century slavery was generally kinder than early American slavery, it's still a shame for anyone to be regarded as the property of someone else.

The word for slave in this verse is *doulos*, a term found 118 times in the NT. "For the Greek in the classical tradition it was well-nigh impossible to use a word of the *doulos* group without some feeling of abhorrence," says Cranfield,[385] and it appears that many Bible translations feel the same way. Whenever possible, many Bibles prefer to translate *doulos* as servant (even though a separate Greek word for servant already exists). It sounds much nicer to us to be called a servant of God than a slave of God (see Acts 2:18 for one of many examples), but I'd rather go for accuracy even if it may sound harsh to us. In a world where public "servants" are often caught only serving themselves, it might be good for all believers to regard themselves as the slaves of God, and not merely his servants. We are not our own, but belong to the Lord.

For his part, Paul is not afraid to speak of slavery. In fact, he calls Jesus a slave in Phil 2:7 (which is also often hidden by English translations). Nor is Paul afraid to speak directly to the slaves—an act that in itself bestows dignity on them. They are not farm tools, beasts of burden, or witless numbskulls; rather, they are responsible members of the body of Christ addressed with the word of God.[386]

Probably the closest most of us get to the slave/master relationship is the employee/employer relationship. The importance of obedience, hard work, and serving the Lord applies to our workplace as well, but we should never forget that it is truly a blessing if we are a slave only to the Lord and not to some earthly master.

Master of all things, I pray that you would set free all those who live in slavery on this day.

²² *Slaves,* **obey in all things [your] lords according to the flesh,** *not by way of "only-when-watched service," as people-pleasers, but in sincerity of heart, fearing the Lord.*

We can't avoid the fact that slaves not only belong to the Lord, but also to another human being. In English, we refer to the owner of a slave as the master. But the Greek word for master is the exact same word translated as "Lord" (*kurios*). The master of a slave is his lord. Bible versions avoid this translation partly because it seems to exalt the slave-owner and besmirch Jesus. By translating *kurios* as "master," however, we might be missing the force of Paul's point. In this paragraph, he seems to be purposely contrasting earthly lords with the Lord Jesus.

We obey earthly lords, not because we fear them, but because of our reverent fear of the Lord Jesus (verse 22). When we work hard, we're not working hard for any earthly lord, but for the Lord Jesus (verse 23). Nor are we working to be rewarded by any earthly lord, but by the Lord Jesus (verse 24). When it comes right down to it, we are not slaving away for any earthly lord at all, but rather for the Lord Jesus (verse 24). The earthly lords nearly become a non-factor for the slave, for all attention is focused on Jesus. If you were a "lord" listening in on these words, you would either be offended that your own concerns as a lord of the slaves was so thoroughly overlooked, or you would be embarrassed to have the same title applied to you that more properly belongs to Jesus. You would realize that you are only a lord "according to the flesh," which is not only an indication of being in a body, but is often an indication of weakness and sin as well.

The slaves are to relate to their lords by obeying them in all things, just as the children were to obey their parents in Col 3:20. Paul is asking them to continue on in a difficult thing, for in his day (as well as ours) having to obey another person—especially with regards to manual labor—was seen as a great humiliation. According to Hay, "Greco-Roman culture tended to regard it as improper for free men to take orders from anyone except their fathers or military commanders and also to regard work, especially manual work, as 'not fitting' for citizens."[387] Cicero said sellers, butchers, cooks, craftsmen and manual laborers did detestable work (*De Officiis* 1.150).

One of the more difficult aspects of obedience for slaves was if their master wanted to sexually abuse them (which unfortunately, was a common problem). It's unclear how Paul would advise them.

Lord, we especially pray on this day for those today who are being trafficked as sex slaves. May their "masters" repent and submit to your lordship.

*[22] Slaves, obey in all things [your] lords according to the flesh, **not by way of "only-when-watched service," as people-pleasers,** but in sincerity of heart, fearing the Lord.*

Here Paul spells out how slaves are to obey their masters by first pointing out what attitudes to avoid, and then indicating what attitudes to embrace.

Paul knows that some of the work we do for others is only done in a way calculated to stay on another person's good side. We are not really concerned about them or the work. We're only concerned about ourselves and how we are perceived. If we can manipulate another person into being pleased with us, even if we didn't care about them or the work, that's sufficient for us. This occurs in many workplaces today and also happened in ancient households. Slaves might excel at manipulation, so that even if they were not good workers, they could make it appear as if they were.

Paul describes this kind of work with the colorful term *ophthalmodoulia*, which literally means eye-slavery. Since this and Eph 6:6 are the first written uses of this term, either Paul coined the term or it was a popular slang word. This word likely means "service done in order to be seen," with the implication that once the master is no longer watching, then the slaves are no longer working. But even if slaves can fool their earthly lords into only seeing them hard at work, the one true Lord sees all things (Heb 4:13).

Along these same lines Paul describes manipulative slaves as people-pleasers—a quality that Paul himself wants to avoid (Gal 1:10; 1 Thess 2:4). Paul is aware, however, of a good kind of people-pleasing in which we try not to give undue offense when proclaiming the gospel. God's message is scandalous enough as it is; there is no need to unnecessarily add to the scandal by aggravating people. So he says in 1 Cor 10:33, "I try to please everyone in everything I do, not seeking my own advantage, but that of many, that they may be saved" (NRSV). What keeps Paul's attitude from becoming the bad sort of people-pleasing is his line about not seeking his own advantage, but that of others. People-pleasing could be good if it were genuinely done for the sake of others, instead of merely to manipulate others for selfish gain. If a servant genuinely wanted to please his master, that would not be what Paul warns against here. Rather, he forbids the kind of people-pleasing that is only a cover for pleasing oneself.

I confess, Lord, that instead of loving and serving others, I spend too much energy merely managing how I am being perceived by them.

²² *Slaves, obey in all things [your] lords according to the flesh, not by way of "only-when-watched service," as people-pleasers, **but in sincerity of heart, fearing the Lord.***

On the positive side, Paul urges slaves to obey with sincerity of heart. Those who act with sincerity have no underhanded motivation for their interactions with others, but instead their heart is an open book.

For instance, while some might have thought the guests at Absalom's party were in on a conspiracy to acclaim him as king, the Greek version of 2 Sam 15:11 says they attended with sincere hearts. And while some might have thought Daniel was trying to advance himself with King Darius, he was delivered from the lions because of his sincerity (1 Mac 2:60).

In the NT Paul tells those who suspect his motives that he preaches the gospel with sincerity (2 Cor 1:12), and he prays that we'd all do the same (2 Cor 11:3). Col 3:22 (echoed by Eph 6:5) calls on slaves to have the same sincerity toward their earthly lords as they do toward their heavenly Lord. Rather than working under false pretenses, with underhanded motives (such as becoming the master's favorite or as a cover for some wrongdoing), they are to do their work in a generous and open way.

Slaves do this because they fear the Lord, the very Lord who knows all and sees all. Although the notion of fearing God or fearing the Lord is very common in the Greek OT (well over 180 references), it's not nearly as common in the NT. Perhaps the NT does not focus on fear because the cross of Jesus gives believers confidence to come boldly before God's throne (Heb 4:16; 10:19-22). Thus, for the Christian, "there is no fear in love, but perfect love drives out fear" (1 Jn 4:18, NIV), "for God gave us a spirit not of fear but of power and love and self-control" (2 Tim 1:7, ESV).

Yet even though the fear of the Lord is not highlighted in the NT, it is still present, as is the case in Col 3:22. Slaves are to do the right thing—not because they fear their earthly masters or the consequences of getting caught—but because of their awe-filled respect for the Lord Jesus. Just as 1 Sam 12:24 (NETS) calls on God's people to "fear [*phobeō*] the Lord and be subject [*douleuō*, to work as a slave] to him," so in Colossae the slaves (*doulos*) are also called to fear (*phobeō*) the Lord by serving him.

And this call to fear the Lord is not just for the slaves. In Lev 25:43 the *masters* are also reminded to fear the Lord by not mistreating their slaves.

Holy Lord, I'm glad I don't have to be scared of you, but I do pray to be taught to fear you with the respect and awe you deserve.

²³ In whatever you do, work from the soul, as for the Lord and not for men, ²⁴ knowing that from the Lord you will receive the reward of the inheritance. Slave for the Lord Christ, ²⁵ for the one doing wrong will receive-back what he did wrong—and there is no partiality.

Earlier, in Col 3:17, Paul said "in all of whatever you do...[do] all things in the name of the Lord Jesus." Here he uses similar words ("whatever you do") to call on slaves to apply that command to their situation. As Sumney says, "In some ways, slaves thus become the paradigm for all who do 'everything in the name of the Lord Jesus.'"³⁸⁸ Although we might think of legitimate exceptions to this, our focus should not be on these loopholes. It's all too easy for the sinful heart to let exceptions and excuses multiply. Rather, Christian slaves are called upon to be consistent in working hard for their masters, not just when the task is enjoyable, but in all things.

But not just any work ethic will do, for the slaves are to "work from the soul." Different translations capture this idea with phrases like "work heartily" (ESV), "put yourselves into it" (NRSV), and "work at it with all your heart" (NIV). This phrase encourages a willing spirit, rather than a begrudging one. This is not the only biblical text about doing an action "from the soul." God's people are also commanded to love God from the soul (Dt 6:5), as well as to seek God (Dt 4:29), obey God (Dt 26:16). turn to God (Dt 30:10), and serve God (Dt 10:12)—all from the soul. Slaves work from the soul not because they really like their master or they find the work so meaningful. Rather, they work from the soul because they are doing it for the Lord (which is the point of the rest of this verse).

According to the last phrase of this verse, slaves (and actually all Christians) are to work "as for the Lord and not for men." Paul is not saying we should work "as if" for the Lord, imagining how we'd behave *if* our master were Jesus and then acting as if this imaginary scene were real. No, for Paul, this scenario *is* real. The one we truly work for *is* the Lord Jesus. Our earthly masters and employers may think we're working for them, but our sights are set elsewhere: on the Lord who is above (see Col 3:1-2)

This perspective radically affects how anyone—slave or free—approaches their workday. Because Jesus is Lord, the earthly lords and employers lose their domination of our lives and fade from view. It is to the Lord Jesus that we devote our work.

Lord Jesus, I dedicate my work to you. In fact, I'm happy to be employed and used by you for your kingdom work.

²³ *In whatever you do, work from the soul, as for the Lord and not for men,* **²⁴ knowing that from the Lord you will receive the reward of the inheritance.** *Slave for the Lord Christ,* ²⁵ *for the one doing wrong will receive-back what he did wrong—and there is no partiality.*

Workers are usually motivated by two things, says Wall: "either we enjoy a good working relationship with the boss or company, or we expect to derive some personal benefit from our work."[389] The previous verse spoke to the first motivator. This verse speaks to the second motivator. While earthly masters might motivate with praise, food, or better clothing (see Xenophon *Oeconomicus* 13.9-12), Jesus offers a far better motivation for his slaves: an eternal inheritance.

One of the disheartening things about being a slave is that even though the basic needs for food and shelter were provided (and some received a stipend), slaves did not really receive a living wage, nor was there much hope of receiving an inheritance in the future. In fact, slaves were not normally allowed to inherit property.[390] As Walsh and Keesmaat put it, slaves were "more likely to *be* part of an inheritance than to receive one," for Lev 25:44-46 says that non-Jewish slaves could be inherited by one's sons.[391] The slaves of the Lord Jesus, however, do receive an inheritance.

Paul talked earlier about the Christian's inheritance when he prayed for the Colossians to be "giving-thanks to the Father for qualifying you for a share of the inheritance of the holy-ones in the light" (Col 1:12). Just as the Promised Land was the inheritance of the liberated Hebrew slaves (Dt 4:37-38), so the kingdom of God is the inheritance of all the slaves who have been liberated by Christ and will be liberated even more in the future. The one who has *received* Christ (Col 2:6) will also *receive* an inheritance.

It is helpful for the slaves to be "knowing" this, says Paul. Without the knowledge of this future hope, the drudgery of daily labor might cause a believing slave to give up in despair. But with the knowledge of such hope, slaves can be more than conquerors.

While this inheritance is called a reward, it's not a *deserved* reward, but one that comes purely by grace (Luke 17:7-10).[392] The only one able to earn the inheritance is Jesus,[393] and now he shares it freely with all of his slaves as a gift of grace.

Though I may complain, Lord, about the earthly compensation for my work, I must confess that I have and will receive from you far more than I deserve.

²³ *In whatever you do, work from the soul, as for the Lord and not for men,* ²⁴ *knowing that from the Lord you will receive the reward of the inheritance.* **Slave for the Lord Christ,** ²⁵ *for the one doing wrong will receive-back what he did wrong—and there is no partiality.*

Most Bibles translate this as a statement using the verb "serve," as, for example in the ESV, "You are serving the Lord Christ." Most commentators, however, believe it should be translated as a command instead,[394] in which case Paul is forming a chain of three commands for slaves: obey in all things (verse 22); work from the soul (verse 23); slave for the Lord Christ (verse 24).

The verb here translated as "slave" is *douleuō*, corresponding to the noun "slave" (*doulos*) used in Col 3:22. Even though "slave" is not often used as a verb in English (except in the verbal phrase "slave away," which usually implies some resentment), it's a much stronger translation than "serve."

The majority of OT verses using *douleuō* refer to serving (or slaving for) God, serving *other* gods, or *not* serving God at all. NT uses of this verb reveal the same God-ward focus of serving: people either serve the Lord (Acts 20:19; Rom 7:6; 14:18; 1 Thess 1:9) *or* they serve non-gods, like sin, their own appetites, and wrongful pleasures (Rom 6:6; 16:18; Gal 4:8-9; Titus 3:3). This choice between the true God and the false gods was highlighted by Jesus who said that no one can be a slave of two masters (Mt 6:24).

Those of us who highly value freedom from any constraints might be offended by the thought of being slaves of Christ, but for Paul, real freedom does not mean doing whatever you want, but being set free from bondage to sin and death.[395] It is only as slaves of Christ that we are truly set free.

Slavery to Christ actually increases our status. All slaves in Paul's day knew that their status was determined, not by their own biological family, but by who their master was.[396] Said Sumney, "If slaves in the emperor's household often wielded considerable power and commanded deference because of who their owner was, slaves of the true ruler of the entire cosmos must enjoy even higher status."[397]

So, in contrast to those slaves who "do not serve [*douleuō*] our Lord Christ, but their own appetites," (Rom 16:18, NRSV), Christian slaves—and that means all of us—have been given the commands of Rom 12:11, "Do not be slothful in zeal, be fervent in spirit, serve [*douleuō*] the Lord" (ESV).

I'd rather not think of myself as a slave, Lord, but I am one. I have to serve somebody, in which case, I know it's far better to be your slave. Bind my heart to yours.

*²³ In whatever you do, work from the soul, as for the Lord and not for men, ²⁴ knowing that from the Lord you will receive the reward of the inheritance. Slave for the Lord Christ, ²⁵ **for the one doing wrong will receive-back what he did wrong**—and there is no partiality.*

As verse 24 mentioned, we are motivated to serve the Lord in part by the prospect of a good payback, a reward. But we are also motivated to serve the Lord by the prospect of a negative payback for failing to do so.

Even though we rightly focus on how slaves have been sinned against, this does not give them a free pass to sin. Just because they are victims does not mean they are allowed to get away with wickedness. Slaves have not only been wronged, but they are also capable of doing wrong themselves.

Paul does not specify what some of these wrongs might be, but slaves were not immune to the sins he listed earlier in this chapter: sexual immorality, covetousness, idolatry, anger, malice, obscene talk, and lying (Col 3:5-9). Watson noted that "the individual slave is frequently in a good position to provide the master with a poor return on his investment, to cheat him, rob him, damage his property, or make him liable to others for property damage, to make disastrous contracts for him, to give damaging reports of him, to exploit him sexually, and even to assault or kill him."[398] Paul calls on Christian slaves, however, to turn from the wrong in order to avoid negative payback for any sins they commit.

Many people today are uncomfortable with Paul here, for they believe the quality of our moral behavior is tainted if we are motivated by either reward or punishment. The Bible, however, would not agree with that. Those who weigh consequences are simply being wise, understanding how life works in God's world. Those who think they are doing the right thing with no regard for reward or punishment are fooling themselves. Possible reward or punishment is always part of the mix in how we make decisions. If it's the *only* criterion for our decision-making, then, yes, our morality would be flawed. Then we'd only be operating as moral mercenaries (only doing the right thing if we're paid) or moral cowards (avoiding the wrong thing only to stay out of trouble). But surely, rewards and punishments are important to consider, which is why Paul brings it to the attention of Christian slaves.

Lord, I'd like to think that I am not at all motivated by the prospects of reward or punishment, but it's not so. Whatever mixed motives I might have, I pray that I would continue to walk in your way.

²³ In whatever you do, work from the soul, as for the Lord and not for men,
²⁴ knowing that from the Lord you will receive the reward of the
inheritance. Slave for the Lord Christ, ²⁵ for the one doing wrong will
*receive-back what he did wrong—**and there is no partiality.***

Lest slaves think that their sins should be excused because they are victims of slavery, Paul reminds them here that there is no partiality (*prosōpolēmp-sia*) on God's part. This is a compound word formed from *prosōpon* (meaning "face") and *lambanō* (meaning "to receive"). Partiality happens when we show a receptive face to some and not to others.

The OT frequently calls on *human* judges to be impartial (see Ex 23:2-3; Lev 19:15; Dt 1:17; 16:19; 2 Chron 19:7; Job 32:21; 34:19; Ps 82:2; Prov 18:5; 24:23; 28:21; Mal 2:9). But Dt 10:17 also highlights *God's* impartiality: "For the LORD your God is God of gods and Lord of lords, the great GOD, the mighty and awesome, who is not partial and takes no bribe" (NRSV).

In the NT James follows the OT's focus on the problem of *human* partiality (Jms 2:1, 9). Peter, however, highlights God's impartiality in Acts 10:34, which he takes to mean that God grants salvation to all kinds of people, not just the Jews. When Paul talks about impartiality, however, as he does here and in Rom 2:11, he is not thinking of how God impartially *saves* both Jews and non-Jews. Rather, he focuses on how God impartially *judges* both Jews and non-Jews.

The Bible recognizes how partiality can cut in both directions. In the matter of justice, some want to give more leeway to the rich and powerful, while others show a preference for the poor and weak. Although God is clearly concerned for the poor and weak (which is James' special concern), yet the poor and weak will also be held accountable for sin. The OT clearly states "Do not show partiality to the poor or favoritism to the great" (Lev 19:15, NIV). Paul says the same to those who are slaves. God will show no favoritism toward a sinner just because they happen to be a slave. One's condition in life, as unjust as it might be, provides no excuse for sin.

We should not think Paul is being too harsh on slaves here, for in Eph 6:9 Paul will point out that the slave owners will also come under God's same impartial judgment. So, whether a person has social power or lacks it, there is no excuse for sin.

Lord, do not let me excuse my sins by somehow thinking I'll get preferential treatment on judgment day. There is no condemnation in Christ, but neither is there any favoritism.

4:1 **Lords,** *give justice and equal-treatment to [your] slaves, knowing that you also have a Lord in heaven.*

After his extended words to slaves, Paul returns to form when addressing the masters by keeping his remarks brief. Perhaps Paul has fewer words for masters because this is actually the third time the same group of men have been addressed, for the slave owners were probably also husbands and fathers.[399] What's most notable here, however, is how Paul says nothing of helping masters be more efficient in running their slaves. Rather, as Garland says, "he is concerned to enhance the mutual solidarity between slaves and masters."[400]

Paul addresses these masters as "lords." This verse is one of the few times in the Bible in which "lord" is written in the plural. Sometimes spiritual powers are called lords: "for although there may be so-called gods in heaven or on earth—as indeed there are many 'gods' and many 'lords'" (1 Cor 8:5). In other verses, political rulers are called "lords" (Isa 19:4; Jer 27:4; 1 Mac 9:25). Those who rule over a household or have a lot of clout might also be called lords (Amos 4:1; Mt 15:27). Owning something might also make a person a lord of that object (Tobit 2:12-14; Lk 19:33). Finally, those who own slaves are also designated as lords (Ps 123:2), as is the case here in Col 3:22 and 4:1, as well as in Paul's parallel discussion of slaves and masters in Eph 6:5, 9.

As mentioned earlier, Paul might refer to them as "lords" because that is the title used in his culture, but it also highlights the contrast between these slave owners and the Lord Jesus. While some made the case that slave owners should be called lords because they are to have the same honor, dignity and authority as the heavenly Lord, this title actually exposes how unlordly they really are. These lords are not at all on the same level as the heavenly Lord. Rather, they are inferior lords, who must submit to the one true Lord. That's the reason both testaments call God the "Lord of lords." Dt 10:17 declares, "For the LORD your God is God of gods and Lord of lords, the great, the mighty, and the awesome God, who is not partial and takes no bribe" (ESV; notice the same theme of impartiality shows up here too). This same title of Lord of lords is also given to Jesus in Rev 17:14 and 19:16.

Since no one can serve two lords (the more literal meaning of Mt 6:24), this means that earthly lords must always defer to Jesus the Lord.

Lord Jesus, whenever I am put in charge of something or someone, remind me again and again that you are Lord of lords.

4:1 Lords, **give justice** and equal-treatment to [your] slaves, knowing that you also have a Lord in heaven.

As the Lord of lords, Jesus has the authority to call on these "lords of the flesh" to give an account. Just as God rebuked the "gods" for their injustices toward the weak and the needy in Psalm 82, so here the Lord warns these "lords" to give justice to the slaves who are in a subordinate position.

Notice that Paul does not call on these "lords" to show *mercy* to their slaves; rather he calls on them to give *justice* to them. If Paul had asked the masters to show mercy, that would imply the slaves don't deserve anything, and that masters can be congratulated for going above and beyond what's expected. But by calling on them to act justly, Paul highlights the rights of slaves to be treated with justice.[401] Instead of thinking about the *rights* which masters have *over* their slaves, Christian masters were to consider instead the *obligations* they had *to* their slaves.[402]

Some ancient philosophers, like Aristotle, did not believe justice applied to the institution of slavery. Aristotle said about slaves, "There can be no friendship, nor justice, towards inanimate things...nor yet towards a slave as slave. For master and slave have nothing in common: a slave is a living tool, just as a tool is an inanimate slave" (*Nichomachean Ethics* 8.11.6-7). Likewise, the Greek historian Xenophon believed that it was proper to starve, fetter, and beat slaves, concluding, "I make their lives a burden to them until I reduce them to submission" (*Memorabilia* 2.1.16-17). The philosopher Plato, however, said that "proper treatment of servants consists in using no violence towards them, and in hurting them even less, if possible, than our own equals" (*Laws* 7.777D-E.).

The word "justice" here is a word rich in meaning in the Bible, but it is especially about justice for those who have no power (see Ps 140:12 for one of many examples). In our day "righteousness" and "justice" have quite distinct connotations. Says Marshall, "'Righteousness' carries the sense of personal ethical purity and religious piety...while 'justice' relates to public judicial fairness and equality of rights."[403] But righteousness and justice belong together in the Bible—and in this text—because they are the same Greek word. Only the oddity of the English language has separated them.

Paul is asking the Colossian slave owners to do the same for their slaves as God does for his (see Ps 119:135, 137). It is not just the slaves who must act justly; doing justice is even more the responsibility of the master.

Lord, forgive us for focusing on personal righteousness to the neglect of social justice, or vice versa. We pray for both to happen in our lives and in our world.

> [4:1] *Lords, give justice **and equal-treatment to [your] slaves,** knowing that you also have a Lord in heaven.*

"Equal-treatment" is the noun *isotēs*, which is often translated as "fairness" or "fairly." Some, however, contend that the translation "fairness" hides Paul's radical message, and so regard "equality" as a better translation.

According to Sumney, "This is one of the clearest places where this table of [household] instructions intentionally signals opposition to the system it seems to support," for "if masters and slaves are equals, there can be no justification for slavery."[404] In *Every Good Man is Free* (79), the Jewish philosopher Philo agreed, for he admired the Essenes who denounced slave owners for "their injustice in outraging the law of equality." In his book *The Special Laws,* Philo calls this equality "the mother of justice" (4.231), for "all that goes amiss in our life is the work of inequality, and all that keeps its due order is of equality" (4.237). But even apart from abolishing slavery outright, Philo believed progress toward equality can be made in other ways: when masters show gentleness and kindness to their slaves, then "inequality is equalized" (*The Decalogue* 167).

Perhaps Paul is encouraging the same moves. While we might be appalled that Paul doesn't reject slavery outright, it's actually astounding that he speaks of equality as something slaves should experience.

Isotēs is not a common word in the Bible. In the Greek OT (not the Hebrew or English OT) it describes the equal proportions of God's pavilion (Job 36:29), the future hope of an equality of grace (Zech 4:7), and the actions of the coming Messiah who "shall lead all of them in equity [*isotēs*], and there shall be no arrogance among them, that any one of them should be oppressed" (Sol 17:41, NETS). The only other use of *isotēs* in the NT is 2 Cor 8:13-14, where Paul says that Christians who have more can share with those who have less, but someday the circumstances may be reversed so that it will all come out equally.

Although Paul does not say so here, *Christian* masters should especially recognize their equality with their *Christian* slaves, for they are equal brothers (or siblings) in God's family. Lev 25:43 warned any Jew who had a fellow Jewish kinsman as a slave, "You shall not rule over him with harshness, but shall fear your God"(NRSV). Paul would issue this same warning to Christian masters in how they treat their kinsmen in the faith.

Lord, I pray for the day when all people will treat one another as equals instead of some assuming superiority over others based on race, nationality, social status, language, or gender.

[4:1] *Lords, give justice and equal-treatment to [your] slaves, **knowing that you also have a Lord in heaven.***

Another reason Christian "lords" should give justice and equal-treatment to their slaves is that they are both fellow-slaves who have to answer to a Lord.

The Roman orator Seneca said something similar, but with a very different meaning. He reminded masters that the slaves are actually "our fellow-slaves, if one reflects that Fortune has equal rights over slaves and free man alike." But while Seneca regards all people as slaves to the whims of Fortune (which doesn't care about us at all), Paul proclaims that all believers are slaves of Christ, who treats us all with justice, love, mercy and respect. Jesus is the Lord *in heaven* (see Col 3:1), a location that doesn't mean Jesus is a distant Master, but a supreme Master.[405]

This may have been a comforting thought to slaves, but it would sound more threatening to masters.[406] With these words, Paul is saying that masters are not really the masters of their slaves, nor even the masters of their own fate. They too are the slaves of Christ, and thus everything said to the slaves in Col 3:22-25 somehow applies to them as well:

Like slaves, master are also required to obey the Lord in everything including acting with justice and equal-treatment (verse 22a). Masters (like slaves) are commanded to obey the Lord at all times, and not just when they think he's looking, for God is always watching (verse 22b). When masters do their Heavenly Lord's bidding of showing justice and equal-treatment, they should (like the slaves) do it from their soul instead of grudgingly (verse 23). And if masters give justice and equal-treatment to others, then they (like the slaves) will be rewarded; but also (like the slaves) there will be a bad payback if they fail to treat their slaves justly (verses 24-25).

The Master of these masters is the Lord and he will show them no partiality, even though society currently grants them power. It is only right that these "lords" would deal rightly and justly with their slaves because, as Paul said in Rom 6:16, 19, all believers are slaves of the Lord and thus "slaves to righteousness leading to sanctification." If these masters fail to act justly, they are failing as slaves of Christ and showing themselves to be nothing but slaves of sin.

These same words apply to all of us who find ourselves in positions of authority over others, whether in the workplace, the home, or the church.

I recognize, O Lord, that you are King of kings and Lord of lords, and that you are my Lord, even when I am exercising authority.

Read Colossians 3:18-4:1 again.

Even though Paul told us not to be conformed to the world in Rom 12:1, some might wonder if his household-instructions only succeeded in con- forming to the power arrangements of typical first century families. Would anything really change if a family of unbelievers was converted? The wife would still be submitting, the children and slaves would still be obeying, and the most powerful figure in the home (the husband-father-master) would be getting his way, although perhaps in a nicer manner.

But according to Paul, real change has happened: Jesus has entered — even intruded—into the household as Lord (notice how often "the Lord" is mentioned in this section). The most powerful figure in the home is no longer the husband-father-master, but the One who exercises power through the weakness of the cross. And this new Lord of the home is also dwelling within each Christian member of the house.

Wives, children, and slaves no longer submit or obey because they have no choice in a hierarchical society. Now they do so because the Lord is in them and they in the Lord. The wives are not pushing to get their way, but are taking up the cross of submission. The children obey because this pleases God. The slaves obey because they look beyond their earthly lord and answer to their true Lord. And the husband-father-master realizes that his power has been diminished, even supplanted, by the Lord, and whatever power he has left is not there for him to dominate others. Rather, he lives by the power of Jesus' cross, a power that works to love his wife sacrificially, to build up his children (rather than tear them down), and to treat his slaves with justice and equality because he too is a slave—a slave of Christ.

Some of us might be offended by our perception of patriarchalism in this text, but perhaps what really offends us is the cross-shaped living it proclaims.[407] Maybe at first it appears as if nothing has changed when the Lord Jesus enters a household—which may be partly what Paul means in Col 3:3 that "your life is hidden with Christ in God."[408] But on the inside, everything has changed, and eventually the inner working of the crucified Lord cannot help but revolutionize the home (and thus even society). It will not be a revolution in which the former oppressor (the husband-father- master) gets put down, only to have new oppressors rise up in his place. Rather, it will be a revolution that changes the family because it changes the hearts of one and all.

Lord, rule my family so that all of us live out your cross-shaped way of
exercising power.

Come, Holy Lord, Into Our Families
to the tune of Langran: *Here, O My Lord, I See Thee Face to Face*
© 2014 David J. Landegent

Come, Holy Lord, into our families;
Fill every spouse with sacrificial grace.
Love and submission bring serenity;
Let every bitter quarrel be displaced.

Lord, send Your Spirit into every child
That they would heed the parents' discipline.
May every conflict soon be reconciled,
So that our homes reflect Your love within.

When family members go to work or school,
Let them see You in every person's face.
May all their work be done as done for You,
Dealing with others justly and with grace.

Commands for life in the world

Colossians 4:2-6

November 28-December 14

*² As for prayer—attend to it, being-watchful in it with thanksgiving, ³
praying at the same time even for us in order that God would open for us a
door for the word, to speak the mystery of Christ for which I have been
bound, ⁴ in order that I may reveal it as is necessary for me to speak. ⁵ Walk
in wisdom before those "outside," snapping up the time. ⁶ Let your word
always [be spoken] in grace, being seasoned with salt, [so as] to know how
it is necessary for you to respond to each one.*

Since Col 3:5, Paul has been using commands to show the Colossian believers what it looks like to live in Christ in the church (Col 3:5-17) and the home (Col 3:18-4:1). But there is yet another sphere in which their life in Christ will have a great impact, namely, in the world of unbelievers. Actually, it's not a great leap to move from the household to the world, for a household in Paul's day was the doorway for engagement with the world. Often the family's home was the location of the family business.

Although there have been many parallels between Ephesians and Colossians, here there is an interesting contrast. In both letters, the household-instructions (Eph 5:21-6:9; Col 3:18-4:1) are immediately followed by commands for believers concerning their relationship to the world and calls for prayer (Eph 6:10-20; Col 4:2-6). Yet the tone is very different. Ephesians conveys a sense of over-against-ness, calling us to pray because we are under threat from a world dominated by spiritual forces of evil (Eph 6:10-20). And it's because the days are evil that we are to redeem the time and walk in wisdom (Eph 5:15-16).

Colossians, however, has a more world-embracing perspective. Instead of putting on armor to close up points of vulnerability (as in Ephesians), the prayer of Col 4:3 is for doors of ministry to be opened. Similarly, the primary need for walking wisely in this world is not to avoid its wickedness, but to convey open graciousness in our conversations with unbelievers.

Modern readers may have their preferences about being more open or closed to the world, and those preferences will be influenced by our personalities, experiences, and cultures. But there is no need to choose between the two. Both are appropriate stances to adopt. We can only guess why Paul's tone differs between the two letters. But one thing is clear: Paul calls us to be cautious of the world's harmful influence on our lives and also openly eager to let the light of the gospel shine forth in that world.

*Protect me, Lord, from the harmful influences of the world, but do not protect
the world from the good influence of your gospel.*

> [2] **As for prayer—attend to it,** *being-watchful in it with thanksgiving*

Prayer was often highlighted by Paul in the opening and closing of his letters to the churches. In the opening, he would report that he was praying for the recipients (see Rom 1:9-10; Eph 1:15-23; 1 Thess 1:2-3), and toward the end he would ask them to pray for him (see Rom 15:30-32; Eph 6:18-20; 1 Thess 5:25; 2 Thess 3:1-2). He follows this same pattern here in Colossians (see Col 1:9-10 and 4:2-3).

Because Paul was a praying man, he was often urging the churches to join him in prayer, which could be regarded as both a ministry and privilege. Here he issues the call to "attend" to prayer (wording that is repeated in Rom 12:12). Attending to prayer includes both the idea of attending to the activity of prayer and attending to the person being prayed to. If we only attend to the activity of prayer, but not the God to whom we pray, prayer quickly becomes a meaningless habit. But prayer remains alive when the focus of prayer is not so much on the activity of it, but on the Lord to whom the prayers are directed.

This, of course, is one of many verses in which Paul encourages—and even commands—Christians to pray (see also Rom 12:12; Phil 4:6; Eph 6:18; 1 Thess 5:17; 1 Tim 2:1, 8). Some might think being commanded to pray is as odd as being commanded to love. Shouldn't prayer be a heartfelt desire to communicate with the God of love? Yes, but just as our love for others is weak enough that we need reminders to do it, so our love for God is weak enough that we need reminders to pray. As Longenecker said, "Prayer is viewed as both an inward response of devotion *and* an outward act of obedience—that is, a reflection of individual spontaneity *and* an ordinance of community tradition."[409]

Because of busyness, weariness, the frustration of thinking it's not helping matters, or other reasons, people frequently neglect prayer. But prayer is vital for the work of God in our lives and in our world, and so Paul reminds us to keep at it. In the further words of Longenecker, prayer is not "something initiated by humans in order to awaken a sleeping or reluctant deity. Nor is it to be understood as negotiating or bargaining with God. Rather, it is always an acknowledgement of dependence on God, a response to what God has done in both creation and redemption, and a declaration of God's goodness in inviting people to present their praise and petitions before him."[410]

Lord, I confess that I have been less than attentive to prayer. Stir me by this command to communicate with you.

² *As for prayer—attend to it, **being-watchful in it** with thanksgiving*

Persistently attending to prayer means "being-watchful" (*grēgoreuō*) in it. To keep watch here means to stay awake, vigilant, and alert. In other words, *attending to* prayer means being *attentive in* prayer.

Jesus tells a number of parables which emphasize the need for his followers to be watchful and awake because the Lord may return unexpectedly like a thief in the night, or a master returning home at an unknown hour (Mt 24:42-43; 25:13; Mk 13:34-35, 37; Lk 12:37). The book of Revelation calls on believers to "wake up [*grēgoreuō*]...If you will not wake up [*grēgoreuō*], I will come like a thief, and you will not know at what hour I will come against you" (Rev 3:2-3, ESV; see also Rev 16:15).

The need to stand watch against temptation is also found in Peter's call to "be watchful. Your adversary the devil prowls around like a roaring lion, seeking someone to devour" (1 Pet 5:8, ESV). In Acts 20:30-31 Paul tells the Ephesian elders to be alert (*grēgoreuō*) for false teachers who are luring believers away from the truth. Paul himself calls on believers to "be watchful, stand firm in the faith, act like men, be strong" (1 Cor 16:13, ESV) and urges them, "let us not fall sleep as others do, but let us keep awake [*grēgoreuō*] and be sober" (1 Thess 5:6, NRSV).

Jesus also spoke of staying awake and watchful on both a physical and spiritual level when he told his sleepy disciples in Gethsemane, "Stay awake [*grēgoreuō*] and pray that you may not come into the time of trial; the spirit indeed is willing, but the flesh is weak" (Mt 26:41, NRSV).

As in the Gethsemane verses, being watchful and being prayerful go hand in hand in Col 4:2. Believers do not watch merely to analyze or critique. They do not watch in order to be suspicious or cautious. They watch in order to pray; they are attentive in order to attend to prayer. And their prayers are shaped by what they see. Unlike the Colossian distortionists who only had eyes for heavenly worship (Col 2:18), Paul wants us to have eyes open to what is going on in the culture around us and the lost people in need. Because we think the things above (Col 3:2), our eyes are watching for what the Lord above is doing on earth in terms of mission, and we are praying for how to participate in it. Our eyes are also open with expectancy because we know what time it is: the Day of the Lord is approaching, the light is dawning, and there's no time for complacent slumber.

Even though I close my eyes in prayer, I ask, Lord, that you would open my eyes to a world in need of that prayer.

> [2] *As for prayer—attend to it, being-watchful in it* **with thanksgiving**

If our watchfulness was merely a matter of caution and suspicion, it would be characterized by fear, for many things would then be seen as a threat. But as it is, the watchfulness of Col 4:2 is characterized by thanksgiving (*eucharistia*). We observe all the things happening around us, all the things God is doing in our midst, and our hearts overflow with prayers of thanks. There is, of course, a place for wariness in watching, as emphasized by nearly all the other NT texts about watching. But Col 4:2 reminds us that not only are the people of God to be cautiously watching for evil things lurking out there, but they are also to be gratefully watching for what God is doing.

"Prayer and thanksgiving can never be dissociated from each other in the Christian life," said F. F. Bruce.[411] Or to put Paul's perspective more positively, Knight said, "requests are made always in the context of conscious expressions of thankfulness."[412] Thus we find them often placed together in Paul's letters, usually when he is telling the churches that he is praying for them with thanksgiving (Eph 1:6; Col 1:3; 1 Thess 1:2; Philemon 4). But three times he also calls on others to follow suit: "in everything by prayer and supplication *with thanksgiving* let your requests be made known to God" (Phil 4:6, NRSV, emphasis mine); "I urge that supplications, prayers, intercessions, and *thanksgivings* be made for all people" (1 Tim 2:1, ESV, emphasis mine), and here in Col 4:2.

While "prayer" basically refers to asking God for something, "thanksgiving" is the gratitude shown to God for already having supplied many needs. Without the element of "thanksgiving," asking-prayers are in danger of turning into a whiny kind of pleading, a pesky sort of complaining, or even a shopping list of demands. Thanksgiving sets a tone of gratitude that's fitting when approaching the Almighty God with requests, and as such, it should not be turned into a technique for improving the odds of having one's prayers granted.

This is the last of six references in Colossians to thanksgiving and gratitude. If Philippians is known as Paul's letter of joy, Colossians could be thought of as his letter of thanksgiving. This emphasis on thanksgiving shows that Paul's letters are not to be interpreted as dictatorial teachings, finicky corrections of error, or moralistic sermons. Rather, his words flow from a heart filled with gratitude for the truth found in Jesus Christ.

Lord, on this day, I want to thank you for all I see you doing in my life and in my world.

[2] As for prayer—attend to it, being-watchful in it with thanksgiving, 3
praying at the same time even for us *in order that God would open for us*
a door for the word, to speak the mystery of Christ for which I have been
bound [4] in order that I may reveal it as is necessary for me to speak.

Paul highlights two basic ways the Colossians can be involved in God's mission in the world: first, by praying for Paul's wider ministry (verses 2-4) and second, by engaging in their own evangelistic conversations with people in their community (verses 5-6). This structure was summarized by Lucas as "Speaking to God about people" and "Speaking to people about God."[413]

This is not the only time a leader has asked others to pray for him. Daniel asked his companions to pray for him so that Nebuchadnezzar's dream would be revealed to him (Dan 2:17-18). Queen Esther asked the Jews to fast (and probably pray) for her before she made the dangerous move of appearing before the king (Esther 4:15-16). In Gethsemane Jesus told his disciples to watch with him while he prayed and to pray also that they would not enter temptation (Mt 26:36-46). But it is Paul who especially called on believers to pray for him (Rom 15:30-32; 2 Cor 1:11; Phil 1:19; Eph 6:18-20; 1 Thess 5:25; 2 Thess 3:1-2; Philemon 22).

Paul asks for prayer in Colossians for two basic reasons. First, prayer is a primary way for other believers to become partners with him in the ministry of the gospel. By praying for him the Colossians are cooperating and assisting him in his work.[414]

Second, Paul wants prayer because he knows his ministry is totally dependent on the power of God, and without that power those who are lost will remain lost. In and of himself, Paul knows he is a weak vessel, a jar of clay (2 Cor 4:7). What has brought people to Christ is not Paul's zeal, his willingness to sacrifice, his understanding of the gospel, or any great oratorical powers (which the Corinthians did not think he possessed anyway). Rather, people believed in Jesus through Paul's ministry only because God was at work. Paul is not a self-sufficient person, the kind who says, "I need nothing" (that was more characteristic of the church in Laodicea later on, as Jesus noted in Rev 3:17). Rather, Paul says, "Not that we are sufficient in ourselves to claim anything as coming from us, but our sufficiency is from God" (2 Cor 3:5, ESV). Paul knows he is "standing in the need of prayer."

I pray, O Lord, right now for Christian leaders that I know, that they would be
encouraged in their work and see your hand at work in their ministries.

*² As for prayer—attend to it, being-watchful in it with thanksgiving, 3
praying at the same time even for us **in order that God would open for us
a door for the word,** to speak the mystery of Christ for which I have been
bound ⁴ in order that I may reveal it as is necessary for me to speak.*

As the people pray for Paul, he especially wants them to pray for an open
door. In one sense, Paul prays for the door to be opened so *he* can go
through it ("that God would open *for us* a door..."). But in another sense, the
door is to be opened so the *word* proclaimed by Paul could go through it
("that God would open...a door *for the word*").

Paul knows that without the Lord's power, there are only walls in front
of him, both literally (for he writes from prison) and spiritually. The hardened hearts of individuals function as obstructive walls to the gospel, and so
do the closed-off attitudes of many communities, cultures, and people
groups. These walls will stand unless God miraculously creates a door of
opportunity for the good news of Christ to break through.

God is often celebrated in Scripture as a God who opens what was
closed, including wombs, ears, eyes, and mouths, but in the NT, the Lord is
especially involved in opening doors. Three times God miraculously opens
literal prison doors, so imprisoned apostles can go free (Acts 5:19; 12:10;
16:26-27). But that's not what Paul prays for here. He wants God to open a
door so others can believe in Jesus (Acts 14:27; 1 Cor 16:9; 2 Cor 2:12). Paul
seeks an open door, not because he is fearful that none will be opened, but
because he knows Jesus has promised to open doors for those who request
it: "Ask, and it will be given to you; seek, and you will find; knock, and it will
be opened to you" (Mt 7:7, ESV). He knows Jesus is the "one who opens
[doors] and no one will shut, who shuts and no one opens" (Rev 3:7, ESV).

But more than wanting to have a door for himself to go through, Paul is
especially wanting the "word" to go through the door, so that even if Paul
never leaves the jail cell, the word which he speaks can continue to move in
mighty ways. As he observes in 2 Tim 2:9, "I am suffering, bound with
chains as a criminal. But the word of God is not bound!" (ESV). God's word
does not sit still, but continues to move across the planet through the
mouths of Christ's followers. One way God answered Paul's prayers (now
seen in hindsight) was by moving Paul to write letters like this one from
prison, letters which have opened doors and hearts throughout the world
and through the centuries.

*Lord Jesus, open a door today in the heart of an unbeliever that I know, so that
your word could get through to that person.*

375

² As for prayer—attend to it, being-watchful in it with thanksgiving, 3 praying at the same time even for us in order that God would open for us a door for the word, **to speak the mystery of Christ for which I have been bound** *⁴ in order that I may reveal it as is necessary for me to speak.*

Echoing Col 1:25-27, Paul here connects the mystery of Christ with speaking. In that earlier reference, he called the gospel of Christ a formerly-concealed mystery that is now revealed to the people of God. Here Paul prays that he may have opportunity to speak (*laleō*) this mystery.

Laleō is a very common verb (over 1,400 uses in the Greek Bible). It often means nothing more significant than "to say" or "to speak." But it's not just a filler word. In at least a third of the instances of *laleō* in the NT, the focus is on speaking authoritatively and boldly as a witness or ambassador for God's message. To "speak" in these verses means far more than engaging in a spiritual conversation or giving a religious opinion.

First and foremost, it is Jesus who speaks God's kingdom truth (Lk 9:11). He speaks what he knows and has seen (Jn 3:11). Because of this, "the words that I have spoken to you are spirit and life" (Jn 6:63, NRSV). Indeed, "in these last days, [God] has spoken to us by his Son" (Heb 1:2, ESV).

But others also speak authoritatively for the Lord, including the prophets, who "spoke from God as they were carried along by the Holy Spirit (2 Pet 1:21, ESV). And after Jesus ascended to heaven, he sent his Holy Spirit to help his disciples also speak God's word boldly. "We cannot but speak of what we have seen and heard," they said (Acts 4:20, ESV). Paul too was empowered to speak the word of the Lord (Acts 16:32) "in words not taught by human wisdom but taught by the Spirit" (1 Cor 2:13, NRSV).

As great and necessary as deeds of love may be, for Paul it is the *speaking* of God's word which gives meaning to those deeds and brings kingdom-transformation to those who hear it. Any attempt to downplay the role of the spoken word of God in the mission of the church completely misses the mark. Our prayer is not for doors to open only so deeds of love could be shown—as good as that might be. Instead we pray that doors would open for God's word to be spoken. After all, Paul is not in prison because he was a kind person, but because he has *spoken* the mystery of Christ. Very few people object to Christians performing acts of kindness. What scandalizes the world, however, is when these loving deeds are accompanied—both before and after—by the spoken word of God.

Lord, send your Holy Spirit to empower me and my church to speak your word to a world that's desperate for the message.

> [2] *As for prayer—attend to it, being-watchful in it with thanksgiving, 3 praying at the same time even for us in order that God would open for us a door for the word, to speak the mystery of Christ for which I have been bound* [4] **in order that I may reveal it as is necessary for me to speak.**

The purpose of Paul's prayer request is that he might reveal the message of Christ. This is of great concern to Paul because he knows it is "necessary" (*dei*) for him to speak this message. *Dei* can also be translated with words like "must," "ought," or "should," but these words often convey a sense of a dreary moral expectation that many people regard as optional. This is seen in phrases like "I should lose a little weight," or "I ought to call my mother more often"—with the speaker having no real intention of doing so. That's why I prefer translations that refer to divine *necessity*. It is God who has laid upon Paul not merely the *opportunity* for him to be a witness of the gospel, but the *necessity* of him being a witness.

For Paul, preaching the gospel was not a mere option, a career choice, or a side-hobby. Rather, God had destined him to preach the gospel, and so it was necessary for him to do so. He could do no other. Paul may be engaged in some word play here. He may be bound or constrained (*deō*) by human captors (as he said in Col 4:3), but far more important is that he is under divine constraint or necessity (*dei*) to preach the gospel (Col 4:4).[415]

Just as it was necessary for Jesus to die and rise (Mt 16:21), so it is necessary for the world to be told of what God has done through Jesus' death and resurrection. Before God's kingdom comes in its fullness, "the gospel must [*dei*] first be preached to all nations" (Mk 13:10, NIV). When the Jewish council tried to stop their preaching, the apostles said, "We must [*dei*] obey God rather than men" (Acts 5:29, ESV). The main point of that verse is not that human commands can sometimes be disobeyed, but that God's command to preach the gospel must of necessity be obeyed.

Prior to his conversion, Paul thought it was "necessary" for him to persecute Christians (Acts 26:9), but after Jesus confronted him on the Damascus Road, he learned of other things it would be "necessary" for him to do, namely, to carry Jesus' name to the world and suffer for that name (Acts 9:6, 15-16). That's why he said in 1 Cor 9:16b, "For necessity is laid upon me. Woe to me if I do not preach the gospel!" (ESV). Since preaching is so necessary, it's also necessary that we "ought [*dei*] always to pray and not lose heart." (Lk 18:1, ESV).

I'm asking, Lord, that those who speak your word today, including myself, would do so with the urgency that such a necessary task requires.

⁵ **Walk in wisdom** *before those "outside," snapping up the time.*

Although Paul sought prayers for his own ministry of reaching the lost, he was aware that the Colossians were also responsible for some form of evangelism (besides praying for him and contributing to his work). God had placed them in their community to bring good news in word and deed to those who were not Christians, and that's the focus of Col 4:5-6.

Given that contemporary church leaders often call on us to evangelize and reach out, we might expect Paul to frequently issue the same call, but he seldom mentions it explicitly—almost as if he thinks the bulk of missional work belongs to apostles like himself and their co-workers.

It's possible that this was his perspective. The church, however, would never have grown as it did if most believers were simply passive recipients of the gospel who left the mission work to the experts. It's more likely, then, that Paul did not often mention the role of every believer in fulfilling the Great Commission because it was already happening extensively through-out the empire: "For not only has the word of the Lord sounded forth from you in Macedonia and Achaia, but your faith in God has gone forth every-where, so that we need not say anything" (1 Thess 1:8, ESV). There was lit-tle need to urge believers to do what they were already doing. Yet here Paul does instruct us on how to best be involved in God's mission.

Verse 5 begins with a brief word about the role of their conduct, more literally, their "walk." Although they had at one time walked in sinfulness (Col 3:7), Paul was praying for them to "walk worthily of the Lord" instead (Col 1:10). He even commanded them to walk in Christ (Col 2:6). Here he issues a command to walk *in wisdom*.

Paul is not talking here about acting according to their own considered judgment, but instead walking according to the wisdom found in Christ.[416] If we do not understand or follow God's wisdom, then we will inevitably stray from the trail of life which God has marked out for us. According to earlier references in this letter, wisdom is a Spirit-oriented understanding that comes about through prayer (Col 1:9). Wisdom can also be taught to believ-ers—even through worship songs (Col 3:16)—so that they can be made complete in Christ (Col 1:28). While some might vainly seek wisdom through various religious practices (Col 2:23), Christ himself is the source of all wisdom (Col 2:3). Walking in wisdom, then, puts us on the same path as walking in Christ and living out the mystery which is revealed in Christ.

Grant me wisdom, Lord, so that in my behavior and conversation I can best represent you to a lost world.

*⁵ Walk in wisdom **before those "outside,"** snapping up the time.*

What Paul emphasizes here is walking in wisdom as we rub shoulders with those who are "outside," presumably because they are watching how we conduct ourselves and drawing conclusions about Jesus from what they see. The thought is similar to 1 Pet 2:12, "Conduct yourselves honorably among the Gentiles, so that, though they malign you as evildoers, they may see your honorable deeds and glorify God when he comes to judge" (NRSV).

The whole notion of "outsiders" can be a dangerous one for believers. Focusing on the distinction between insiders and outsiders leads to unholy forms of exclusivism, which take a sick delight in ostracizing, condemning, rejecting, mocking, or even persecuting those—even other Christians—who are not like us. Yet as much as the outsider/insider mentality can be dangerous, there is no avoiding the fact that such language can be biblical.

Who is Paul regarding as an "outsider"? Obviously for Paul, no one should be regarded as an outsider because of their ethnicity or social class (Col 3:11). The more immediate context suggests that an outsider is anyone on the other side of the door that Paul is praying to be opened, someone who has not yet heard or believed the gospel of Jesus (Col 4:3).

Ultimately, Christ is the dividing line between insider and outsider. People are either in Christ or not. Insiders are holy ones and brothers and sisters in Christ (Col 1:2), while outsiders do not belong to the Lord or his family. Insiders have been relocated to the kingdom of God's Son, while outsiders are still enslaved under the authority of darkness (Col 1:13). Insiders are reconciled through Christ and remain in the faith, while outsiders remain alienated from Christ (Col 1:21). Insiders know the mystery of "Christ in you, the hope of glory" (Col 1:26-27), while outsiders do not have Christ within them, nor the hope that he grants. Insiders walk in Christ, rooted, built up, and established in him, while outsiders are captivated by human traditions and elemental-orders (Col 2:6-8). Insiders are in Christ to such an extent that they have died with him to sin and have been raised with him to new life, but outsiders are still dead in their sins (Col 2:11-14; 3:5-17). Insiders are fully alive, joined to Christ as a body to the head, while outsiders are disconnected from Christ, perhaps living in a flimsy shelter of religiosity (Col 2:16-23). Whenever the insider/outsider dynamic is found in this letter, Christ is the dividing line.

Lord, I am thankful to be "in" you and in your family, and I pray for all those who do not yet know this blessing.

⁵ *Walk in wisdom **before those "outside,"** snapping up the time.*

Some might conclude from this "outsider" talk that Christianity is just another exclusive religion fostering hatred and bigotry. But they may be overlooking the most important element of the insider/outsider dynamic, namely, that being an "outsider" is not meant to be a permanent condition. Even if many people are outside of Christ, we are not to be smugly content with that situation. Rather, we are called to invite outsiders to enter in.

Every outsider is a potential insider, a "future fellow-believer," as Barth put it,[417] and we eagerly join the Lord in working to see that happen. Some unbelievers might still be offended by this perspective because they don't think of themselves as outsiders who need to be drawn inside; that cannot be helped. Yet this perspective is far better than the insider mentality that wants to keep others out.

In the OT we see that Abraham was chosen to be God's "insider," not so he could hoard God's blessings, but so all the outsider nations of the world could be blessed through him (Gen 12:2-3). Many OT stories, for example, celebrate the "outsider" who becomes part of God's family and kingdom, including the Canaanite Rahab (Joshua 2), the Moabitess Ruth, the Syrian general Naaman (2 Kings 5), and others.[418] The psalms joyfully anticipate the day when all the "outsider" nations become "insiders" (Ps 86:9). The prophets have the same hope: "I will make you as a light for the nations, that my salvation may reach to the end of the earth" (Isa 49:6b, ESV).

When Jesus came, he was especially concerned for outsiders within the nation of Israel: the prostitutes, the tax collectors, the lepers, the prodigals, the lost sheep, the disabled, the women, the children. If people were on the outside, Jesus wanted to invite them in, even if that meant excluding those who had been on the inside before (Lk 13:28-29). And Jesus wanted this invitation extended to the whole world, which is why he charged his disciples to bring all nations into the circle of insiders (Mt 28:19-20).

Paul, of course, took this commission seriously. He affirmed in 1 Cor 9:19-23 that he must do whatever it takes to win all outsiders to Christ. He joined Jesus in preaching "peace to you who were far away and peace to those who were near" (Eph 2:17, NIV), for his aim was to "present every person complete in Christ" (Col 1:28).

Lord Jesus, protect me from exclusivist attitudes that shun those who are unlike me. And when I meet those who are outside of you, use me to draw them in.

⁵ *Walk in wisdom before those "outside," **snapping up the time.***

Time has both a quantitative aspect (seconds, minutes, hours, days, weeks, etc.) and a qualitative aspect (such as the opportune moment, the hour of decision, the day of discovery, and the momentous occasion). Here Paul focuses on the qualitative aspect, dealing with the issue of what time is for.

In this case, time is for snapping up (*exagorazō*), which is a marketplace term for buying (*agora* is Greek for marketplace). Paul twice used it in reference to Christ purchasing or redeeming people (Gal 3:13; 4:5). The other two uses of *exagorazō* are about purchasing time (here and its parallel in Eph 5:15-16, both of which also speak of walking in wisdom).

Time is not a resource under our control. Rather time belongs to *God*, who makes it available to us to obtain, purchase, and snap up. We are not snapping up extra hours, days, and years in order to extend our lifespan. Rather, we are snapping up opportune times sent by God to be used for God's purposes. This verse has very little to do with learning techniques for time management, but it has everything to do with timely obedience.

In the context of Colossians, God provides opportune times for walking wisely before outsiders as witnesses of the gospel. "Snapping up the time," then, is Paul's way of saying "Seize the day"—not for personal purposes and dreams, but for God's purposes of reaching out to a lost world.

When God makes opportune-times available to us, we must snap them up, or they'll disappear. Unlike many plastic goods that have a long shelf-life, opportune-times have a short shelf life. If we don't "buy" them at the right moment, we often will not have another chance. That's one reason we are to pray with a watchful spirit (Col 4:2), so that we will be able to see (and snatch up) the opportunities God provides. Doing general good deeds is fine, but a good deed done too late has little value, and a good deed done instead of the deed that was really needed at the moment also misses the mark. What's needed is that we act in response to God-given opportunities.

To walk wisely before others means that we will not be pushy witnesses, nor will we be overly-cautious, passing by every opportunity because we fear it's not the right time.[419] Perhaps we could learn from Clare De Graaf's *The 10-Second Rule*: when you sense Jesus calling you to do something, you should respond to it immediately, for if we give ourselves too much time to respond, we will think of excuses not to do it. Procrastination is not a friend of obedience.[420]

Lord, when an opportunity happens today for me to be a witness to your grace, help me see it and respond immediately.

*⁵ Walk in wisdom before those "outside," snapping up the time. ⁶ **Let your word always [be spoken] in grace,** being seasoned with salt, [so as] to know how it is necessary for you to respond to each one.*

Walking in wisdom before outsiders often leads to opportunities for conversation. The term "word" has already been used four times in this letter to refer to God's word (Col 1:5, 25; 3:16; 4:3). Here, however, Paul talks about "your" word, which likely refers to ordinary conversations, whether or not they contain an explicit reference to Jesus. These conversations are part of "all of whatever you do—in word or in work" that is to be done in the name of Jesus (Col 3:17).

Here Paul urges the Colossians to speak their words "in grace." Although a pleasant and courteous message and tone of voice may be a part of this (see Ps 45:2; Eccles 10:12; Lk 4:22), the goal is not to be well-liked, but to draw others to Christ.[421] So it's more likely that Paul is talking about a word that conveys the gracious love of God to others. Both the Word of God and the words spoken by Christians can convey God's grace.

When a Christian abides in Christ and is mindful of extending good news to all the world, then even in conversations about the weather, sports or politics, our words and the tone of our voice can come from a heart filled with the grace of God toward a sinful world. Since "the Word became flesh...full of grace and truth" (Jn 1:14, NRSV), then believers filled with this Word-made-flesh can also speak words full of grace and truth.

And when we speak our words "in grace," then those who hear us will experience this same grace: "Let no corrupting talk come out of your mouths, but only such as is good for building up, as fits the occasion, that it may give grace *to those who hear*" (Eph 4:29, ESV, emphasis mine). In Colossians 3 Paul has already provided a few examples of what this grace-filled language sounds like (verses 12-17) and what it does not sound like (verses 8-9). Perhaps his instruction to be "speaking the truth in love" in Eph 4:15 (NIV) best summarizes what grace-language is like.

And this grace-filled talk is not only for certain occasions or audiences. It is not only for those moments when we know the microphone is on. Grace-filled speech is to be spoken "always," says Paul. While it's possible for the tone of our voice to convey sarcasm, anger, meekness, insistence, gentleness, indifference, etc., according to Paul, no tone of voice or choice of words is appropriate if it does not convey grace.

I ask, Lord Jesus, that you would not only tame my tongue, but fill it with words of grace.

*⁵ Walk in wisdom before those "outside," snapping up the time. ⁶ Let your word always [be spoken] in grace, **being seasoned with salt,** [so as] to know how it is necessary for you to respond to each one.*

Paul describes gracious language as "seasoned with salt." In our day, salty language refers to the profanity of sailors. In Paul's day, however, salty language was more often associated with wittiness, and any boring speech was criticized as being unsalted. The Latin orator Quintilian said that the salt of wit "serves as simple seasoning of language, a condiment which is silently appreciated by our judgment, as food is appreciated by the palate, with the result that it stimulates our taste and saves a speech from becoming tedious...in the case of those who have the salt of wit there is something about their language which arouses in us a thirst to hear" (*The Institutio Oratorio* 6.3.19).

But Paul is not merely calling on Christians to be charming, witty, or funny—the kind of people who successfully navigate cocktail parties. Being a wit and being a witness are not necessarily the same thing. It would be more helpful to look at biblical references to salt for clues about what Paul means. And we'll do that in today's reading and tomorrow's.

- Salt has purifying power. This is seen by the custom of washing newborns with water and rubbing them with salt (Ezek 16:4). Another instance of salt's purifying power is found in the short story of Elisha transforming a city's bitter water supply by throwing salt into the spring (2 Kgs 2:19-22). Thus, Paul might mean that our words should have a purifying effect on those who hear them, rather than a corrupting effect. In Eph 4:29 Paul said that our mouths should not be filled with "corrupting talk," but with words that impart grace.
- Salt can function as a fertilizer. In ancient Israel, as well as in many parts of the world today, according to Bradley, "salt accelerates crop growth and development, increases crop yield, minimizes damage to plants and promotes environmental sustainability."[422] Salt can also prevent piles of dung from losing their fertilizing capacity too soon, which is why Jesus said that salt which has lost its saltiness is of no use for the manure pile (Luke 14:34-35). The words of Christians, then, do more than keep the world from decaying; they also cause life to spring up, promoting growth in barren places.[423]

Use my words today, Lord, to encourage and build up those who are often knocked down.

*⁵ Walk in wisdom before those "outside," snapping up the time. ⁶ Let your word always [be spoken] in grace, **being seasoned with salt,** [so as] to know how it is necessary for you to respond to each one.*

Here are some other ways that our words can function like salt.

- Salt was required for some sacrifices. This was especially true of grain offerings (Lev 2:13) and the burnt offerings to be sacrificed in the New Jerusalem (Ezek 43:24). Says Brown, "Once salted, the sacrifice is transferred [from the realm of what's clean] to the holy and thus to the priests' share."[424] Perhaps Paul wants to transfer our common words into holy words, salted offerings for the Lord which are pleasing to him.
- Salt was a factor in the making of covenants. According to 2 Chron 13:5, "the Lord God of Israel gave the kingship over Israel forever to David and his sons by a covenant of salt" (ESV, see also Num 18:19). Somehow salt functioned in the sealing of a covenant. Perhaps it meant that the promises spoken were to be as long-lasting as salt.[425] By seasoning our words with salt, we pledge ourselves to be truthful in what we say.
- Salt can enhance the flavor of food. Job 6:6 (NIV) asked, "Is tasteless food eaten without salt?" Possibly then, Col 4:6 is calling us to use tasty, winsome, appealing, enlivening words, so that others are drawn to "taste and see that the Lord is good" (Ps 34:8, NRSV).
- Salt is associated with peace. Jesus said, "Have salt in yourselves, and be at peace with one another." Nothing ruins a meal or a conversation more than quarrels. If our words are spoken in grace, then they will be seasoned with the tasty salt of peace.
- Christians are to function as the salt of the earth (Mt 5:13). Presumably, we are to let our saltiness be experienced by others—not hiding it in a salt shaker, but spreading it around for the world to receive. When we speak, we are to be conscious of the missional impact of our words.

There may be no way to know exactly what Paul meant by seasoning our words with salt, and that's okay. When the biblical writers use a word picture, it's often to open up new possibilities for understanding, rather than setting careful limits on what is meant. In any case, Paul would not approve of Christians being only interested in church matters and thus unable to even engage in "small talk" with an unbeliever.[426]

I would ask, Lord, that you would put me in a conversation with an unbeliever and that my words would be just right for the moment.

*⁵ Walk in wisdom before those "outside," snapping up the time. ⁶ Let your word always [be spoken] in grace, being seasoned with salt, **[so as] to know how it is necessary for you to respond to each one.***

To understand what Paul means we should take note of three terms here:

- Necessary. Not only was it necessary for *Paul* to speak the gospel (Col 4:4), but here we see that it's also necessary for *us* to "respond" to people with God's gracious news.
- Respond. Although this word is often translated as "answer," that could give the impression that Paul is only thinking of question-and-answer conversations, perhaps even a debate or a hostile inquiry. To translate it as "respond" leaves more room for a wide variety of interactions that happen in conversation.
- How to. In our world, "how to" is all about technique and efficiency, and relies on a one-size-fits-all perspective. The gospel, however, is about God's love for each individual with all the unique elements that make each person who they are. We do not respond to the lost as a generalized mass of people in need of a cookie-cutter solution. Rather, we are to respond to "each one" in all their uniqueness. As Eugene Peterson said, "We cannot use impersonal means to do or say a personal thing—and the gospel is personal or it is nothing."427

Speaking with grace, then, will help us know best how to respond to various individuals. In spiritual conversations we don't always know where the other person is coming from. Perhaps they are sincerely seeking truth; maybe they just love to argue; or possibly they are hoping to get evidence to use against us. Some want what they see in our lives; others relish an opportunity to prove they are better than we are. Even those who earnestly want to know the truth may be motivated by different factors, such as alleviating guilt, seeking a purpose for living, or overcoming loneliness.

We cannot know in advance just what a person needs to hear in order for them to respond well to Jesus, but we can always speak in a grace-filled way, wanting to bless the other person with the love and truth of Jesus. And as God's grace operates through our words (and our listening), God's Spirit will make it clearer to us what they need to hear.

Help me, Lord, to get to know others in all their uniqueness, so that I would know how to respond to them wisely and compassionately.

With Watchful Eyes and Thankful Hearts
to the tune of Azmon: *O For a Thousand Tongues to Sing*
© 2014 David J. Landegent

With watchful eyes and thankful hearts, we come again in prayer.
We pray for those lost in the dark, who need to know You care.

Break through their walls of doubt and sin by opening a door.
Your Word goes out, it draws them in; that they may be restored.

Proclaim the mystery of Christ to all who are confused.
Reveal His saving sacrifice, through those who preach Good News.

You give us opportunities before the watching world
To live our faith consistently, according to Your Word.

Let all our conversations, Lord, convey Your vibrant grace,
So that our lives will evermore reflect Your glorious face.

Parting words: grace be with you

Colossians 4:7-18

December 15-31

⁷ Tychicus, the beloved brother and faithful servant and fellow-slave in the Lord, will make known to you all the things about me. ⁸ Him I sent to you for this [reason]: in order that you may know the things concerning us and that he may encourage your hearts. ⁹ [I sent him] along with Onesimus, the faithful and beloved brother, who is one of you; they will make known to you all the things here.

¹⁰ Aristarchus my fellow-prisoner-of-war greets you, [as does] Mark, the cousin of Barnabas (about whom you have received commands; if he comes to you, welcome him), ¹¹ and Jesus called Justus—these alone being from the circumcision who are [my] fellow-workers in the kingdom of God, [and] who have been a comfort to me. ¹² Epaphras, who is one of you, a slave of Christ Jesus, greets you, always striving for you in his prayers in order that you may stand, complete and being fully-assured in all the will of God. ¹³ For I testify for him that he experiences much hardship for you and those in Laodicea and those in Hierapolis. ¹⁴ Luke the beloved physician greets you, and [so does] Demas.

¹⁵ Greet the brothers [and sisters] in Laodicea and Nympha and the church in her house. ¹⁶ And when this letter is read to you, make [arrangements] in order that it be read in the church of the Laodiceans, and that you read the one [forwarded] from Laodicea. ¹⁷ And say to Archippus, "See to the service which you received in the Lord in order that you may fulfill it." ¹⁸ The greeting is [written] in my—Paul's—hand. Remember my chains. Grace be with you.

According to Dunn, Paul's letters could feature up to five different components, at least two of which are found in every letter. Only 1 Corinthians and Colossians, however, have all five components: travel plans of Paul or associates (7-9), greetings from Paul and others (10-15), final instructions (16-17), a personal note (18ab), and a benediction (18c).[428]

A number of scholars have pointed out the diversity revealed in the names in this section: a woman, free men, a former slave, a doctor, Jews and non-Jews. Seven of the eleven personal names in this section also appear in the short letter to Philemon, indicating that the two letters were written about the same time to nearly the same recipients.

Lord, I want to call to mind right now many people by name who helped me grow in my faith; bless them, Lord.

[7] **Tychicus, the beloved brother and faithful servant and fellow-slave in the Lord, will make known to you all the things about me.** *[8]* *Him I sent to you for this [reason]: in order that you may know the things concerning us and that he may encourage your hearts.*

Paul brings his letter to a conclusion by commending two people who are hand-delivering it to the Colossians. It was necessary to find people to deliver messages in that day because the Roman postal service only functioned for officials and not private citizens.[429]

The first messenger named is Tychicus, whom Paul also sent to the Ephesians (Eph 6:21; 2 Tim 4:12) and to Titus (Titus 3:12). He was also one of two workers from the province of Asia (the western end of modern-day Turkey) who accompanied Paul when he traveled from Greece back to Jerusalem (Acts 20:4).

Paul's appreciation for Tychicus is seen in the three phrases he uses to commend him. First, Paul describes Tychicus as a "beloved brother," loved by God and by other believers. The love from God which is now extended toward one another is what causes Christians to regard each other as family members, beloved brothers and sisters in Christ.

Tychicus is also commended as a "faithful servant." God is often described as faithful (Dt 7:9), and so is Jesus (Rev 1:5). People in the Bible were also described as faithful in their various roles as friends, brothers, messengers, witnesses, soldiers, prophets, wives, leaders, martyrs, slaves, household managers, and servants. The latter are not only faithful to the one they serve, but are also faithful with whatever has been entrusted to them. Tychicus, then, is faithful to Paul and faithful with whatever tasks Paul has entrusted to him.

Finally, Paul commends Tychicus as a "fellow-slave in the Lord." Paul does not act like the slave in Jesus' parable who abused his fellow-slaves (Mt 24:49). Instead, he worked together with Tychicus, as they were fellow-slaves in Christ. For Tychicus to be called both servant and slave in this verse fits well with Jesus' words: "But whoever would be great among you must be your *servant*, and whoever would be first among you must be *slave* of all" (Mk 10:43b-44, ESV, emphasis mine).

Lord, I pray that you would transform me into being the kind of person that Tychicus was: beloved and faithful in serving you alongside others.

*7 Tychicus, the beloved brother and faithful servant and fellow-slave in the Lord, will make known to you all the things about me. 8 **Him I sent to you for this [reason]: in order that you may know the things concerning us and that he may encourage your hearts.***

While Paul likely entrusted many tasks to Tychicus, including the delivery of this letter to the Colossians, the main task mentioned in verse 7 is that of informing the church of other details about Paul and his ministry.

It was common for letter carriers to convey extra information. For example, when a woman sent a letter to a man named Zenon describing how someone was mistreating her son, she added, "The rest please learn from the man who brings you this letter. He is no stranger to us."430 Likewise, Cicero wrote to his wife, "Be sure you keep well, and send me letter-carriers to let me know what is being done and how you all are" (*Epistulae ad Familiares* 14.1.6). In the case of Colossians, it may be that Paul gave very few written details about his situation so he did not "jeopardize" his upcoming trial.431 If so, Tychicus would provide the details.

There is a natural human desire to know about the lives of other people. Sometimes this desire is corrupted and turns to gossip—we learn things about others (some true, some false) in order to tear them down and build ourselves up. Some might take the opposite stance and talk about ideas instead of people. But as important as ideas might be, people *are* indeed endlessly fascinating and there's nothing wrong with asserting that. We would all be very interested to hear what Tychicus would have to say about the apostle, for there's no denying that many of our "ideas" and teachings about Jesus come wrapped in this very human package named Paul. While knowing about others can lead to gossip, pride, and slander, our knowledge of others can also lead to more prayer for them, increased love for them, greater joy concerning them, and further wisdom in how to live as fellow-slaves of Christ.

What Tychicus was sent to share, of course, was not tidbits of celebrity gossip, but the kind of information about Paul that would encourage the Colossian church. In Col 2:2 Paul spoke of the same thing using the same verb for encouraging. In that earlier text and here, information about how the Lord is helping Paul in his trials will also encourage the Colossians in their trials.

Lord, whenever I hear information about someone else, teach me to turn that into a prayer on their behalf.

⁹ [I sent him] along with Onesimus, the faithful and beloved brother, who is one of you; they will make known to you all the things here.

Along with Tychicus, Paul also sent Onesimus, "who is one of you," that is to say, he is from Colossae. This is the same man who had been a slave of Philemon, a member of the Colossian church. Onesimus was a common name for slaves because it means "useful one." Slaves were usually named or renamed by their masters when they were purchased. According to the Roman author Varro, slaves were commonly named after the person who sold them, the location where they were purchased, or some particular quality (*On the Latin Language* 8.21).

Onesimus had run away, but then became a Christian through Paul's ministry, and somehow helped Paul. The apostle then wrote to Philemon asking him to liberate Onesimus with perhaps a hint that he be allowed to continue working with Paul (a letter now included in the Bible). Some scholars wonder if Tychicus and Onesimus were bringing both the letter to Philemon and the letter to the Colossians with them. But this is doubtful because here in Col 4:9, Onesimus is introduced matter-of-factly as if any tensions about his situation had already been resolved. Much more likely is that Onesimus had earlier been sent back to Philemon, along with that letter, and in response Philemon freed Onesimus to continue his work with Paul. In this new position, Onesimus now returns to Colossae with Tychicus.

No matter how we interpret Paul's earlier words about slaves and masters (Col 3:22-4:1), the fact that Paul praises a former runaway slave as a faithful and beloved brother speaks volumes of the social changes stirred up by the gospel. Says Moo, "Here we find a practical example of the principle that in the new creation there is 'no...slave or free' (3:11)."[432]

In commending Onesimus to the church, Paul uses words that are very similar to the ones he used to describe Tychicus. Both of them are called "faithful" and "beloved." It is interesting to note, however, that while Tychicus is called a faithful *servant* and fellow-*slave*, the former slave named Onesimus is called a faithful and beloved *brother.* The free man is called a slave, while the ex-slave is called a brother. This calls attention to the reversal of roles that Paul spoke of in 1 Cor 7:22, "For whoever was called in the Lord as a slave is a freed person belonging to the Lord, just as whoever was free when called is a slave of Christ." (NRSV).

Lord, it's tempting to be skeptical of new Christians like Onesimus. I get suspicious of their sincerity and their motives. But I pray that I would welcome them as openly as Paul did.

¹⁰ **Aristarchus my fellow-prisoner-of-war greets you,** *[as does] Mark, the cousin of Barnabas (about whom you have received commands; if he comes to you, welcome him),* ¹¹ *and Jesus called Justus—these alone being from the circumcision who are [my] fellow-workers in the kingdom of God, [and] who have been a comfort to me.*

Following the commendations of those who are bringing the letter to Colossae, Paul also relays greetings from others on his ministry team. By mentioning these coworkers, Paul shows that he's a team player and not an "authoritarian apostle."[433]

The sending of greetings from others was very common in ancient letters. Paul did not do it often in his letters, except when he was trying to make connections with churches that he was less familiar with, like the ones in Rome and Colossae. Here the greetings from his ministry team include three Jewish Christians (Aristarchus, Mark, and Jesus called Justus) and three non-Jewish Christians (Epaphras, Luke, and Demas).

The first one sending greetings is Aristarchus, a Macedonian from the city of Thessalonica (Acts 27:2). As a faithful traveling companion of Paul's, he often got into trouble right along with Paul. For instance, when a rioting mob in Ephesus could not find Paul, they seized Aristarchus—and another Macedonian named Gaius—and dragged them into the theater, but no action was taken against them (Acts 19:29). After Paul was sent to Rome as a prisoner, Aristarchus accompanied him and experienced the same fateful shipwreck in Malta (Acts 27:2).

Paul refers to Aristarchus as a fellow-prisoner-of-war. Neither of them may have felt they were making war against the Roman empire (according to Eph 6:12, we don't fight against flesh-and-blood enemies), but some in the empire felt threatened by their message anyway. These people of the empire likely regarded the proclamation of Jesus as Lord as subversive to the empire and arrested its spokesmen, like Paul and Aristarchus.

By joining Paul in prison, Aristarchus is showing his loyalty to Christ and to Paul. He is not one of those fair-weather friends, whom the Latin writer Seneca described as deserting one "at the first rattle of the [prison] chain" (*Epistle* 9.9). Instead, his commitment to Paul is on display. According to Dunn, "In a culture dominated by ideas of honor and shame, the willingness to accept the stigma of prison...would indicate a high degree of personal commitment to Paul" and to Christ.[434]

Lord, I wonder about how loyal I will be to you and your people when it involves suffering. Strengthen my courage and loyalty for whatever lies ahead.

*¹⁰ Aristarchus my fellow-prisoner-of-war greets you, **[as does] Mark, the cousin of Barnabas (about whom you have received commands; if he comes to you, welcome him),** ¹¹ and Jesus called Justus—these alone being from the circumcision who are [my] fellow-workers in the kingdom of God, [and] who have been a comfort to me.*

Another person sending his greetings is John Mark, a man with many connections in the early church. Mark's mother was named Mary, and it was to her house that Peter came after an angel miraculously rescued him from prison (Acts 12:12). Furthermore, Mark was a cousin to Barnabas, a leader in the early church who was originally named Joseph but was called Barnabas, "son of encouragement," because of his ministry style (Acts 4:36).

Barnabas was the one who had introduced the newly-converted Paul to the leadership in Jerusalem (Acts 9:27). Barnabas was later sent by the Jerusalem church to encourage the church in Antioch (Acts 11:22). To help him with his work in Antioch, Barnabas first recruited Paul (Acts 11:25) and later had his cousin Mark join them (Acts 12:25).

Not long afterward, the church in Antioch obeyed a prophetic word to send Barnabas and Paul on what would later be called Paul's first missionary trip (Acts 13:1-3). Mark accompanied them on the first leg of this trip, but left them early on and returned to Jerusalem (Acts 13:13). When Paul and Barnabas were preparing for a second missionary trip, Barnabas wanted to give Mark another chance, but Paul did not think that was a wise choice. They had such a sharp disagreement that they parted ways, and Paul went on this second trip with Silas instead (Acts 15:39).

At some point during the intervening dozen years or so, however, Paul must have had a change of heart about Mark, and Mark himself probably matured, for in Col 4:10 and Philemon 24 Paul describes Mark as a fellow-worker. Paul later told Timothy, "Get Mark and bring him with you, because he is helpful to me in my ministry" (2 Tim 4:11, NIV). Their personal reconciliation is a marvelous example of the "cosmic reconciliation" initiated by Jesus (Col 1:20).⁴³⁵

Mark also became a helper for Peter, who passed along greetings from Mark and referred to him as his son in 1 Pet 5:13. Church tradition suggests that Mark wrote the gospel bearing his name, especially relying upon eye-witness testimony from Peter.⁴³⁶

Lord, teach me today to give a second chance to those who have disappointed or angered me.

¹⁰ *Aristarchus my fellow-prisoner-of-war greets you, [as does] Mark, the cousin of Barnabas (about whom you have received commands; if he comes to you, welcome him),* ¹¹ **and Jesus called Justus—these alone being from the circumcision who are [my] fellow-workers in the kingdom of God, [and] who have been a comfort to me.**

One more person sending greetings is Jesus called Justus, a man who appears only here in the Bible. The only thing we know about him is that he, along with Aristarchus and Mark were "from the circumcision"; in other words, they were Jewish Christians. In fact, at this point in time, these three are Paul's only co-workers who were Jews; the rest were non-Jewish.

We cannot tell from his wording if Paul is (1) expressing disappointment that other Jewish-Christians had abandoned him; (2) simply stating what was the case; or (3) pointing out the remarkable fact that his ministry among non-Jews has been so successful that he doesn't have to rely much on Jewish-Christians for help.

Paul calls these three Jewish-Christians "fellow-workers." They were not merely traveling companions, nor were they Paul's personal helpers (as if he were their boss). Rather, they were involved in the work of ministering the gospel along with Paul—although they probably ministered *to* Paul as well, as indicated by the last phrase in this verse.

Paul does not describe these men as fellow-workers in *his* ministry, which might reveal a self-serving perspective. Rather, they are fellow-workers in *the kingdom of God*. The King does not do all the kingdom work, but instead raises up workers to announce the kingdom (Mt 4:17), heal diseases (Mt 4:23), sow the seed of the Word (Mt 13:31), act as harvesters (Mt 20:1), grow good fruit (Mt 21:43), help the needy (Mt 25:34), invest God's resources wisely (Lk 19:15), walk in a manner worthy of God (1 Thess 2:12), and so much more.

Paul closes his description of these Jewish co-workers by saying that these men "have been a comfort" to him. Paul finds comfort in knowing that these men join him in ministering *to others*. He also finds comfort in how these co-workers (and others) minister *to him*. They visit and encourage churches on his behalf (Phil 2:19-24), help him write letters (Rom 16:22), refresh his spirit (1 Cor 16:18), collect offerings (2 Cor 8:16-24), minister to his physical needs (Phil 2:25), and bring him needed items (2 Tim 4:13).

Thank you, Lord Jesus, for all the workers that you have raised up to do kingdom work in my local church. Encourage them, Lord, on this day.

¹² Epaphras, who is one of you, a slave of Christ Jesus, greets you, always striving for you in his prayers in order that you may stand, complete and being fully-assured in all the will of God. ¹³ For I testify for him that he experiences much hardship for you and those in Laodicea and those in Hierapolis.

Paul also conveys greetings from three non-Jewish co-workers. The first is Epaphras, who was probably the first person to bring the gospel to Colossae and organize the church there (see Col 1:7).

Paul's glowing words about Epaphras assure the Colossians that they had done well in believing his gospel message and that they should continue to follow his leadership. Paul, in fact, believes that Epaphras' work mirrors his own—in at least three ways.

For one thing, both of them were striving (*agōnizomai*)—Paul striving for the sake of all (Col 1:29), and Epaphras striving in prayer for the Colossians (Col 4:12). Prayer often involves striving, struggling, and wrestling. In prayer we may be striving with God, or with a world dominated by the devil, or with our own sinful desires. Jacques Ellul believes combat is the most basic form of prayer. It is combat against distractions, doubts, a consumer-mentality, religiosity, heresy, lies, evil, and self-absorption. It is even a combat against God as we call upon him to be the God he promised to be.[437]

Secondly, both men also aimed to present people complete (*teleios*) in Christ—Paul aims to present (*paristēmi*) all people complete (Col 1:28), and Epaphras prays that the Colossians would stand (*histēmi*) complete (Col 4:12).

Finally, both want the Colossians to experience full assurance—Paul wants them to have full-assurance (*plērophoria*) of understanding (Col 2:2), and Epaphras prays for them to be fully-assured (*plērophoreō*) in God's will (Col 4:12).

Since both Paul and Epaphras are striving toward presenting people complete and fully assured in Christ, there may be a sense in which this would be a good goal for all Christian leaders, and even all Christians. There is no place for being lackadaisical in our interactions with people. Rather, we love others with a purpose of moving them toward Christ and hope that others love us with the same aim.

Lord Jesus, show me where my mission field is, and empower me by your Spirit to do the work each day.

12 Epaphras, who is one of you, a slave of Christ Jesus, greets you, always striving for you in his prayers in order that you may stand, complete and being fully-assured in all the will of God. **13 For I testify for him that he experiences much hardship for you and those in Laodicea and those in Hierapolis.**

Paul commends Epaphras further by testifying that he experiences much hardship (*ponos*) on behalf of the Colossian believers and the neighboring churches of Laodicea and Hierapolis.

Most translations opt to translate *ponos* as a reference to hard work, as if Paul appreciates Epaphras' good work ethic. But most biblical uses of this word refer to unwanted pain or hardship which has either been inflicted upon us or which we have foolishly brought upon ourselves. There are a few verses in which *ponos* obviously refers to work, but some of these point to the negative side of work, such as the painful labor of the Hebrew slaves (Ex 2:11) and the curse of working hard in the field only to see it taken by other nations (Dt 28:33).

Thus it seems most likely that Epaphras is commended because of his willingness to suffer hardship for the church. If this is the case, then once again Paul is highlighting how Epaphras' ministry echoes his own. Paul rejoices in his sufferings for the church (Col 1:24), and now he commends Epaphras for the similar action of enduring "much hardship for you" (Col 4:13).

The phrase "for you" is more significant than may appear. Of the twenty-five times the Greek phrase "for you" is found in the NT, about half of them are used in contexts of suffering for others. At the Last Supper, Jesus used it to describe the purpose of his death (Lk 22:19-20; 1 Cor 11:24). At that same meal Peter foolishly claimed he was willing to lay down his life for Jesus (Jn 13:37), but later he confessed that it was Christ alone who suffered "for you" (1 Pet 2:21). Paul knew he was not crucified for other believers (1 Cor 1:13), but he was a prisoner for them (Eph 3:1), suffered for them (Eph 3:13; Col 1:24), and struggled for them (Col 2:1). In a similar way, Epaphras struggled and experienced hardship for the Colossians (Col 4:12-13). Perhaps his hardship included a recent stint with Paul in prison, for he was called a "fellow prisoner in Christ Jesus" in Philemon 23 (NRSV).

Lord Jesus, I sometimes resent being inconvenienced by the people and ministries of my local church. Expand my love, so that I am willing to go the extra mile for your people, even to the point of suffering for them.

^{14} Luke the beloved physician greets you, and [so does] Demas.

Two other non-Jewish Christians who greet the Colossians are Luke and Demas, who also sent greetings in Philemon 24.

There is only one further reference to Luke in the NT—2 Tim 4:11, which states that Luke was the only one staying with Paul at that point. Luke never refers to himself by name in the gospel that bears his name, nor in the book of Acts, which he also wrote. This verse is also our only evidence that Luke was a physician, which was not a common profession.[438] One can only wonder what Luke, trained as a physician, thought of all the faith healing he witnessed and heard about among Christians.

Since Luke was not a Jew, but had a great awareness of Jewish matters in his writings, he may have been a God-fearer (a non-Jew who worshiped in the synagogue) before becoming a Christian.[439] That would explain why Luke often mentions God-fearers in his writings. Scholars attempt to trace Luke's movements in the book of Acts by noting the times when he refers to "we," meaning that Luke and others who were accompanying Paul. If this is the case, then Luke was with Paul on his second missionary journey in Macedonia (Acts 16:8-17), on the return voyage to Israel at the end of his third missionary journey (Acts 20:5-15; 21:1-18), and on the voyage to Rome that was shipwrecked (Acts 27:1-28:16).

It might be surprising to learn that Demas appears as often as Luke in the Bible, three times. Twice he's with Paul and expresses his greetings (here and in Philemon 24). His only other appearance in Scripture, however, is as a no-show: "For Demas, in love with this present world, has deserted me and gone to Thessalonica" (2 Tim 4:10, NRSV). Paul was in a lonely mood when he wrote this, and he expressed some bitterness about Demas' disloyalty.

Many preachers have used Demas as an example of falling away from the faith. It's unclear, however, if Demas forsook his faith in Jesus, or simply forsook Paul because of other "worldly" commitments. Perhaps in Paul's mind they were the same thing, but Demas' love for this present world could have ranged from living the wild life of a prodigal to simply returning back home to take care of some family matters. In any case, we should not be too hard on Demas, for even those who desert the Lord's mission can still come around—and a prime example of this is Mark, whose story of desertion and restoration we just noted in Col 4:10.

I pray, Lord Jesus, for those I know who appear to have forsaken the faith.
Restore them, and use me to do so if it be your will.

¹⁵ Greet the brothers [and sisters] in Laodicea and Nympha and the church in her house. ¹⁶ And when this letter is read to you, make [arrangements] in order that it be read in the church of the Laodiceans, and that you read the one [forwarded] from Laodicea.

After passing along greetings from others, Paul concludes his letter with directions of a more personal nature. First, he wants to make sure that the family of believers in Colossae does not isolate itself. Thus, he calls on them to make contact with the church in Laodicea by passing along Paul's greetings. The local church should not regard itself as a single cell, but as part of the larger body of Christ. Or to use Paul's imagery here, they are not to think of themselves as an isolated nuclear family, but as brothers and sisters in God's extended family. In today's jargon, Paul wants the Colossian church to network with the one in Laodicea.[440]

Paul also wants the Colossian church to greet a woman named Nympha and the church that meets in her home. In the first century, churches did not own their own worship facilities (that did not start happening until about 250 AD).[441] Therefore, believers commonly gathered in a home, usually the larger home of a wealthier person or couple, which could fit 30-50 people in the largest room.[442] At least in some cases, the home belonged to a wealthy woman, either single, divorced, or widowed. Just as Jesus' needs were supplied by a corps of women when he was traveling throughout the land (see Lk 8:1-3), so also the first Christians were often hosted by women believers.

The NT does not give us much information about this, but it would not take much imagination to think of the following hospitable women as hosting a church in their home: the sisters Mary and Martha (Lk 10:38-41); Lydia, a merchant of purple goods (Acts 16:14-15); Dorcas (Acts 9:36-42); and perhaps Euodia and/or Syntyche (Phil 4:2-3). Couples involved in hosting these house churches likely included Priscilla and Aquila (Acts 18:1-3, 26) and Apphia and her husband (although it's hard to tell from Philemon 1-2 who her husband is). It's difficult to assess what kind of leadership Nympha had in the church that met in her home. Whether or not she served in an official capacity, such as overseer or elder, is unknown, but minimally, by hosting the church in her home, Nympha would still lead by setting the tone for church gatherings.

Lord, I dedicate my home to you, making it available for ministries of hospitality within the church and among the lost.

[16] And when this letter is read to you, make [arrangements] in order that it be read in the church of the Laodiceans, and that you read the one [forwarded] from Laodicea.

While it was customary for churches to follow the synagogue's practice of reading the Scriptures aloud during worship (see Lk 4:16-17), churches probably also read letters and documents written by the apostles and other early church leaders (see Acts 15:31; 2 Cor 1:13; 1 Thess 5:27). Not all letters, however, seemed to have survived, for we do not have the letter Paul wrote to Corinth before 1 Corinthians (see 1 Cor 5:9), nor the letter to the Laodiceans mentioned here.

In this case Paul strengthened the ties between churches by writing separate letters to Colossae and Laodicea, and then having the two churches swap letters. This must have become a common practice later. A similar situation is found in Revelation 2-3, which contains seven letters to seven churches, each of which could also be read by the others.

Paul did this because he knew the content of his letters would be relevant to more churches than the one who first received it.[443] Seitz states, "Paul has become aware that his letter writing is a form of apostolic ministry with its own integrity and afterlife, especially in the form of letters" being collected together.[444] Knowing that he intended his letters to be read beyond those who first received them must have affected what he wrote.[445] This would mean that we need to read each letter of Paul's in light of other letters written by him.

This practice of sharing letters also happened in Roman and Greek culture. Cicero noted that it was common for upper class people to make copies of letters they received and then pass them along to others. If a host read a letter he had received, guests might even request a copy for themselves (*Letters to Atticus* 8.9). One could easily imagine a similar situation happening in churches. A visiting Christian might hear a letter written to that church and request a copy to take back to his own church.[446]

This scenario, however, might give the impression that a collection of Paul's letters happened haphazardly through Christians gathering copies from various recipients. It's quite likely, however, that Paul himself kept copies of his letters, for that was the standard procedure for many writers in that day. If so, then Paul's own collection of letters he had written would have easily come into the hands of his ministry team after his death.[447]

Thank you, Lord, for inspiring Paul's letters and still speaking their truths today.

¹⁶ And when this letter is read to you, make [arrangements] in order that it be read in the church of the Laodiceans, and that you read the one [forwarded] from Laodicea.

In our world most reading is done silently and privately. But in Paul's day, public reading was far more common. And this is precisely what Paul wanted the churches to do with his letters. In 1 Thess 5:27 he solemnly charged the church, "I put you under oath before the Lord to have this letter read to all the brothers" (ESV). It was *not* to be a private correspondence for private consumption.

In some respects, the church was only doing what was done throughout Roman culture. In the ancient world, the upper classes would gather to hear something read to the group, and after people would comment on it—both questioning and defending it—they might request it to be read again, followed by more commenting, and input from a teacher. Sometimes those in the reading group would even compete for giving the best interpretation.[448] One can easily imagine similar readings happening among Christians, with a key difference that those lacking in social power would also be included in the discussion of apostolic writings.

In part, this oral reading was done because many members of the church would have been unable to read and would need the letter read to them. Estimated literacy rates were between 10-20%, with a higher percentage among the Jews.[449]

Reading in a group also changes the dynamic of listening—and can change it for the better. Instead of a private reader merely taking in (or rejecting) information on a page, a public reading makes the letter much more relational, for the listeners are encountering Paul through someone's living voice and the group is experiencing Paul's voice together. Through public reading, relationships are being transformed, either for better or worse. Public reading, then, doesn't just provide informational knowledge, but also relational knowledge.

There's also an advantage to reading what is written to someone else. If someone writes to correct us, our guard will be up and we will listen very defensively. But if we listen in on someone else being corrected in a letter, we are actually more open to its correcting words. By listening in on what's written to someone else, we actually become better listeners.

Open my ears, Lord, so that I can be attentive, instead of defensive, in listening to what you say to the churches through Scripture.

¹⁷ And say to Archippus, "See to the service which you received in the Lord in order that you may fulfill it."

Paul adds one more personal note to an individual named Archippus. He is likely the same man named as Paul's fellow soldier in Philemon 2. He is somehow connected to Philemon and a woman named Apphia (perhaps as their son) and the church that meets in their home.

At an earlier time Archippus had received a calling from God to some ministry, and now Paul encourages him in this work. The word used for this ministry is *diakonia*, the normal NT noun for service. For Paul, there is a wide variety of services to which Christians are called (1 Cor 12:5), and each Christian should be dedicated to whatever their form of service is (Rom 12:7). Many of these would involve serving other believers (1 Cor 16:15; Eph 4:12) and even serving Paul himself (2 Tim 4:11).

We might think of service as something imposed upon us, as if we were coerced into it. Paul, however, says we "receive" these opportunities for service, presumably as a gift from the Lord. But it's not a gift for us to hoard for our own private enjoyment, but for us to live out for the sake of others. In Col 2:6 Paul used this same word for "receive" to say that as we have received Christ, so we should walk in him: do not receive Christ in vain, but act upon that relationship. Likewise, he tells Archippus, do not receive a form of service in vain, but act upon it.

Perhaps Paul gives this encouragement to Archippus because he knows how easy it is to become weary in well-doing. Although he claimed he had not lost heart in performing his service (2 Cor 4:1), Paul knew others might lose heart. Thus he called on Timothy to "fan into flame the gift of God, which is in you through the laying on of my hands" (2 Tim 1:6, NIV), so that he would fulfill his form of service (2 Tim 4:5). It's possible Archippus had also become discouraged in his service and needed this word of encouragement. By encouraging Archippus in a letter read to the whole church, he is not trying to shame him into doing the work, but is rather hoping that the rest of the believers will also encourage him.

Paul calls Archippus to "see to the service...in order that you may fulfill it." A partially-completed service is not what God has in mind. He has called us to press on to completing or fulfilling our assignment. So just as Paul encouraged Timothy in 2 Tim 4:5 to "fulfill your ministry" (ESV), so here he encourages Archippus to "fulfill it."

Lord, prompt me today to encourage someone I know who is in ministry so that they would not become weary in well-doing.

> *18 The greeting is [written] in my—Paul's—hand. Remember my chains. Grace be with you.*

Paul concludes his letter by writing out his own personal greetings. He mentions this also in 1 Cor 16:21, Gal 6:11, and 2 Thess 3:17. The implication, of course, is that the rest of the letter was probably penned by a secretary. These were usually people who could write neatly enough to be read and small enough to avoid using too much expensive papyrus.[450] We know Paul used a secretary for his letter to the Romans because the secretary Tertius identified himself as such in Rom 16:22. It was likely Paul's practice with other letters as well.

Paul believed it was important to personally sign his letters, not only to make the letter more personal, but also to reassure people that it was genuine. In 2 Thess 2:2 Paul counsels the church "not to be quickly shaken in mind or alarmed...by...a letter seeming to be from us" (ESV), and so he ends that letter with his autograph, adding, "This is the sign of genuineness in every letter of mine; it is the way I write" (2 Thess 3:17, ESV).

While writing this final verse with his own hand, Paul cannot help but think about how his hand is restrained by chains, as if to say, "Remember that the hand that writes this is a chained hand."[451]

The three main forms of Roman custody were imprisonment, military custody, and free custody. *Imprisonment* meant being in a dark, unsanitary dungeon (often in chains) with many other prisoners. Under *military custody*, a prisoner was usually kept in an ordinary room, chained to military guards (who took turns in this duty), but friends and servants might move about freely in helping the prisoner. In *free custody*, the prisoner was detained but without chains under the supervision of non-military personnel. When writing Colossians, Paul was likely under military custody.[452] Paul knew that being in chains was part of the price to pay in following Jesus: "The Holy Spirit testifies to me in every city that imprisonment and persecutions are waiting for me" (Acts 20:23, NRSV). But even in prison Paul was able to proclaim the gospel (see Phil 1:13), although he'd rather not be so confined (see Acts 26:29).

It is these miserable chains that Paul wants the Colossians to remember. When they remember his chains, they will remember to pray for him, and they will remember that they themselves may face suffering in the future.[453]

I'm remembering before you, Lord, those many believers who are persecuted and even imprisoned because of their faith in you.

18 The greeting is [written] in my—Paul's—hand. Remember my chains.
Grace be with you.

Paul does not end his letter focusing on his bad situation. Instead his thoughts are on the Colossians and his desire for them to experience God's grace. This is not just a wish on his part, for he believes that his words of benediction not only speak of grace, but convey it.

Just as Paul began this letter with a word of grace (Col 1:2), he now concludes it with a similar word. He moves from grace to grace. He would have agreed with John 1:16, "For from [Christ's] fullness we have all received, grace upon grace" (ESV). It's no wonder grace is featured at the end of *every* letter he wrote.

In eight of Paul's thirteen letters, he explicitly states that this grace comes from the Lord Jesus Christ. In Ephesians, Colossians, 1 and 2 Timothy, and Titus, however, he speaks only of grace. This does not mean Paul has forgotten the source of grace and now believes in the power of a vague, sentimental love. The letter of Colossians may not explicitly say that grace comes from Jesus, but it does declare that Jesus is the source of redemption and forgiveness (Col 1:14; 2:13; 3:13); reconciliation and peace (Col 1:20, 22; 3:15); hope and glory (Col 1:27); wisdom and knowledge (Col 2:2-3); resurrection life and victory (Col 2:12, 15; 3:4). If that's not grace, nothing is.

The thrust of this blessing is that Jesus' grace would be "with you." Paul's benedictions all repeat some form of this phrase, always using the preposition for "with." Unlike the opening line of his letters, which include some form of "grace *to* you," Paul always concludes by saying "grace *with* you." This movement from "grace *to* you" in the beginning to "grace *with* you" in the end is so consistent that it's as if Paul is visually portraying the movement of grace. When Paul "appears" at the beginning of the letter, he brings the Lord's grace with him and extends it to those who are gathered: *grace to you.* Then when he "takes leave" at the end of the letter, he doesn't take the Lord's grace back with him, but instead leaves it behind to remain with his listeners: *grace with you.* That's important because we do not live by occasional encounters with Jesus' grace. Rather, we are sustained by this grace that goes "with us" on our journey of faith.

And that is my prayer for you. This book and this year may be ending, but may the grace of the Lord continue with you all.

Thank you, Lord Jesus, for sending your grace that has accompanied me this past year and will do so into eternity.

Grace Be With You
to the tune of Glorified: *Lord, Be Glorified*
© 2014 David J. Landegent

As God's fam'ly—grace be with you, grace be with you;
Brothers, sisters—grace be with you today.

As God's servants—grace be with you, grace be with you;
Kingdom workers —grace be with you today.

Tell the hurting—grace be with you, grace be with you;
Those who suffer—grace be with you today.

Hear this promise—grace be with you, grace be with you;
Know God's kindness—grace be with you today.

Works Cited

Anderson, G. A.
2009   *Sin: A History*. New Haven: Yale University Press.

Arnold, Clinton E.
1996   *The Colossian Syncretism*. Grand Rapids: Baker Book House.

Atkins, Anne
1987   *Split Image: Male and Female After God's Likeness*. Grand Rapids: Eerdmans.

Aune, David E.
2001   "Prayer in the Greco-Roman World." Pp. 23-42 in *Into God's Presence: Prayer in the New Testament*. Edited by R. N. Longenecker. Grand Rapids: Eerdmans.

Balla, P.
2003   *The Child-Parent Relationship in the New Testament and Its Environment*. Peabody, MA: Hendrickson Publishers.

Barclay, William
1959   *The Letters to the Philippians, Colossians and Thessalonians*. Daily Study Bible Series. Philadelphia: Westminster Press.

Barth, Karl
1956a   *Church Dogmatics* I.2. Edinburgh: T. & T. Clark.

1956b   *Church Dogmatics* IV.1. Edinburgh: T. & T. Clark.

1957   *Church Dogmatics* II.1. Edinburgh: T. & T. Clark.

1958   *Church Dogmatics* IV.2. Edinburgh: T. & T. Clark.

1960a   *Church Dogmatics* III.2. Edinburgh: T. & T. Clark.

1960b   *Church Dogmatics* III.3. Edinburgh: T. & T. Clark.

1961a   *Church Dogmatics* III.4. Edinburgh: T. & T. Clark.

1961b   *Church Dogmatics* IV.3.1. Edinburgh: T. & T. Clark.

1962a   *Church Dogmatics* IV.3.2. Edinburgh: T. & T. Clark.

1962b   *The Epistle to the Philippians*. Richmond: John Knox Press.

1969   *Church Dogmatics* IV.4. Edinburgh: T. & T. Clark.

1981   *The Christian Life: Church Dogmatics* IV.4, *Lecture Fragments*. Grand Rapids: Eerdmans.

Barth, Marcus and H. Blanke
1994   *Colossians*. The Anchor Bible 34B. New York: Doubleday.

Bauckham, Richard
2006   *Jesus and the Eyewitnesses: The Gospels as Eyewitness Testimony*. Grand Rapids: Eerdmans.

Beasley-Murray, George R.
1962   *Baptism in the New Testament*. Grand Rapids: Eerdmans.

Beetham, Christopher A.
2008   *Echoes of Scripture in the Letter of Paul to the Colossians*. Leiden: Brill.

Behm, J.

1967   *"Nēstis, nēsteuō, nēsteia,"* Pp. 924-935 in *Theological Dictionary of the New Testament*, Vol. IV. Edited by G. Kittel. Grand Rapids: Wm. B. Eerdmans Publishing Company.

Berkouwer, G. C.
1969   *The Sacraments.* Studies in Dogmatics. Grand Rapids: Eerdmans.

1976   *The Church.* Studies in Dogmatics. Grand Rapids: Eerdmans.

Berlin, Adele
2000   *"Numinous Nomon:* On the Relationship between Narrative and Law," Pp. 25-31 in *"A Wise and Discerning Mind": Essays in Honor of Burke O. Long*—Brown Judaic Studies 325. Edited by Saul M. Olyan and Robert C. Culley. Providence, Rhode Island: Brown Judaic Studies.

Blackwell. Ben C.
2014   "You Are Filled in Him: Theosis and Colossians 2-3." *Journal of Theological Interpretation,* 8: 103-113.

Bonhoeffer, Dietrich
1954   *Life Together.* New York: Harper & Row, Publishers, Inc.

1955   *Ethics.* New York: Macmillan Publishing Company.

1963   *The Cost of Discipleship.* New York: Macmillan Publishing Company, Inc.

Boulton, Matthew M.
2008   *God Against Religion: Rethinking Christian Theology Through Worship.* Grand Rapids: Eerdmans.

Bradley, Anthony B.
2016   "You Are the Manure of the Earth." *Christianity Today.* 60/8 (October): 72-76.

Brown, William P.
1996   *Character in Crisis: A Fresh Approach to the Wisdom Literature of the Old Testament.* Grand Rapids: Eerdmans.

1999   *The Ethos of the Cosmos: The Genesis of Moral Imagination in the Bible.* Grand Rapids: Eerdmans.

Brownson, James V.
2007   *The Promise of Baptism: An Introduction to Baptism in Scripture and the Reformed Tradition.* Grand Rapids: Eerdmans.

Bruce, F. F.
1964   *The Epistle to the Hebrews.* New International Commentary on the New Testament. Grand Rapids: Eerdmans.

1984   *The Epistles to the Colossians, to Philemon, and to the Ephesians.* New International Commentary on the New Testament. Grand Rapids: Eerdmans.

Brueggemann, Walter
1997   *Theology of the Old Testament: Testimony, Dispute, Advocacy.* Minneapolis, MN: Fortress Press.

Brunner, Emil
1956   *Faith, Hope, and Love.* Philadelphia: Westminster Press.

1960   *The Christian Doctrine of the Church, Faith and the Consummation. Dogmatics : Vol III.* Philadelphia: Westminster Press.

Caird, G. B.
1976   *Paul's Letters from Prison: Ephesians, Philippians, Colossians, Philemon.* New Clarendon Bible. London: Oxford University Press.

Carson, D. A.

2004   "Mystery and Fulfillment: Toward a More Comprehensive Paradigm of Paul's Understanding of the Old and the New." Pp. 393-436 in *Justification and Variegated Nomism. Volume 2—The Paradoxes of Paul.* Edited by D. A. Carson, P. T. O'Brien and M. A. Seifrid. Grand Rapids: Baker Academic.

Cassidy, R. J.
2001   *Paul in Chains: Roman Imprisonment and the Letters of St. Paul.* New York: The Crossroad Publishing Company.

Chambers, Oswald
1935   *My Utmost for His Highest.* Uhrichsville, OH: Barbour Publishing, Inc.

Cranfield, C. E. B.
1975   *A Critical and Exegetical Commentary on the Epistle to the Romans,* Vol. 1. The International Critical Commentary. Edinburgh: T & T. Clark Limited.

De Graaf, Clare
2010   *The 10-Second Rule.* New York: Howard Books.

Deissmann, Adolf
1926   *Paul: A Study in Social and Religious History* (2nd edition). New York: George H. Doran Company.

Detwiler, David F.
2001   "Church Music and Colossians 3:16." *Blbliotheca Sacra* 158 (July-September):347-369.

Dibelius, M.
1975   "The Isis Initiation in Apuleius and Related Initiatory Rites" (originally published in 1917). Pp. 61-121 in *Conflict at Colossae.* Edited by F. O. Francis and W. A. Meeks. Missoula, MT: Society of Biblical Literature and Scholars Press.

Duguid, Iain M.
1999   *Ezekiel.* The NIV Application Commentary. Grand Rapids: Zondervan.

Dunn, James D. G.
1996   *The Epistles to the Colossians and Philemon: A Commentary on the Greek Text.* New International Greek Testament Commentary. Grand Rapids: Eerdmans.

Ellul, Jacques
1970   *Prayer and Modern Man.* New York: The Seabury Press.

1976   *Ethics of Freedom.* Grand Rapids: Eerdmans.

Fee, Gordon D.
1994   *God's Empowering Presence.* Peabody, MA: Hendrickson.

2000   *Listening to the Spirit in the Text.* Grand Rapids: Eerdmans.

2007   *Pauline Christology: An Exegetical-Theological Study.* Peabody, MA: Hendrickson Publishers.

Fitch, D.
2008   "Missional Misstep." *Christianity Today,* 52/9 (September): 36-39.

Francis, F. O. and W. A. Meeks
1975   *Conflict at Colossae: A Problem in the Interpretation of Early Christianity Illustrated by Selected Modern Studies* (rev.). Missoula, MT: Society of Biblical Literature and Scholars Press.

Gamble, Harry Y.
1995   *Books and Readers in the Early Church: A History of Early Christian Texts.* New Haven: Yale University Press.

Garland, David

1998   *Colossians and Philemon.* The NIV Application Commentary. Grand Rapids: Zondervan Publishing House.

1999   *2 Corinthians.* The New American Commentary 29. Nashville: B & H Publishing Group.

Gill, David

2000   *Becoming Good: Building Moral Character.* Downers Grove: InterVarsity Press.

Gorday, P.

2000   *Colossians, 1-2 Thessalonians, 1-2 Timothy, Titus, Philemon.* Ancient Christian Commentary on Scripture, New Testament IX. Downers Grove, IL: InterVarsity Press.

Gorman, Michael J.

2001   *Cruciformity: Paul's Narrative Spirituality of the Cross.* Grand Rapids: Eerdmans.

2015   *Becoming the Gospel: Paul, Participation and Mission.* Grand Rapids: Eerdmans.

Guthrie, S. R.

2014   "Love the Lord with All Your Voice." *Christianity Today* 58: June 2014, 44-47.

Hafemann, Scott

1990   *Suffering and Ministry in the Spirit: Paul's Defense of His Ministry in II Corinthians 2:14–3:3.* Grand Rapids: Eerdmans.

Harris, Murray J.

1991   *Colossians & Philemon.* Exegetical Guide to the Greek New Testament. Grand Rapids: Eerdmans.

Hartman, L.

1995   "Code and Context: A Few Reflections on the Parenesis of Col 3:6-4:1." Pp. 177-191 in *Understanding Paul's Ethics: Twentieth Century Approaches.* Edited by B. S. Rosner. Grand Rapids: Eerdmans.

Hay, David, M.

1973   *Glory at the Right Hand: Psalm 110 in Early Christianity.* Nashville: Abingdon Press.

2000   *Colossians.* Abingdon New Testament Commentaries. Nashville: Abingdon Press.

Hendricksen, William

1964   *Colossians and Philemon.* New Testament Commentary. Grand Rapids: Baker Book House.

Hengel, Martin

1977   *Crucifixion.* Philadelphia: Fortress Press.

Hering, James P.

2007   *Colossian and Ephesian* Haustafeln *in Theological Context: An Analysis of Their Origins, Relationship, and Message.* (American University Studies VII: Theology and Religion, Vol. 260). New York: Peter Lang Publishing.

Horrell, D. G., C. Hunt and C. Southgate

2010   *Greening Paul: Rereading the Apostle in a Time of Ecological Crisis.* Waco, TX: Baylor University Press.

Houlden, J. H.

1970   *Paul's Letters from Prison: Philippians, Colossians, Philemon and Ephesians.* The Pelican New Testament Commentaries. Middlesex: Penguin Books.

Johnson, Luke T.

1998   *Religious Experience in Early Christianity.* Minneapolis: Fortress Press.

Johnson, William A.
2009   "Constructing Elite Reading Communities in the High Empire." Pp. 320-330 in *Ancient Literacies: The Culture of Reading in Greece and Rome*. Edited by William A. Johnson and Holt N. Parker. New York: Oxford University Press.

Keck, L.
1988   *Paul and His Letters*. Proclamation Commentaries. Second edition. Philadelphia: Fortress Press.

Knight, George W., III
1992   *The Pastoral Epistles: A Commentary on the Greek Text*. New International Greek Testament Commentary. Grand Rapids: Eerdmans.

Koester, Helmut
1971   "The Structure and Criteria of Early Christian Beliefs." Pp. 205-231 in *Trajectories through Early Christianity*. Edited by James M. Robinson and Helmut Koester. Philadelphia: Fortress Press.

König, Adrio
1982   *Here Am I: A Believer's Reflection on God*. Grand Rapids: Eerdmans.

1989   *The Eclipse of Christ in Eschatology: Toward a Christ-Centered Approach*. Grand Rapids: Eerdmans.

Landegent, David J.
1999   "The Lust for Certitude." *The Reformed Journal* 14 (June/July): 11-13.

Lewis, C. S.
1943   *Mere Christianity*. New York: Macmillan Publishing.

1946   *The Great Divorce*. New York: The Macmillan Company.

1948   *Beyond Personality*. New York: Macmillan Co.

1961   *The Screwtape Letters*. New York: The Macmillan Company.

1970a   "The Laws of Nature." Pp. 76-79 in *God in the Dock: Essays on Theology and Ethics*. Grand Rapids: Eerdmans.

1970b   "The Sermon and the Lunch." Pp. 282-286 in *God in the Dock: Essays on Theology and Ethics*. Grand Rapids: Eerdmans.

Lincoln, Andrew T.
1978-79   'Paul the Visionary': The Setting and Significance of the Rapture to Paradise in II Corinthians XII.1-10." *New Testament Studies* 25: 204-220.

1981   *Paradise Now and Not Yet: Studies in the Role of the Heavenly Dimension in Paul's Thought with Special Reference to His Eschatology*. Cambridge: Cambridge University Press.

2000   *The Letter to the Colossians*. Pp. 551-669 in *The New Interpreter's Bible* XI. Edited by Leander Keck. Nashville: Abingdon Press.

Litfin, D.
2012   "You Can't Preach the Gospel with Deeds and Why It's Important to Say So," *Christianity Today,* 56/5 (May): 40-43.

Lohse, Eduard
1971   *Colossians and Philemon*. Hermeneia. Philadelphia: Fortress Press.

Longenecker, Richard N.
2001   "Prayer in the Pauline Letters." Pp. 203-227 in *Into God's Presence: Prayer in the New Testament*. Edited by R. N. Longenecker. Grand Rapids: Eerdmans.

Lucas, Richard C.

1980　　*The Message of Colossians & Philemon.* The Bible Speaks Today. Downers Grove, IL: InterVarsity Press.

MacLeod, G. P.
1955　　"The Epistle to the Colossians: Exposition." Pp. 132-241 from *The Interpreter's Bible* 10. Nashville: Abingdon.

Maier, Harry O.
2005　　"A Sly Civility: Colossians and Empire." *Journal for the Study of the New Testament* 27: 323-349.

Marshall, C.
2001　　*Beyond Retribution: A New Testament Vision for Justice, Crime, and Punishment.* Grand Rapids: Eerdmans.

Martin, Ralph P.
1974　　*Colossians and Philemon.* New Century Bible. London: Marshall, Morgan & Scott.

Melick, R. R.
1991　　*Philippians, Colossians, Philemon.* The New American Commentary 32. Nashville: Broadman Press.

Milgrom Jacob
1990　　*Numbers Commentary.* The JPS Torah Commentary Project. Philadelphia: The Jewish Publication Society.

Moo, Douglas
1996　　*The Epistle to the Romans.* New International Commentary on the New Testament. Grand Rapids: Eerdmans.

2008　　*The Letters to the Colossians and to Philemon.* Pillar New Testament Commentary. Grand Rapids: Eerdmans.

Moore, R.
2012　　"A Purpose Driven Cosmos." *Christianity Today* 56/2 (February): 31-33.

Moule, H. C. G.
1898　　*Colossian and Philemon Studies: Lessons in Faith and Holiness.* London: Pickering & Inglis Ltd.

Newsom, Carol
1985　　*Songs of the Sabbath Sacrifices: A Critical Edition.* Atlanta: Scholars Press.

O'Brien, Brandon
2009　　"To Kill or To Love—That Was The Question." *Christianity Today* 53/7 (July): 42-44.

O'Brien. Peter T.
1982　　*Colossians, Philemon.* Word Biblical Commentary 44. Waco, TX: Word Books.

Oswalt, John N.
2003　　*Isaiah.* The NIV Application Commentary. Grand Rapids: Zondervan.

Pao, David W.
2012　　*Colossians and Philemon.* Zondervan Exegetical Commentary on the New Testament 12. Grand Rapids: Zondervan.

Payne, P. B.
2009　　*Man and Woman, One in Christ: An Exegetical and Theological Study of Paul's Letters.* Grand Rapids: Zondervan.

Peterson, Eugene
1991　　*Answering God: The Psalms as Tools for Prayer.* San Francisco: HarperSanFrancisco.

2005 *Christ Plays in Ten Thousand Places: A Conversation in Spiritual Theology.* Grand Rapids: Eerdmans.

2006 *Eat This Book: A Conversation in the Art of Spiritual Reading.* Grand Rapids: Eerdmans.

2007 *The Jesus Way: A Conversation on the Ways that Jesus is the Way.* Grand Rapids: Eerdmans.

2008 *Tell It Slant: A Conversation on the Language of Jesus in His Stories and Prayers.* Grand Rapids: Eerdmans.

Pokorný, Petr
1991 *Colossians: A Commentary.* Peabody, MA: Hendrickson Publishers.

Reumann, John
1990 "Colossians 1:24 ('What is Lacking in the Afflictions of Christ'): History of Exegesis and Ecumenical Advance." *Currents in Theology and Mission.* 17/6: 454-461.

Richards, E. R.
2004 *Paul and First-Century Letter Writing: Secretaries, Composition and Collection.* Downers Grove, IL: InterVarsity Press.

Rosner, Brian S.
2007 *Greed as Idolatry: The Origin and Meaning of a Pauline Metaphor.* Grand Rapids: Eerdmans.

Saller, Richard P.
1994 *Patriarchy, Property and Death in the Roman Family.* Cambridge: Cambridge University Press.

Sappington, T. J.
1991 *Revelation and Redemption at Colossae.* Sheffield, England: JSOT Press.

Schweizer, Eduard
1982 *The Letter to the Colossians.* Minneapolis: Augsburg Publishing.

Seitz, Christopher R.
2014 *Colossians.* Brazos Theological Commentary on the Bible. Grand Rapids: Brazos Press.

Smedes, Lewis
1978 *Love Within Limits: A Realist's View of 1 Corinthians 13.* Grand Rapids: Eerdmans.

1983b *Mere Morality: What God Expects from Ordinary People.* Grand Rapids: Eerdmans.

Smith, Gary V.
2001 *Hosea/Amos/Micah.* The NIV Application Commentary. Grand Rapids: Zondervan.

Smith, James K. A.
2010 *Thinking in Tongues: Pentecostal Contributions to Christian Philosophy.* Grand Rapids: Eerdmans.

Spina, F. A.
2005 *The Faith of the Outsider: Exclusion and Inclusion in the Biblical Story.* Grand Rapids: Eerdmans.

Spivey, Steven W.
2011 "Colossians 1:24 and the Suffering Church." *Journal of Spiritual Formation and Soul Care* 4: 43-62.

Stählin, G.
1967 "The Wrath of Man and the Wrath of God in the NT." Pp. 419-447 in *Theological Dictionary of the New Testament,* Vol. V. Edited by G. Friedrich. Grand Rapids: Wm. B. Eerdmans Publishing Company.

411

Stott, John
1986   *The Cross of Christ.* Downers Grove, IL: InterVarsity Press.

Sumney, Jerry L.
2008   *Colossians: A Commentary.* The New Testament Library. Louisville: Westminster John Knox Press.

Talbert, Charles H.
2007   *Ephesians and Colossians.* Paideia Commentaries on the New Testament. Grand Rapids: Baker Academic.

Thielicke, Helmut
1974   *The Evangelical Faith: Volume One: Prolegomena: The Relation of Theology to Modern Thought Forms.* Grand Rapids: Eerdmans.

1977   *The Evangelical Faith: Volume Two: The Doctrine of God and of Christ.* Grand Rapids: Eerdmans.

1979   *Theological Ethics. Volume 1: Foundations.* Grand Rapids: Eerdmans.

1982   *The Evangelical Faith: Volume Three: The Holy Spirit, The Church, Eschatology.* Grand Rapids: Eerdmans.

Thompson, Marianne M.
2005   *Colossians and Philemon.* The Two Horizons New Testament Commentary. Grand Rapids: Eerdmans.

Tidball, Derek J.
2011   *In Christ, In Colossae: Sociological Perspectives on Colossians.* London: Paternoster.

Torrance, Thomas
1976   *Space, Time & Resurrection.* Grand Rapids: Eerdmans.

Turner, P.
2003   "The Ten Commandments in the Church in a Postmodern World." Pp. 3-17 in *I Am the Lord Your God: Christian Reflections on the Ten Commandments.* Edited by C. E. Braaten and C. R. Seitz. Grand Rapids: Eerdmans.

Verhey, Allen
1984   *The Great Reversal: Ethics and the New Testament.* Grand Rapids: Eerdmans.

Wall, Robert
1993   *Colossians and Philemon.* The IVP New Testament Commentary Series 12. Downers Grove, IL: InterVarsity Press.

Walsh, Brian J. and S. Keesmaat
2004   *Colossians Remixed: Subverting the Empire.* Downers Grove, IL: InterVarsity Press.

Watson, Alan
1987   *Roman Slave Law.* Baltimore: The John Hopkins University Press.

Wiedemann, Thomas
1981   *Greek and Roman Slavery.* Baltimore: The John Hopkins University Press.

Willimon, William H. and Stanley Hauerwas
1996   *Lord, Teach Us: The Lord's Prayer & the Christian Life.* Nashville, TN: Abingdon Press.

Wilson, R. M.
2005   *Colossians and Philemon.* International Critical Commentary. New York: T&T Clark International.

Wink, Walter
1986   *Unmasking the Powers.* Philadelphia: Fortress Press.

1992   *Engaging the Powers*. Minneapolis: Fortress Press.

Witherington, Ben

1998   *Grace in Galatia: A Commentary on Paul's Letter to the Galatians*. Grand Rapids: Eerdmans.

2004   *Paul's Letter to the Romans: A Socio-Rhetorical Commentary*. Grand Rapids: Eerdmans.

2007   *The Letters to Philemon, the Colossians, and the Ephesians: a Socio-Rhetorical Commentary on the Captivity Epistles*. Grand Rapids: Eerdmans.

Wright, N.T.

1986   *The Epistles of Paul to the Colossians and to Philemon*. Tyndale New Testament Commentaries 12. Grand Rapids: Eerdmans. Reprinted in a new format 2008.

1994   *Following Jesus: Biblical Reflections on Discipleship*. Grand Rapids: Eerdmans.

Yoder, John H.

1972   *The Politics of Jesus*. Grand Rapids: Eerdmans

[1] Tidball 2011: ix.
[2] Pokorný 1991: 29-31.
[3] Thompson 2005: 112.
[4] Cranfield 1975: 47.
[5] Garland 1999: 47.
[6] Richards 2004: 128.
[7] See Richards 2004: 19-31.
[8] M. Barth and Blanke 1994: 141.
[9] Witherington 2007: 17-19.
[10] Aune 2001: 36-37.
[11] Pao 2012: 50-51.
[12] Thielicke 1979: 343.
[13] Brunner 1956: 13.
[14] Dunn 1996: 57.
[15] W. Barclay 1959: 128-129.
[16] Bonhoeffer 1954: 21-24, 35.
[17] G. Smith 2001: 357.
[18] Peterson 1991: 91.
[19] Wall 1993: 51.
[20] Fee 1994: 641-42, and 2000: 33-35.
[21] K. Barth 1958: 376.
[22] Gorman 2015: 196.
[23] Sumney 2008: 48-49.
[24] Brunner 1960: 303.
[25] Brown 1999: 248-249.
[26] M. Barth and Blanke 1994: 181.
[27] Smedes 1978: 2-10.
[28] Walsh and Keesmaat 2004: 40.
[29] Bruce 1984: 48.
[30] Lucas 1980: 40.
[31] Witherington 2007: 125.
[32] Adapted from a sermon by Martin Luther, cited by Seitz 2014: 64.
[33] Russell Moore 2012: 33.
[34] Fee 2007: 296.
[35] This is a paraphrase of Walsh and Keesmaat 2004: 226.
[36] From Kuyper's 1880 inaugural address at the Free University of Amsterdam.
[37] See C. Arnold 1996: 20-89, 104-157 for examples.
[38] Garland 1998: 99.
[39] C. S. Lewis 1943: 56.
[40] Walsh and Keesmaat 2004: 85-86.
[41] C. S. Lewis 1948: 5.
[42] C. S. Lewis 1970a: 77.
[43] König 1989: 53.
[44] M. Barth and Blanke 1994: 201.
[45] K. Barth 1960b: 458-459.
[46] Walsh and Keesmaat 2004: 86.
[47] Hendricksen 1964: 74.
[48] Moo 2008: 66.
[49] Wink 1992: 67.
[50] C. Arnold 1996: 265.
[51] Bruce 1964: 6.
[52] Walsh and Keesmaat 2004: 87.
[53] Garland 1998: 106.
[54] Wink 1986: 146.
[55] H. C. G. Moule 1898: 78.
[56] Walsh and Keesmaat 2004: 88.
[57] Torrance 1976: 142.
[58] Wright 1986: 78-79.
[59] W. Barclay 1959: 142.
[60] Caird 1976: 175.
[61] Cranfield 1975: 267.
[62] Pao 2012: 103.
[63] Horrell, Hunt, and Southgate 2010: 128.
[64] Berkouwer 1976: 135.
[65] Maier 2005: 333.
[66] Hengel 1977: 22-32.
[67] Fitch 2008: 37-38.
[68] Wall 1993: 78.
[69] Lucas 1980: 59-60.
[70] Thielicke 1977: 192.
[71] Chambers 1935: September 1.
[72] König 1989: 97-98.
[73] Moo 1996: 356.
[74] Bruce 1964: 118.
[75] Hay 2000: 68-69.
[76] Wright 1986: 90-91.
[77] Houlden 1970: 180.
[78] Reumann 1990: 456.
[79] Walsh and Keesmaat 2004: 227.
[80] Spivey 2011: 56-57.
[81] Stott 1986: 322.
[82] Witherington 2007: 146.
[83] K. Barth 1957: 40.
[84] Carson 2004: 427.
[85] Witherington, 2007: 143.
[86] Wright 1986: 95.
[87] Adolf Deissmann 1926: 140.
[88] Pokorný 1991: 104.
[89] Litfin 2012: 40.
[90] K. Barth 1981: 264-265.
[91] Witherington 2007: 148.
[92] Seitz 2014: 111.
[93] Caird 1976: 187.
[94] Richards 2004: 130.
[95] Dunn 1996: 130.
[96] Walsh and Keesmaat 2004: 129-131.
[97] Walsh and Keesmaat 2004: 130.
[98] Landegent 1999: 11-13.
[99] Wright 1986: 99.
[100] K. Barth 1956a: 10-11.
[101] Caird 1976: 184.
[102] Schweizer 1982: 120-121.
[103] Cited by Richards 2004: 124.
[104] Harris 1991: 87.
[105] R. P. Martin 1974: 77.
[106] P. T. O'Brien 1982: 106-107.
[107] Garland 1998: 140.
[108] Lohse 1971: 96.
[109] C. Arnold 1996: 208.
[110] Moo 2008: 193.
[111] Garland 1998: 158.
[112] Thompson 2005: 55.

[113] Garland 1998: 145.
[114] K. Barth 1956b: 176.
[115] Sappington 1991: 204.
[116] Blackwell 2014: 113.
[117] Lohse 1971: 101.
[118] Wright 1986: 108.
[119] C. Arnold 1996: 295.
[120] König 1989: 124.
[121] Stott 1986: 276.
[122] Walsh and Keesmaat 2004: 157-58.
[123] C. Arnold 1996: 297.
[124] Witherington 1998: 456.
[125] Beetham 2008: 161.
[126] Dunn 1996: 156.
[127] Caird 1976: 194.
[128] K. Barth 1956b: 296.
[129] Bonhoeffer 1963: 99.
[130] Lewis 1946: 98-102.
[131] Seitz 2014: 126.
[132] K. Barth 1969: 160.
[133] Cranfield 1975: 304.
[134] Berkouwer 1969: 117.
[135] K. Barth 1981: 145.
[136] M. Barth & Blanke 1994: 320.
[137] Gorman 2001: 124.
[138] Brownson 2007: 138.
[139] G. Beasley-Murray 1962: 159.
[140] Thielicke 1974: 155.
[141] Thielicke 1982: 10-11.
[142] Dunn 1996: 163.
[143] Marshall 2001: 67.
[144] Wright 1986: 115.
[145] Sumney 2008: 143.
[146] Schweizer 1982: 148.
[147] Thielicke 1977: 187.
[148] G. F. Moore, cited by Anderson 2009: 96.
[149] Anderson 2009: 15-26.
[150] Lohse 1971: 110.
[151] Lohse 1971: 110.
[152] Lincoln 2000: 625.
[153] P. T. O'Brien 1982: 126.
[154] Lucas 1980: 106.
[155] K. Barth 1958: 544.
[156] Sumney 2008: 147.
[157] König 1982: 13.
[158] Garland 1998: 153.
[159] Lewis 1961: 3.
[160] König 1989: 126.
[161] Hafemann 1990: 20-21.
[162] Maier 2005: 334-336.
[163] Lincoln 2000: 628.
[164] Wright 1994: 19.
[165] K. Barth 1956a: 107.
[166] Garland 1998: 187-199.
[167] Thompson 2005: 9.
[168] Dibelius 1975: 90.
[169] *Metamorphosis* XI, 29, cited by L. Johnson 1998: 84-89.
[170] Wall 1993: 120-121.
[171] C. Arnold 1996: 213.
[172] Behm 1967: 926.
[173] Cited by C. Arnold 1996: 215, from Gnilka's German commentary on Colossians.
[174] Lohse 1971: 115.
[175] Witherington 1998:361-62.
[176] Beetham 2008: 202-203.
[177] Sumney 2008: 154.
[178] Francis 1975: 167-168.
[179] Bruce 1984: 117.
[180] See L. Johnson 1998: 94-97.
[181] K. Barth 1969: 618-619.
[182] K. Barth 1960b: 480-481.
[183] Sappington 1991: 65-70.
[184] Newsom 1985: 16.
[185] See C. Arnold 1996: 9-10, 20-30, 48-50 for more examples of this.
[186] Lincoln 1978-79: 215.
[187] MacLeod 1955: 205.
[188] Hay 2000: 113.
[189] K. Barth 1958: 59.
[190] Sumney 2008: 169.
[191] Helmut Koester 1971: 231.
[192] Lincoln 2000: 633.
[193] Pao 2012: 192.
[194] Sumney 2008:158.
[195] Moo 2008: 233.
[196] K. Barth 1960a: 621.
[197] M. Barth and Blanke 1994: 353-54.
[198] Lucas 1980: 126.
[199] Ellul 1976: 239.
[200] Thompson 2005: 68.
[201] Seitz 2014: 140.
[202] K. Barth 1956b: 448.
[203] K. Barth 1956b: 450-451.
[204] Lucas 1980: 112.
[205] C. S. Lewis 1943: 65.
[206] Bruce 1984: 125.
[207] Boulton 2008: 73.
[208] Boulton 2008: 196.
[209] Ellul 1976: 238-239.
[210] C. Arnold 1996: 219.
[211] Thompson 2005: 65.
[212] Peterson 2005: 243.
[213] K. Barth 1961a: 348.
[214] Smedes 1983b: 252.
[215] Lucas 1980: 130.
[216] Bruce 1984: 129.
[217] Wall 1993: 130.
[218] Thompson 2005: 69, emphasis mine.
[219] Harris 1991: 136.
[220] Moo 2008: 233, 245.
[221] K. Barth 1958: 59.
[222] Hendricksen 1964: 140.
[223] Thompson 2005: 70.
[224] Lincoln 1981: 116.

[225] Duguid 1999: 268.
[226] Thompson 2005: 70.
[227] Willimon and Hauerwas 1996: 38.
[228] Hay 1973: 15.
[229] Sietz 2014: 149.
[230] K. Barth 1960b: 438.
[231] J. Smith 2010: 111, 114.
[232] Pokorný 1991: 160.
[233] Moo 2008: 248.
[234] K. Barth 1962a: 936.
[235] Sumney 2008: 180.
[236] Gorman 2001: 34, 46.
[237] K. Barth 1962b: 103.
[238] Brueggemann 1997: 401.
[239] Peterson 2008: 250.
[240] K. Barth 1962a: 722-725.
[241] W. Barclay 1959: 177.
[242] K. Barth 1958: 289.
[243] Caird 1976: 202-203.
[244] Gorman 2001: 46.
[245] Keck 1988: 75-78.
[246] Dunn 1996: 208.
[247] Bonhoeffer 1955: 217-218.
[248] Seitz 2014: 153.
[249] K. Barth 1958: 300.
[250] Dunn 1996: 209.
[251] Gill 2000: 119.
[252] Witherington 1998: 379.
[253] Walsh and Keesmaat 2004: 156-157.
[254] Berlin 2000: 25, 30.
[255] Moo 1996: 818.
[256] Thompson 2005: 156-161.
[257] Hay 2000: 135.
[258] Wright 1986: 138.
[259] Pokorný 1991: 158.
[260] Turner 2003: 3-4.
[261] Witherington 1998: 404.
[262] Moo 2008: 254.
[263] Hendricksen 1964: 144.
[264] Wright 1986: 133.
[265] K. Barth 1956a: 261.
[266] Garland 1998: 203.
[267] Witherington 2007: 175-76.
[268] Walsh and Keesmaat 2004: 160.
[269] Rosner 2007: 21-47, 159-65.
[270] Rosner 2007: 169.
[271] Rosner 2007: 174.
[272] Moo 2008: 258.
[273] Stählin 1967: 425.
[274] M. Barth and Blanke 1994: 406.
[275] Verhey 1984: 65-66.
[276] Garland 1998: 224.
[277] Smedes 1983b: 213.
[278] Wright 1986: 142.
[279] Bruce 1984: 146.
[280] Thompson 2005: 78.
[281] Melick 1991: 295.
[282] Witherington 2004: 160.

[283] Philo's On Dreams 1.224-225.
[284] Philostratus' Life of Apollonius 4.20.
[285] K. Barth 1962a: 530.
[286] K. Barth 1961b: 249.
[287] Bonhoeffer 1955:17-20.
[288] Thielicke 1979: 152.
[289] Cited by Hay 2000: 127.
[290] Oswalt 2003: 216.
[291] B. O'Brien 2009: 44.
[292] Caird 1976: 206.
[293] Maier 2005: 340-345.
[294] See Talbert 2007: 80-82 for many quotes about this.
[295] Witherington 2007: 177.
[296] Thompson 2005: 185.
[297] Schweizer 1982: 200.
[298] Gill 2000: 118.
[299] Hartman 1995: 189-190.
[300] K. Barth 1969: 6.
[301] Brown 1996: 8.
[302] Moo 2008: 276-77.
[303] M. Barth and Blanke 1994: 418.
[304] Sumney 2008: 212.
[305] Wall 1993: 201.
[306] Sumney 2008: 213.
[307] Hay 2000: 131.
[308] M. Barth and Blanke 1994: 421.
[309] Garland 1999: 427.
[310] Gill 2000: 138-139.
[311] Dunn 1996: 230.
[312] Dunn 1996: 230.
[313] Peterson 2007:184-185.
[314] Melick 1991: 300.
[315] Caird 1976: 207.
[316] Smedes 1978: xi-xii.
[317] Marshall 2001: 266-268.
[318] Marshall 2001: 261.
[319] K Barth 1958: 785.
[320] Apuleius' Metamorphosis (XI, 581).
[321] Sumney 2008: 218.
[322] Walsh and Keesmaat 2004: 173.
[323] Gorday 2000: 49.
[324] Peterson 2006: 115.
[325] Garland 1998: 201.
[326] Sumney 2008: 220.
[327] Garland 1998: 212.
[328] Walsh and Keesmaat 2004: 176.
[329] Paraphrased by Dunn 1996: 236.
[330] Dunn 1996: 235-236.
[331] Fee 1994: 656-657.
[332] Detwiler 2001: 366-367.
[333] Peterson 2005:176, 178.
[334] K. Barth 1962a: 867.
[335] Detwiler 2001: 362-363.
[336] Detwiler 2001: 368.
[337] Bruce 1984: 160.
[338] Thielicke 1979: 21.
[339] Thompson 2005: 243.

[340] K. Barth 1981: 170-171.
[341] Talbert 2007: 63-64.
[342] Garland 1999: 481.
[343] Talbert 2007: 24.
[344] Original words and music by Dennis Jernigan © 1991 Shepherd's Heart Music/BMI.
[345] Garland 1998: 261.
[346] Pao 2012: 279.
[347] Dunn 1996: 243.
[348] Yoder 1972: 172-173.
[349] Schweizer 1982: 213.
[350] Hering 2007: 83.
[351] Hering 2007: 79-80.
[352] P. T. O'Brien 1982: 220.
[353] Seitz 2014: 168.
[354] P. T. O'Brien 1982: 215.
[355] Dunn 1996: 244.
[356] Caird 1976: 208.
[357] Garland 1998: 243.
[358] Lewis 1970b: 286.
[359] Garland 1998: 257.
[360] Payne 2009: 281-282.
[361] Hering 2007: 82.
[362] Atkins 1987: 172.
[363] Wright 1986: 151.
[364] Moo 2008: 302.
[365] Sumney 2008: 242.
[366] Pao 2012: 267.
[367] Garland 1998: 245.
[368] Smedes 1983b: 70-71.
[369] Balla 2003: 33-34, 75.
[370] Hendricksen 1964: 173.
[371] Moo 2008: 307.
[372] Balla 2003: 46.
[373] Saller 1994: 133-153.
[374] Saller 1994: 144.
[375] Saller 1994: 139, 150.
[376] Wright 1986: 153.
[377] Garland 1998: 267.
[378] K. Barth 1961a: 256.
[379] K. Barth 1961a: 282.
[380] Moo 2008: 298, 309.
[381] Pao 2012: 271.
[382] Hering 2007: 84-85.
[383] Moo 2008: 296.
[384] Lincoln 2000: 656.
[385] Cranfield 1975: 50.
[386] Garland 1998: 248.
[387] Hay 2000: 146.
[388] Sumney 2008: 249.
[389] Wall 1993: 162.
[390] Wright 1986: 154.
[391] Walsh and Keesmaat 2004: 207.
[392] Marshall 2001: 192.
[393] M. Barth and Blanke 1994: 448.
[394] Moo 2008: 313.
[395] Thompson 2003: 95.
[396] Wiedemann 1981: 1.
[397] Sumney 2008: 251.
[398] Watson 1987: 1.
[399] Dunn 1996: 259.
[400] Garland 1998: 248.
[401] Schweizer 1982: 227.
[402] Thompson 2003: 96.
[403] Marshall 2001: 36.
[404] Sumney 2008: 252.
[405] Sumney 2008: 254.
[406] Dunn 1996:260.
[407] M. Barth and Blanke 1994: 436.
[408] Hay 2000: 148.
[409] Longenecker 2001: 209.
[410] Longenecker 2001: 224.
[411] Bruce 1984: 172.
[412] G. W. Knight 1992: 115.
[413] Lucas 1980: 171.
[414] P. T. O'Brien 1982: 236.
[415] Hay 2000: 152.
[416] Pao 2012: 295.
[417] K. Barth 1962a: 495.
[418] See Spina 2005 for an extensive exploration of this theme.
[419] Lucas 1980: 174-175.
[420] De Graaf 2010: 70.
[421] Garland 1998: 285.
[422] Bradley 2016: 75.
[423] Bradley 2016: 72-76.
[424] Brown 1999: 94.
[425] Milgrom 1990: 154.
[426] Dunn 1996: 267.
[427] Peterson 2007:2.
[428] Dunn 1996: 269.
[429] R. M. Wilson 2005: 296.
[430] Cited by Richards 2004: 183.
[431] Garland 1998: 275.
[432] Moo 2008: 336.
[433] Hay 2000: 165.
[434] Dunn 1996: 276.
[435] Thompson 2005: 106.
[436] Bauckham 2006: 114-239.
[437] Ellul 1970: 139-178.
[438] P. T. O'Brien 1982: 256.
[439] Pao 2012: 318.
[440] Pao 2012: 325.
[441] P. T. O'Brien 1982: 256.
[442] Dunn 1996: 285.
[443] Dunn 1996: 286.
[444] Seitz 2014: 37.
[445] Seitz 2014: 191.
[446] Richards 2004: 158.
[447] Richards 2004: 217-218.
[448] W. Johnson 2009: 324-329.
[449] Gamble 1995: 4-10.
[450] Moo 2008: 353.
[451] Bruce 1984: 186-87.
[452] Cassidy 2001: 37-43.
[453] Walsh and Keesmaat 2004: 232.